To Bro. E. Lij

Read, learn, –

Omega History and Fraternal life on the "Mother Pearl"

Bro. Robert Gaander

> Friendship is Essential to the Soul!
> Manhood, Scholarship, Perseverance, Uplift, and "Service," the "Fifth Cardinal Princple."*
> "Let it be said of Omega of the future that we live to serve our fellow man."
> *Founder Oscar J. Cooper, December 17, 1941

Friendship is Essential to the Soul

Manhood, Scholarship, Perseverance, Uplift, and "Service," the "Fifth Cardinal Principle." "Let it be said of Omega of the Future that we live to serve our fellow man."

*Founder Oscar J. Cooper, December 17, 1941

# 50+ OMEGA INSPIRED YEARS:

## TRACING AN OMEGA LEGACY TO 1931

### Rohulamin Quander

Washington, DC

Printed in the United States of America

ISBN 978-1-63315-229-8

© 2014 Rohulamin Quander

All rights reserved

No part of this book may be reprinted without the written permission from the publisher or copyright holders, except for a reviewer who may quote brief passages in a review; nor may any part of this book be reproduced, stored in a retrieval system, or transmitted in any form or by any means electronic, mechanical, photocopying, recording or other, without written permission from the publisher or copyright holders.

The author can be reached and orders can be placed via
info@quanderquality.com

Cover Design: Legacy Program Consultants

First Edition, June 2014

# DEDICATION

These Omega Memoirs are dedicated to Bro. James W. Quander (1918-2004, Alpha Omega 1958), loving and dedicated father, husband, and friend, and Joherra Rohualamin Quander, always loving and devoted mother, both of whom inspired me throughout my entire life to go forth and achieve. They are also dedicated to Bro. Joseph P. Quander, Sr. (1907-1969, Theta Psi 1931), godfather and uncle, who inspired both dad and me to pursue Omega, and who further instilled in me the importance of Fraternity and Friendship.

# ACKNOWLEDGEMENTS

The creation of these Omega-inspired memoirs would not have been possible without the encouragement and sustained support of Carmen Torruella Quander, my beloved wife and life partner, Rohulamin D. Quander, my son and technical supporter. I am most appreciative of each of them, and again thank them for believing in me, and that I could achieve this unique result – an Omega-inspired memoir of 50+ dedicated years of service. Thank you!

A special word of thanks to those whose photographs made this memoir possible:
> Bro. Jamal Parker
> Bro. Emanuel McRae
> Bro. Kirk Weems
> My Dear Wife, Carmen Torruella Quander
> My Devoted Son, Rohulamin D. Quander.

DREAMS

*Die young, die middle-aged, die old –*

*Remember that the most abundant life is*

*The one in which one dreams dreams*

*That will never completely come true and chooses*

*Ideals that forever beckon but forever elude.*

*To seek a goal that is worthy …,*

*So all-consuming, and so challenging*

*That one can ever completely attain it,*

*Is the life magnificent; it is the only life worth living.*[1]

---

1 *Rev. Bro. Dr. Benjamin E. Mays, Alpha Chapter 1920.*

# CONTENTS

Letters of Greeting...................................................... i

I     Omega Psi Phi – 100 Years in The Making........................ 1

II     My Early Life................................................................ 7

III     Omega, In the Beginning.............................................. 13

IV     Omega Called To Social Action, 1930s, 40s & 50s................... 27

V     Realizing the Depth Of Omega, 1958.............................. 41

VI     The Birth of Les Jeunes Hommes.................................... 49

VII     Omega's Golden Anniversary, My 1st Jubilee, 1961............ 63

VIII     On To Howard University........................................... 81

IX     Transferring To Lincoln University................................ 85

X     Upholding Omega During The Civil Rights Era................. 93

XI     The Tone of Appreciation & Induction Into Omega............ 107

XII     An Omega Man At Last................................................. 151

XIII     Beta Chapter A 50th Anniversary Celebration.................... 167

XIV     Refocusing On the Academic Mission............................. 177

XV     Graduation and Entering Law School Starting Over ......... 201

XVI     Continuing With My Legal Career .................................. 227

XVII     The Middle Period, The 1980s & My Second Jubilee........... 233

## CONTENTS

| | | |
|---|---|---|
| XVIII | Coming Into my Own, A Diversity of Experiences............ | 237 |
| XIX | Just Beneath the Surface, Unique Interaction with AKA… | 245 |
| XX | People, Places, and Things and the World Abroad............ | 265 |
| XXI | Planning Omega's Centennial, My Third Jubilee, 2011….. | 279 |
| XXII | Centennial Countdown....................................................... | 301 |
| XXIII | Planning a Centennial History Exhibit.......................... | 317 |
| XXIV | Reflecting on the Centennial History Effort....................... | 329 |
| XXV | Founders Day, Nov. 17, 1911 to Nov. 17, 2011.............. | 335 |
| XXVI | Alpha Chapter Celebrates its Centennial, Dec. 15, 2011..... | 343 |
| XXVII | Omega, A Continuum of Service................................. | 351 |
| XXVIII | Omega, in its Second Century, 2012 and Beyond............ | 359 |
| XXIX | Homecoming Stretch..................................................... | 375 |
| XXX | Omega Men Gather at the White House....................... | 383 |
| XXXI | Salute to Colonel Charles Young................................. | 387 |
| XXXII | Omega Verses Alpha, Who is Number One.................... | 397 |
| XXXIII | Fifty Years in Omega................................................. | 403 |
| XXXIV | My Parting Words..................................................... | 415 |
| XXXV | Our Founders – A Retrospect........................................ | 427 |

Founders: Frank Coleman, Oscar J. Cooper, Ernest E. Just, Edgar A. Love

### Omega Psi Phi Fraternity, Inc.
Dr. Andrew A. Ray, 39th Grand Basileus
3951 Snapfinger Parkway, Suite 202
Decatur, GA 30035
404.284.5533 office 404.284.0333 fax
grandbasileus39@oppf.org
www.oppf.org

April 4, 2013

Bro. Rohulamin Quander, Esq.
1703 Lawrence Street NEW
Washington, D.C. 20018

Bro. Quander,

I extend congratulations to you on the completion of your memoirs. Your fifty plus years in Omega is indeed a milestone to be noted. Your chronology of moments in time, wherein you share those experiences that have shaped your life, work in Omega and the broader community will be of value for those who will follow you. As the moving finger writes and moves on; there will be no need to cancel out any of the many lines that contribute to Omega's History.

May God's Grace be with you in your continuous walk in Omega.

Fraternally,

*Andrew Ray*

Dr. Andrew A. Ray,
39th Grand Basileus

*"The Best Grand Basileus is one who never forgets what it is to be a Grand Brother"*

# Omega Psi Phi Fraternity, Inc.
*3951 Snapfinger Parkway, Decatur, Georgia 30035*

From - The Office of the Grand Keeper of Records and Seal          April 4, 2013

To -    Bro. Rohulamin Quander
       Alpha Omega Chapter

Dear Bro. Quander:

I am most pleased to pen this letter of congratulations to you, as you enter your 50th year of membership in and service to the Omega Psi Phi Fraternity, Inc. When our Four Founders – Ernest E. Just, Oscar J. Cooper, Edgar A. Love, and Frank Coleman gave life to Our Beloved Fraternity they conceived the creation of a lifelong brotherhood of men of like minds and life goals; men who would labor together and help one another in a united and focused effort to uplift all of humanity. More importantly, they envisioned a fraternity set apart from all others by its watchword, "Friendship" which "..is essential to the soul"! In other words, the Founders envisioned a fraternity of men who labor through both good and difficult times to overcome all obstacles, to include petty differences, and ever strive to truly become and remain friends.

Now, more than 100 years after Omega was founded and fifty years since you were initiated let us pause to reflect and reminisce a bit on just how well the objectives of our Four Founders have been realized. But more importantly, we need to reflect and consider the work that still lies before this brotherhood of ours if Omega is to not only survive but to thrive for centuries to come. I salute your service and applaud the effort capture and codify your fifty years in Omega. It is because of the many Omega men like yourself, that I am confident the best days of Our Beloved Fraternity lie ahead and that Omega will achieve even greater heights; thereby proving what you and I already know - Omega Men are truly special people!

I look forward to reading your Memoirs and to enjoying your perspective about what it means to be a Son of Omega. Thank you for this invitation and opportunity to be a part of your reflective journey. May God continue to Bless You, and may your travels through life continue to take you to interesting places with even more interesting people.

Fraternally,

*Curtis A. Baylor*

Curtis A. Baylor
Grand Keeper of Records and Seal

# The Omega Psi Phi Fraternity, Inc.
## Third District

OFFICE OF THE DISTRICT REPRESENTATIVE

April 4, 2013

Bro. Rohulamin Quander, Esq.
Alpha Omega Chapter
Omega Psi Phi Fraternity, Incorporated
Washington, DC

Dear Bro. Quander,

As your presiding Third District Representative, it gives me a unique pleasure to congratulate you as begin your $50^{th}$ year as a member of the Omega Psi Phi Fraternity, Incorporated. You and I share another great legacy, having both been initiated into the Brotherhood of Omega by way of Alpha Chapter, our Mother Pearl, which gave both birth and nurture to Omega, and from which all else has flowed. I have known you for the better part of my adult life, which coincides with my tenure in Omega, and I have always looked at you as a treasured Friend and mentor, both Fraternally and professionally.

Fifty years! Indeed, this is an outstanding accomplishment and testament to your faith in our Fraternal Brotherhood as well as your perseverance to continue on as one of Omega's proudest sons. Whenever I preside over the initiations of new Brothers, I always advise them that the sacred oath is just that, "sacred," and that the oath just taken must mean something to each one of us.

Omega is both a lifelong journey and a way of life, and you are one of Omega's shining examples of someone who is dedicated to preserving and fostering that way of life. I am proud and honored to know you and to fully realize that you are indeed a worthy Brother, who continues to demonstrate that you are likewise a true Omega Man.

On November 17, 1911, our Four Founders envisioned an organization that would endure. They understood that in order to realize that objective, Omega would need many men like you, who fully appreciated that *Friendship is Essential to the Soul.* Whether working individually or collectively, these men would do what is necessary to uphold what is near and dear in the hearts of all Omega Men. As you begin your $50^{th}$ year in Omega, let me once again congratulate you and extend best wishes on behalf of myself and the entire Third District.

In Friendship,

Robert C. Warren, Jr., Esq.
$27^{th}$ Third District Representative

*iii*

**OMEGA PSI PHI FRATERNITY, INC.**
LLOYD J. JORDAN
36th GRAND BASILEUS

April 4, 2013

Bro. Rohulamin Quander,
Alpha Omega Chapter

    Re: Your 50 years of Omega Brotherhood

Dear Bro. Quander:

I extend my sincerest congratulations to you as you enter your 50th year as a member of the Omega Psi Phi Fraternity, Inc., where *Friendship is Essential to the Soul*. To have a friend is a sweet experience, but to be a friend, is life sustaining. I count you among my friends, and believe that the brotherhood that we share, by reason of Omega and otherwise, is one of the most sacred and beloved assets that two men can have.

When you told me that you were writing your Memoirs, and that it would be Omega-focused, I realized that you are a man of the world, someone who has done a considerable bit for others, and that you are still focused upon and dedicated to that mission of service. This is reminiscent of what our Four Founders – Ernest E. Just, Oscar J. Cooper, Edgar A. Love, and Frank Coleman – believed was the measure of the man. Rendering service to others makes life worth living and the burden upon those who are served is reduced.

As April 4, 2014, approaches, and you enter the Inner Sanctum of Omega, called "Senior Brothers," please know that it is because of men like you, who have upheld and dedicated themselves to the sacred oath that they took on the day of their inductions, that Omega remains strong, focused, and diverse. Indeed, because of men like you, and others of like mind, the future for Omega is most promising.

May God continue to bless and keep you – Today and Always.

Fraternally

*Lloyd J. Jordan*

Lloyd J. Jordan, Esq.
36th Grand Basileus

264A G STREET S.W. WASHINGTON, D.C.

*iv*

# Omega Psi Phi Fraternity, Inc.
Dorsey C. Miller, Ed.D., 35th Grand Basileus

April 4, 2013

Brother Rohulamin Quander

Alpha Omega Chapter

Washington, D.C.

Re: *50 years of Omega Brotherhood*

Dear Brother Quander:

When I heard that you were writing your memories, and that your focus would be upon your 50+ years of membership and affiliation with our beloved Omega Psi Phi Fraternity, Inc., I immediately thought: "What a great idea! More of our brothers should do likewise." It is readily apparent that Omega means a great deal to you, and that the sacred oath that you took on April 4, 1964, was a lifelong commitment. Otherwise, you would not have undertaken so ambitious a project.

I am confident that your efforts will result in a great success. From what I know of you, you have quite a story to tell, tracing your Omega Legacy to Joseph P. Quander (Theta Psi, 1927), your uncle/godfather, and through James W. Quander (Alpha Omega, 1958), your dad. What a legacy! It is one that is full of recollections, advice, and encouragement. If only more Omega sons would do likewise. We have a rich history, one of outstanding, stellar contributions, both as individual Omega Men and collectively as a fraternity.

You are indeed a part of both components, and I am proud to be a small part of this effort by you to document, protect, and share your Omega Legacy.

Fraternally,

Dr. Dorsey C. Miller

35th Grand Basileus

P.O. Box 1738, Fort Lauderdale, FL 33302-1738
Phone (954) 332-0366
Fax (954) 332-0368
Cell (954) 298-4042
E-mail: DCMA@bellsouth.net

Omega Psi Phi Fraternity, Inc.
Dorsey C. Miller, Ed.D., 35th Grand Basileus

April 4, 2013

Brother Rohulamin Quander

Alpha Omega Chapter

Washington, D.C.

Re: *50 years of Omega Brotherhood*

Dear Brother Quander:

When I heard that you were writing your memories, and that your focus would be upon your 50+ years of membership and affiliation with our beloved Omega Psi Phi Fraternity, Inc., I immediately thought: "What a great idea! More of our brothers should do likewise." It is readily apparent that Omega means a great deal to you, and that the sacred oath that you took on April 4, 1964, was a lifelong commitment. Otherwise, you would not have undertaken so ambitious a project.

I am confident that your efforts will result in a great success. From what I know of you, you have quite a story to tell, tracing your Omega Legacy to Joseph P. Quander (Theta Psi, 1927), your uncle/godfather, and through James W. Quander (Alpha Omega, 1958), your dad. What a legacy! It is one that is full of recollections, advice, and encouragement. If only more Omega sons would do likewise. We have a rich history, one of outstanding, stellar contributions, both as individual Omega Men and collectively as a fraternity.

You are indeed a part of both components, and I am proud to be a small part of this effort by you to document, protect, and share your Omega Legacy.

Fraternally,

Dr. Dorsey C. Miller

35th Grand Basileus

P.O. Box 1738, Fort Lauderdale, FL 33302-1738
Phone (954) 332-0366
Fax (954) 332-0368
Cell (954) 298-4042
E-mail: DCMA@bellsouth.net

Jon E. Love, Sr.

9 Strand Court

Owings Mills, MD 21117

April 4, 2013

Bro. Rohulamin Quander,

Alpha Omega Chapter

Washington, D.C.

Re: Your 50 years in Omega

Dear Bro. Quander:

It is both humbling and an honor for me to write this letter of congratulations to you as you enter your 50th year as a member of our shared brotherhood in the Omega Psi Phi, Inc. It was the vision and continuing prayer of my father, Bishop Edgar A. Love, when he, along with Ernest E. Just, Oscar J. Cooper, and Frank Coleman, co-founded the Omega Psi Phi Fraternity on November 17, 1911, that men of like mind would come together in a sacred and sustained brotherhood.

For most of my life, I have had the esteemed privilege of being in the company of the caliber of men that my dad envisioned would be the lifeblood and continued future of Omega. As I understand it, you too have a long, shared legacy in Omega, tracing from 1927 through Joseph P. Quander, Sr., your uncle and godfather, and then James W. Quander, your dad, from 1958.

One of the greatest strengths of Omega is their vested interest in carrying on the legacy of membership from father to son, uncle to nephew, and friend to friend. It gives me the greatest pleasure to be able to call you "Brother," and to know that in doing so, I have helped to fulfill my dad's hopes and dreams that Omega would be a place where men, who desired to be of service, to share both brotherhood and friendship, and who were likewise focused and determined to help one another, could call "Home."

Thank you for this special honor, and God Bless you today and always.

Fraternally,

*Jon E. Love, Sr.*

Jon E. Love, Sr.

Son of Bishop Edgar A. Love, Founder

*David H. Reid, Jr., M.D.*
*5109 Myrtleleaf Drive*
*Fairfax, Virginia, 22030*

April 4, 2013

Bro. Rohulamin Quander
Alpha Omega Chapter
Washington, D.C.

Re: Your 50 years with Omega

Dear Bro. Quander:

I am delighted to send you greetings and best wishes, as you begin your $50^{th}$ year of membership, service, and devotion to our beloved Omega Psi Phi Fraternity, Inc. It hardly seems that long since you and my son, David, III, were inducted into Omega Brotherhood by way of Alpha Chapter, on April 4, 1964. But, looking back over these many years, I guess that indeed it has been just that long ago.

I still remember the day that I was inducted into Omega in November 1927, by way of Upsilon Chapter, Wilberforce University, Ohio. I was overjoyed at becoming a member of this special brotherhood, and I am still overjoyed at being a member for now more than 85 years. Who would have ever thought that such was possible?

You have been a faithful and loyal son of Omega, just like your father, Jim before you. Together you have carried Omega's torch forward, just as my son, David, your line brother, and I have done over these many years. Omega's future looks very bright, and the realization of that future depends upon brothers like yourself, and your efforts to document, protect, share, and preserve that history. All the best to you!

Fraternally,

David H. Reid, Jr., M.D.
Upsilon 1927; Alpha Omega
Age 103 years

# I - Omega Psi Phi, 100 Years In The Making

On the evening of Thursday, November 17, 2011, I arrived at Cramton Auditorium, Howard University, at about 5:30 p.m. The day was not like any other than I had experienced in life. Today was special, very special. We had been planning for this event for months, years actually, as reminiscent of what had occurred on this same campus on a rainy Friday evening 100 years ago to the date, when three young students at Howard, aided and advised by a youthful faculty member, conceived the idea of what would become an internationally known and respected organization of Brotherhood and Friendship.

On that fateful evening, November 17, 1911, the Omega Psi Phi Fraternity was born, and with it the hopes, dreams, and goals of men of like attitudes began to seek higher achievement within a structure that was designed to foster such, and also serve as "home" to their life and ambitions. The objective of my Omega-focused Memoirs, then, is to look back over these past 100 years, and to give my personal impression about Omega, including my historical introduction to the fraternity through the Omega legacies of my uncle/godfather, Joseph Pearson Quander, Sr., (1907-1969) and my own dad, James W. Quander (1918-2004), both of whom were proud, active and involved Omega men.

Uncle Joe was inducted into Omega in 1931, by way of Theta Psi chapter (formerly the original Kappa Chapter) at West Virginia Collegiate Institute (now West Virginia State University). Influenced and impressed by the many outstanding Omega men from Washington, D.C., most all of whom were affiliated with the Paul Laurence Dunbar High School in some way, he graduated from this hallowed institution about June 1929, with a strong sense of worth and a desire to achieve, qualities that the men and women of the Dunbar faculty, and those who had matriculated there previously, managed to instill and foster in their young charges in the Washington, D.C. segregated public school system.

## 50+OMEGA INSPIRED YEARS

As Uncle Joe related to my father in later years, he first became aware of Omega through Dunbar, reflecting that Omega seemed to have the best men, men who were dedicated to their families and to our race. Opportunities were very limited then, and the colored citizens were largely restricted as to what we could do and how far we could go. But the Omega men at Dunbar seemed determined to press the limits, to be more focused upon reaching beyond, not content to settle and accept the limitations that the white society tried to place on our heads. He said, "I never accepted that. My attraction to Omega was created and fostered by these many Omega giants, who stood so tall among even their great peers. So when I graduated, I was already looking forward to the day when I could join these men in this sacred brotherhood."

It would be many years, though, before my dad, James W. Quander, would join his older brother in the Omega fold. Although he was caught up in the Spirit of Omega at a very young age – serving as the team "mascot" for the Omega summer baseball league in the early 1930s - his induction was long postponed due to health reasons and related concerns about what was expected of him, in the process of seeking Omega's light. A juvenile diabetic from at least age three, his health was always fragile, with a medical diagnosis that death was likely before he reached age 10 years. Graduating from Dunbar in the Class of 1936, he enrolled and graduated from Miner Teacher's College in 1940.

There was no chapter of Omega at Miner at the time, but in observing the rigorous physical and psychological demands of pledging Kappa Alpha Psi Fraternity, which did have a chapter on campus, he was apprehensive about what deleterious effects pledging Omega might have upon his health. In plain English, he was afraid to pledge, although longingly looking at Omega from a distance, and greatly admiring those stellar men who had endured the process and become Omega Men. As he indicated to me,

> Omega Men just stood apart. They seemed to be different, and came to the fraternity already with a focus. I believe that they managed to take that focus, and when joined with other Omega Men, became even stronger. I did not realize at first how many

**OMEGA PSI PHI 100 YEARS IN THE MAKING**

*of my teachers at Dunbar and Miner were Omega men, but in later years I came to know that. I then better understood their dedication and determination to mold us, their young charges, into what we each became.*[2]

Citing men like Walter Smith (Dunbar principal), Eugene Clark (President of Miner Teacher's College), Cato Adams (Armstrong High School, Assistant Principal), and Edwin Bancroft Henderson (Dunbar educator and sports legend) as but four examples of the caliber of men who founded Alpha Omega Chapter in 1922, dad always remained enthused about Omega. When he was accorded the opportunity and was inducted by way of Alpha Omega chapter on July 9, 1958, his life and purpose took on additional meaning.

In this first chapter of my personal Memoirs, one of my objectives is to establish that my Omega lifelong journey is a *Legacy*, a Legacy of a son who followed the pre-ordained path set by his uncle/godfather and his father, both proud and dedicated Sons of Omega Psi Phi, and who, following in their footsteps, not only seeks to enhance, preserve, protect, and share their Omega stories, but to enhance his own Omega legacy, by sharing his own personal story for all others to appreciate and enjoy.

I came into my own as a member of the fraternity on April 4, 1964, by way of Alpha Chapter, Howard University. I was inducted into the "Mother Pearl" chapter, the founding chapter that was personally conceived, nurtured, and preserved by three young students, all dedicated men, to wit, Edgar Amos Love, Oscar James Cooper, and Frank Coleman, guided by their knowledgeable and focused faculty advisor, Ernest Everett Just, who in most respects was Omega's brainchild. Just knew Latin and Greek and was able to help Love, Cooper, and Coleman put structure to their raw concept, to put greater focus upon their less clear references to forming a sacred brotherhood of men of like goals, seeking to attain for the common good.

---

[2] *Conversation with Bro. James W. Quander, Alpha Omega Chapter, c2002.*

## 50+OMEGA INSPIRED YEARS

Over the next several chapters, I will relate my own Omega life and my own Omega experiences. But my focus, my determination, is to share with my readers, and particularly my Omega brothers, what Omega has meant and still means to me. For many of my Omega brothers, their lives and association with the fraternity began shortly before they were actually inducted. For me, that was not the case. And as I weave my story together, to include the founding of *Les Jeunes Hommes*, the Omega interest group in 1960, to my three Omega Jubilees to date (1961, 1986, 2011), my objective is to underscore the significance of Omega's legacy, and to reassert that no matter what, *Friendship is Essential to the Soul*.

As I review the many components of my life to date, there are naturally many activities that I am or have been associated with that have nothing to do with Omega directly. For example, my work on researching and preserving the Quander Family's stellar history, documented from the 1670s in the Maryland, Virginia, and Washington, D.C. area, including ancestors being in service to President George Washington at the Mount Vernon Plantation. As well, my sustained service to the Martin Luther King Holiday efforts and now working in effort to combat illicit human trafficking in India, are not Omega-related

### Omega's Purpose

*No better words can be found to express the purpose of Omega Psi Phi than those of the preamble of the original constitution, which reads, "Believing that men of like attainment and of the same ideals of fellowship, scholarship and highest manhood should bind themselves together in order to approach these ideals, we have banded ourselves together under the name 'Omega Psi Phi.' " The motto of the fraternity, "Friendship is essential to life," involves a truth which becomes more apparent to us as the years add themselves. The men who founded Omega were friends. They knew the value of friends. They knew that only men of like ideals could be really friends. They were aware that close association was necessary for the development of friendship."* - Extract from Statement made by Founder Edgar A. Love, The *Oracle*, March 1937, P. 4.

## OMEGA PSI PHI 100 YEARS IN THE MAKING

But in a sense they are all related, because Omega has helped me to focus on what it means to have a friend, and more importantly, what it means to *be* a friend. I could not live in isolation. I would not want to go through life not focused upon or dedicated to helping others. And when demands are presented that require my efforts to further Dr. King's message of love, peace, and nonviolent protest, and when I further understand the plight of the Dalit people in India, commonly referred to as "the Untouchables," my heart cries out for justice.

Yes, Omega is very much a part of all of these ancillary activities on my part. *Manhood! Scholarship! Perseverance! Uplift!* These are the Four Cardinal Principles under which Omega was founded in 1911. These are likewise, my personal constitution. And as Omega Founder Oscar J. Cooper noted in a 1941 letter written to George Isabel, Omega's 10th Grand Keeper of Records and Seal, in retrospect Omega might have added a Fifth Cardinal Principle – *Service!* [3] He noted, and I fully embrace his thinking, that Service can be implied in the appreciation, adopting, and a life lived that embrace the other Four Cardinal Principles. A Life of Service requires that one exhibit Manhood, pursue Scholarship, Persevere in seeking what you believe, and always Uplift those who need it. And for me, that should be enough.

Adelante!

---

*3 Extracts from the referenced letter will appear later in this Memoir.*

## 50+OMEGA INSPIRED YEARS

# II - MY EARLY LIFE

**My Parents Meet and Marry**

The Memoirs that I have undertaken to write are Omega focused, and as such, will present my perspective of what my life has been to date with the fraternity's badge of affiliation being kept upper most in my mind. Likewise, I want my readers to appreciate how and in what ways I have been influenced throughout my teenage and adult years by my knowledge of, and later affiliation with the Omega Psi Phi Fraternity, Inc.

But I was not always an Omega Man. Nor was I born with any concept of what Omega was all about. That came later. So understand that I had a life before Omega, and still have a life that is not specifically Omega-focused, although most of what I do at this time is done in a manner that is consistent with and influenced by Omega's Four Cardinal principles – *Manhood, Scholarship, Perseverance,* and *Uplift.* They are the foundation for my personal constitution, and guide me in most everything that I do. So at the outset of my Omega Memoirs, allow me to digress in this chapter and tell you something about me, who I am, where I came from, and how I was shaped into becoming the man that I am.

I was born on December 4, 1943, in the colored ward of Garfield Hospital, located at Eleventh Street and Florida Avenue, N.W., Washington, D.C. At that time, even the hospital wards were segregated. My father, James William Quander, was an African American, called "colored" or "Negro" at that time, born and raised in that city. He was both a proud Dunbar High School and Miner Teacher's college graduate. His father, John Edward Quander, migrated into Washington, D.C. from Upper Marlboro, Prince George's County, Maryland, the ancestral state from which the Quander family traces its stellar history, documented from the 1670s.

His wife and my grandmother, Maude Pearson Quander, migrated to Washington, D.C. from Walterboro, South Carolina in 1890. Her primary Caucasian lineage was Scottish, being descended from the famed Frazier/Frasier family of that area, which distinguished itself during the

American Revolution.[4] Her great uncle was Charles Frazier, the Civil War artist who achieved fame for going out into the field of battle and painting Civil War battles while in progress.

My mother, Joheora Rohualamin Quander, was born in Barbados, British West Indies, and immigrated to New York, arriving on December 4, 1934, nine years to the day of my subsequent birth. Her ethnic heritage was very mixed. Her mother, Oquindo O'Brien, was of longstanding Barbados heritage, mostly descended from Ireland and Scotland, with some African heritage, about which nothing is known. In early 1920, she was married at 16 to Mohammed Abdul Rohualamin, a 1913 immigrant to Barbados from Houghley-Calcutta, India. He was 32 years old and a Muslim merchant who previously had lived across the street from the O'Brien family when my grand-mother was a young girl. A joint Catholic-Muslim wedding, it was presided over by an imam who performed the ceremony mostly in Arabic. Of this union, seven children were born, of which my mother was the first.

James and Joherra Quander, My Parents

Because of the impending fury that would be World War II, most men of my dad's immediate age group were called to arms. However, because he had an extreme case of diabetes (now identified as Juvenile Diabetes), he was exempted from military service. The year 1942 was a whirlwind for my parents. They met in early January 1942, three weeks after my mom came to D.C. from New York, just after the

---

*4 Her lineage is beyond the scope of this document, except to note that her mother, Hannah Frazier (c1839-1926) was the daughter of Frederick Frazier and his enslaved woman, Mary Ellen. Hannah married William Pearson (? – d1890), thus extending and expanding their joint mixed mulatto and Scottish ancestries.*

## MY EARLY LIFE

Pearl Harbor attack of December 7, 1941. They started keeping company, and got engaged in June, and were married on December 6, 1942, at St. Augustine Catholic Church, then located at 15th and M Street, N.W., on the site of the present Washington Post building.

In early August 1950, about one month before entering the Sacred Heart parochial school, I was invited to a birthday party for my new friend, Richard Washington. Our dads had grown up together at St. Augustine church, and graduated from Dunbar one year apart. This was Richard's first birthday party. He was six. There was several children at the party, but not knowing them previously, I can only recall four others – Richard Washington, the birthday boy, Jackie Evans, and two Latino children who did not speak any English.

I had better watch what I say here, because I could be inheriting a world of trouble. The Latinos were brother and sister. The boy's name, as I would later learn, was Ramberto Antonio Torruella. His little sister was Carmen, who had just turned five years old the prior month. Their mother, Juana Campos was from the Dominican Republic, while their father, Juan A. Torruella, was Puerto Rican.

I am told that I was immediately smitten with her, following her around everywhere. Later, when we were playing "Hide 'N Seek" down in the unfinished basement at the home, located at 11th and Monroe Streets, N.W., I apparently followed her into a big box that had contained a just delivered appliance, perhaps a refrigerator or a washing machine. My recollection is a little fuzzy after 64 years, but apparently I tried to kiss her in this box. My efforts did not meet with success, although I had a couple of bruises to confirm the attempt.

Little did I know at that moment that this incident, minor in my mind, would lead to a lifelong commitment. I had no inkling at ages six and five years old, that I had just met my future wife. Of course it would take years before we marched down the aisle at the Sacred Heart basilica, but what started as an innocent attempt with a kiss, blossomed into a long-term successful marriage to the love of my life. More on that later.

## 50+OMEGA INSPIRED YEARS

What we, as little children, did not know on that birthday party afternoon, is that our parents had separately made the decision to enroll the four of us – Richard, Ramberto, Carmen and me – into Sacred Heart. It was a natural. Richard's mother, Luisa, was also Dominican. So we had four devout Catholic families electing to enroll their children in Sacred Heart. Only Juana Campos, Ramberto and Carmen's mother, had no idea about the former segregated status of the school. All she knew was that she now lived in the neighborhood and wanted her children in a Catholic school. Although they were quite brown, their features and hair was not typical of African Americans. As "foreign blacks," connected to the Embassy of her country, had the schools remained segregated at that time, they still might have been able to get into Sacred Heart.

I matriculated at Sacred Heart from the second to the eighth grade, graduating in June 1957. I enjoyed Sacred Heart very much, and met and have maintained many of my lifelong friends from that era. In addition to Carmen, Richard, and Ramberto, my friends included Reggie and Laura Smith, siblings, Denis Noble (deceased), and Robert (Bobby) Wilson and William Ralph Young, the latter two also being Quander cousins.

None of the above-named were Caucasian. They were all children of color. Although I did have a couple of white "school friends," there was nothing of any of those relationships that lasted beyond the confines of the school and playground. There were occasional birthday parties given by white classmates, but in my entire seven years at Sacred Heart, I was never invited to a single one of those parties.

My summer activities while in elementary school were varied, as my mother looked for activities in which to enroll me. When I was younger, I generally stayed at home, doing chores, going to Banneker swimming pool. Aunt Ruth, my grandmother's maiden sister, lived with us and kept a smoothly running house, as did Evelyn, our housekeeper, and later Florence, both of whom did the chores, aided by my help from a list my mother created.

In June 1954, Mrs. Lorraine Heathcock, mother of my playmate, Virgil, and a Latin teacher at Banneker Junior High, transported and enrolled us in the Bunker Hill summer day camp, located in the

## MY EARLY LIFE

Brookland section of D.C., with the main entrance at 14th and Otis Streets, N.E. Bunkerhill was the site of a now gone Civil War fort, one of many that ringed Washington, D.C. during that turbulent time, created to protect the core of the city from Confederate attack. This fort was named in memory of Fort Bunkerhill from the American Revolutionary war.

I initially met several future friends at Bunkerhill, but did not formally establish ongoing friendships and relationships with some of them until I was a little older, perhaps in early high school. Friends who were at Bunkerhill include: Gilbert Douglass; Betty and Jane Davis, sisters; Linda Aikens; Joycelyn and Michael Mason, siblings; Brenda Baker; and Buddy and Brenda Parish, siblings. I also met David H. Reid, III, who would later be my Omega line brother in 1964. Mike Mason and I met while playing some sport. I do not recall which one, but it was probably dodge ball. We were on the same team. I did not then know his name, but he was friendly enough.

It was barely one month after the *Brown* decision which desegregated the D.C. public schools. I have been joking about "colored week" for the past several years, as I attempted to determine whether the camp was still segregated or integrated as early as June 1954, only weeks after the *Brown* decision. My inquiries with the D.C. Department of Recreation only further confused the issue, as I received no consistency in their responses on what they city government did to address the issue of the formerly segregated summer camp system in June 1954, as they had less than three weeks from the May 17th decision of the Supreme Court to institute an integrated summer camp program.

In summer 1955, I returned to Bunkerhill, and Mike and I picked up where we left off the prior year. As they say, "school friends," for we had no further contact beyond camp, and probably never thought that we would see each other again after my two years at the camp. But fate would decide otherwise, when I enrolled at Archbishop John Carroll High School in September 1957, and he followed, enrolling in September 1958. Although we had known each other since 1954, it was not until 1958 that we had sufficient independence to pursue a friendship, to interact with each other's families, and to go on many double dates through our high school years. We even had one girlfriend in common, Janet Coleman. I did not take her from him, though. Their relationship had ended and she had another boyfriend when I came on the scene later and interrupted.

As we passed through our teenage years into adulthood, we learned that our families had been interacting for several years, and perhaps even for generations. They were not necessarily friends, but went to the same churches (St. Augustine and Holy Redeemer), the same high schools (Dunbar and Armstrong) and colleges (Howard and Miner), and with families being larger than they are now, always knew some of the Moss or Quander family members. As well, either Nellie or Susie Quander, both teachers of longstanding in the D.C. public schools, most likely taught a Moss or Quander at Shaw or Garnet –Patterson junior high schools. Sixth years after our June 1954 first meeting, we are best of friends, and I am privileged to be the godfather of his son, Mathew.

The John Carroll years were great fun too, combined with a lot of hard work. My parents put me into this newly constructed, predominantly white high school at their personal expense, and I felt the obligation to do well academically. And I did. Although the four years, 1957 – 1961, went by fairly quickly, I met many new friends, black and white, and have sustained several of these relationships, now for more than 50 years. Unlike Sacred Heart, I have developed and maintained friendship with several of my white classmates, including Fr. John Mudd, the retired Director of Development at Carroll; Michael Richardson; James Porter; Stephen Sawyer; and Laurenzo Cristaudo, the latter two of whom also attended Sacred Heart. Our friendship blossomed after we left Sacred Heart and went to high school.

Along the way, I was in the Carroll musical play twice, sang in the glee club, ran track, and ran for political office, although I did not win the race to become a junior class representative. My slogan, "Do not wander! Vote for Quander!" But they wandered, and although I came in second, still it was a great experience. Beyond Carroll, I founded *Les Jeunes Hommes,* the Omega Psi Phi Fraternity's interest club in January 1960. The club was dedicated to service and was successfully functioned for 11 years. There is more information about *Les Jeunes Hommes* in later chapters.

# III – Omega, In the Beginning

On November 17, 1911, on a rainy evening, three young ambitious Howard University students met with their faculty advisor in his office, located in Science (now Thirkield) Hall to form a new fraternity; based upon a foundation of Friendship and supported by pillars of Manhood, Scholar-ship, Perseverance and Uplift. Thus the Omega Psi Phi Fraternity was born. A month later, on December 15th, eleven of their care-fully chosen friends, fellow students of "like attainment and of the same ideals of fellowship, scholar-ship and manhood," were brought into the Fraternity to form Alpha Chapter, "The Mother Pearl," our Fraternity's first chapter. [5]

In the Beginning
(a historically acurate dipiction of the Founding Day of Omega in the Office of Founder Ernest E. Just) - Carmen Toruella Quander, artist

## The Challenge

*Following the Great War, we are now in an era of universal reconstruction. This nation, all nations, must play a part; we men of Omega Psi phi, all men must play a part. Earth, old traditions, hopes as old as man himself, ay, and prejudices too, our heritage from ages gone, part of the price we pay for our evolution, all of these are in the balance. Many of these must and shall go; we tremble lest others go. The world is well nigh hysteria. Under the shock of these last four years, civilization, fresh from the rim of Hell is convulsive; orderly activity is*

---

[5] Welcome to the Mother Pearl of Omega, Celebrating 100 Years of Alpha Chapter, Extracted from "This is Alpha Chapter," a Statement prepared by Bro. Jonathan Matthews (Alpha Chapter, 1983), 2013 Alpha Chapter, Omega Psi Phi Fraternity Inc. All Rights Reserved.

*difficult indeed in these hyper-excitable times. What shall we do? These times demand clean men, of clear vision, or straight thinking, of unselfish doing. And every Omega man must accept this challenge.* - Statement of Founder Ernest E. Just, Initial Issue of the ORACLE, 1919

Still, there was not yet an organizational structure to accommodate these men remaining a part of Omega, other than the undergraduate chapters, i.e., Alpha at Howard University, Beta Chapter at Lincoln University, Pennsylvania, Gamma Chapter in Boston, and Delta Chapter at Meherry Medical School. Yet those brothers located in Washington, D.C. and elsewhere still found a way to continue their affiliation with Omega for several years post-graduation. While the formalization of graduate chapters did not initially materialize until 1920 (Lambda Chapter, now Lambda Omega, Norfolk, Virginia), it is safe and correct to assert that Omega brothers were functioning on a post-undergrad level for several years, most probably beginning as early as 1913, when the first of the undergrads earned their degrees.

Most every Omega brother knows that Beta Chapter was established at Lincoln University in February 1914 by a delegation of three Alpha Chapter brothers, Oscar J. Cooper (Founder), Griffith Brannon (Alpha 1912), and John McMorris (Alpha 1913), a delegation commissioned by the Grand Conclave/Alpha Chapter. They were each recently graduated men when they traveled to Lincoln University.

Likewise, with the establishment of the two War Chapters, one each at Fort Des Moines, Iowa (1917), and Camp Howard, Howard University, Washington, D.C. (1918), both largely consisted of men who had already graduated from college, and now were in leadership training for the Great War. They were young adults who had been selected for leadership training. They had been evaluated for their maturity, ability to inspire others, and certain characteristics deemed to be necessary and desirable for wartime activity. Therefore, they certainly were not solely college level students.

# OMEGA, IN THE BEGINNING

## The War Chapters

### Fort Des Moines, Iowa

*Permission was obtained from the Grand Basileus, Mr. McMorris, to establish a War Chapter of the Omega Psi Phi Fraternity at the R.O.T.C. at Ft. Des Moines, in order to grant to these members of the fraternity an opportunity to enjoy the privileges of meeting together and taking among themselves such men as they thought were qualified to partake of, and live up to the spirit of Omega. . . . The fraternal organizations which have as their sincere purpose the salvation and uplift of men have readily launched out upon the new course of fraternalism. The Omega Psi Phi Fraternity has been on the alert for every opportunity that would enable her to become a greater and more beneficial servant of the young Negro men. Her change to a new course is one for which she has long been preparing.* - Extracts from the minutes of the first meeting of the men of Omega Psi Phi Fraternity at Fort Des Moines, Iowa, 1917; the *Oracle,* first edition, June 1919, P. 15.

### Camp Howard, Washington, D.C.

*On August 1, 1918, the War Department established a special officer training camp for students from Negro colleges, this time placing it at Howard University. Operating under the name, "Camp Howard." The purpose was the same as the 1917 operation a Fort Des Moines, except that the selected men were apparently still enrolled in school, making them a year or two younger than those previously selected. Recognizing that this assemblage at Howard also could foster a spirit of comradeship to bring students from Negro colleges together in a true spirit of inter-collegiate cooperation, Omega immediately saw another opportunity to bring several of these students together in a foundation of a closer relationship, that would include being initiated into the Omega brotherhood. Thus on September 1, 1918, 27 young men, all of who were still enrolled in southern-based colleges (Fisk, Virginia Union, Shaw, Talladega, Atlanta, Biddle, Morehouse, and West Virginia), were called to Omega's brotherhood.*

## 50+ OMEGA INSPIRED YEARS

*The induction ceremony was conducted at the Alpha Chapter Fraternity house, then located at 322 T Street, N.W., Washington, D.C. The report on Camp Howard, written by Bro. J.A. Thomas, Jr., Howard 1918, and Basileus of the Camp Howard Chapter, did not specifically anticipate the same level of life-long affiliation with Omega, and thus the eventual creation of graduate chapters, as clearly was the case as enumerated in the Report on Fort Des Moines. However, Bro. Thomas's language would seem to anticipate the same result, eventually, when he said, in anticipation of the southern schools' eventual acceptance of fraternities on their campuses, "When the barriers that prevent their existence in the great schools of the South are broken down, Omega will be first to place her banner there and her sons will strive harder to maintain the high ideals upon which it is constructed. May the day soon come when tis will be possible and the name of Omega stand as an incentive to inspire her sons to higher ideals and greater accomplishment."* - the *Oracle*, first edition, June 1919, P. 20.

## The Birth of Alpha Omega, 1922 and the Graduate Chapters, Alpha Chapter

*As the older men are passing beyond the confines of college life, the work of the organization is being taken up by younger men who are eager to give their services in the maintenance of its high ideals. They realize the power of organization and the great obligation which rests upon them to preserve it.* – "The History of Alpha Chapter," Luther O. Baumgardner, the *Oracle*, first edition, June 1919, P 9.

Omega had a "problem." But not one that was unsolvable. What should we do with this talent, these Omega men and others seeking Omega, that we can channel into creditable and useful service? Already, it was known that several of these post-graduate men were continuing to socialize, remaining close to each other, and convening on occasion in activities that were for the more mature guests and members. Many were in their late 20s, some older, and the appeal for spending time with the undergrads was simply not there. So they often met, ate, socialized, and planned other life events from a more mature perspective. It was only a short leap to officially form what would become known as "graduate chapters."

In the fall of 1922 when Alpha Omega Chapter was formally launched, Omega Psi Phi Fraternity was only 11 years old, a youth with a lot of questions both about itself and about everything around it. Just two years earlier, the fraternity had come up with an answer to one of the most burning questions facing it: How could a young Omega build a structure that would allow members who had received so much from their undergraduate experience to continue to derive benefits and the "good fellowship" as they moved into their careers and on to graduate education? As Bro. Herman Dreer wrote in *The History of Omega Psi Phi Fraternity*, "They wanted the place of their new abode to feel the transforming power of Omega."[6]

The solution was to charter graduate chapters, with the first one being Lambda of Norfolk, Va., in November 1920 (now Lambda Omega). By 1922, Grand Basileus J. Alston Atkins would restructure the system for assigning names to chapters, adding the word "Omega" to the names of graduate chapters and tying them to the name of the undergraduate chapter in the city. For Washington, D.C, the birthplace of Omega and the location of its Alpha Chapter at Howard University, this new system meant that the graduate chapter carried the name "Alpha" as a tribute to the first chapter and the name "Omega" to distinguish it as a graduate chapter. Not surprising, many of the earliest members of Alpha Omega were men who had entered the fraternity through Howard University.[7]

In researching for this publication, I was drawn to the readily apparent, i.e., that the older brothers located in Washington, D.C. had already considered themselves as "graduate brothers" at least by 1920, and probably earlier. This state existed despite the delayed formal establishment of a Washington, D.C.-based graduate chapter (Alpha Omega) and no issuance of a chapter charter until October 1922. Why was that? I do not know, and have found no answer to this

---

[6] As stated in *The History of Alpha Omega Chapter*, from the Alpha Omega Chapter website, Ivory Gene Cooper, c1997.

[7] *The History of Alpha Omega Chapter*, from the Alpha Omega Chapter website, Ivory Gene Cooper, c1997.

question during my research. I am comfortable in concluding that to them, the issuance of a chapter charter document was a formality for the historical record, because already the graduate level men had long been functioning as though they were a separate entity from Alpha Chapter, despite not yet having a document so designating.

An underscoring of this point is found in the October 1929 Issue *Oracle*, noting the death of Bro. Charles Herbert Marshall, Sr., M.D., the primary founder of Alpha Omega Chapter and its first basileus. The post-death article referred to him as having been initiated into Omega in 1920, by way of "Alpha Omega" Chapter. However, I take note of the obvious fact that there was no Alpha Omega Chapter in 1920, and thus no way for Bro. Marshall to have been inducted into Omega in Washington, D.C., other than through Alpha Chapter, an undergraduate entity. He was born on May 15, 1862 in Amissaville, Virginia, and was 58 years old when inducted via the undergraduate chapter.[8]

Surely, it was not his intent to be and remain an undergrad again. But there was no other formal structure to obtain membership at that time, other than through an undergraduate chapter. Therefore, he elected that route, which included an unusual anomaly of pledging under the sponsorship of his own son, Bro. C. Herbert Marshall, Jr., who was inducted into Alpha Chapter in 1917. How unusual is that? Another example. Bro. Edwin Bancroft Henderson, an outstanding educator and athlete, is noted as another Alpha Omega chapter founder. No record of when he was inducted into Omega has been located, but undoubtedly it was through Alpha chapter, at a time when "E.B." was about 45 years old.

Bro. Marshall was an outstanding leader in the local community on many fronts, and naturally his leadership abilities drew him to the top of the Omega leadership. So enthused about Omega was Bro.

---

8 "Brother Charles Herbert Marshall, Sr., M.D. (1862-1929), Chartering Basileus, Alpha Omega Chapter," a biographical statement by Bro. Rohulamin Quander, prepared for Alpha Omega's 90th Anniversary Celebration, November 2, 2012, itself based in significant part upon an article about Bro. Marshall that appeared in the Fall 1929 Oracle.

## OMEGA, IN THE BEGINNING

Marshall Sr. that he did not mind having to pledge under the guidance of 18 to 20 year old men. However, his love of Omega did not stop there. Spurred on by the desire to make Omega more than just a college-era experience, he called to his side mature men of like ideas and the desire to create and sustain Omega as a life-long journey. From the outset of his membership, and in discussions and regular meetings convened by some of the older brothers, he determined that the newly established concept, known as "the Graduate Chapter," but as yet non-existing in Washington, D.C., should likewise take hold. Several of these men had pledged Alpha Chapter at Howard. Others had pledged elsewhere, including on the two War Chapter pledge lines during the Great War. At any rate, they were determined to remain as brothers and to move forward in life as a closely-knit unit of determined, focused men who had life goals that they wanted to achieve, despite the limitations that the larger society placed upon them because of the color of their skin.

Thus, on October 1, 1922, Alpha Omega, now Omega's largest graduate chapter, was formally chartered, under Bro. Charles Herbert Marshall Sr.'s direct guidance, at last putting a formal structure to what the more senior brothers had already been enjoying informally for well more than his personal two years of membership. With no intent to compromise Lambda Omega's justified claim and entitlement to be recognized as Omega's *First* chartered graduate chapter, what would later be titled "Alpha Omega Chapter" had already been functioning as a separate and "more adult" group of Omega men from at least the 1917-1918 War Chapter period, and continued so doing, possibly intermittently, until delayed formalization in October 1922.

> *The idea for a graduate chapter in Washington, D.C., "had its birth in the minds of men in the spring of 1922," said Brother Spurgeon Burke during an interview in 1975, and was formed and launched in fall 1922. "Alpha Omega evolved from the Alpha Chapter because as we advanced through the academic curriculum in the college or from the professional schools, we became graduates of the university," Burke said. "Many of us lived in the District of Columbia, and we did not want to lose*

*our relationship with Mother Omega. And out of our combined yearning to continue in the service of Omega, these graduates decided to build the Alpha Omega Chapter."*

*Burke added, "The actual desire was extended to the point that we felt that there was an opportunity for leadership in this city among adult citizens who were out in the world and in many instances had already made their mark, and we wanted to have their association and support. In those instances we made it our business when we first made an effort to organize Alpha Omega Chapter to select the leadership." Among the charter members of the chapter were Bradshaw Marshall, Campbell C. Johnson, Leonard Johnson, C. Herbert Marshall, Edwin B. Henderson, Robert Mattingly, Gene Clark, Guy Wilkerson, Kyger Savoy, Clyde McDuffie, Walter Smith, G. David Houston, Cato Adams, and Howard Long, as well as Burke.*[9]

The founders of the Alpha Omega Chapter had diverse educational and professional backgrounds. Several of these men were already or soon would become fixtures in the local community, and even beyond, in some cases. Some were school principals, a college president and professors, language instructors, authors, and officials in the physical education department of Washington, D.C.'s segregated school system. C. Herbert Marshall, M.D., Founding Basileus, was a medical doctor, who was widely loved, admired, and

---

[9] *Comments made by Bro. Spurgeon Burke, (Alpha 1914) during a 1975 interview. It is not known who conducted the interview. Note, however, that Bro. Burke does not mention either Bro. George Brice (Alpha 1915) or Bro. William H. Bradshaw, as among the Alpha Omega Chapter original charter members, as noted on other lists. Perhaps it was just an oversight. Further, Bro Burke referred the above delineated brothers as "Among the charter members of the chapter were ..." which accommodates the apparent conclusion that Alpha Omega's initial chapter membership included more than the 15 brothers who were specifically listed by name. Bro. Brice, who died in 1962, was an outstanding sportsman, and businessman, among other accomplishments.*

## OMEGA, IN THE BEGINNING

respected, both for his medical prowess and community service. "These men had already made excellent records, were outstanding, and had been accepted by community leaders," said Bro. Burke during his 1975 interview. Brother Cato W. Adams was the chapter's first Keeper of Records and Seal.

Dr. Charles Herbert Marshall, Sr. (Alpha 1920), Founding Basileus, held that position until 1928, when failing health dictated that he should step down. He died in 1929. The Fall *Oracle* of that year, reflecting on Bro. Marshall's sustained contributions to many organizations, Omega being principal among them, stated "As a man of the church, a worker in the community, a husband, a father, a Brother of Omega, Dr. Marshall gave the world the highest exemplification of a life well lived. He rendered an acceptable service. God in Heaven exacts no more from Man."[10]

Referring to the noted men who were among the charter members of Alpha Omega, I found reference to several of them, and no information as to others, as noted herein. Bradshaw Marshall (no information); Campbell Carrington Johnson (Alpha 1913), eventually the 18th Grand Basileus, and high ranking military leader, served this nation in a critically significant position during World War II; Charles Leonard Johnson (Alpha, pre-1920, no information); Edwin Bancroft Henderson was an outstanding teacher, athlete, and author; credited with introducing the sport of basketball to African Americans in 1904, after studying physical education at Harvard University; Robert Nicholas Mattingly (no information); Eugene A. Clark, President, Miner Teachers College; Garnett Crummell Wilkerson , an outstanding administrator, was the superintendent of the Colored Division of the D.C. Public Schools during segregation; Alfred Kyger Savoy was also an educator and served as principal in the D.C. public school system; Clyde C. McDuffie (no information); Walter L. Smith was the principal of the Paul Laurence Dunbar High School; G. David Houston (Honorary 1915), was principal of Armstrong High School; Cato Wesley Adams (Alpha 1917) was the assistant principal of

---

[10] *The contents for the above statement were derived from several sources, including a personal statement written by Dr. Marshall, Sr., newspaper clippings, and the Fall 1929 issue of the Oracle.*

## 50+ OMEGA INSPIRED YEARS

Armstrong High School; Howard Long (no information); Walter Spurgeon Burke (Alpha 1914, no information); George E. Brice (Alpha 1915, no information); Howard Long (no information); and William H. Bradshaw (no information).

Bro. Brice, along with Bro. Campbell C. Johnson, Bro. Jesse Heslip, Bro. William Stuart Nelson, and William I. Barnes had a meeting with President Woodrow Wilson in 1916 to discuss establishing a Negro Officer Training Program. Although they were scheduled for only a 10 minute conference, the meeting went well beyond the time. President Wilson was so impressed that he stated, "Gentlemen, I do not know where the camp will be. I do not know when it will be established, but I promise you that it will be established, and in a few days you will hear from me."[11] In June 1916, within a few days of the meeting, President Wilson subsequently communicated with George W. Cook, Secretary of Howard University, and advised that a military camp would be established there. However, the War Department selected Fort Des Moines, Iowa, for the first camp, established in 1917, and Camp Howard's establishment did not occur until 1918. A significant number of these men had some connection to the Paul Laurence Dunbar Senior High School. Some were graduates, others were teachers or administrators. Further, in many instances, the founding brothers of Alpha Omega Chapter's Dunbar connection was in all three capacities.

For 92 years (1922-2014), Alpha Omega Chapter has had a distinguished history in Washington, D.C., and has consistently been the largest or second largest chapter of the fraternity in terms of total financial membership from its outset. Alpha Omega's members have won national recognition for their ambitious programs and reclamation efforts. The chapter has been home to Founders Edgar A. Love and Frank Coleman, several national officers, including former Grand Keeper of Records and Seal Bro. Robert Fairchild, former Grand Keeper of Finance Bro. Kenneth A. Brown, former Grand Chaplain Rev. Bro. H. Albion Ferrell. As well, Alpha Omega was the

---

*11 The History of Alpha Phi Alpha; A Development in College Life, Charles H. Wesley, 6th Edition, Foundation Publishers, Washington, D.C, 1950, Chapter VIII - "The War Interlude" Pg. 107.*

## OMEGA, IN THE BEGINNING

home chapter of the first National Executive Secretary, Bro. H. Carl Moultrie I. During this time period, Alpha Omega has hosted or co-hosted four Grand Conclaves, in 1924 (13th), 1945 (31st), 1986 (75th), and 2011 (the 77th, the Centennial Celebration).

It was into this atmosphere that Joseph P. Quander, Sr. (1907-1969) was initially introduced to Omega. While there is no specific written record or even any oral traditional of how he came to know of Omega Psi Phi, and what specifically attracted him to the fraternity, the mere presence and involvement of such men as noted above, was more than a sufficient incentive to draw towards itself those young men who were seeking – seeking more. These were young, teenaged men, attending and graduating from the famed Dunbar High School, who had to look no further than their immediate surroundings for personal guidance, inspiration, and motivation. There was a multitude of great men and women who were in their immediate environment, many of whom were or had previously served on the Dunbar faculty, or as administrators. To name a few, any listing must include Founder Ernest E. Just, Bro. Ernest B. Henderson, Bro. Carter G. Woodson, Bro. Walter Smith, Bro. A. Kiger Savoy, and Bro. Garnett C. Wilkerson.

As well, Joseph was assuredly influenced by determined women who were likewise focused upon improving the self-confidence and ability of our race, despite the troubled adverse conditions that characterized their daily living. Women such as Mary Church Terrell (Delta), Anna Julia Cooper(AKA), Eva Dykes (Delta), Julia Brooks (AKA), Susie Quander (Zeta), and Nellie Quander(AKA), in their own respective ways, most certainly played significant roles and exercised some influence upon young Joseph, his contemporaries, and their immediate surroundings. All of them were either M Street/Dunbar graduates, were on the Dunbar faculty at one time, or served in both capacities prior to Joseph's enrollment there in c1925-26.

Without question, the Dunbar circle most assuredly impressed the young Joe Quander. Their education, knowledge in many disciplines, oratorical skills, focus and determination, were talents that served as a great personal inspiration to this young man. His own parents, John E. Quander and Maude Pearson Quander, while loving, caring, and devoted to their six children, did not themselves have the education, connections, and self-confidence that were so highly valued among the up and coming generation of young Negro students in the 1920s. Yet John and Maude both knew enough to respect and appreciate the opportunity that was being offered to young Joseph at Dunbar, and to likewise appreciate, at a later time, that four of their six children would be Dunbar graduates, and that the other two children would have good educational opportunities at Armstrong High School, the academic alternative to Dunbar.

Inducted into the Omega brotherhood at Theta Psi (formerly Kappa) Chapter, West Virginia State College, in 1931, the neophyte was duly proud and excited. He was, by oral accounts, already a "big man on campus" and adding the brand, "Omega Psi Phi," seemed only to add to this luster. All institutions were rigidly segregated in those days, and despite West Virginia having split off from Virginia in 1863 over the issue of slavery, the social and racial attitudes of most West Virginians were traditional to those states of the deeper South. Quander knew what he could and could not do, and stayed within the confines that the race–focused local society dictated were the limits of what was acceptable.

## Theta Psi Chapter

*Our chapter is small, numbering eighteen active members and five who are not as yet connected with the chapter. We have been thoroughly convinced that quality and not quantity counts, for though few in number we have made Omega the outstanding fraternity on the campus.....*

*The social calendar for Omega last school term was the most outstanding feature of the social life of the campus. On May 10th, 1929, it closed in grand style as the ladies came in vying with Venus for their place in the records of Omega. Omega boys moved with the grace of magic gods as they danced with their sweethearts. Thus it was long to be remembered as the most picturesque and charming aspect of social life at this college.*

*The voice of Omega has cried in West Virginia and as the days, months, and years go by, a forceful echo and re-echo in the form of applicants for pledgeship resound, until today we stand as the*

## OMEGA, IN THE BEGINNING

*most formidable fraternity in West Virginia and boast of the best group of aspirant available. Twenty-four have been pledged since September and there are any number who are just waiting for the O.K. behind their name.* – Theta Psi Chapter Report, the *Oracle,* April 1930, P. 7.

# 50+ OMEGA INSPIRED YEARS

# IV – Omega Men Called To Social Action

**Omega in the 1930s**

With the Great Depression in full swing and the U.S. economy in prolonged dire straits, the plight of the African American sank to a new low. Jobs were hard to come by, and with institutional racism still the order of the day, many an Omega man was either unemployed or underemployed. Still, we as a group persevered, continued to keep our eyes on the universal justice prize, ever more determined to win the day when all of us, as African Americans, would be rightfully accorded our place in the sun as full citizens of this great nation.

Begrudgingly, the majority population was slowly coming to terms, and giving a modest realization that we, as a group of people, had earned our way through centuries of uncompensated labor, but now we were beginning to straighten our backs in ways hither to not previously possible, and demanding our right places in every phase of American life. Still, it would be decades before the greatest measures of that recognition would come, but with every little step taken, every picket, civil rights demand, and the exercise of some small increase in voting rights, things began to change at last.

A typical dichotomy is the way that Omega men enjoyed their fraternal relationships during the 1930s, focused upon the concepts of Fraternity and Friendship, yet at the same time with increased awareness of the obligation to lift others up, as we ourselves collectively climbed. These two varied thoughts were captured in 1935 and 1941, by comments made by Founders Love and Cooper, respectively, demonstrating both the social side of Omega, and the emerging Social Action side of what it meant to be a true friend, which included rendering service to others.

The latter statement, provided by Founder Cooper was a comment that was rendered after Omega has begun to refocus in the 1930s, to become more social action oriented, noting that we serve no real purpose if our sole objective is to only enjoy the company of ourselves, while others of our race, who were less fortunate, continued to suffer great indignities in their daily lives. Therefore, we, as Omega man banded together, must face and fight head on the denials that are sustained, thus relieving some of the misery that had become Negro life in the larger colored population throughout our nations. As educated professional men, it still would not be easy, but we have contacts and societal involvements that take us to places in the society where many of the Negro masses have never yet experienced.

## The Omega Program

*No better words can be found to express the purpose of Omega Psi Phi than those of the preamble to the original constitution, which I quote. 'Believing that men of like attainment and of the same ideals of fellowship, scholarship and highest manhood should bind themselves together in order to approach these ideals, we have banded ourselves together under the name, Omega Psi Phi upon the ideals of the Fraternity.'*

*The motto of the Fraternity, 'Friendship is essential to life,' involves a truth which becomes more apparent to us as the years add themselves. The men who founded Omega were friends. They knew the value of friendship. They knew that only men of like ideals could really be friends. They were aware that close association was necessary for the development of friendship. They had in mind the development of friendships in the local chapters which would carry on down through the years. They aimed at the establishment of such ideals in the Fraternity, as being adhered to, would make all men connected therewith, feel drawn toward one another. . . .*

*We need make no apology to anyone for the type of organization which is ours - an organization of intelligent men with high ideals. Nevertheless if we were only that, the raison d'etre for our continued existence as a national body of undergraduate and graduate chapters might be seriously questioned. We must therefore have a national program which will give this large body of intelligent men with high ideals the opportunity of contributing to the sum total of human progress and happiness*

## OMEGA MEN CALLED TO SOCIAL ACTION

*through the disseminating of our own ideals throughout the whole social order. Such a program appears to me to be set forth in the June issue of the Bulletin. To carry on such a program necessarily requires money and that money should be gladly advanced by the men of Omega.* - By Rev. Edgar A. Love, Founder – Special Article, The *Oracle*, December 1935, P. 4.

### The 1940s and 1950s,
### Omega Men Called To Take Up Social Action

*This decade saw the adoption of a set of social action principles and the effectuation of an immense administration reorganization. Z. Alexander Looby [Alpha chapter 1920], a Nashville attorney, was the leader of a succession of Grand Basilei who shared credit for this development. This era saw frequent adjustments demanded by the World War II situation and its aftermath. However, despite this grave situation, new chapters continued to be chartered.*

*Within the limits of its intellectual, administrative and financial resources, the Fraternity committed the members to a national program of mass education on the felt needs of the Afro-American in the areas of health, housing, employment, social security, law, civil rights, public education, and cultural relations, and the means by which they should be satisfied. The Social Action program became the third of four major programs of the fraternity.*[12]

The 1950s in America is generally associated with the thrust for social change. Of course there were many ongoing changes well before that decade, as Omega men and African Americans (then generically referred to as "Negroes" or "Colored") refused to accept the Jim Crow limitations that the greater society had placed upon us. Actually, it was during the decade of the 1940s that the sleeping giant

---

[12] *Extracted from the 75th Anniversary Diamond Jubilee 68th Conclave, Washington, D.C., "Omega Psi Phi Fraternity, An Historical perspective," unnumbered page, co- authored by Bro. William Clement, Grand Marshal, Bro. Kenneth A. Brown, Deputy Grand Marshal, Bro. Herbert B. Dixon, and Bro. Rohulamin Quander.*

finally awoke and demanded to be heard. A few of these remarks are enumerated here, to underscore the changed attitude and continuing efforts to make the larger society come to grips with how unfairly and unjustly it had been treating its sable brothers and sisters.

Already, we had prepared ourselves, announced ourselves, and begun to move forward on a number of fronts. However, as the United States approached the half century mark, and with the world recovering from the effects of World War II, through the Marshall Plan, there were many changes in the air. The military had been integrated in 1948, and the new push for official access to all reaches of the American Dream was taking hold.

### Bro. Arthur Davis Heads Scholarship Program

*Appointed new chairman of the Scholarship Commission at the Fortieth Grand Conclave, Brother Arthur P. Davis has announced his plans for a dynamic and all-out campaign to raise undergraduate scholarship in Omega. ... One of the gravest problems confronting our fraternity is this alarming drop in scholarship among the college chapters. If it continues, it will eventually and inevitably result in a loss of position and prestige for Omega. Bro. Davis sincerely feels, however, that if the undergraduates themselves can be made to realize the seriousness of the situation they – and only they – can do something about it. If any person in Omega can persuade college students to see the light on these matters, it is Brother Davis. Very few men in Omega are better qualified with respect to training, personality, and experience to deal with undergraduates than Brother Davis –*the Oracle, Vol. 94, No. 1, March 1952, P. 12.

The federal G.I. bill that Congress adopted had the mission of extending the right to attain a home to every American who had fought to preserve democracy. Housing was to be made plentiful, affordable, and readily accessible. But with this convenience, and the creation of many up-to-date new towns, came additional challenges. What about jobs? Who was available to fill them? And schools? Were we going to continue keeping our schools racially segregated? And why? After all, the black men and women had fought side-by-side, proven themselves time-after-time, yet were still denied many of the basic tenets of citizenship, including the right to vote, to be educated, and freedoms of association. This had to change.

### Omega Man of the Year Award

*When the District of Columbia's Alpha Omega chapter tapped the Pittsburgh Courier's Washington, editor Robert L. Taylor for one of its 1950 Achievement Awards, for his crusading journalism, it paid tribute to one of Omega's most successful and inspiring careers. One of five sons of a Washington minister, Brother Taylor was reared and educated in the public schools of the District. He is a product of Hampton Institute and Miner Teachers College, in Washington. He also did graduate study at Howard and Columbia Universities. ... [D]rafted in 1941, ... wide travel and broad experience as [a] Transportation Corps officer, he recalled, influenced him to seek an effective medium to fight discrimination and intolerance This is how he hit upon newspaper work, he said. Within two years he worked his way up from the status of reporter to his current job [Washington, D.C. editor of the Pittsburgh Courier.] Washington began to feel the impact of this new career when in 1946 Brother Taylor ... launched the now famous "End Segregation In the Nation's Capital" campaign, reverberations from which rang around the country, and paved the way for other subsequent frontal attacks... - Oracle,* Vol. 41, Vol. 2, Sep. 1951, P. 2.

Although there had always been a focus upon uplifting the race from the very first date of Omega's founding, there was a stronger push to refocus this effort, to make it less generic, and to be more specific in terms of short and long term goals, and how to achieve them. Brother Frank S. Horne, Special Assistant to the Administrator, National Housing Authority, addressed the 33rd Grand Conclave, held in Fort Worth, Texas, on December 29, 1947. Among his remarks, he noted that in 1946, the prior year's conclave, the fraternity accepted a recommendation and created the Nation Social Action Committee (NSAC).

## 50+ OMEGA INSPIRED YEARS

The recommendation stated: "A socio-economic program shall constitute a major permanent function of Omega Psi Phi beginning with 1945." Such fields as public education, housing, health, full and fair employment, civil rights, the franchise and social security were among the recited purpose and matters considered appropriate for inclusion in this program. The supervision of this program was made the responsibility of a permanent National Social Action Committee (NSAC) to consist of the Supreme Council, District Representatives, the Director of the Achievement Project, the Chairman of the Housing Authority and Scholarship Commission, and five additional members to be appointed by the Grand Basileus.[13]

> *I am compelled to render unto Alpha Chapter my highest commendations for pursuing one of the finest achievement programs I have been privileged to witness. In presenting the Alpha Chapter Choral Ensemble, composed of 45 voices, under the direction of Bro. Valerian E. Smith, I feel confident without exaggeration I've never heard a finer group of singers and to think they were all members of Alpha Chapter. I don't believe any other chapter in either a fraternity or sorority can lay claim to such a distinction. Bro. Dr. Charles Drew was the speaker of the evening. The highlight of the evening was the awarding of the Scroll of Honor to Mr. Eugene Meyers, Editor of the Washington Post.* - Minutes of the 34th Grand Conclave, Detroit, Michigan, December 27-30, 1947, from the Report of Harry Penn, Third District Representative, May 7, 1947, P. 62.

> *The Chapters at the Third District Conference urged their members to communicate with their legislator in support of Civil Rights legislation, and that the local chapters take leadership in stimulating all people of the respective communities to do likewise. The guest speaker at the Press Luncheon held at Banneker Junior High School was Senator [Hubert] Humphrey of Minnesota. He stated that a concerted drive will be made in Congress to get some of President Truman's Civil Rights*

---

[13] *The Oracle, March 1947, P. 11.*

## OMEGA MEN CALLED TO SOCIAL ACTION
*Programs passed in this session.-* Minutes of the 36th Grand Conclave, Boston, Massachusetts, 1950, from the Report of Harry T. Penn, Third District Representative, 1949, P. 65.

It was clear then that Omega was already putting into place the appropriate mechanisms that would be required in order to be prepared for what was forthcoming. On February 23, 1946, the Committee, called to assembly by Grand Basileus, Colonel Campbell C. Johnson, met at Howard University. It was determined that the work and efforts of the Committee would fall into four primary areas: 1) employment and social security; 2) legislation and civil rights; 3) education and cultural relations; and 4) health and housing. The overall direction of the program was assigned to Brother Dr. Ira De Reid of Atlanta, with Brothers John Davis, Albert Dent, William Hastie, and Frank S. Horne, each of whom were nationally-known and respected men in their professional fields, and designated as chairman of one of the program committees.[14]

> *The local problems to be overcome in achieving housing for Negroes and other minority groups constitute a challenge to the best that we can provide in leadership, in skill and in vigorous local action. The Omega Psi Phi Social Action Committee provides a structure for the challenging of our efforts. Here is a method whereby the few who have had opportunity for training may identify themselves with all segments of the community, a possibility for the closing of the gap which often grows between the trained and untrained, and between people of various income levels. This is one field in which [Omega] can justify the claim of leadership which should be the responsibility of those who have had the advantage of advanced formal training -* The *Oracle*, March 1947, P. 15.

It was readily apparent that the strongest seat of Omegadom rested with the concentration of Omega men who lived and worked in the Washington, D.C. area. Not only was the city the capital of the nation, its sustained history as a community where formal education

---

[14] *The Oracle, March 1947, P. 11.*

among the Negro was highly prized and the opportunity for housing, cultural associations, and better medical care, all bred an atmosphere where the city and its environs were deemed to be among the best places to live. The presence of Howard University and Miner Teachers' College had prepared the best and brightest of our race for the challenges of life, and imbued in them the responsibilities of lifting as they themselves were blessed and climbed higher along life ladders. These men constituted "Who's Who in Colored America," and held many key positions in both the government and in the professional world.

Omega men present certificate of appreciation to President Harry S. Truman, Fall 1952

Consequently, in 1949 Omega established a national headquarters at 107 Rhodes Island Avenue, N.W., Washington, D.C., which helped to stabilize the day-to-day and national administration of the fraternity. Bro. H. Carl Moultrie I, (Beta, 1933), was installed as the National Executive Secretary (later National Executive Director) of Omega at that time, a position that he held until 1972, when he was named as an associate judge of the Superior Court of the District of Columbia. In 1978, he was named as the first African American Chief Judge of the Court, a position that he held until his death in 1986. After his death, the brothers of Alpha Omega Chapter, supported by

## OMEGA MEN CALLED TO SOCIAL ACTION

other chapters and members of the community at large, succeeded in their effort to have the court building renamed in honor of the memory and contributions of Bro. Moultrie.

### Preparing for Integration

*The new social justice pattern which the present generation of students face will have a great significance for our survival. The Supreme Court decision outlawing segregation in our school system will have an important role in the future of many of our so called Negro institutions and organizations. The new generation of American youth will have a new view of all matters pertaining to race and color of peoples. We can see signs of this new era now with a decrease in membership in certain areas. The predominantly Negro fraternities must now look to the future and gear their programs to be more inclusive. We are living in an age of competition, and must set our aims and objectives with higher ambitions. ... The Omega Psi Phi Fraternity will have to meet this challenge by enlarging its objectives, raising its standards and enforcing its principles under which it was organized. Scholarship must be attained at all levels, so that we might secure in our membership the best students in schools. How then shall we compete with these [other white] fraternities? There are several suggestions which can be offered:*

*1. Enlarge our programs and objectives.*

*2. Encourage higher scholarship among our undergraduates.*

*3. Step up our public relations programs .*

*4. Develop an interest in national and civic programs.*

*5. Assist and work with our undergraduates.*

*6. Continue our interest as alumni members and support them morally, financially, and spiritually.*

*7. Place our organization before the public and encourage leadership among our members.* – "How Omega Can Prepare To Meet Integration." by Lawrence A. Hill – *Oracle*, Vol. 95, No.1, March 1955, P. 16.

It was inevitable that, given time, and the accumulation of enhanced legal supports as the federal government slowly moved in a direction that accorded African Americans our just rights and due, that society at large would slowly make many much needed changes. At various times in the late 1940s and well into the 1950s, several Omega brothers in this district were in key positions to make a major difference in Washington, D.C. and elsewhere in the Third District to help put those changes into effect. For example, Campbell Carrington Johnson, a native Washingtonian, and subsequently the 18th Grand Basileus, repeatedly distinguished himself and served Omega and the larger community on many fronts.

Initiated into the fraternity in 1917, during the first Officers Training Camp at Des Moines, Iowa, his military and community service are both legendary. Others included Grant Reynolds, 21st Grand Basileus, William H. Hastie, first black federal judge, and John A. Davis, civil rights leader. Each of these men were giants in their fields, shared their enormous talents, and were, respectively, long-standing contributing members to Omega, always upholding the Cardinal Principles. As well, each of them was either a native to Washington, D.C., or rendered his most critical public service while residing in this immediate area, or both.

> **Omegas Pay Near $11,000.00 in NAACP Life Memberships**[15]
> *I am happy to report to the brothers of Omega that since the official resolution adopted at the Los Angeles Conclave to have chapters of Omega become Life Members in the National Association for the Advancement of Colored People, forty-three chapters of Omega have enrolled. ... Ten [chapters] have paid their $500.00 memberships in full, [including] Delta Omega, Petersburg, Va.; Lambda Omega, Norfolk; Pi Omega, Baltimore, Md.; ... and Zeta Iota, Portsmouth, Va. ... Thus Omega has sent a total of $10,811.06 to the NAACP in recent years. –* Oracle, *Vol. 97, No. 1, March 1957, P. 5.*

NSACs recited purpose was initially received in 1946 with great enthusiasm. With the second world war just ended, and the nation refocusing upon the need for rebuilding our nation and helping other

---

[15] *Extracted from a 1957 Report filed by Bro. Roy Wilkins, Executive Director, NAACP.*

## OMEGA MEN CALLED TO SOCIAL ACTION

nations as well, including the vanquished Germany and Japan, Omega too stepped into the fray. During the 31st Grand Conclave, held in December 1945 in Washington, D.C., the issue of what Omega should do was adopted as a resolution for a more expanded commitment to service. And from the adoption of this resolution was created the National Social Action Committee, and with it a recited determination to make it a component of what many brothers said needed to become a key component of an Omega with a re-branded image.

Although the initial spark was hoped to be enough to sustain the fires of more than luke-warm enthusiasm it would not be so. The magnitude of the undertaking, to include the sustained involvement of each presiding brother chairman, plus the annual changes in fraternal leadership, rendered the successful operation of so ambitious an undertaking as less than realistic. Lacking a permanent organizational structure such as a foundation, with necessary financial and other resources to keep it going, the initial enthusiasm gave way to burdensomeness of the task of trying to keep the mission of the NSAC fully operational.

> *Perseverance in Uplift –* All of our chapters should endeavor to sponsor socially acceptable conduct. This would include improvement of manner as well as refraining from activities which are reflections on our organization. A special emphasis should be placed upon respect to womanhood. In all of this the attitude should be that we endeavor to aid brothers who have erred, not to condemn them. - Summary of Findings, Third District Conference, Virginia State College, April 29, 30, and May 1, 1955, P. 3.

> *Social Action Committee-* The Social Action Committee recommends that the Third District of Omega Psi Phi Fraternity reaffirm the Social Action Program advocated by the Grand Chapter at the 1955 Conclave in California. Also, that we continue our full support to the NAACP, the Urban league, and other groups working for integration of the races economically, socially, politically, and spiritually. Further, that we give financial support as well as moral support to those organizations

## 50+ OMEGA INSPIRED YEARS

*and that we press with renewed vigor our Fraternity program to increase the vote.* - Minutes of the Third District Conference, Norfolk, Virginia, April 20-21, 1956.

The challenge to keep going soon faded, with uneven pursuit of the mission becoming the order of the day. In an effort to stem the loss of interest and to revive the NSAC and its mission, several national level brothers made an effort to keep everything in place. Led by former Grand Basileus Harry T. Penn, their efforts proved to be far less than hoped for, as the continuing interest of the brotherhood seemed to fade. However, all was not lost, as the concept of Omega as a service organization, a thought which initially began to take a firm old in the 1930s, found itself to becoming entrenched in the minds and thoughts of Omega's sons who wholeheartedly undertook locally-focused service projects as a viable and expected component of membership with the fraternal brotherhood.

### Editorial by Harry T. Penn, Former Grand Basileus, Roanoke, Va.

*It was rather stimulating and encouraging to know there are others who recognize that the Omega Psi Phi Fraternity must assume quite a different role if it expects to survive. There are still a few members who remember our extra-ordinary National Social Action program which began in 1945 and lasted until 1950, then slowly ebbed away like a dream. Those were the days when District Representatives performed almost miraculous tasks, each vying for the coveted award of the Outstanding District Representative of the year. I recall with sorrow, while attending the 1952 conclave in Cincinnati, the futile efforts of few of us to rejuvenate our social action program. Unfortunately many of our brothers were thinking only of the social side of our Fraternity.*

*Brothers, time and action must be a predominate factor in our lives during these crucial days. Can we afford to sit idly by watching the babbling brook, while so many of our fellowmen are in dire need of our talents, a portion of our time, and above all, the virtue of our charity? The spirit of most individuals is likened unto a river. When nothing disturbs it, it flows gently*

## OMEGA MEN CALLED TO SOCIAL ACTION

*along its banks, showing no interest whatsoever. Suddenly, a dam is constructed in its path, the opportunity for alertness or greatness is witnessed. Cities, town and various industries are serviced with electrical power, recreation areas are established, all because of the opportunity to display its potential strength. We have lived to see miracles occur during our days. There are too many factors aligned in our direction until it is almost unthinkable that so many of us are unaware of our potentials for service.*

*Let us return to the ideals of the Founders of our Fraternity. Let us remember Brother Just, who gave his life for a cause, and the living founders who are giving daily of their lives to mankind. We hold it to be self-evident that all men are created equal, this is right and good, but the Bible speaks of another truth, "To whomsoever much is given, of him shall much be required." Let no brother think that he is an island unto himself. Omega and Omega men can do much – much more. –* The Oracle, Vol. LI, No. 4, Dec. 1962, P. 2.

**50+ OMEGA INSPIRED YEARS**

# V - Realizing The Depth Of Omega, 1958

### Extracts from the Citation to Oliver Hill
### "Omega Man of the Year" for 1957

Oliver W. Hill, counselor, gentleman, scholar, champion of the rights of the Negro, humanitarian, and Christian – Omega is proud to claim you as its son. Truly have you exemplified the four cardinal principals of our beloved fraternity: Manhood, Scholarship, Perseverance, and Uplift. ... When Howard University conferred upon you the Bachelor of Laws Degree in 1933, straightway did you utilize this training, opening your law office. The successes which you have had in the legal field are attested to by your forthrightness, tenacity, courage, and high ethical code. Numerous are the cases which have devolved upon you:

    1. Cases which tested constitutionality of laws in the school segregation cases;
    2. Cases which tested Virginia's poll tax laws;
    3. Cases which sought the preservation of the NAACP;
    4. Cases which tested the mythological doctrine of "Separate but Equal";
    5. Cases which opened to Negroes public facilities of your state;
    6. Cases which challenged seating of Negro passengers on public carriers.

... Your active service to your people and the citizens of Richmond are known to all men – and in every capacity where you have served with dignity and humility; you have wept at segregation and discrimination; ... in your wise and unremitting efforts, you have moved America towards the goal of real equality and justice; you, as that great Roman Counselor, Cicero, have held steadfastly to the dictum that "we cannot advance ourselves by crushing others." Oliver, Omega is happy tonight to pay you this public tribute in awarding you its highest honor, "Omega Man of the Year." On behalf of the Supreme Council, and the entire brotherhood of Omega, I *present to you this plaque which reads, "OLIVER W. HILL – Scholar, gentleman, leader, diagnostician, practitioner, and surgeon in the field of race relations." –* The *Oracle,* Vol. 98, No. 3, March 1958, P. 10.

On July 9, 1958, my dad, James W. Quander, was inducted into the Omega brotherhood by way of Alpha Omega Chapter, Washington, D.C. His recruiter and sponsor was Bro. Ernest Mercer, Alpha Omega chapter member and future basileus. They had been pals for years, and Ernest had spoken to my father on a number of prior occasions about becoming a member of the fraternity. One day Mercer said to him, "James, I don't see why you haven't taken steps to become an Omega Man. Your brother, 'Turkey' (the nickname of my uncle, Joseph P. Quander), joined Omega years ago, and the frat has grown and diversified a lot since then. A man like you, with a lot of focus, energy, and a strong sense of community, you ought to be Omega."

As my dad later related to me, he was a little hesitant. A juvenile diabetic, with symptoms manifested since 1921, when he was just three years old, and with a confirmed diagnoses from 1924, just before his sixth birthday, he had always been interested in Omega membership since his teenage years, but was apprehensive of what the demands of pledging entailed. He asked himself, "At my age, 40, would I be subjected to some form of physical harassment? Would the time requirements incidental to pledging and later to membership be too great? And as a diabetic, would the process involved towards obtaining membership adversely affect my health?" These were all questions and real concerns that he gave consideration to, and discussed with my mother, Joherra, who was not a native-born American, knew very little about Omega and black Greek organizations, and what seeking membership entailed. As well, she knew nothing about the demands of maintaining the membership, once that status had been obtained.

*The world of 1961 is very different from the world if 1911. The conscience of the free world is quickening. The hitherto backward nations are waking and asserting their desire to be free and assume their rightful place among the peoples of the earth. To*

## REALIZING THE DEPTH OF OMEGA

*our younger brothers, I would say that the advance must be far greater in the next ten years than in the last fifty. That place of which we have dreamed, we must achieve, and we must hold such high ideals of manhood, patriotism, and citizenship that we shall deserve it.* – Fiftieth Anniversary Oracle, Statement of Frank Coleman, Founder, to Dr. Benjamin E. Mays, 1961, reprinted Fall 1972, *Oracle*.

He explained to her what he knew about the process that the Scroller pledgees of Kappa Alpha Psi, the only fraternity that was present at Miner Teachers College, went through back in the 1930s, when he was a college student. A lack of sleep, an irregular schedule, a life not your own – at least for the several months of the pledge period. She asked him a few questions. First, why would anyone want to go through such an ordeal just to say that they were now a "brother?" "Surely," she added, "there must be more than that. After all, you are 40 years old, and that rah, rah of college days is long gone. Haven't you mentioned to me too, that several of the most prominent colored men in America are also Omegas?"

He replied in the affirmative. She then added, "Well, they don't seem to be cut from that same cloth that you describe was the 'horror' of pledging when you were in college. And why didn't you pledge Omega when you were in college?" That of course beget other questions, requiring him to rehash his earlier private thoughts about his health, the time demands, and the irregular schedule. And of course, there was no Omega chapter at Miner at that time. Her retort, "No! Not anymore. I can't believe that they would require this of you now, a married man with four children. There's got to be more to it than that."

She modified the subject and asked, "Didn't we have a great time at the Mardi Gras in February? I've never been to such an affair on this grand a scale. Do they do that every year? I hope so! I'm not a Washingtonian, not even an American by birth, but I saw some of the people there that I am certain were 'the best' of what being a Washingtonian means." And by the end of this conversation, dad's mind was made up.

## 50+ OMEGA INSPIRED YEARS

*In an atmosphere enhanced by beautiful women, handsome men, excellent music, loads of refreshments and plenty of room for dancing, Washington's Alpha Omega chapter was host to upwards of 4500 who enjoyed festivities at the annual Mardi Gras Ball, at the mammoth National Guard Armory in the Nation's Capital on February 7th. The Afro-American Newspaper's society columnist Margaret Stewart, who acclaimed the affair as one of the best in Omega history, said: "If there were a contest to determine which organization has given the best affair this year, certainly the Omegas would rate number one. I am sure you know one reason for this was the incomparable music of Count Basie and Wild Bill Davis. Could you ask for anything more?"*

*Mrs. Pearlie Cox, another well-known society columnist, used many superlatives in her comment, in which she lauded " ... members of Omega, gracious hosts who left nothing to be desired by their guests, cut handsome figures in their gold tunics, purple-trimmed and their rich black-braided trousers· ... " Continuing her report, Mrs. Cox said: Heading the welcoming band of Alpha Omega was Basileus William D. Martin. Serving as co-chairmen of the festivities were U. S. Attorney Fred Durrah and Frank P. Bolden. Other committee members were Harry Landers, Dennett Harrod, Ernest Johnson, Tommy Robinson, T. T. Bouleware, Ralph Humphries, Fred Thomas, William Porter, S. Bruce Brown, Joseph Love, Edward Patterson, Basil Oliver and others. Brother Martin attributed the great success to the hard work by chapter members; and the excellent cooperation poured into the joint effort by the brothers, the Omega Wives and a host of Omega friends.*[16]

---

[16] *"Omega Mardi Gras Makes Social History," in Washington, D.C., Winter Oracle, 1958*

## REALIZING THE DEPTH OF OMEGA

Still, dad had one more lingering thought. And it was this! He recalled his early teen days, back about 1931 or 1932, when his older brother, Joe, was playing an outfielder position on the Omega summer baseball league team. Joe seemed so enthused, so gung-ho about Omega, but now is hardly active, maybe totally inactive. Dad called his 11-year older brother and asked him why he was no longer active with the frat. He never did get much of an answer, as my uncle fumbled about, stating something about being "too busy" or "too tired." But he never said anything negative about Omega, adding that he had great memories of being active in the frat, and that several of the locally-based Omega men were also nationally prominent and movers and shakers for our race. Now, once he learned of my dad's revived interest, he encouraged him to pursue membership, adding, "Who knows, maybe you will be the cause of my getting active again, and maybe, just maybe, I should."

Memorial brick to Bro. James W. Quander, Howard University

With his older brother's seal of approval, dad picked up the telephone and called his buddy, Ernie Mercer, and said, "I'm in! Oh, I don't mean that I'm in Omega – yet, but I mean I am game for pursuing membership. I already have the application that you gave me earlier, so I'll fill it out and get it to you promptly." And he did. The exact date that he submitted the application is unknown, but it was around April 19, 1958, the date of my dad's 40th birthday. Looking at the calendar for April 1958, I note that April 19th was the third Saturday of the month, the then and still current date of the monthly Alpha Omega chapter meeting. Therefore, I suppose that dad got the application to Mercer just in time for consideration at the chapter's monthly meeting.

Shortly thereafter, my dad was notified that his application for membership had been favorably considered, and that the 60-day pledge period would begin in early May. He was given a few further instructions about what to anticipate and what was expected of him as a prospective for induction into Omega. He related to me that there was nothing onerous, although it was clear that a time commitment was expected. As a member of the Lampados Club, he had to prove his willingness to make some sacrifices on behalf of both Omega and his fellow line brothers, and likewise he must show some dedication to the causes that Omega is already committed to. As well, one of the correspondences referred to the Four Cardinal Principles of Omega. Relating this to me some years later, he could not recall whether the Principles just appeared on the letterhead, or were they actually mentioned in some detail in the contents of the document.

He added, though, that it was readily apparent that what he was about to undertake was serious business, and that the rah, rah of college days was nowhere evident. He asked himself, "Had Omega grown up, or have I?" On a date unrecalled, but in early May 1958, my dad and his three line brothers (names unrecalled) met for the first time. The other three were strangers to him, but they bonded quickly, acted in concert, supported one another, and mutually determined that the "us" against "them" mandated that they had to work as a unit in order to impress the many brothers of Alpha Omega that each of the four was worthy to attain membership.

### Achievement Week – Its Background and its Purpose

*The annual observance of National Achievement Week was set for November 17-25 [1957] with the theme "Desegregation Changed the Practices: Integration Must Establish the Values." [The] purpose of the observance is to raise the prestige of Omega by providing a worthwhile project to which all chapters may direct their energies, thereby simulating and enriching the communities where chapters are located. This year's theme was chosen as a means of pointing out specific methods and techniques which can be used to obtain integration and to show all Americans that it is their job to use these techniques which will make for a united nation. Achievement Week was inaugurated at the ninth Grand Conclave at Nashville, Tenn., and the programs have endeavored to remove any inferiority complex that may be impeding the progress of Negro masses by*

## REALIZING THE DEPTH OF OMEGA

*having them realize that the Negro has achieved and must continue to do so. – Oracle, Vol. 97, No. 4, December 1957, P. 7.*

They persevered, made the rounds to meet the big brothers of Alpha Omega, and engaged in a community service effort that was focused on helping middle school students from lower income families improve their reading comprehension skills. Recall, if you will, most all of these students had been educated in segregated schools, and the facilities in most of these schools were inferior from the outset. They started from a disadvantageous position, and, after four years, were falling farther behind. So the objective of this four-man team, all of whom were or had been teachers, was to work with these children for several weeks, including beyond their July 9, 1958, initiation into Omega, to help them better understand what they were reading, and to learn how to appreciate the relationship between what they were reading and extend it to other applications.

As my dad related to me, "We didn't just want them to learn to read better. We wanted them to understand what they were reading, and to see how what they had just read had some applicability in their further lives. I think that we were successful, but it was more of a short tutorial, not an intent to be a full academic course." Once a member of Omega, dad took that enthusiasm and continued. He joined a couple of chapter committees, including the Mardi Gras committee, which was his favorite chapter involvement for several years. As well, he would later serve as Alpha Omega's moderator of *Les Jeunes Hommes*, the chapter's group of young high school aged boys, helping to mold them into responsible young men.

### Alpha Omega Gives $1,000 to NAACP

*Alpha Omega Chapter of Washington, D.C., ended its local activities for 1960 at its December 17 meeting at the Omega House. At the party, the NAACP was presented a check for $1,000 by Alpha Omega Chapter to aid in meeting legal expenses. Attorney Spotswood Robinson, III, dean of the Howard University Law School and a member of the legal staff of the NAACP accepted the gift on behalf of the recipient organization. In accepting the donation he emphasized the dire*

## 50+ OMEGA INSPIRED YEARS

*need of money for legal expenses by the NAACP in view of its extensive litigation in civil rights cases dealing for the most part with school desegregation. A large number of appeals growing out of these cases require considerable funds and money for proper prosecution. Alpha Omega is dedicated to an active and vigorous social-action program, and the gift to the NAACP is just one of the chapter's many steps in furtherance of this program. For example, at the Annual Achievement Week Banquet, of November 10, the Omega chapters of Washington, presented a $1,200 unrestricted scholarship to Howard University. – Oracle,* Vol. 50, No. 1, March 1961, P. 12.

# VI – Birth of Les Jeunes Hommes

## Creation of an Omega Youth Interest Group

A desire by some neighborhood boys to do community service led to the sponsorship by Alpha Omega chapter of an innovative program designed to both satisfy this desire and to enable the chapter to influence the identification and development of several future Omega men. The name of the organization, *Les Jeunes Hommes* (the Young Men) (LJH) came from me. By way of context and background, in later years I stated to Bro. Marlon Allen, Alpha Omega chapter and *Les Jeunes Hommes* historian that my inspiration for the creation of such a group came when my parents and I attended the 45th annual Grand Conclave (December 27-30, 1959) held in New York City. As I said to Marlon, "I was studying French at the time, and it seemed a perfect name because that's what we were--young men. ... One reason that the idea caught on was that D.C. is a perfect club town. Lots of guys were into clubs, as were girls. The idea of belonging to something and having some kind of name to it was important."[17]

As I further indicated to Marlon, "I came back from the Conclave and felt we needed to have a youth group that could take the principles of the fraternity and get young men in high school involved in the same things as the [fraternity's] cardinal principles called for and get them to take on the responsibilities that went with doing that. I suggested to my dad that a club that would offer those things and could also be an interest group for the frat. I felt that even if they didn't become members [of the fraternity], we would still have the name of the fraternity out there, taking interest in youth." The long term objective of the club was to always provide volunteer community service, primarily in Washington, D.C.[18]

---

[17] "History of Les Jeunes Hommes, a Community Service Organization, the Alpha Omega Chapter Omega Interest Group," by Bro. Marlon Allen, Alpha Omega Chapter, c1996.

[18] "History of Les Jeunes Hommes, a Community Service Organization, the Alpha Omega Chapter Omega Interest Group," by Bro. Marlon Allen, Alpha Omega Chapter, c1997.

## 50+ OMEGA INSPIRED YEARS

Three weeks later, *Les Jeunes Hommes* held its inaugural meeting on January 17, 1960, at the Quander home, located at 3714 13th Street, N.W., Washington, D.C., about one mile north of Howard University. The preserved records of the founding meeting, created and maintained by Bro. James Quander in a scrapbook reflect that the nine (9) young founders of the group, all attendees at the first meeting, were: Rohulamin Quander, Primary Founder, Harold Boyd, Alfred Neal, Denis Noble, William Reid, Michael Russell, Ernest Smith Jr., Edward Webster, and Robert Wilson. All of the original founders were students at Archbishop John Carroll High School, located in Washington.

While interviewing me in anticipation of writing the history of *Les Jeunes Hommes*, I told Bro. Allen that I was inspired by the same four Cardinal Principles upon which Omega was founded – Manhood, Scholarship, Perseverance, and Uplift – and that we could be an interest group for the fraternity. I felt that even if some of us never did become members of the fraternity, we would still have the name of the fraternity out there, demonstrating that they were taking an interest in youth.

> *My name is Bryant L. VanBrakle. I pledged The Omega Psi Phi Fraternity Inc. in 1965, at Alpha Chapter on the campus of Howard University during my sophomore year. I later graduated from HU's Law School in 1970 and then completed a 43 year career with different components of the Federal Government before retiring as member of the Senior Executive Service.*

> *My first exposure to Omega Psi Phi Fraternity Inc. began sometime around 1959 when I was 13 or 14 years old when I learned about a youth organization sponsored by the Alpha Omega Chapter of Omega Psi Phi Fraternity Inc. This youth organization was named the Les Jeunes Hommes and was led by my future fraternity brothers James Quander and Cutie Carter and some other chapter members of Alpha Omega.*

## BIRTH OF LES JEUNES HOMMES

*LJH, like Omega, was a service organization patterned after the Fraternity's own Cardinal Principles of Manhood, Scholarship, Perseverance and Uplift. Membership in LJH was limited to good students with GPA's of 3.0 in the 9th thru the first year of college, who expressed interest in helping others. As I recall, continued membership required good character, academic excellence and active participation. Membership could be terminated if you failed to meet these standards or when you completed your first year of college, which coincidentally, during the 1960's, is when one generally became eligible to join the fraternity.*

*I remember fondly attending LJH meetings at 1231 Harvard Street, N.W., the fraternity house, in a coat and tie and planning public service activities, with our sponsor's assistance that we performed throughout the community. We painted houses for the needy, planted gardens, collected food and provided what I now know to be UPLIFT to those in need.*

*It was not all work and no play for the members of LJH. We were often sought out to be escorts for young ladies who were "coming out" in cotillions sponsored by the Girl Friends and other social groups. We were invited, often as a group, to our fair share of Jack and Jill events and house parties, and we sponsored a few of our own at 1231 Harvard. One of our social events of the year was the annual Alpha Omega Chapter Mardi Gras. While we were much too young to participate in the festivities, LJH members made lots of money and met many, many people carrying in food and drink into the DC Armory where the event was held. I can't begin to describe all of the liquor and food I carried into this venue for a tip ranging from 5 to 20 dollars.*

*What I learned as a longtime member of LJH provided the springboard for joining Omega in April of 1965 as the 14th member of the "Seldom Seen 17" at the Mother Pearl on the campus of Howard University. I shall never forget my first day on campus as an entering freshman when I stood around the Dial and marveled as my future Brothers circled the Dial and marched and sang many songs that I have learned to cherish.* - Bryant L. VanBrakle, 14-65-Alpha; Alpha Omega

What I did not then know then is that Alpha Omega had previously demonstrated an interest in having a young male group made up from the sons and nephews of brothers of the fraternity. In a chapter report issued for the May 8-9, 1959, Third District Meeting in Portsmouth, Va., Alpha Omega Basileus William D. Martin Sr. wrote that among the social affairs held by the chapter during the preceding year were two parties for sons of Omega men. He stated further, "The chapter provided the Omega house, the house hi fi system, invitations, and refreshments for the sons of Omega parties." He added that these socials were planned by seven Omega sons who were still in the high school, graduating in the class of 1958. The first party, which was given in September (probably 1957), provided the sons with an opportunity to get acquainted with Omega before going to college, while the second party, which was given during their Christmas vacation (again, probably 1957), served as a reunion."[19]

LJH's second meeting convened on February 21, 1960, also at the Quander home, as the group began developing its constitution and bylaws, using samples of others documents. Similar to Omega's Cardinal Principles, the five aims of the club were: 1. Scholarship; 2. Perseverance; 3. Social Maturity – Manners and Truthfulness; 4. Manhood; and 5. Good Citizenship, to include service. Membership dues were set at 50 cents a week. James Quander, as well as John Oliver and Basil Oliver, all members of Alpha Omega, attended the second meeting and provided advice. The nine founders, with the aid and support of Bro. Quander and the brothers Oliver, prepared to petition Alpha Omega chapter for official recognition. As well, elections were held. Alfred Neal, the only senior, was elected the first president, while Rohulamin Quander, a junior, became vice president. Denis A. Noble, a junior became secretary, and William Reid, a junior, served as treasurer.

---

[19] *"History of Les Jeunes Hommes, the Alpha Omega Chapter Omega Interest Group," by Bro. Marlon Allen, Alpha Omega Chapter, with some editing by Bro. Rohulamin Quander, c1996.*

## BIRTH OF LES JEUNES HOMMES

Subsequently, on Saturday, March 19, 1960, Bro. James W. Quander, while attending the monthly meeting of Alpha Omega, introduced a novel idea and plan and then made a specific request of the chapter. He explained to the brotherhood that the program that he was about to put before them had grown out of a desire expressed by his son, Rohulamin, in December 1959, during the 45th Annual Grand Conclave. He and several other boys in his neighborhood wanted to do some community work.

The novel idea was that Alpha Omega take on official sponsorship of a male youth group, explaining further that the purposes of doing so would be multiple. He added that beyond the obvious, i.e., setting the stage for recruitment of qualified young men who would become members of the fraternity in due course, there were several other benefits to be gained.

First, sponsorship of young men would further the fraternity's dedication to its four Cardinal Principles. Second, the chapter would serve as a mentor to this group of youth, who would in turn share and propagate the same sense of responsibility to those who were less fortunate. Third, it was an opportunity for these young men to extend themselves into the community by providing youth-to-youth services, in a way that the chapter, as a group of older men, could not easily do. Fourth, this was a very positive way to extend the name, "Omega Psi Phi," and all positive things associated with the name, into the larger community. Fifth, as racial integration was beginning to take effect, having Omega and its sponsored youth group be on the forefront of this fundamental change in American society, was a critically social and civic opportunity that the members of the fraternity, many of whom were already accredited and publicly recognized in the larger community for their civic and civil rights work, should not miss.[20]

---

[20] *These additional comments on the background for the establishment of Les Jeunes Hommes and the adoption of the club as an officially sponsored program of Alpha Omega Chapter were made by Bro. James W. Quander in 2004, as related to his son, Rohulamin Quander (Alpha 1964), when they were writing Bro. Quander Sr., autobiography, The*

## 50+ OMEGA INSPIRED YEARS

The chapter, voting overwhelmingly, elected to establish a program, which its young charges had already identified and called "*Les Jeunes Hommes*" (The Young Men). Alpha Omega's added objective, at least in part, was to develop an interest group among local prospective college entrants. They hoped to stem the tide of local men's continued attraction towards the Kappa Alpha Psi Fraternity, which was not founded at Howard University, yet was very successful in recruiting many of D.C.'s best men to its fold.

As my dad later explained to Bro. Allen during an interview, "My son Ro was in high school at [Archbishop John] Carroll and had boys interested in community service work who were good friends of his."

> *They wanted to do community service work. The first meeting was at my house [around my dining room table]. . . . [Many of them] were in my scout troop. I asked the fraternity about its interest in doing work with the less fortunate and elderly. [Members of Les Jeunes Hommes] did tutoring and other kinds of things. They came from public and private schools. Some men in the fraternity thought this program had potential for bringing new blood into the fraternity. Stated separately, Bro. James Quander noted that this was an ideal opportunity to counter the image that D.C. was a "Kappa Town," as the city was experiencing a strong surge of undergraduate men toward pledging Kappa Alpha Psi at both Howard University and D.C. Teachers College.* Interview of Bro. James W. Quander by Bro. Marlon Allen, *Les Jeunes Hommes* historian.

The next day, Sunday, March 20, 1960, the club held its monthly meeting, at which time four new members were admitted. They were Ramberto Torruella, Richard Washington, Ernest Gardner, and Ray Young.

On Sunday afternoon, April 10, 1960, at 3:00 p.m., and as a result of Alpha Omega's agreement to become official sponsors, the young club members met for the first time at the Washington, D.C., chapter house, located at 1231 Harvard Street, N.W. Alpha Omega Chapter

---

*Quander Quality, The True Story of a Black Trailblazing Diabetic*, published in 2006.

## BIRTH OF LES JEUNES HOMMES

members present that Sunday afternoon included brothers Everett "Cutie" Carter, William F. Aden, Sr., Basil Oliver, and James W. Quander. At this meeting, William F. Aden, Jr., George Bumbrey, Charles Henry, John Harrod, Denis Parker, and Thomas Newman were admitted to membership. As of this moment, the club's membership had increased to approximately 20 young men.

Then on Sunday, May 8th, at the following monthly meeting, the group approved its constitution and by-laws and adopted its crest, "Rodin - The Thinker," which would subsequently be used as the design for a pocket patch worn by members on special occasions, to reflect that they were members of *Les Jeunes Hommes*. The crest was drawn by Denis A. Noble, a founding club member.

The first activity that the club held was on a cold Friday evening in early February 1960. In 1958 Alpha Omega revived what had been the Omega Mardi Gras, a signature event which was initially started in 1923, but held intermittently since then. However, since 1958, the Mardi Gras has been held every year, and is a primary revenue source to underwrite Alpha Omega's many social service programs. Included were academic scholarships and monetary awards for the chapter's annual essay program, the Talent Hunt, and other community service outreach.

In those days, the Mardi Gras was held at the D.C. National Guard Armory. Moderator James W. Quander came up with the idea that the group's members could provide the dance guests with a valuable service. They could park cars and also help guests to carry in bags and boxes containing food and adult beverages directly to their assigned tables. Naturally, only those club members who had drivers licenses would be entrusted with a vehicle. The idea worked marvelously, with all tips received put into the central pot to benefit the fledgling club treasury.

The club repeated the service for several more years. Brother Kenneth A. Brown (Delta Theta 1971), former Grand Keeper of Finance, whose older brother, Charles, was in *Les Jeunes Hommes*, remembers him coming home from the 1961 Mardi Gras and the excitement in his voice as he talked about the people he had seen and the costumes they wore. Kenny recounted, "He got in around 2 o'clock in the

## 50+ OMEGA INSPIRED YEARS

morning, and all he could talk about was all the purple and gold that was all around the room and all the things he had seen and done that evening, just seeing several of the men that he had seen in the community."

## Les Jeunes Hommes Is Youth Group of Washington Omegas

WASHINGTON, D. C.

LES Jeunes Hommes, teen-age Omega interest group under the sponsorship of Alpha Omega chapter, entertained the visiting high-school sons and daughters of Omega men during the 50th Anniversary Grand Conclave held in Washington, D. C., from August 14th through 18th. Host activities included: participation in the Omega family boatride, 3-teen-age dances, a splash party, and trip to Glen Echo amusement park.

Les Jeunes Hommes restricts its membership to boys who demonstrate potentiality for mental growth and development in assuming community responsibilities. Boys 15 to 18 years old, high school juniors and seniors, planning to go to the college and college freshmen, are eligible for membership.

Club activities consist of aiding personnel of the Washington Merriweather Home for Children; youth forums on pertinent local, national and international issues; competitive sports (baseball, football, basketball) and games (chess, checkers); ice and roller skating; theatre parties (concerts, plays, dance recitals); teen-age informal and formal dances.

Two members of the club have been awarded college scholarships: Barrington Parker—Yale University, New Haven, Connecticut; John Robinson—George Washington University, Washington, D. C. Three other members will be attending schools outside D. C., Earnest Gardner—Rockhurst College, Kansas City, Missouri; Alfred Neil—Morehouse College, Atlanta, Georgia and Robert Reid — Windsor Mountain, Lenox, Massachusetts.

### Visiting Brothers
(Continued from Page 5)

registration was kept simple in Washington. They had enough capable people on duty at the designated hours to keep the line moving. The clock-like precision eliminated long ques at the registration desk. Thoughtful brothers who sent in advance registration, about 100 of them, made a single stop. The kit was ready and waiting.

UNDERGRADUATE LUNCHEON — This was a thrilling experience. Just imagine, if you will, returning to your undergraduate chapter, to sit once again with the youth of our fraternity at a table set aside for the chapter in which you were initiated . . . and to sit again with those with whom you shared undergraduate responsibilities. The addresses by Brother Walter N. Ridley, president of Elizabeth City State Teachers College (N.C.) and Brother Robert H. Tucker, who later was elected second vice grand basileus, were invigorating.

OPEN LUNCHEON—A beautiful and effective setting for a brilliant address by Brother Robert C. Weaver, Federal housing administrator, who spoke on, "The Influence of Scholarship in the Space Age."

CEREMONIAL REDEDICATION — Many brothers believed this to be the most impressive feature of the Washington Conclave. A spinetingling experience, the brothers who were there, left better Omega men.

FORTY-YEAR MEN—While a separate story on the "Forty-Year Men" being honored at this Conclave, appears elsewhere in this issue, visiting delegates were impressed to see those Omega men, many who walked with unsteady pace, return to demonstrate their love for Omega.

ALUMNI BREAKFASTS—Prior to the Undergraduate Closed Luncheon, one chapter (Mu Psi of A and T College) had called together the alumni members of that chapter for breakfast. Twenty-two of the 26 original members present from that chapter showed up for what many thought an unreasonable 8:00 A.M. engagement. There will be more of these at future Conclaves.

DAILY NEWSPAPER—A daily newspaper to acquaint brothers with happenings each day, tabbed "The Golden Que," was delivered each day just before the end of the afternoon session. The delegates thought them important to prepare full and detailed reports for their chapters.

TEENAGERS—A varied program of entertainment for teenagers coming with their parents to the Conclave was carefully planned. They were kept happy and busy during the entire event.

BOAT RIDE—The cruise down the Potomac on the S. S. Mount Vernon, the first real organized social event, was a fine "ice-breaker." The kids, teenagers, wives and brothers had the time of their lives.

These were the extras, many of them never thought of until the Washington Omegas began planning and planning.

MEET THE LES JEUNES HOMMES

These are members of Les Jeunes Hommes, a youth group organized by the Alpha Omega Chapter, Washington, D. C. Representing a new trend in the Fraternity's expanding program, the youth groups, operating under several different names, have worthwhile projects and programs. In the group from left to right are: 1st row—Brothers Baisel Oliver, Wm. F. Aden Sr. Everett Carter, James W. Quander (adult leaders); 2nd row—Earnest Gardner, Harold Boyd, Michael Mason, Rehulamin Quander; 3rd row—Phillip White, Ramsey Torella, Michael Russel; 4th row—Reginald Smith, William Reid, Charles Brown; 5th row—Ray Young, Dennis Parker, George Bumbrey; 6th row—Ferman Faxio, Dennis Noble, David Reid, Last row—Charles Smith, Bennie Carter, Robert Reid, Wm. F. Aden Jr.

## BIRTH OF LES JEUNES HOMMES

After the club had been functioning for a little more than a year, Wendell Morgan, Alpha Omega Basileus, penned a letter to Grand Counselor Carl A. Earles, dated May 23, 1961, inquiring whether the chapter could incorporate the name *"Les Jeunes Hommes."* Brother Morgan noted that the group was set up with the intent of counteracting a "strong trend in Washington of local college boys toward one of the other fraternities. The project has been successful. The club, known as the *Les Jeunes Hommes,* numbers among its membership sons of Omega men as well as sons of other fraternity and non-fraternity fathers. Our chapter includes the activity in our regular budget, and the group uses the fraternity house as its meeting place for business and social meetings." Morgan, in raising questions about incorporation as a way to reserve the name for Omega's exclusive use, said his hope was that other graduate chapters would set up similar programs under this name.

In his response, dated June 5, 1961, Grand Counselor Earles said, "Incorporation alone would not necessarily secure the exclusive use of the name for all purposes, but it could be protected by the [chapter's] uninterrupted use [of the name] for a given period of time. . . . What period of time necessary to bring about this particular effect depends upon the facts and circumstances surrounding the use of the name by the fraternity." He continued, "In other words, if another person or organization attempts to use this name, we may be able to succeed in preventing its use by showing that the fraternity and or chapter has used it for a period of time as that name acquires a secondary meaning, thus creating property rights in the fraternity. It may be well also that this matter be presented to the Grand Conclave in the form of a resolution, so that all chapters with interested groups such as yours will be required to use the name."

The Grand Counselor further advised that before any attempt was made to use the name throughout the fraternity, that Alpha Omega should "initiate the program and use it for perhaps one or possibly two years and then present the matter to the Grand Conclave to have the same become part of its national program. I believe that in that way, there would be greater chance for success." However, nothing further resulted from this inquiry and response. Still the club continued to flourish and to attract quality membership.

# 50+ OMEGA INSPIRED YEARS
## A Personal Experience in Civil Rights

Even from the date of its founding, January 17, 1960, LJH was always committed to rendering service to the local Washington, D.C. community. Indeed, the existence of the club likewise enhanced the image of Omega in the local community as well, since many knew of the fraternity's sponsorship and of the many social service projects that the youth group was committed to. To them it was no surprise to learn of a *Les Jeunes Hommes* connection, although small by comparison to the gravity of the issue, to the plight of the parents and children of Prince Edward County, Virginia, when the white Board of Education voted to close the entire public school system of the country, rather than to integrate the schools, pursuant to the Supreme Court decision in *Brown vs. the Board of Education of Topeka, Kansas.* As the issue expanded, with numerous court cases that eventually required action by the U.S. Supreme Court, it also became a story of how several great Omega men played key roles in regaining the rights of the local black community to their educational system.

One evening in early September 1960, the home telephone rang. I answered. On the other end was Ernest Johnson, a member of Alpha Omega chapter. Bro. Johnson was a Theta Psi chapter 1931 line brother of my uncle, Joseph P. Quander, Sr. His wife, Mignon, an active member of Delta, was also a fabulous Omega wife, always ready and willing to serve whenever and wherever there was a need.

Johnson related to me that he and Mignon had taken in a young man, about 15 or 16 years old, who was from Farmville, Virginia, Prince Edward County, and that he would be living with them for at least the full school year, because the board of education had decided to close all of the county public schools in the county, rather than integrate. I was 16 years old, just entering my senior year in high school, already looking forward to making college applications. The very idea of closing the school system down, thus denying all of the Negro children the opportunity for a public education, was hard to imagine. At the time I was completely unaware of the full magnitude of the struggles that many of our race were facing, particularly in the states of the old Confederacy, in trying to obtain just the basics in education. And Prince Edward County was a prime example.

## BIRTH OF LES JEUNES HOMMES

Johnson asked to speak with my dad, and when they got into their conversation, it was animated indeed. I recall my father saying, "What! Those bastards! How could they do such a thing? Those damn crackers will stop at nothing." Then he added, in response to Bro. Johnson's query, "Why of course. We'd love to have him join the *Les Jeunes Hommes.* This will be an opportunity for the young men in the club to really understand and appreciate how it really is out here. Many of them might take certain things, like education, for granted. But here we have a situation where the basic right to a decent education had been removed. And for no reason other than the color of their skin. Those bastards! They are going to burn in hell for this."

I had seen my dad animated on racial issues on many prior occasions, but this one really got his ire up to the max. After the call ended, he sat me down and fully explained the details of what had already been noted in the black press. He added that Ernie and Mignon had taken in a boy for the school year, and that he would be coming to the next club meeting on the forthcoming Sunday. Already, we were in the earliest stages of planning for our first anniversary party for March 1961, and the fraternity's Golden Anniversary Conclave, scheduled for the following August.

We took in a few new members at that meeting, and he was among them. Regretfully, now more than 50 years later, none of the club alumni can recall his name. We do recall, however, his relating the story of what happened, a story that I have since read up on and gathered more detailed information about. I now relate the essence of what he said, enhanced by my further research as footnoted below.

In May 1954, the U.S. Supreme Court in ruling in the *Brown vs. the Board of Education of Topeka* case, unanimously found that maintaining separate schools for white and black children was inherently unequal, and likewise unconstitutional. The *Brown* case was consolidated with four other related cases, of which *Davis v. County School Board of Prince Edward County,* 103 F. Supp. 337 (1952) was the Virginia case. Four of the five main counsel, Oliver W. Hill, William H. Hastie, James Nabrit, and Spottswood W. Robinson, III, were brothers of Omega Psi Phi. The fourth major counsel, Leon A. Ranson, was a member of Kappa Alpha Psi. Brother Hastie had won the Spingarn Medal in

1943, while Bro. Hill (Alpha Chapter 1927) would later garner the Medal in 2005.[21]

One of the other five desegregation cases was *Bolling vs. Sharpe*, the District of Columbia's case. When the Court, ruling in the plaintiffs' favor, ordered full desegregation, it did not choose to impose a date certain by which that goal was to be achieved. Rather, the Court chose the term, "with all deliberate speed," which subsequently allowed those previously segregated states and school systems a multi-year window in which they could and did drag their feet, in essence ignoring the Court, and thinking that they could forever ignore the otherwise very clear directive.

In 1959, five years later, there was still no movement towards racial consolidation, to merge into one integrated system for everyone. Faced with a federal court order to desegregate its schools by fall of that year, the all-white Prince Edward County school board elected to withdraw from the public school business, allowing white only private "academies." Prince Edward's black citizens lacked both the financial reserves to open their own schools and influence with county decision-makers on the school issue. Initially, the black citizens could not fathom that the county would resort to such extremes

While we did not know it at the time, i.e., September 1960, it would take until 1964 for the Supreme Court to finally order the public schools to reopen to everyone. Nearly 2,700 black students were locked out of public schools for this five year period. Fewer than 500 received some formal education outside the county, of which our fellow LJH brother was one of the fortunate few.[22]

---

21 *The Spingarn Medal is awarded annually by the National Association for the Advancement of Colored People (NAACP) for outstanding achievement by an African American. Founder Ernest E. Just won the first Spingarn Medal in 1915, while Bro. Col. Charles Young earned the second Medal in 1916.*

22 *Southern Stalemate: Five Years without Public Education in Prince Edward County, Virginia, Christopher Bonastia – Associate Professor at Lehman College and the City University of New York Graduate Center April 24, 2012.*

## BIRTH OF LES JEUNES HOMMES
### Our First Anniversary

On March 3, 1961, LJH held its first annual anniversary celebration at the headquarters building of the National Association of Colored Women's Clubs (NACWC), 1601 R Street, N.W., Washington, D.C. It was a grand affair with about 150 persons in attendance. Each club member received two invitations (for two couples) which they could give to their expected guests. The dress was "semi-formal" and mandated a party dress for the ladies and a coat and tie for the young men. By then, many of the club members, including myself, had acquired old gold colored blazers, to which we affixed our Rodin the Thinker felt patch over the upper left pocket on the jacket. This "uniform" quickly became a symbol of LJH membership, which we wore with great pride and a sense of purpose as to who we were, what we were about, and our intention to do something with ourselves in life.

While I cannot recall whether we had a live band to play at our first anniversary celebration, photos taken and preserved for the second annual celebration, held at the same location on March 9, 1962, confirm that the El Corals Band, a very popular music group, played the night away. As well, we had singers who harmonized in the best of the doo wop form that was the rage at the time, plus an impromptu floor show of male and female dancers, who really put the icing on the cake. It was grand, grand, grand indeed.

**50+ OMEGA INSPIRED YEARS**

# VII –Planning Omega's Golden Anniversary, My First Jubilee, 1961

In early 1961, the club devised and undertook a plan to serve as hosts for the forthcoming Golden Anniversary Jubilee celebration of the founding of Omega Psi Phi. Although the members were young, generally between 15 and 19 years of age, the enthusiasm was very high and the cooperative abilities were nowhere greater. The club members saw this as an opportunity to showcase not only the club itself, but the many attributes and offerings of Washington, D.C., the nation's capital city. Segregation was still very much the law of the land, and was particularly still the case in much of the surrounding Maryland and Virginia suburbs.

But in Washington, D.C., as a result of a court ruling in *District of Columbia v. Thompsons's Restaurant,* 92 U.S. App. D.C. 34, 203 F.2d 579 (1953), the practice of denying Negroes access to all public accommodation facilities in D.C. was invalidated. At last, African Americans could enjoy full access to D.C.'s hotels, restaurants, and entertainment locales without fear of being turned away and embarrassed. By 1961, we as a group of people were just comfortably settling in to the idea that we could go everywhere and enjoy all of the Nation Capital's public facilities on an equal basis. Remember that forced public school integration had only occurred in 1954, as a result of the *Brown v. Board of Education,* 347 U.S. 483 (1954) decision.

This was just seven short years before the Golden Anniversary Grand Conclave convened at the Sheraton Park Hotel, one of the District's grandest hotels. For Omega to convene its 50th Anniversary celebration at the Sheraton Park Hotel may not seem like that much of a milestone now, looking back to 1961, but my reference back to the 10 prior conclaves reflects that most all of them were either held in a northern location, where there was greater access to public facilities, or convened in Southern locales at a college or university site, with hotel accommodations sometimes being held in black-owned or smaller hotels. Indeed, being able to stay in the Washington, D.C. flagship hotel was a major milestone for Omega's brotherhood and their families.

## 50+ OMEGA INSPIRED YEARS

At the time several members of LJH remembered what it was like to be forced into an all-black public school. Most all of the club's membership at the time had started their primary education in segregated public schools, and although they were generally enrolled in the lower to middle primary grades, they still understood what it was to be separated into an educational environment that was limited and defined by their race, and not by their academic abilities.

My personal recollections of those heady days, and the many then forthcoming events that would follow still bring many smiles. I was elected as the second president of the club in September 1960, after our first president, Alfred Neal, had gone off to Morehouse College. I was a 16 years old senior at John Carroll High School, full of life and looking forward to whatever would unfold, including a hopeful induction into the Omega Psi Phi Fraternity in due course. We were well aware that Omega was soon going to have its 50th Anniversary Celebration. Already committees were in place and the talk was of making this Omega's grandest celebration to date. Fifty Years! And what progress among our race had been made? Much indeed!

My father was deeply involved with the plans of several committees, including *Les Jeunes Hommes* activities, and Alpha Omega's social committee. All of the committees were making big plans to accommodate the brothers and their families during the entire time that they would be at the big event. Dad was creating and editing many documents incidental to the forthcoming activities. Typically his efforts would be directed to creating a program for an assembled meeting or one of the many celebratory banquets.

Whether consciously or not, the club set out to make their contributions to the celebration a grand one, to create a true "Week to Remember!." The club members, with the assistance of their Alpha Omega chapter mentors, and also seeking the input from the mothers of these teenagers, began convening their own planning meetings, in addition to the club's regular monthly meetings.

The Washington, D.C. area planning committee gave the club a charge – You are to plan the entertainment for the teenage youth and young adults who will be here with their families during the conclave celebration. And we proved to be worthy to the challenge. We organized basketball games, splash parties at the hotel's large and

## OMEGA'S GOLDEN ANNIVERSARY, MY FIRST JUBILEE, 1961

inviting swimming pool, and were assigned a good size party room for entertaining young people in the evenings. We had at least three evening dance parties in the room, and danced to the latest 45 RPM records.

We also worked with both the Omega brothers and the Omega wives to coordinate daytime tours of the city, with several of the club members accompanying our visitors, both teen and adults, to help explain the significance of many of the sites. As expected, many of the attendees were first-time visitors to the national Capital City. Everything was well planned and executed without a mishap, as we played our roles as youth ambassadors for Omega, while the Men of Omega stopped and reflected upon what had been accomplished over the prior 50 years, and rededicated themselves towards what could be accomplished in the future.

> *The theme was simple, "Dedicated to Our Founders," but Bro. William D. Martin, Grand Marshal, captured the fraternal dedication for the future in his Welcome Remarks. He stated, "Let us at this 50th Anniversary Grand Conclave, rededicate ourselves anew to the principles of the Omega Psi Phi Fraternity and take worthwhile actions which will give evidence of our determination that Omega will continue to grow and flourish during the coming fifty years."*[23]

One less than pleasant recollection of this grand celebration is called to mind. On Monday, August 14, 1961, the second official day of the Golden Anniversary Grand Conclave, we gathered for an Omega boat ride on the "S.S. Mount Vernon," a large river boat that daily plied the Potomac River from Washington, D.C., departing from the Maine Avenue, S.W., pier. The capacity of the boat was about 1,500 people. Still, it was not large enough to accommodate all in attendance. Live music was provided by the Bobby Felder Band, which has since become a musical institution in Washington, D.C., and is still flourishing after more than 50 years.

---

[23] *Statement of William D. Martin, Golden Jubilee Grand Marshal, as noted in the Souvenir Journal, August 1961.*

### 50+ OMEGA INSPIRED YEARS

The Omega brothers set aside a portion of the tickets for LJH members, their dates, and a few friends. Consequently, there was a significant presence of youth on board. It was a beautiful afternoon when we departed shortly after 5:00 p.m., heading past Haines Point and due south for the three-hour sunset cruise. At that point, the word "South" took on an entirely different meaning.

As noted above, Washington, D.C. was forced open to public accommodations in the *Thompson Restaurant* case, decided in 1953. So we could enjoy full facilities in D.C., including all of the accommodations that the Sheraton Park had to offer. Such was not the case in the D.C. suburbs. Some places were more open and welcoming than others, but for the most part, facilities were still closed to blacks. We locals knew that, and were accustomed to the same "S.S. Mount Vernon" not stopping at the still whites-only Marshall Hall amusement park, whenever a black group chartered the entire boat.

Conversely, when the boat was not rented out, and took on all paying passengers for an afternoon or evening cruise down the river, it was traditional for the boat to stop at the amusement park, and for several passengers to disembark to get on the rides, eat hot dogs, and enjoy a cool fresh squeezed lemonade or cotton candy. A later boat would stop by and pick them up for the return trip to D.C. But for us of the sable persuasion, this option did not exist.

Being a local Washingtonian, whose family had previously been in involuntary servitude to President George Washington at the Mount Vernon Estate and Gardens (the Plantation), I was, and still am, a fairly frequent visitor to the Plantation. I would take visiting out of town relatives and friends down there, to visit the Plantation, which was open to all races, to show them some of the places where

## OMEGA'S GOLDEN ANNIVERSARY, MY FIRST JUBILEE, 1961

the Quander ancestors had worked when enslaved. I recall on more than one occasion when the "S.S. Mount Vernon," while en route to the Mt. Vernon Plantation, stopped at Marshall Hall. A white crew member would be stationed at the disembarkation area to monitor who was getting off, planning to go ashore to partake in the amusements.

Although I never attempted to go ashore, because I was fully aware of the park's segregated status, others of our race were not as fortunate or aware. I observed a few of them attempting to disembark, drawn by the lights and the pleasant smells, only to be tersely advised, "Only white people can go ashore!" What an embarrassment! To make such a public statement was wrong, and to make it in the form of a targeted announcement was a complete humiliation. This was a rude awakening for many who had never been in the south, or had never been on this boat before. To be told, "No Negroes allowed!" was a reminder that racism still ruled the day.

But for at least this evening, August 14, 1961, we were spared such an indignity. The boat made no stops, just a raucous, bacchanalian three hour cruise, with many adults, most of whom were Omega men, joyous at being present to observe and celebrate Omega's 50th. They hardly paid attention to the fact that impressionable youth were present. Still, the brothers did mind their manners for the most part, although "Omega Oil" flowed freely, and likewise loosened their tongues.

While the details of the Golden Anniversary Conclave are beyond my intentions in this Memoir document, my reference to the Golden Anniversary Souvenir Journal is significant for what it reflects. On page one appears a photo of President John F. Kennedy, who only seven months previously, had been inaugurated as the 35th President of the United States. Oddly, though, the statement that appears below his photograph was not from President Kennedy, but was crafted by Bro. Otto McClarrin, the Chairman of the Souvenir Program Committee.

## 50+ OMEGA INSPIRED YEARS

Between August 13-18, 1961, there were:
- worship services;
- at least two concerts;
- an open house at the local fraternity house;
- several committee meetings;
- welcoming addresses;
- district reports;
- Supreme Council reports;
- golf tournaments;
- plenary sessions;
- a memorial service for brothers who reside in Omega Chapter;
- a smoker;
- the Talent Hunt;
- election of officers;
- a tour of Howard University, the site of Omega's founding in 1911;
- symposia addressing social action concerns, including housing, religion, education, and civil rights; a rededication ceremony by Omega brothers; and
- a visit to the grave of Founder Ernest E. Just.[24]

As well, no Omega conclave gathering would be complete without numerous opportunities to fellowship. Among those events were:
- the Get Acquainted Dance (music by the Gay Clefs);
- the Pan Hellenic Dance (music by Wild Bills Davis Combo and the Eddie McDermon Orchestra);
- the Golden Anniversary Ball (music by the Duke Ellington Orchestra);
- the Founders Banquet and ball (music by the Bro. Count Basie Orchestra); and
- the Auf Wiedersehen Dance (music by the Bro. Count Basie Orchestra).[25]

---

[24] See the *50th Anniversary Grand Conclave Golden Anniversary Souvenir Journal, created by the Planning Committee, Bro. William C. Martin, Sr., Grand Marshal, August 1961.*

[25] See the *50th Anniversary Grand Conclave Golden Anniversary Souvenir Journal, created by the Planning Committee, Bro. William C. Martin, Sr., Grand Marshal, August 1961.*

# OMEGA'S GOLDEN ANNIVERSARY, MY FIRST JUBILEE, 1961

As would be expected, there were many nationally accredited speakers during the celebratory week, all of whom were men and women whose historical significance and contributions are secure in American history. To mention but a few: Robert F. Kennedy, U.S. Attorney General, the keynote speaker at the Founders Banquet; Carl T. Rowan, Assistant Secretary of State; Bro. Robert C. Weaver, then Federal Housing Administrator, and later Secretary of Housing and Urban Development, the first African American to serve in a presidential cabinet; Bro. Otto McClarrin, U.S. Commission on Civil

## 50+ OMEGA INSPIRED YEARS

Rights; Woody W. Hayes, Coach, Ohio State University; and Bro. Oliver W. Hill, Esq., civil rights attorney and later a Spingarn Medal winner.

Further, several former or future grand basilei, as well as Bro. H. Carl Moultrie, National Executive Secretary, spoke, issued reports, or otherwise charged the Omega brotherhood to continue their respective life journeys in pursuit of Manhood, Scholarship, Perseverance, and Uplift. The Golden Anniversary Souvenir Journal reflects that among them were: Bro. Milo C. Murray (20th Grand Basileus, 1949-1951); Bro. Herbert E. Tucker, Jr. (23rd Grand Basileus, 1955-1958); Bro. I. Gregory Newton, 24th and then current Grand Basileus (1958-1961); Cary D. Jacobs (25th Grand Basileus, 1961-1964); George E. Meares (26th Grand Basileus, 1964-1967); and James L. Felder (then serving as Second Vice Grand Basileus, an undergraduate elected position).

I am confident that there were several other former grand basilei and current and former Supreme Council members in attendance, men who faithfully served Omega from the earliest days of its initial founding, lovingly shaping her, making the Cardinal Principles a living and breathing roadmap, and standard for a long and successful life. However, their names were not specifically noted as speakers or presenters in the printed Souvenir Journal that was published.

As well, all three of the then living Founders were in attendance: Founder Edgar Amos Love (First and Third Grand Basileus, 1911-1912, and 1913-1915); Founder Oscar J. Cooper (Second Grand Basileus, 1912-1913); and Founder Frank Coleman. Many glowing tributes were likewise given to Founder Ernest E. Just, who died in 1941.

I think back to those special days with a great smile on my face. I had just graduated from Archbishop John Carroll high school in June, taken on a summer job with the Library of Congress, and was finalizing my plans to enter Howard University in the forthcoming September. But the big and most important event of that period was not Howard or my educational future, although quite important and worthy of concentrated consideration. The focus was on the forthcoming 50th Anniversary Conclave. I was not even an Omega – yet – but somehow most of my thoughts and all of the concentrated

## OMEGA'S GOLDEN ANNIVERSARY, MY FIRST JUBILEE, 1961

planning was focused on the single week –August 14 – 18, 1961 – and the culmination that it would represent.

My summer job was at the Library of Congress, working as a "Deck Attendant," mostly on Deck 42, filling book request orders, returning books to their proper places, and reading shelves to verify that the books were not misfiled or out of numerical order, which could easily occur when having so many books to reshelve within a short space of time. A misfiled book could give the impression that the book was checked out, even if the library card files said otherwise. This was also the summer that I met Bro. Frank B. "Frankie P." Patterson, another fellow deck attendant, who had just completed his freshman year at Howard.

He and I had some perfunctory discussions about Omega, with him expressing an interest in pledging the fraternity, despite his father being a Kappa. I did not yet appreciate how serious a problem that could pose in certain families. I recall his saying that his dad did not really care, anyway, since he was not active with his own fraternity. Frank said, "My dad told me to make up my own mind on the decision of what fraternity to seek out, and then to do it." And Frank then added, "I've made up my mind, and Omega is it."

Neither of us had any inkling that someday Frank Byron Paterson would be a "Living Legend" in Omega, a man who has devoted more than 50 years to the betterment of the fraternity, knowing about as many Omega men across the country as anyone else in the fraternity. I doubt if he has ever missed a Grand Conclave, and I was very proud of him when in July 2012 he received his 50-year pin and recognition at the78th Grand Conclave, held in Minneapolis, Minnesota. As well, both Alpha Omega and the Third District each gave "Frankie P." a special recognition for his 50 years of hard work and dedicated service to Omega on the national, district, and chapter levels.

We both missed being on the inside of the Golden Anniversary celebration. However, "Frankie P." would have the honor of being inducted into Omega via Alpha Chapter on the "Slick 21," in April 1962, on the first post Golden Anniversary Celebration pledge line at the Mother Pearl. Bro. Dennis Parker, who was a *Les Jeunes Hommes* member, and one of the first two club members to enter Omega's sacred fold, was likewise Frankie P.'s line brother.

## 50+ OMEGA INSPIRED YEARS

I was busy too, on the personal side. I was always a social person, went to some of the "best" affairs in town, met many of the so-called "right" people, although that would often prove to be very shallow. And as I have matured into adulthood and now as a senior citizen, I more fully appreciate the significance of values, standards, goals, and that the friendship and respect of good, decent, and honest people is what really counts in life. And for those lessons learned, I am most appreciative. But naturally, at 17 years of age, I was hardly thinking much about "values" and "standards." At senior prom time, mid-May, I had one girlfriend, Antoinette "Toni" Watson. By conclave time I had asked Carmen Torruella, with whom I had attended elementary school, to be my date for the entire week.

Carmen had always liked me, ever since we met in August 1950 at Richard Washington's sixth birthday party. I was already six, and Carmen had just turned five. We had no idea that month that in September, the following month, that she and I, plus Richard and Carmen's brother, Ramberto, would integrate the Sacred Heart elementary school, as part of the Archdiocese of Washington's decision to integrate the formerly segregated parochial school system.

When I asked Carmen to be my Conclave week date, she readily accepted. She was a Latina, and heavily supervised and chaperoned by her mother, Juana Campos, and the Latin community. However, her mother always liked me and my family. So she consented. Not only did she consent, she proceeded to create a wardrobe, to include three new party dresses for the evening socials. In writing this memoir, I asked Carmen, who is now my beloved wife of many years, if she could remember what the dresses looked like. She looked at me as though I had two heads, and said, "1961! How do you expect me to remember what I wore more than 50 years ago to a party?" But after putting our heads together, we did remember at least one of the dresses, particularly because of a unique feature.

It was a canary yellow strapless dress made of a jersey fabric. Gathered around the waist, it opened up below into a flair. What was unique about it though, and recalled by her, was that in place of sleeves, her mother, Juana Campos, made wide matching upper arm bands, puffy and of the same color. These arm bands were faux

## OMEGA'S GOLDEN ANNIVERSARY, MY FIRST JUBILEE, 1961

sleeves, but were not attached to the dress. She received several favorable comments about the uniqueness of the idea.

This entire celebratory week was quite an eye opener for her too. Being of Dominican Republic and Puerto Rican background, she had been closely sheltered and supervised, and had not been allowed much social mixing. So, for her to be allowed to spend her time with me and my family was a new experience for her too. About to enter the 11th grade, it was her first real opportunity to interact with African Americans (we were still called "Negroes" and "colored" at the time) on such a wide basis. Her world was socially small, limited to the tightly knit Latino community that was present in Washington, D.C. at that time.

What we did not realize at that time, though, was that the 1961 Omega conclave was our first Omega Jubilee, which we have now observed every 25 years. Although I was not yet a part of the fraternity officially, we both were integral to the celebration by virtue of my position as president of *Les Jeunes Hommes* and the complete component of activities that we planned for our teenage and young adult guests. Later, in 1986, we would work together to contribute to the success of Omega's 75th Anniversary Diamond celebration, also held in Washington, D.C. That was our second jubilee.

I was the primary author of the Omega Statement that appeared in the Souvenir Journal that year, but had able editing and input assistance from Bro. William Clement, Grand Marshal, Bro. Herbert B. Dixon, and Bro. Kenneth A. Brown. But Carmen, too, played a major role in the preparation of the document, as she edited, commented, and helped me put the document together intermittently, before the others saw what I was producing. Further, as a professional artist, she designed the Diamond Jubilee Souvenir Journal cover.

And our third jubilee in 2011! That was the Centennial Celebration, of course, and together we made it quite a personal celebration in addition to all the other things that were ongoing. I am cognizant that I am discussing events that occurred well beyond the events of the 1961 grand conclave, but I thought it relevant and appropriate to mention the second and third jubilees in the present context, because it is important to realize that my dedication to Omega and her support of both Omega and me, has been ongoing for

## 50+ OMEGA INSPIRED YEARS

quite some time. We are looking forward to our fourth jubilee, Omega's 125th Anniversary Celebration, to be celebrated in Washington, D.C. in 2026. I will revisit both the second (1986) and third (2011) jubilees later in this book.

From the outset of *Les Jeunes Hommes* in 1960 and during the ensuing 11 years, the club's activities were focused on continued community service projects, but always with a stirring in of some athletic and social events, particularly the annual anniversary party, a much coveted event. Among the service projects were: regular public affairs forums, youth-focused programs; a D.C. Department of Recreation Gardening Project; visits to Capitol Hill in February 1962 to lobby the U.S. Congress on behalf of D.C. Public Schools; health fundraising, volunteer visits and work at senior citizen homes; the "Mississippi Survival Project" clothing drive, sponsored by the Student Nonviolent Coordinating Committee (SNCC); weekly supervising younger children at the Banneker Recreation Center, to provide guidance and opportunities to develop healthy sportsmanship; and public service painting projects, including painting the basement of the historic Mary L. Merriweather (Marie L. Merriwether)[26] Home For Children, a 100-year institution, located on Euclid Street., N.W., across from Howard University.

### Alpha Omega Teenage Group Marks 3rd Year

*Les Jeunes Hommes, teenage Omega interest group, sponsored by Alpha Omega Chapter, Washington, D.C., held its third anniversary celebration on March 8th, at the headquarters of the Federation of Colored Women. One objective of the club is to provide area youth with opportunities for growth and development in assuming community responsibility by actively participating in worthwhile community service projects. Trips have been made to Capitol Hill to make Congressmen aware of the needs of the District Public Schools. Members of "Les Jeunes Hommes" have also appeared on television youth forums such as*

---

[26] *The spelling variation for Mrs. Merriweather's given as "Mary" and "Marie," is due to different spellings noted in various resources and citations. The same is true for the varied spellings of Merriweather and Merriwether.*

## OMEGA'S GOLDEN ANNIVERSARY, MY FIRST JUBILEE, 1961

*"It's Academic" and "Youth Speaks Out." Plans are currently being made to entertain patients at St. Elizabeth's mental hospital and displaced children living at Junior Village. Academic pursuit and achievement beyond the high school level are stressed. Although the club's membership is comprised predominantly of high school boys, there are Les Jeunes Hommes attending the following institutions of higher learning: Howard University; District of Columbia Teachers College, Catholic University; George Washington University; Lincoln University, Pa.; Morehouse College; Williams College; Providence College; Central State University; Yale University; Princeton University; and Notre Dame University. Adult moderators of the club are Everett W. "Cutie" Carter, Basil B. Oliver, James W. Quander, and Fred Aden. –* Oracle, Vol. 78, May 1963, P. 32.

*Les Jeunes Hommes* also played a significant and lasting role in promoting racial understanding and greater harmony between black and white residents of this city. In what were probably the first interracial visits scheduled at the fraternity house, the second city-wide interracial visits occurred on Sunday afternoon, October 18, 1964, under the umbrella of a program known as "Interracial Home Visit Day." The *Washington Afro American* issue of October 24, 1964, noted that approximately 4,000 residents of the Washington Metropolitan area participated in this unique event and opportunity. About 2,500 of the participants lived in Washington, D.C. Noting that 37 young adult groups and many individuals participated city-wide, the article focused on *Les Jeunes Hommes*, noting that the 24 club members played host to the young Caucasian students, many of whom, like *Les Jeunes Hommes'* membership, were in high school or just staring college.

> *There was seldom a lag in the exchange of questions and answers as each person tried to explain his feelings about racial prejudice and the effects it has on the entire nation. Frequently the white youngsters were amazed by historical events or contributions of colored people that have been carefully obscured in most school texts in this country. The*

*interchange of ideas was stimulating and down to earth. No punches were pulled on either side. The topics discussed included interracial marriage, religion, education, and economics.* – "Teenagers Exchange Ideas On Important Racial Issues," The *Washington Afro American*, October 24, 1964.

The *Afro* article estimated that there were about 200 people present at the Omega Psi Phi-sponsored event, subdivided into 12 groups, with *Les Jeunes Hommes* members serving as discussion leaders and participants. James W. Quander, the club's adult moderator stated that the success of the event at the Omega house was due in large measure to the efforts of *Les Jeunes Hommes'* members, who worked tirelessly with Alpha Chapter, located at Howard University, Omicron Gamma Chapter, located at D.C. Teachers College, and other brothers of the fraternity, to assure that the event would be both successful and beneficial. According to an October 19, 1964, *Washington Post* article, the object of the home visit program was to "discuss ways of bridging the gap between the races." A *Catholic Standard* article on the same event, reported that under the organized plan whites visited Negro homes during this visit cycle, but that it was planned that Negroes would visit white homes during third visit, then planned for Spring 1965.[27]

At least one chapter of the fraternity inquired about the club and its program. Rho Psi Chapter at Tennessee State University wrote James W. Quander on September 1, 1961, asking for a copy of *Les Jeunes Hommes'* constitution and any other items Quander could provide. Rho Psi Basileus Philmore Graham said the chapter had an interested group of 175 students in four schools near the Tennessee State campus. Quander sent the chapter the information but never heard whether it actually set up its own *Les Jeunes Hommes* program.

## Members Who Entered Omega

About 15 men entered Omega as a result of their prior *Les Jeunes Hommes* membership. Further, several more non-club members, including Kenneth A. Brown and Larry Brown, became Omega men

---

[27] *The Catholic Standard, October 23, 1964.*

through their introduction to the fraternity via some affiliation with *Les Jeunes Hommes*. Among the men who entered Omega Psi Phi after being members of *Les Jeunes Hommes* were Rohulamin Quander, David H. Reid, III, Bryant Van Brakle, Flavius Galliber, and Dennis Parker, all of whom entered through Alpha Chapter. As well, Alfred Neal, the group's first president and a graduate of Morehouse College, was inducted through Psi Chapter. Some of the other men inducted were Jonathan White, Phillip White, Raymond Young, and Tony Taylor. There were other inductees also, but time has passed and memory faded, so their names are not now recalled.

> *What it meant was that these young men had identified with the frat through the organization, and now they were coming forth to make active application for membership. We had [about 20 or more] fellows who came into the fraternity. In fact, being a member of Les Jeunes Hommes ultimately became an advantage for these young men. While mention of the organization during an interview for membership in Omega Psi Phi did not guarantee acceptance into the pledge clubs . . . the mention of the organization was, in general, seen as more of a plus among members of the chapter where the young man was seeking membership than as a negative.* - Interview of Rohulamin Quander by Bro. Marlon Allen, c1996.

The group moved from vibrancy to life support by 1969, while Bro. James W. Quander, its initial mentor and adult founder, entered the Roman Catholic seminary, studying to become a Permanent Deacon. No one from Alpha Omega stepped forward with the same zeal, and shortly thereafter, the chapter found itself unable to carry on the full program, which required a continued sustained commitment to the club established history of rendering service. Thus *Les Jeunes Hommes* faded away around 1971. Besides the brothers not stepping up to keep the club afloat, it was also a victim of the Black Power Movement and many students' attitudes and feelings that black fraternities were no longer relevant. When the history of *Les Jeunes Hommes* was being written in the late 1990s by Bro. Allen, Bro. James Quander stated to him, "We need the organization more now than ever, given the issues facing society. It should never have broken up."

## 50+ OMEGA INSPIRED YEARS

Most importantly, *Les Jeunes Hommes* made a lasting contribution for 10 solid years. Its principles and legacy were largely the same as those adopted by Omega in 1911.[28] These five "Aims" served us well as both a beacon and guiding light. We were young men who were formulating our life goals and objectives, and were privileged to have been a part of this club and beyond. As well, there were many others, both young men and young women, who were likewise influenced by the integrity standards for which the club stood and was known.

We were always challenged by the occasional buffet of those who did not understand the many purposes for which the club was created, or those who were not invited to join. Contrary to some of those adverse and negative assertions, it was not a club for "doctors and lawyers sons" as one detractor stated to me, in an attempt to make us both bourgeois and irrelevant. Nor was it club for the sons of "rich Omegas." Rather, *Les Jeunes Hommes* was always focused upon introducing young men of like mind and college-bound, to certain principles, all of which were to be found in Omega Psi Phi and beyond. And service to others was at the top of the list.

Even today, 54 years after the club was founded, and about 43 years after its dissolution, many of these former club members continue to interact and live a life consistent with the true purposes for which the club was established. I am happy, content, and proud the count myself as among that group.

Whether they are Omega men, and some did pledge at least Kappa or Alpha, or never joined a fraternity, the sense of place and the need to render service to others is still a valuable component of their lives, an aspect and characteristic which they share and will continue to share with their family, friends, and peers. Indeed, *Les Jeunes Hommes* did make a lasting impression and contribution to not

---

[28] *The five aims of the club were: 1. Scholarship; 2. Perseverance; 3. Social Maturity – Manners and Truthfulness; 4. Manhood; and 5. Good Citizenship, to include service. The club members felt that the slightly modified purposes (the aims) were more descriptive, and suited them more accurately and specifically in 1960, when the club was being formed. However, the members were ever mindful of Omega's Four Cardinal Principles and did not want to deviate from them.*

**OMEGA'S GOLDEN ANNIVERSARY, MY FIRST JUBILEE, 1961**
only its members and the brothers of Omega Psi Phi, but to society at large. This is our club's lasting legacy, of which the club's alumni are most proud.

## 50+ OMEGA INSPIRED YEARS

# VIII – On To Howard University

I graduated from John Carroll High School in June 1961. All of my immediate family, and many from my Barbados family were present at the commencement exercise. Carmen made it a point to be present too, as her like for me was evident by that time. I had another girl who I was squiring around at the moment, but Carmen, who was very friendly with my family, made her physical presence felt, regardless of another woman being on the scene. Funny though, for whatever the reason, my then girlfriend, Antoinette, was not present that afternoon. Why? I cannot recall at this time.

Entering Howard University in September 1961 was a bit anticlimactic, after the high level festivities and excitement of celebrating Omega's Golden Anniversary, as above detailed in my chapter on the history of *Les Jeunes Hommes.* Still, ordinary day-to-day events are part of life, and no one should reasonably expert that every minute of every day would be "fabulous" However, entering Howard was a unique experience for me. I was 17 years old, and full of life. Other than during the first grade in the old D.C. segregated educational system, I had never had a black teacher.

Further, having just graduated from a predominantly white high school, where there was nothing Afro-centric, and not even a hint of any contributions to the world that people of the African Diaspora ever contributed, entering Howard was a real eye-opener. Many of my entering classmates came from cities and towns where the number of Negroes was very small, and in some cases, almost nonexistent. They too got a rude awakening for their own betterment. I know that I did.

Although I was part of the D.C. social scene, having been a regular invitee to certain parties, an escort in several Girl Friends and Bachelor Benedict-sponsored cotillions, and a member of a good family with a name of longstanding, arriving at Howard was somewhat overwhelming. So many pretty girls, so many diverse attitudes and activities, so many clubs to join. I knew that I was there for serious business, and had to limit myself to what I could handle.

## 50+ OMEGA INSPIRED YEARS

At one of the earliest weekly freshman assembly activities, one of the deans addressed the class, with a famous, but discouraging statement. He said, "Look to your left. Now look to your right. Next year, one of the three of you will not be here." I was insulted. Why would he think so little of us, I wondered? But what I did not yet understand is that he was absolutely right. Many a classmate, good people and new friends, did not return the following year. For some, the money ran out too soon. Others lost interest in college. But a significant percentage of them simply did not cut it academically. In simple works, they flunked out.

Later, when I saw one of my former classmates at Homecoming 1962, the year that I had transferred to Lincoln University, Pennsylvania, I asked him why he did not return to Howard. Looing glum, he replied, "I had too much fun. I simply could not buckle down and study. Too many distractions. The women!" Only then did the remark of the dean fully sink in. Fortunately, although I did have my academic challenges, I was never in danger of flunking out, and never so distracted that I lost sight of the reason why I was there.

My freshman year at Howard University was an eye opener. This was my first sustained international experience as a young adult. Although there were foreigners and recent immigrants during my elementary years at Sacred Heart (1950-1957), and likewise in high school (1957-1961), this time it was different. Because the students were all adults, while there was some clannishness among certain groups, most of the students were interested in reaching out and being a part of the Howard community beyond just the classroom. As a freshman, I did not belong to either the Campus Pals or the International Pals, but I found myself among several students from diverse backgrounds. This enabled me to learn something about their respective homelands and cultures, and opened my eyes further to the realization that we might have some shared interests, and were all in pursuit of higher education, but we were not all the same.

At that time I was focused on studying medicine, so my course load reflected introductory science courses, including Biology 101, which was offered in the Biology Building, which is now the Ernest E. Just Hall. As well, survey courses in the social sciences were the order of the day for all Howard freshman enrolled in the college of liberal

## ON TO HOWARD UNIVERSITY

arts. I enjoyed everything, including my new found freedom as a young adult. Still, I longed for the "away" experience, and when the opportunity was presented to go away to another university, I elected to pursue that option.

# 50+ OMEGA INSPIRED YEARS

# IX – Transferring To Lincoln University

Although I was not unhappy with Howard, still I had a yearning for the away college experience. My dad knew a lot of Lincoln men, including Bro H. Carl Moultrie (Beta Chapter, 1933) and we found ourselves being invited to the annual Lincoln alumni dinner. There I met several more Lincoln men, including several students who had come down from campus. We were entertained by the Lincoln Chorale, which I learned was heavily populated with Beta Chapter brothers and members of the Lampados Club. I liked the idea of going away, and my parents liked the idea of my not going too far away. Lincoln was only 99 miles from D.C., less than two hours away. I completed my freshman year at Howard in June 1962, and was accepted to enter Lincoln as a transfer student beginning in September 1962.

Lincoln was a very different place from Howard. It was isolated, and had just become a co-ed institution. There were no residence halls for women. The few that were enrolled lived off campus. Some of them were local and lived at home, while other co-eds lived with local families, including faculty and administrators' families. I lived in room 212 McCrary Hall, sharing a dorm room with Jimmy Smith, an older student, from Pittsburgh, who had just gotten out of the military.

Campus life was one of the first differences that I observed at Lincoln. Less pretentious, and still not use to having women on the campus, the "just men" attitude made for a far more relaxed atmosphere than was the case at Howard. For example, the dress and behavioral patterns between Howard and Lincoln men were far and away not the same. The trend at Howard was shirt and tie, but not everyone, and not every day. Further, we mostly carried attaché cases for our books, setting a psychological tone for what we hoped would unveil in our future careers.

Conversely, Lincoln men did not feel the need to dress for success or to impress. It was just a bunch of fellas, hardheads in jeans and old clothes. That was still the prevailing atmosphere. But of course Lincoln men did know how and when to dress, such as on weekends of particular events. Following that trend, the Lincoln brothers of Beta Chapter seemed to be less polished than their Alpha Chapter brothers, but no less enthusiastic about Omega, They dressed down, were rougher in their actions, and carried the chapter appellation "Bloody Beta" very well.

### Beta Chapter

*Beta Chapter of the Omega Psi Phi looks back with pride to February 6th, 1914, the day of its birth. Some of the more sober mindset men of the campus wished to enjoy the privileges of true fraternalism and conferred with one another concerning this matter. As a result of their untiring efforts, Beta Chapter was established. Twenty men who emphasized in their daily life the principles for which Omega stands, were chosen for membership. Like in every other new movement for principle and progress, difficulties were encountered. However, under the staunch leadership of men like Stewart, Anderson, Saulter, and others, we were successful and a very high fraternal ideal was thereby set up. – "Beta Chapter," C.R. Saulter, the* Oracle, *first edition, June 1919, P 11.*

Beta was also a singing chapter. Alpha chapter was as well. However, at Lincoln, with less distractions, singing took on a more serious tone. The brothers would gather outside of McCrary, Rendell, Houston, and other locations, and just sing. There was no one in particular to impress, unless it was a subtext for recruiting the next pledge line, by showcasing what the Beta brothers could do, given the appropriate musical forum.

One song that they routinely sang, and which I loved then and still do, is *This is Omega*. It was not a song unique to Lincoln, as we sang it at Howard too, but Beta's spirit seemed extra special to me. It goes like this (as best as I can remember):

*This is Omega, grandest on earth*
*This is Beta Chapter, second of our birth*
*To there we pledge our allegiance*
*Omega into the fold*
*For this is Omega, to have and to hold*

## TRANSFERING TO LINCOLN UNIVERSITY

The pledging cycle at Lincoln was also different. They had authority to take two lines per year, although the one that was formed in the Spring was more popular and larger. With the spring line, there was a summer intermittency, and then initiation in the fall, generally late October to early November. The winter line, conducted entirely during the academic semesters, did not have that long break in between.

My mind was already set on Omega. I watched every pledge-related movement with intensity. What was the purpose of those lamps that the Lampados were carrying into the woods after dinner? Just what was happening in those woods anyway? I was very impressed by how focused and dedicated the pledgees were. Then hell week arrived, the last week before induction into the fraternity. The guys were as tired as they could be. They looked as though they had not slept in at least two weeks, and maybe they had not.

To the untrained eye, to the unknowing mind, hell week was just a lot of foolishness. But to me it represented the final test in order to qualify for Omega brotherhood. I did not know the guys when they were inducted into the Lampados club in the spring of 1962, since I had not yet arrived at Lincoln. However, by the time they went over in that fall, under the name, "The Roaring 19," I could see a transformation between September, when I arrived, and the date of induction, several weeks later. Indeed, before the school year ended in June 1963, I counted several of these Omega men as friends, and am still loosely in touch with several of them.

They were not just a bunch of male college students. Seemingly, they were transformed into adult Omega men over night. Now an integral component of Beta's proud and historic Omega brotherhood, the demarcations between them and balance of the Lincoln University enrollees was readily apparent. Of course I would be remiss if I failed to note that this newly acquired status also went to the heads of some of these young men. Most of them were about 20 to 21 years old, and were still in training in what it meant to be responsible adults.

Omega men are taught discretion, but when mixed with testosterone, alcohol, and the woods, some indiscretions occurred. Still such behavior was a valuable learning step in the life process. In my personal opinion, many of the brothers, and likewise their fellow non-Omega classmates, did not respect women. Such was the prevailing attitude in the early 1960s, but the general atmosphere and location was particularly suited for acting out, and in many cases not measuring up to the standard of personal behavior that I would have expected from an Omega Man.

Maybe I am using the wrong set of eye glasses for viewing the situation. I doubt that I felt that way back in 1962, and committed a few indiscretions myself. But now that I am older, I believe that things should have been different in attitude about the ladies. They guys ragged on each other terribly if you had a less than attractive woman on the campus. One particular song was popular at the time, and found itself being the daily pronouncement, characterized by hearing several voices singing, but not seeing anyone or knowing from where the sound was coming. Accredited to Jimmy Soul, although many performers sang it with equal gusto, it went like this:

> *If you wanna be happy for the rest of your life*
> *Never make a pretty woman your wife*
> *So from my personal point of view*
> *Get an ugly girl to marry you*
> *A pretty woman makes her husband look small*
> *And very often causes his downfall*
> *As soon as he marries her then she starts*
> *To do the things that will break his heart*
> *But if you make an ugly woman your wife*
> *you'll be happy for the rest of your life*
> *An ugly woman cooks meals on time*
> *And she'll always give you peace of mind*

Imagine how embarrassing that could be if you are walking around campus with the lady that you love, who is very nice and devoted to you, but not the most physically attractive. You are more mature than to place too much emphasis upon physical beauty, because you have grown to love, respect, and appreciate the inner person, when suddenly you hear these hurtful words, coming from out of the blue. What do you say to her at a moment like that? Fortunately, I was spared that humiliation. When I went to Lincoln, I

## TRANSFERING TO LINCOLN UNIVERSITY

was going with Janet Coleman, a very attractive young lady. I left her in D.C. but still thinking that there might be a sustained future for us.

However, she had just graduated from high school in 1963, and wanted to get married, and decided not to wait until I graduated, or even less for me to enter graduate school. She found someone else, married him, and that was the end of that. I met several other ladies and began hanging with them, although there was no long-term relationship. I always hoped, and likewise feared, that some guys might act up, and start singing the song. But it never happened to me.

### Getting to Know Omega Better Through Beta Chapter

Lincoln was one of the universities where two pledge lines a year were permissible, so there was sometimes a spring and a fall induction. Although this two-lines-per-year practice was common on some campuses, it was abolished at Howard in about 1959, and reformatted to solely one spring line per year. By now it was painfully apparent that many chapters were not mature enough to maintain an eternal pledge club. Perhaps the pledge process was too long and had already created a life of its own, which interfered with the academic purpose of attending college in the first place.

As well, the issue of hazing was always of paramount concern, attracting more negative attention to the fraternities and sororities than was healthy. The image of what being a member of a fraternity typified, was increasingly negative, as many of the non-members would chide the frats about being "elitist brutes," which *nom de plume* we certainly did not want or need, given the good that the Black Greek-letter organizations have done for so long, and continue to do for the benefit of African Charles Woodard (later the Basileus), Reggie Gillian, Gene Hedge, Kenneth "Dido" Williams, Phil Taylor, David Closson, Chester Fortune, Michael Frank, Thomas Guyden, and Wyatt Johnson were but a few of the "Roaring 19" initiates whom I befriended during my short tenure at Lincoln. From the following line there was Harvey Marshall and Charles Spain, both good friends. And then there was the "Neoteric Nine," which rendered Leon Dash into Omega's fold. Leon would go on to became an internationally accredited news reporter, and university professor.

## 50+ OMEGA INSPIRED YEARS

Beta was a singing chapter, and had many great voices, several of whom also belonged to the Lincoln choir. This discipline helped the Omegas in the choir to tone and maintain their voices, with the result that every time the Omega choir brothers would separate themselves into a chorale, typically after an away football game, they would sing Omega songs in true harmony. It was just beautiful to listen to them. Everyone marveled at their capacity, and the women just swooned about those great Omega men and their melodic renditions.

Although I was not yet aware of it, the Omega chorale at Lincoln, and the acceptance and praise for their abilities, were reminiscent of the glory days of the Alpha Chapter Omega Chorale from about 1947 until 1955. Initially led by Bro. Valerian Smith (Alpha chapter 1945), the Alpha Chapter Chorale gave repeated sold out and standing room only concerts. They recorded several songs, which are preserved on a CD, which several brothers currently proudly own.

While Lincoln was a great experience, affording me the opportunity to go away to college, I had great difficulty with chemistry, and faced a hard reality, i.e., that the challenges imposed upon me by the sciences was only going to get harder and more demanding. After discussing the situation with my parents, and an impending "D" grade, if I could hold onto that, it was decided that I should change my major to something that I really liked and enjoyed, i.e., political science. I switched majors for the second semester, and, quite a surprise to me, I went onto the dean's list and my grade point average for that semester was very high. But by the time I learned of my new achievements, I was on my way back to "H.U."

I was always interested in governmental process and how nations operated, from the smallest locally derived municipal considerations, to the demands of running the largest and most diverse countries and political entities in the world, including the United Nations. Lincoln's political science department was not particularly strong at the time, so the real consideration was whether to transfer away from Lincoln and return to Howard University, whose political science department was internationally known and respected. The credentials and visibility of the faculty was established, but recent graduates and current students were continuing to gain recognition for their points of view and intellectual curiosity, which was paying off in several ways on

## TRANSFERING TO LINCOLN UNIVERSITY

national and international levels. Ralph Bunche, undersecretary of the United Nations and winner of the Nobel Prize for Peace in 1949, and Eric Williams, Prime Minister of Trinidad and Tobago, had created and left great legacies during their 1940s era tenure at Howard. And the university was committed to maintaining that standard, by adding such professors as Bernard Fall, Vincent Brown, and Emmett Dorsey, to name but a few.

I made the decision to leave Lincoln and to return to Howard in the Fall of 1963. Although I had some regrets, they were few in the wake of my newly refocused academic intentions. I formed many friendships while at Lincoln, not all of whom were Omega men. But I realized too, that if I was to improve my personal self, I would have to go in a different direction, both academically and professionally. Time would prove over and again that my decision to return to Howard was correct.

I had made an application for a summer job in the federal government. Because I was making the application from Pennsylvania, where I was completing my one year at Lincoln University, I did not have personal access to trying to tailor my job to any particular agency or type of program. Still, I was selected, but then assigned to work in the U.S. Postal Lock shop, making postal locks for mailboxes and canvas mail bags. It was production line work, repetitious and boring to me. But it was also beneficial. There were many men and women there, mostly African American, whose entire careers were spent in the postal service. They often had limited educational opportunities, yet managed to raise their families by working in such menial jobs as making postal locks.

And for them I have the greatest respect, as they pursued decent moral work, in the face of racial and possibly other adversities, and demonstrated to the rest of us the true value of work and the work ethic. But the monotony of this work, like my other ventures with the postal service, only reaffirmed to me that I needed to take advantage of what was being offered, get my degrees, and make something of myself for the long term. So this lock shop experience was all to the good.

**50+ OMEGA INSPIRED YEARS**

# X – March On Washington, The Civil Rights Era, 1963

Arriving back in D.C. in early June 1963, getting back into the D.C. swing of things, I learned that Kappa Psi Chapter, an intermediate chapter of the fraternity, was planning to induct a summer line. Kappa Psi was one of Omega's most historic fraternal chapters. It was founded in 1926 by Bro. Dr. W. Montague Cobb, a graduate of Amherst College, class of 1925, an intellectual of the highest order, and former director of Omega's national scholarship program. Bro. Cobb determined that there was a need for Omega to accommodate younger men, most of whom were in graduate or professional school at Howard University, seeking medical and law degrees, or engaging in graduate study programs.

As well, there were other men who were recent college graduates, and who likewise still wished to join and affiliate with Omega. Noting that this group often did not share much in common with the older Omega men, many of whom were often already in their 40s, Bro. Cobb determined that something dramatic must be done. At the time complaints were already rising that some of the older men were too set in their ways, and would not give ear to the younger men's interests and ideas. As well, Bro. Cobb recognized that there were eligible young men who were attending other colleges and universities where Omega had no chapter, and that an intermediate chapter could serve the needs of this entire group. Thus the intermediate chapter concept was born in Washington, D.C., and served Omega well for many years.

My enthusiasm for becoming an Omega was such, that I made application to Kappa Psi for induction into the Lampados Club. An interview was held at the fraternity house on a Sunday afternoon in mid-June 1963. The chapter brothers were affable towards me, and most all of them knew my dad or my uncle, as well as me. In August 1962, the prior summer, I drove my parents Chevrolet station wagon to New York for the annual Omega Show Boat, sponsored by Kappa Omicron chapter. A couple of the Kappa Psi brothers even hitched a ride with me and shared the same hotel room. So there was no hostility towards me when I showed up for a June 1963 interview for a hopeful induction into the Lampados Club.

But there was one big obstacle. I had just left a university where there was already an existing chapter of Omega that was in good standing, and was next headed to another university, Howard, where there was also an Omega chapter in good standing. After the universal first questions posed by the chapter interviewers, i.e., "Tell us something about yourself and why do you think that you should be allowed to pursue membership in our fraternity, Omega Psi Phi," I was next hit, not once, but several times, by varied versions and aspects of the same question, to wit, "Why can't you wait, and seek Omega through your undergraduate college initiation program?" "Why do you think that we should make an accommodation to you now, when there is a perfectly good chapter of Omega for undergrads already at Howard?" "Do you think or feel entitled to some special privilege or consideration because your dad and uncle are Omegas?" "Wouldn't it be better to be inducted into an undergraduate chapter, where you would be exposed to all the traditional activities associated with undergraduate pledging?"

It was pretty clear to me from that point, that there was no way that they were going to accept me into the Kappa Psi Lampados Club program for that summer. What was not yet clear, however, is the blessing that I received from these Omega men, in the form of a rejection letter. The letter was not hostile. They did not use the word "Rejection," but rather phrased it as an easy let down. While I cannot recall the exact words now, more than 50 years later, the turn-down was philosophical, wishing me the very best, and suggesting that I pursue brotherhood in Omega through the next Howard University undergraduate chapter initiation program.

They started the pledge line in July, and initiated four new Omega men on September 8, 1963, two weeks after the famed D.C. March on Washington for Jobs and Freedom. With Omega's commitment to service, and the forthcoming March on everybody's mind in this city, being a member of the Lampados Club presented an ideal opportunity for these four men to render valuable service to the larger community, helping the big brothers of all of the host chapters to prepare for the incoming large crowds.

## MARCH ON WASHINGTON, THE CIVIL RIGHTS ERA, 1963

Logistics was the major component, including figuring out and planning, in conjunction with several other people, how to accommodate the large crowd, how to feed them or direct them to where they could get food, attending to the older Omegas and their spouses, making certain that their needs were met, especially if it was a particularly hot or humid day. Fate smiled on these four men, and they played their designated roles well, and fittingly demonstrated that they were each of the caliber that Omega expected of her sons.

The inductees were Robert Adams, Ewan A. Brown, Harold Lloyd, and Michael A. Proctor. The only one that I do not know is Lloyd. I used to date Bob's sister. I attended Carroll High School with Proctor. And while I did not know Brown at that time, at present he is my Brookland neighbor, and a co-member of the Greater Brookland Garden Club. Carmen and I visit his home on regularly.

Of course I was hurt by the non-acceptance, but now realize that it was for the better, since a Howard initiation into Omega through the Mother Pearl offered much significance. I was 19 years old at the time, and induction through Omega's Mother Pearl at Alpha Chapter, Howard University, did not yet have the unique historic meaning to me. In retrospect, though, my formal introduction to Omega through the Mother Pearl would prove unique and a blessing of the highest order. And for that "rejection" at the time, I am most thankful to the brothers of Kappa Psi. Their turn down helped me to focus, become more determined, and imbued me later with a greater appreciation of the significance of Omega brotherhood. Later the sacred oath that I would eventually take on April 4, 1964, would become a lifelong pledge to Omega and to her Four Cardinal Principles – Manhood, Scholarship, Perseverance, and Uplift. When Kappa Psi said no to me, it was a personal test to demonstrate how I would handle the significance of these four principles as I continued my journey.

I believe that I handled all of them well: demonstrating MANHOOD in the face of the adversity related to not being accepted, yet determined to still pursue Omega, no matter what; SCHOLARSHIP to make certain that I met Omega's academic standards from the outset; PERSEVERANCE until I was deemed qualified to begin the Omega journey; pursuing and UPLIFT to myself and others, to continue to share myself with others less fortunate, to continue in the vein of the interracial home visit program that *Les Jeunes Hommes* engaged in to bring about greater racial harmony between "Negroes" and whites.

One thing that I do not recall hearing at the time of my turn down from Kappa Psi, was whether there was a requirement or policy that addressed the issue of allowing someone to pledge Omega at another chapter, when they were matriculating or about to, at a college where there was already a chapter in good standing. At the present item, there is such a regulation that directs that men seeking Omega while in undergraduate school, must first pursue membership through the undergraduate program at their current college. This requirement makes perfect sense, since a major purpose of Omega is to foster brotherhood at the undergraduate level, and most specifically at the site where the intended brother is located. But whether such was the state in 1963, is uncertain to me.

The year 1963 is often considered to be the year in which the Modern Civil Rights Movement was launched. I was enrolled at Lincoln during the first half of the year, preparing to transfer to Howard in September. Of course, there was always resistance to the ribald forces of racial discrimination and denial of equal access to the law from our fellow black ancestors, who never acquiesced to the many indignities that they were subjected to. But something was rapidly changing in 1963, as a newer generation of young blacks came to the forefront, supplementing the tireless work of Dr. Martin Luther King, Jr., and Malcolm X, both of whom were legendary and about whom we already know much.

But there were many others too, including John Lewis (now a senior member of the U.S. Congress), Stokely Carmichael (Student Non-Violent Coordinating Committee (SNCC), Marion Barry (former mayor of Washington, D.C. and SNCC), Medgar Evers (field secretary for the NAACP in Mississippi), Fannie Lou Hamer (Mississippi Freedom Democratic Party and SNCC), and Dr. Dorothy I. Height (NCNW). Each of them rendered a most valuable service to the cause, even if some of their actions were controversial at the time and widely questioned regarding the wisdom of the undertaking. Indeed, Evers suffered the ultimate sacrifice on June 12, 1963, when he was slain on his front lawn in Jackson, Mississippi by a member of the White Citizens Council.

Then on September 15, 1963, just two weeks after the famed March on Washington for Jobs and Freedom, August 28, 1963, at which event Dr. King rendered his timely, but legendary, *I Have A Dream* speech, four little girls were killed and many others injured on a Sunday morning at the Sixteenth Street Baptist Church, Birmingham, Alabama. Four members of the Ku Klux Klan set off a bomb in the church basement. Yes, 1963 was a horrible year for black folk. I vividly remember seeing the July 1963 photos in the *Washington Post*, and other media, of firefighters, employees of the government, turning fire hoses on black and sympathetic white citizens as well, repelling them from the exercise of their First Amendment rights to freedom of speech.

The photos of these atrocities against African American citizens and their white sympathizers were seen around the world, underscoring that the flowery words embodied in both our Declaration of Independence and later by the U.S. Constitution, were just that, "words," not universally applied to everyone. I recall some of my fellow international students, both at Lincoln and Howard, commenting that American was a racist hellhole, and that this country has refused to come to grips with the reality of the true situation, and would never really make great progress as a nation, until we did so. This was a difficult time to be both an American of color and to hold one's head up. One nation – divided between black and white. Yet, there was still reason to be hopeful. Indeed, most all of my associated knew within our heads and hearts that right was on our side, and that meaningful and lasting change was going to come. But when?

While I was greatly concerned about what was going on in the deep South, and even occurring in the nearby regions of Maryland and Virginia, I took no active role in the demonstrations. When at Lincoln, located in Pennsylvania, there did not seem to be much interest in getting into the active civil rights act. I do not recall any student group or agitation towards that objective.

On the other hand, when I returned to Howard in September 1963, I discovered that a number of students in the Howard community had become involved in several of the Freedom Rides and the restaurant sit-in demonstrations, but their numbers were small. The great majority of the Howard community simply was not focused on that affiliation, although the *Hilltop,* the university student paper, carried story after story of what was going on with the Movement. I credit this malaise to a greater concern with getting our formal education completed, and preparing to make our way into the rapidly changing new world.

We were the future doctors, lawyers, business leaders, and the mood at Howard was not that activist when I was initially a Howard student for the 1961-1962 academic year, and again when I returned in September 1963. But, I could see changes. There were opportunities to participate in the Freedom Rides and the sit-ins, with signs posted of how to get involved, students that were coordinators for planned protests, and weekend trips to places further south. Some of these trips did not go very far, as many locations in both Maryland and Virginia refused to serve Negroes, so one did not need to travel to North or South Carolina, Alabama, or Mississippi, to register their protest.

When I mentioned to my dad in late September/early October that Howard had a small, but active contingent of students who were volunteering and engaging in civil rights activities, he was very negative towards my getting involved. Although he had been on the local forefront of demonstrations against the People's Drug stores and Safeway, regarding their non-hiring-of-blacks policies, these were not violent picketing efforts. As well, he was vigilant in the protests against George Washington University for its initial "whites only" policy for admission to the then newly opened Lisner Auditorium. That was, from his perspective, a different era. He was not having any part of any possible violent or confrontational demonstrations, electing to continue fighting in his own way, which did not include my participating on the active level.

As noted above, the "March on Washington for Jobs and Freedom" rally occurred on the National Mall on August 28, 1963. Approximately 200,000 citizens, mostly African American, converged on Washington, D.C., decrying that although the slavery ended on January 1, 1863, more than 100 years later, African Americans were still suffering from a two-tier system in most every aspect of

## MARCH ON WASHINGTON, THE CIVIL RIGHTS ERA, 1963

American society. Overt racial and economic discrimination were practiced in the South, denying the black man the right to vote, confining him to "Negro jobs," and restricting where he could live, most often with the expressed approval of the legal system, both legislatively and judicially.

Regretfully, discrimination in the North was not much better. Many of the same problems plagued our people who resided north of the Mason-Dixon Line, but getting at the problem, defining it, and then tackling a just solution, often proved to be illusive. Where you could visibly observe the discrimination, you could foster a plan of action to bring down those walls. When the separation was subtle, it demanded a different approach, one that is politically savvy, appealing to the conscience of the public at large, to bring about change.

On my "Regret List," I have the missed opportunity of participating in the March. Preparing to transfer from Lincoln and go back to Howard, my summer job ended about one week before registration began at Howard. A Lincoln classmate invited me to visit his family in Atlanta, and this week was the only time available. So while the final plans for the March and the event itself were occurring, I was out of town. In retrospect, and now fully appreciative of why the March on Washington was held and necessary, I regret that I was not sufficient politically aware of its significance, and why I should have participated. Being 19 years old, and more focused on being "Joe College," I did not place enough emphasis upon what I was about to miss or the importance of the Civil Rights Movement. Truth be told, I could have gone to Atlanta another time, and been just as pleased then to be in the Old South.

The *Oracle* of September 1963 reflects at Page 5, that hundreds of Omega brothers and their families participated in the March, starting from the fraternity house. While noting the presence and participation of Founder Frank Coleman and several current and former members of the Supreme Council, the focus of the article was upon Bro. Hiram F. Jones, then Third District Representative, and my father's former junior high school gym teacher. The author observed that while the March planners were busy attending to every detail, in order to make the March a great success, both in terms of its meaning and focus, and in drawing a large crowd of peaceful demonstrators, Omega Psi Phi was nowhere to be seen on the original list of sponsors and supporters.

### Hiram F. Jones, 3rd District DR, Initiates Omega March

*Brother Jones, while working on the March's local Finance committee, and approaching churches, civil and fraternal organizations, did not find Omega Psi Phi Fraternity listed among the supporters. He, filled with the desire that Omega be associated with other organizations in such an historic movement, contacted all local chapters and the National Executive Secretary and found that none were supporting groups. Touched by, the lack of spirit, he decided that the Fraternity must be represented in this social revolution since it encompasses one or more of the cardinal principals, especially that of "Uplift." Officers of the 3rd District and Bro. Moultrie were contacted for approval and guidance as to registering the 3rd District as a supporter. The District was so enrolled and all 3rd District basilei, the Supreme Council, District Representatives, and national chairman were notified by card that the 3rd District would march to uplift America. A committee of four was formed to put the program into action. Henry Smith, III, of Kappa Psi served as social action chairman for the project; Brother Dent, Basileus of Kappa Psi, was in charge of badges and publicity; Brothers Everett W. Carter and Wallace Perkins of Alpha Omega took care of after March refreshments; and H. F. Jones served as general chairman. The effective functioning of this committee resulted in the Fraternity's being well represented in the August 28th March on Washington for Jobs and Freedom. The conduct of the marchers, numbering more than 200,000 can be summed up as "magnificent."*- the *Oracle*, Vol. 52, No. 3, September 1963, Page 5.

Appreciating the historical significance of the upcoming event and likewise the need for Omega to not only be a part of this effort, but to be likewise visible in every respect, Bro. Jones' enthusiasm materialized on several Omega-related fronts. First, as the *Oracle* article noted. Bro. Jones was shocked and dismayed to learn that, up to that point, none of Omega's local chapters was involved in rendering support. Nor had the fraternity, through the office of the National Executive Secretary, who was Bro. H. Carl Moultrie, made any movement in that direction.

Well, if you knew Bro. Hiram Jones, and I knew him reasonably well, you also knew that he did not take "No!" for an answer when he was determined to make something of significance happen. Likewise, this spirit, focus, and determination directly contributed to how and why Bro. Jones capably served the Third District as its elected District Representative for six years in the late 1950s-early 1960s Penned as "Bro. Jones' Idea," the *Oracle* article noted that, "Hundreds of Omegas Participate in 'March' Starting at Frat House."

As the date for the March drew closer, Alpha Omega brothers were likewise drawn to the fray, pressed into service to assure that the many brothers and their families, who were coming to town, would be accommodated, kept safe, provided food and refreshments, and given proper directions regarding protocol, including how to find their source of transportation again, after the March was concluded. With so many people coming to Washington for this massive demonstration, seeking redress of their many legitimate grievances, and wanting to air their deep-seated and continuing frustrations, there was genuine concern that the entire event might degenerate into a street riot, with "the blacks," as many racist Southern congressmen would call them, bent on destruction. These opponents attempted to stir up a frenzy, to scare even the African Americans away, to get them to stay at home and not support the March. Several very racist comments were made by those who opposed the March, many of whom were themselves elected officials who swore to uphold the U.S. Constitution, which guarantees the right of all citizens to assemble to redress their legitimate grievances.

Everyone in the community at large was not in favor of or in support of the forthcoming March on Washington, electing to characterize it as an upcoming brawl, an event where rowdy Negroes would be prowling the streets, looking to rape, pillage, and plunder. It was a first class scare tactic, but it never caught fire within the black community.

## 50+ OMEGA INSPIRED YEARS

My dad volunteered to work with the planning committee. I recall his heading to the fraternity house, which was just a few black from our own home, located at 3714 13th Street, N.W. He would return home, excited about what was in the planning stages, and encouraged my mother to likewise get involved. The call was going forth for the Omega Wives and other volunteers to work with the local chapters, to attend to the needs of our expected out of town visitors. It was noted that this occasion was not the time for a big party, as the serious nature of the March dictated a likewise serious demeanor in our personal conduct. However, we must also realize and appreciate that where two or three Omegas are gathered, there must likewise be an exchange, a sharing of brotherhood, and usually the breaking of bread.

Working within Alpha Omega, calling upon the other local chapters of the fraternity to step forward in this effort, and likewise asking all of the Black Greeks to work in concert, the efforts of the organizers for a peaceful, well-attended March now began to take on its final shape. A few days prior to the big day, I recall my dad making telephone calls to other chapter brothers, and also utilizing his Pan-Hellenic connections, many of whom were men and woman who had attended the Paul Laurence Dunbar High School and/or Miner Teacher's College with him. Esther Robinson (Alpha Kappa Alpha) and Gerri Elliott (Sigma Gamma Rho) were two of his favorites, when it came to getting the Pan Hellenic chapters of Washington, D.C. to adopt a plan of action.

My dad refused to be deterred or intimidated by these thinly veiled threats. As a culmination of his untiring efforts, both my father and mother participated, bringing with them, Joherra, my sister age 15, John, my brother, age 12, and Ricardo, my youngest brother, age 8. My parents were not afraid. They expected nothing but a peaceful rally, one that would amply demonstrate that the Civil Rights Movement was committed to a nonviolent, and thus more intellectual struggle and success, than even the most racists opponents of the event could imagine.

At the appointed time, everyone assembled with the Alpha Omega chapter brothers, other Omegas, Omega wives, and non D.C. friends too, at the fraternity house, preparing to go to the March *en*

## MARCH ON WASHINGTON, THE CIVIL RIGHTS ERA, 1963

mass. There was much excitement on that hot Wednesday, August 28, 1963. They left the fraternity house that late morning, marching under the banner of the Omega Psi Phi Fraternity.

### Hundreds of Omega Participate in "March" Starting At Frat House, Washington, D.C., Bro. Hiram F. Jones' Idea

*The sun rose high in the east as the first Ques arrived at the Fraternity House from Pittsburgh, Pa. Founder Frank Coleman, Forty Year Man Cato Adams, and Third District Representative, Hiram F. Jones were on hand to meet them and all other brothers. Among the early arrivals were, Brothers: George E. Meares, Brooklyn, N.Y., first vice grand basileus; Jesse Jackson, Greensboro, N.C., second vice grand basileus; H. Carl Moultrie, I., Washington, D.C., national executive secretary; J. Quentin Mason, Altadena, Calif., DR for the 12th District, and Herbert E. Tucker, Boston, Mass., chairman of the Omega Social Action Committee, and former grand basileus. The newly designed Third District Banner held the eyes of all who looked upon it for the first time. The background is gold with purple letters and border. It contains the four cardinal principles, the name of the Fraternity, the shield and the name of the Third District. Its dimensions are six feet by eight feet. This banner was one of the largest and most colorful ones in the March. – the Oracle, Vol. 52, No. 3, September 1963, Page 5.*

Of course the highlight of the day was the "I Have a Dream" speech that was so brilliantly delivered by Dr. Martin Luther King, Jr., on the steps of the Lincoln Memorial. Recalling many of the injustices that African Americans had suffered and continued to suffer at the hands of the white majority, Dr. King called upon all Americans to push forward, and not to let up until all Americans, black and white, could share equally in the American Dream. There was much more to his famous speech than I have recorded here, but the essence was to demand our basic human rights which were still being denied to Negro Americans 100 years after the January 1, 1863, Emancipation

Proclamation. He asked, How long is it going to take to realize what was promised, and when will it come to pass?

While the brilliance of his speech can never be underestimated, I later learned that Dr. King publicly acknowledged on many occasions that Omega Brother Dr. Benjamin E. Mays, former dean of the School of Religion, Howard University, and then president of Morehouse College during Dr. King's matriculation there, was one of his greatest mentors, and a man who was majorly responsible for King's being able to present himself as he did on so many occasions and in all types of circumstances.

I returned to Washington just after the March ended, and heard all about it. During the overnight train trip from Atlanta, I met Bro. Dosh Jackson, Jr., and a native Atlantan, who was returning to Hampton Institute (now university). He was a member of Gamma Epsilon chapter of Omega. I would see him several times thereafter, and later learned that his dad, Dosh, Sr., was one of the oldest members of the fraternity, now 102 years old at the time that I am writing this Memoir. I had the privilege of spending an afternoon with Bro. Jackson, Sr., in June 2013, when I, as an at large member of the International History and Archives Committee, was visiting our international headquarters in Decatur, Georgia, for an Omega history research project.

Learning the details of the March on Washington and the great success and significance of the events, I immediately I regretted not being in attendance. In several significant ways, I had missed the boat on that one. Looking back, I was still in my "Joe College" frame of mind, not yet appreciative of the full impact of why the March was necessary in the first place. I vividly recall how nasty many of the Southern members of the U.S. Congress were about the march, and how they tried to frighten the general population with threatening words, including that the streets of Washington, D.C. would be filled with roving bands of young, angry Negroes, and that no white person, particularly females, would be safe in the national Capital City.

Comments such as these, all too often supplemented by agreeable newspaper columnists, infuriated the African American population further, making them determined to have the March and assure that it

## MARCH ON WASHINGTON, THE CIVIL RIGHTS ERA, 1963

would be a peaceful demonstration, despite the calls for riot police and heavy armament to be placed in the streets at strategic locations where the blacks were due to demonstrate. If nothing else, to carry out such a request and turn it into a plan would have been an intimidation. The call for staging such heavy security was rejected. While that fear may have caused a few to stay away, the efforts to stir up the hatemongers and to frighten would-be-marchers backfired. Looking back, I was impressed by my dad's diligence and dedication to make the event a resounding success. Because of him, and others with a similar mind, many of whom were proud and accomplished Omega men, he had nothing to be ashamed of when the results were tabulated.

**50+ OMEGA INSPIRED YEARS**

# XI – Induction Into The Omega Psi Phi Fraternity, April 4, 1964

Returning to Howard in September 1963, many of my Howard friends were happy to see me again, not knowing why I had been missing from campus during the prior academic year. Some commented that they thought that I was "the One," that had been mentioned several times while in Freshman Assembly, held on each Tuesday afternoon at 1:00 p.m. Being mostly young students, although significant numbers of classmates had recently completed military duty and were only now enrolling in college, courtesy of the G.I bill, they were referring to those occasions, more than once, when a dean or a professor, had said, "Look to your left. Now, look to your right. Next year, one of you is not going to still be here." What a backwards way to encourage self-discipline and focus, plus strive for academic excellence.

No, I assured them, I was not "The One." In fact, having changed my major during my second semester at Lincoln, I made the dean's list and was recognized at the annual Dean's List Convocation, that was held in September 1963. Because I was no longer enrolled at Lincoln, I became aware of the convocation and awarding of certificates of achievement when a friend mentioned it to me. Being only 19 years old, I was not sufficiently motivated to contact Lincoln and have the certificates mailed to me. Apparently no one at Lincoln thought it sufficiently important to do so either, as I never received the certificates, written recognition of my academic accomplishments during my second and final semester at Lincoln.

Man, was it great to be back at Howard. It was truly a new beginning. I felt invigorated with my new major, then called "Government," but later changed to "Political Science." Howard's Government/Political Science department had a very good reputation. Beyond Ralph Bunche and Eric Williams, mentioned above, the department's professors included many well respected professors, all of whom were distinguished in their own right. While I never lost sight of the fact that I came to get a college degree, I was likewise focused upon becoming an Omega man. But how should I approach the effort from this point?

Although I already knew several college-level Omega men, I also knew many of the Alpha Omega graduate chapter men too. They were my dad's and uncle's friends. Joseph P. Quander, my uncle and godfather, pledged Theta Psi Chapter, West Virginia State University, in 1931. He had a number of Theta Psi alumni brothers also in Alpha Omega, one of whom, Ernest Johnson, was his line brother, and one of my favorite Alpha Omega brothers. When he would see me, Johnson would say, "Young fella, don't lose sight of Omega. Your turn is coming, and when it does, you have a life-long assignment in front of you!" His wife, Mignon, member of Delta Sigma Theta, was a great lady as well, very stylish, and active in the Omega Wives. She was the cousin of one of my fellow Lincolnites, Bro. Howard Wright, Jr., whose dad was president of Allen University. Bro. Dr. Howard Wright, Sr., was a great Omega man as well.

Now my turn was approaching. Beginning with my return to Howard in September 1963, I immediately felt some pressure. Was it a psych? Were some of the Alpha Chapter brothers already trying to pledge me underground, making veiled threats about my alleged assumption that I had it made, could just walk into Omega, because my father and uncle were both quite active, visible, and well known in city Greek circles? Further, everyone knew that I had founded *Les Jeunes Hommes* in 1960, and was president from June 1960, until September 1962.

I was even told not to bother to come to an interview, as they did not want me, because I was not "Omega material," and probably could not withstand what was called for, in order to be an Omega Man. It was not hard to see through all of this. I knew what I wanted, and did not believe that there was any reason why I should not be given the opportunity to prove it to myself, as well as to them. But what was I to do now? It was still September, and there was no line and pledge opportunity until the third week in February 1964.

I know what I'll do! I became scarce. Being a D.C. boy, many of my high school friends, several of whom I had known since summer day camp during our later elementary school years, had recently pledged or were planning to pledge Kappa Alpha Psi on the spring

## INDUCTION INTO OMEGA PSI PHI FRATERNITY, APRIL 4, 1964

1964 line. I kept hearing repeatedly, and to some extent it was true, "D.C. is a Kappa town, and you should become one of us." And also, "Omegas, they are not much, and besides, they have the lowest academic average on campus." I never knew whether that was a true statement at the time, although I would later learn, during my tenure in Alpha Chapter, that maintaining a sufficient academic average, befitting and in keeping with the Cardinal Principle of "Scholarship," was a continuing problem. I listened, went to the many parties, almost weekly, at the Kappa House, located at 1708 S Street, N.W., Washington, D.C., but never committed myself to pursue it further.

In about mid October 1963, a couple of buddies and I drove down to Virginia State University for its homecoming day. We went to the parade and then the football game – Howard vs. Virginia State. I cannot recall who won, but it made no difference as far as the enthusiasm was concerned. This was my first coed post-football game experience on a campus besides Howard University. After the game, the Greeks assembled in their respective locations and began to sing. The Omegas did their thing, as did the Deltas and other Greek-letter organizations. But what really impressed me the most and got my lasting attention is when the Omegas and Deltas joined together for a joint sing.

While I do not recall all of the songs, and not all of the words in the songs, two lines caught my particular attention. They were, "Ques and Deltas, sisters and brothers, Ques and Deltas love one another. Oh, Oh, Oh ….." and "In the beginning, the beginning, there were only two. Eve was a Delta and Adam was a Que." As I stood on the sideline and gazed, I felt a warm rush coming over my entire body. So this is what they meant when it was noted that the Ques and Deltas are brother-sister organizations. I had no clue about this prior to that day, and only learned later than there is nothing official or established with reference to their friendly relationship. Rather, the connection emerged from some personal relationships between two Omega Founders and two Delta Founders, one of which resulted in marriage. But that's getting ahead of my story, and I will return to this issue later.

I returned to D.C. more focused on Omega than ever. But I had to keep cool, maintain my distance, and not get too friendly with the

## 50+ OMEGA INSPIRED YEARS

Alpha Chapter brothers. Because many of them seemingly knew who I was, I also did not want to ignore them. The pendulum swings in both directions, and I did not want to suffer from an affliction of uppitiness or seeming arrogance, which could likewise assure that I would garner a negative vote. Once I eventually became a brother, I noted that this appellation was sometimes applied to prospective lamps, and some of them suffered a rejection, due to having given the impression, whether accurate or note, of not being sufficiently humble. Yet Omega could have greatly benefitted from what these men had to offer, as many of them did go on in later life to achieve great things. It would have been nice to add "Omega Psi Phi" to their resumes, indicative of our being adult enough to recognize the difference between the strength of character, and just plain snooty attitudes displayed by some of these prospective brothers.

As 1963 drew to a close, I found myself traveling in a largely different circle. Already the sub-terra lines for the competing fraternities were taking shape. Who was going Kappa? Who was going Alpha, or Sigma, or Omega? The fraternities themselves were doing some recruiting on the QT. This type of pre-pledge campaigning, although not too widespread, was not prohibited, as is the case today. There was no harassment, implied threats, or pressure being applied. In a way, I felt slighted. Wouldn't you think that the brothers of Omega would be reaching out to certain individuals, particularly someone like me that many of them already knew was a good prospect for the fraternity?

Well, it did not happen. It made me think about it a lot. For years, the Kappas had been declaring about town that D.C. was a "Kappa town," and they wanted to keep it that way. This attitude seemed to matter little to the Alpha Chapter brothers, most all of whom were not from D.C., and apparently had no sensitivity as to whether this was truly a big issue. Why was *Les Jeunes Hommes* created in the first place? To offset the Kappas overt aggressiveness in recruiting eligible D.C. guys for Omega. After all, Omega was founded right here at Howard University. One would think, at least from my perspective, that there would be a conscious effort to counter Kappa's annual push for D.C. men. The existence of a group of young men who had been exposed to Omega through the local graduate chapter, were prime for

## INDUCTION INTO OMEGA PSI PHI FRATERNITY, APRIL 4, 1964

the picking. The question then, was "Who was going to pick them, Kappa or Omega?" And indeed, Kappa did grab a few of our club members right from under Omega's nose.

At the time I did not realize that the frat still had the deeply ingrained, "Men seek Omega! Omega seeks no one!" attitude. But here it was in full regalia, alive and well, at least with regard to me, personally, and my childhood friend and future line brother, David H. Reid, III. He too experienced the same as I, and but for our fathers' respective involvement in Alpha Omega chapter, a constant reminder of the fraternity, its purpose and programs, both of us might well have drifted elsewhere.

Here at last! It's almost 1964, and my world is about to change significantly, to open wider and head into a totally different direction. I was completing another round of working at the U.S. Post Office, helping to handle the Christmas rush mail. We were all working in the main postal building, then located at the corner of North Capitol Street and Massachusetts Avenue, N.E. It was a short assignment, perhaps two weeks only, beginning at about 4:00 p.m., and lasting until anywhere from 8:00 p.m. to 10:00 p.m., depending upon the daily load. From about December 10, 1963, until about December 23rd of that month, I worked with the mail. It was dirty work sometimes, unloading heavy mail bags off the trucks and dragging them onto rolling carts, where the contents would be sorted, separated according to whether it was locally bound or out of town. If local, we were assigned to stand in front of trays for several hours, sorting according to zip code.

This work was repetitive, monotonous at the least, but good still in a way, First of all, it was honorable work, and one of the few means by which our forebears, my dad included, were able to support their families. The U.S. post office, along with the government printing office, cafeteria and elevator operator work, plus messengers at various government agencies, were often the only work that the colored men and women could get in the prior ages.

As 1963 came to a close, with the Civil Rights Movement in full swing, sit in demonstrations were catching ahold in the South. Many college students joined others in militant, but nonviolent protests, demanding the right to vote, equal educational, job, housing, and enjoyment of life opportunities, and public accommodations nationwide. While I was not fully aware of everything, I did realize and appreciate what the protesters were enduring, and further, what indignities and insults, and denials our parent and grandparent forebears had endured even before then. Still, they were determined to accomplish, and many did so, for our benefit, so that we would eventually have full access to all aspects of American society, and no longer be relegated to so-called "Colored jobs," as the U.S. postal service was considered to be.

Working at the post office was a physical challenge. As college students, we were not universally prepared to meet the demands of some of what unfolded as a component of these temporary Christmas rush jobs. I recall specifically one evening, and there were also other evenings after this one, when the supervisor came to our unit, told all of us to stop doing what we were doing and to follow him. We proceeded to the loading dock, which was located on the same floor. Although the loading dock was technically inside the building, the huge truck bay doors were kept open to the cold air since postal vehicles were coming and going 24 hours a day. Our supervisor directed each of us to offload very heavy and dirty mail bags, and to place then onto the canvas-sided carts, and then push them into the area where they would be initially processed. The bags had just come from local mailboxes, and had not been processed.

I was one of the first to tackle a bag, and got the surprise of my life. It was so heavy, as were all of the other bags, that I could not lift it. I was pulling and pulling, and making very little progress. The supervisor called to one of the women, who was a full time postal employee, and directed her to show us how it should be done. The woman was smaller than I, and I am only five feet, seven inches tall. She grabbed that bag in such a way, which I never quite understood, swung it forward, flipped it up in the air, and turned it much like a shot-put player would do during a match. The bag went flying, right into the mail cart. Needless to say, I was humiliated and embarrassed, as everyone laughed, mostly at me. For the most part, we were all college students, with a heavy dose of students from Howard, many of whom already knew what I was just learning. As some later told

## INDUCTION INTO OMEGA PSI PHI FRATERNITY, APRIL 4, 1964

me, they could not have done any better themselves, except that they had the distinction of not being the first to try.

Trying to mimic the technique that has just been demonstrated about how to lift, handle, and swing the loaded mail bags, we pretty much caught on, although it was still quite a challenge to lift 80-pound bags of dead weight. That same night I gained an even greater appreciation for why I was in college – to not have to do this for the rest of my life. Further, I gained more respect for my dad and my uncle for what they had to endure. Each of them supported their families by working in the post office, and while they may not have worked on the loading dock, they both handled mail, delivered mail in all kinds of weather, and kept their self-respect, by knowing that this was the best that they could do at the time, solely because of the limitations that had been placed upon them due to their race and the color of their skin.

My dad delivered mail for about 18 months, and then left that "Colored job" for another "Colored job" in the U.S. government printing office. My uncle, who was studying to become a doctor at the Meherry College of Medicine, Nashville, Tennessee, was forced to leave medical school during the Great Depression of the 1930s. My grandfather lost his business, and the family needed to be supported. Unfortunately, the best laid plans sometimes go astray, and his intentions to return to Meherry and finish his medical training to become a doctor, never came to fruition. All was not lost, however. His elder son, Joseph P. Quander, Jr., (Kappa Psi Chapter, 1959), did graduate from Howard University School of Medicine in 1961, following in his dad's intended footsteps. My uncle was always and rightly proud of his son, realizing that his own efforts to save the family in a time of great need, made it possible for Joseph, Jr., to graduate in 1951 from the Paul Laurence Dunbar High School, Washington, D.C., as the Salutatorian, and have Yale and Harvard Universities each vying for his enrollment. He elected Yale and graduated from there in 1956.

This adventure with the mail bag was my second 1963 experience working for the postal service. During the first experience, the prior summer, I worked in the postal lock shop, working on a production line, making locks for mail boxes and mail bags. It too was boring big time, but at least I was inside an air conditioned building, and the hours were daytime only. Later, in December 1964, I was assigned to carry mail in zip code 20010. The mail bag was heavy at the outset, and the weather was cold and wet on occasion. It was only a two week assignment, so I made it.

But as I look back on these three postal experiences, I realized it then, and appreciate it now, that I was most fortunate to be able to attain a college education and degree and then go to law school, so that I would not have to face the drudgery of everyday work of that type. While I have the greatest respect and admiration for the men and women who served us via the postal service, that was not the type of work that interested me. I was looking for something more challenging and diverse, and changing from loading dock, to zip code boxes, to making postal locks just was not for me.

But I did get a chance to do a lot of "thinking on my feet." And naturally my mind turned towards Omega. I even found myself humming or singing some Omega and Delta songs, but careful not to be too loud, as several members of Alpha Chapter were working alongside me, and I did not want to appear to be too presumptions.

My parents were very social, and one of the highlights of each year was the Alpha Omega Christmas party. My mom was a great seamstress, a talent that she inherited from her mother and grandmother, both from Barbados, as was she. They all knew how to sew extremely well. My mother would make a beautiful dress, and then wear it to the Omega party or annual Mardi Gras that same evening. Over the years, she even made her own prize winning costumes. Including first place winners, for the annual Mardi Gras. I recall coming home one evening from the postal assignment, just as they were departing for a party at the fraternity house. My dad was on the organizing committee, and wanted to make certain that everything went just right. He was like that. He had many Omega and Omega-connected friends, several of whom he already knew from Dunbar High School and Miner Teacher's College days. Some were men, and others were elegant ladies, fashion plates who prided themselves in being some of the grand dames of D.C. Society.

I knew some of them myself, due to my youthful legacy's connection to Alpha Omega. Many of these ladies dressed fabulously,

## INDUCTION INTO OMEGA PSI PHI FRATERNITY, APRIL 4, 1964

as was the style at the time. It became a joke that they were the "Fabulous Omega Wives," well known for their annual fashion show in the spring of each year. In the view of some brothers, the wives even eclipsing their husbands in visibility in the society and community at large. At least to the social pages of the *Washington Afro American,* it seemed to be that way. I overheard my dad commenting to my mother that several of the men felt that they needed to "tame" the wives, and "pull them back," because they were becoming more prominent and visible than their own husbands, who were the reason why the Omega Wives existed in the first place.

Who were some of these "Fabulous Omega Wives?" In no particular order, and at the risk of overlooking some of the most prominent, I name but a few. In some instances, I cannot recall the ladies first names, or who their husbands were. They include – Ethel Oliver (Basil); Isabel Durah (Fred); Pauline Elmoe (?); Daris Hopkins (Jimmy); Edna Robinson (Harry); Esther Robinson (Thomas); Emma Carter (Everett "Cutie"); Frances Bolden (Frank Page); Mignon Johnson (Ernest); Katherine Wright (Grant); Grace Jones (Hiram); Grace Dent (Tim); Geri Elliott (?); Louise Bouleware (Theodore); Rachel Reid (David); Golda Douglas (Winston); Oveta Jewel (Harold); Hilda Wesley (Henry); Travola Adams (Cato); Algetha Quander (Joseph); and Joherra Quander (James). All of them were fashion conscious, hat and fur coat-stole wearers, and leaders in their respective organizations, to include churches, sororities, alumni clubs, and communities at large. They were also family oriented. I realize that I neglected to include many other ladies, and for that I apologize.

These were ladies who were able to make a difference in the Washington, D.C. black society at their time, and they made very favorable impressions. It was also a time when there was much competition with other auxiliary groups, including the Kappa Silhouettes and the Alpha and Sigma Wives as well. Who was going to be "most fabulous?" And indeed, the Omega Wives had nothing to apologize for. In today's context, some might judge all of this as irrelevant, but placed in its proper context, it's important to realize and appreciate that we were just coming out of segregation, and the perception of black men and women by the larger white society was not favorable overall. It was a time when we, as black folk, had a lot to prove, both to others and ourselves. We had to demonstrate that we had nothing to apologize for, and that we too knew how to do, had accomplished much, and were continuing to accomplish.

It was an important time in our black "society," and being what is today called, derisively, "Negro fabulous," was an important component of just who we were. In the long term, it made a positive difference, contributing mightily to what we as a race are today, even to the point of having a black man and woman, Barack Hussein and Michelle Obama now as our 44th U.S. President and First Lady.

There will always be critics of what someone else does, but before they criticize, they should walk a few miles in the other groups' shoes. These ladies, and others similarly situated, whether they were sorority sisters, the medical-dental wives, the lawyers wives, female teachers association, and the like, all set a valuable tone, critical to creating and sustaining the black middle class. Some might summarily dismiss them as "bougie" or elitist, and to some extent, they certainly were. But when viewed in the context in which they were operating, I believe that they served a valuable purpose in building up our presence in places in our local and then national societies where we needed to be not only physically present, but likewise visibly prominent.

Perhaps I have gotten a little off the mark in my expression of self, as I prepared to pursue membership in Omega, but this is what I knew, had been exposed to for several years, and expected to become a part of, beginning in 1964. None of the above is isolated into a particular date, time, or place, but rather an evolved story that transcended over time, involved many people and events, and caused me to receive many blessings in the process. And for that I am eternally grateful.

The shortest verse in the Bible is at the Gospel of St. John, Chapter 11, Verse 35, just two words – "Jesus wept!" Be brief! That was my own personal constitution for the period between September 1963 and February 1964 – I studied! I earned greater than a 3.0 grade point average that September – January semester. So as far as Omega's Cardinal Principles were concerned, I was at least displaying Scholarship. The Alpha Chapter jury was still out on whether I would

# INDUCTION INTO OMEGA PSI PHI FRATERNITY, APRIL 4, 1964

be judged to possess at least the rudiments of Manhood, Perseverance, and Uplift.

### The Omega Mardi Gras[29]

*The Mardi Gras dance is an annual feature of the social program of the three chapters of Washington. It is marked by its hilarity, good music, proper amount of Omega oil, and the distinctive costumes, etc., worn by the guests. . . . Two prizes were awarded to the ones with the best costumes, and souvenirs were distributed to all of the guests. Brothers from Richmond, New York, Lincoln University, Philadelphia, Virginia State and other nearby points journeyed to the Capital for the night of festivity. -* The *Oracle,* March 1939, P. 21.

The above statement is a reference to the fact that the Omega Mardi Gras, initiated in 1923, was a well-established, although periodically scheduled event of the fraternity. The Lincoln Colonnade, located on V Street, N.W., was the traditional venue for this fabulous affair. Since 1958, and every year thereafter, people in Washington mark the first Friday in February on their calendars, as they do not want to miss the Alpha Omega Mardi Gras, the chapter's major fundraiser, which benefits the chapter's scholarship and social action programs. The Mardi Gras celebration is almost as old as the chapter, with the first one being held in 1923 at the Lincoln Colonnade on V Street.

The idea for the Mardi Gras came from one of the members of the chapter, who had gone to New Orleans to Mardi Gras, and thought the chapter should host such an event. The Mardi Gras was held intermittently between 1923 and 1957. On February 7, 1958, Alpha Omega revived the Mardi Gras after a period of dormancy, with a celebration at the National Guard Armory and Count Basie as the guest artist. The Mardi Gras has been held every year since then, moving from the Armory to the Sheraton Washington and now to the Washington Hilton.

---

[29] *The History of Alpha Omega Chapter, from the Alpha Omega Chapter web page, c1997.*

## 50+ OMEGA INSPIRED YEARS

Every year, Alpha Omega's Scholarship Commission, a fraternity mandated program, provides up to $20,000 in scholarships to deserving young men graduating from the Washington, D.C., public, private, and parochial schools to help them attend college. In total, the chapter has given more than $90,000 in college scholarships over the last 10 years. The chapter has also provided emergency grants to undergraduate and graduate students who are members of the fraternity. This is just one example of what Alpha Omega has continued to accomplish during its 92 year history in Washington, D.C. The chapter has set a high standard for fraternity life, and the members feel they are ready for the next challenges and opportunities life in Omega offers.

I approached the first Friday in February 1964 with great anticipation. While I cannot recall whether this was the same year that my mother won first prize in the individual costume awards, it was about this time. Looking through several international magazines for a picture that would inspire a costume, she found one of a Balinese dancer from the island nation of Indonesia. Copying the photo, she made a beautiful gold Balinese dancer costume dress. Actually, it was a two-piece outfit, with a fitted blouse and balloon pants. The outfit had wide well adorned cuffed sleeves, and likewise an adorned hem at the bottom of the pantaloons. Anyone who sewed, and anyone who did not, could easily recognize that this costume was an original, not a rental, and likewise a work of art. She put a lot of time and effort into it, and it showed. But what would such a beautiful outfit be like, without the proper head dress. And slippers. Fortunately, she found the golden slippers with turned up tassel points at a local store in downtown D.C.

My dad called upon his friend, Artie Bell, who was a society page editor and milliner who was also known for her personal hats that were really headdresses. They put their heads together, did some research, and came up with an authentic design for the perfect headdress for mom's costume. Artie called upon her contacts and arranged to have the headdress custom-made. Constructed mainly of metallic gold sequence, with large jewels embedded throughout, it was a three-point head covering, with two small pyramid-type points on the left and right sides, and another one of like size in the back. It

## INDUCTION INTO OMEGA PSI PHI FRATERNITY, APRIL 4, 1964

also had a pointed tower which reached at least 12 inches above the basic "hat." Everything was mounted on a lightweight invisible wire frame, so that the shape and height would remain constant. It was a work of art that complemented mom's metallic gold outfit, which itself was adorned with hanging clusters of multi-colored jewels. When the photographs of the costume competition appeared in the *Washington Afro American* the following week, mom and her costume were prominently featured, with the notation that the costume was made by her, and was authentic.

It is unfortunate that this tradition of wearing beautiful costumes to the annual Omega Mardi Gras has faded. The essence of the true meaning of the event is to play masquerades, and by not doing so, the flavor of what the event should be is diluted to the point that it is just another dance. I would hope that as the years progress, that the brothers could find some way to inspire the guests to go back to wearing beautiful costumes, which would revive the true flavor of the meaning of "Mardi Gras."

Brother James Quander with Mardi Gras Committee, c1959

## 50+ OMEGA INSPIRED YEARS

I attended the Mardi Gras event that year, held on Friday, February 7, 1964. It was the night before the Alpha Chapter smoker, and less than one week before the fraternity initiation interviews. I was quite nervous about a lot of things. While the dance was an open event, available to all who had a ticket, still I could not help but wonder how would my presence be perceived. Several Alpha chapter undergrads were in attendance at the cavernous National Guard Armory building, the location where the event was held for several years. They were sitting together at tables they purchased, and visibly close to where my parents' table was located. I do not recall whether I had a date that night, but I cut a sharp image in my tuxedo, which I had acquired a few years before, when I was making the round of high school proms and later going to some dress-up affairs in my early college years.

I was old enough to legally drink alcohol, as the legal age at that time was 18 years old. Therefore, I needed to maintain my discretion and not drink too much. I put my best face forward, danced with the ladies, and gathered around when the brothers collected themselves in the center of the dance floor to sing *Omega Dear*. I hummed along with them, but would not dare to let anyone see my lips move, for fear that this might be misinterpreted in terms of just who I thought I was. It was a great night, and the first time that I attended the Mardi Gras as a guest.

In prior years, beginning in February 1960, and continuing in 1961 and 1962, I, along with my *Les Jeunes Hommes* brothers, had been in service, unloading the guests' vehicles, carrying the boxes and bags, ladened with food and adult beverages, directly to the assigned tables. Indeed, in 1960, when the club was about three weeks old, this was the first activity that we did, serving as valets, relieving them of this burden while dressed in their finest, and the ladies in high heels. The club made some good tips too, which helped to start our treasury. But for me, I had been there and done that, so now it was my time to just enjoy.

Unlike now, with the annual event staged in a hotel, the Mardi Gras was then a 10:00 p.m. until 4:00 a.m. affair. It was a grand party, but still a major undertaking to be at party speed for so long. It was not until several years later, when the Alpha Omega brothers moved

## INDUCTION INTO OMEGA PSI PHI FRATERNITY, APRIL 4, 1964

the event into a hotel, that the time was adjusted, generally to begin at 9:00 p.m., and ending at 2:00 a.m.

The next two days, Saturday, February 8th, and Sunday the 9th, were super busy. I attended the Alpha, Kappa, and Omega smokers, two of which were held on Saturday, and one on Sunday. Truth be told, the Alpha smoker was the best, and the food, homemade chili con carne, was outstanding. Alpha Phi Alpha did a great job of explaining what the Alpha fraternity was, including that its Beta Chapter was established in 1907 at Howard. They mentioned in detail who some of their most prominent members were and what they were doing, both for Alpha and in the community at large. I had never considered pledging Alpha, and was not interested this time either. But, because I received a specific invitation to attend, and there was no obligation, I decided to go. The Alpha House was located on New Hampshire Avenue and S St., N.W., while the Kappa House was located at 1708 S Street, diagonally across the street from the Alpha House.

Had the events been immediately sequential, I could have gone from one event to the other. But Alpha was in the early afternoon, about 2:00 p.m. to 4:00 p.m., while Kappa did not convene until the evening. So I returned to the area for the Kappa smoker, to see what they had to say. Kappa's approach was more of the same, with more emphasis upon parties and socialization than I thought it should be, especially since scholarship and high achievement was the watchword for all of the fraternities. Each claimed that its members were scholarly, had a better academic average than their competitors, and that the men of that fraternity had continued to prove themselves after college, by a sterling record of accomplishment. It has been a long time since that Saturday night, and my recollection is not the best. Still, I vividly recall that Xi Chapter, Kappa Alpha Psi, placed more emphasis upon their D.C. connections, urging that D.C. was a "Kappa Town" and less focus upon achievements of Kappa men. I had already decided that Kappa was not for me, anyway, but the outcome of their smoker only served to reinforce that. My mind was already made up. Omega was my goal and destination – provided they would have me. Whatever Kappa was offering seemed to hit the mark, though, for both Kappa and Alpha lines for 1964 were significantly larger than what Omega would assemble. Go figure!

Sunday afternoon, Omega had their smoker at the fraternity house. I arrived there at the exact advertised time. I immediately noticed a changed attitude from the brothers. Although they had not been particularly distant in relationship to me, this time they put on their friendly faces, and expressed delight at my being present. I am certain that they realized that there was a great competition for members, that many of us were attending more than one smoker, and that this was the final opportunity to make a favorable impression with the young perspectives before the official pledge period began.

"Welcome to the Omega House. Make yourself at home. We are delighted that you have decided to give Omega a look, before you make up your mind," was the pervasive attitude that afternoon. It was fine with me, relaxed me somewhat, and made me believe that indeed I was both welcome and wanted. I don't recall the menu, nor the program, except that a graduate brother from Alpha Omega Chapter was the guest speaker, and was most impressive. The following year, however, February 1965, when I was a neophyte, I had a hand in planning the recruitment smoker. We were honored to obtain as guest speaker, Bro. Dr. C. Herbert Marshall, Jr., (Alpha Chapter, 1917), whose dad, Bro C. Herbert Marshall, Sr., had pledged in 1920, under the sponsorship of his son, and later became the Founding Basileus of Alpha Omega Chapter in 1922.

The interviews were scheduled for that same week, all in the evening. I do not recall which day I took my interview, but I remember the scary event like it was yesterday. Arriving at the fraternity house, perhaps about 6:30 p.m., I entered the living room, where maybe eight to 10 other young men were sitting, waiting for their respective turns to be interviewed. You would have thought that someone had died. I have rarely seen such a more somber, long faced crowd. They were scared to death, and I among them. As outsiders, we did not understand that the funereal tone that the Alpha Chapter brothers set was no more than a big psych, designed to frighten us. Maybe, just maybe, they could make me believe that Omega did not really want me, or that at least they were not that particularly

## INDUCTION INTO OMEGA PSI PHI FRATERNITY, APRIL 4, 1964

interested or pressed into having me on the pledge line or in the fraternity.

As we watched the interviewees come down from the second floor, where the interviews were being held, and observed their body language, it was disconcerting. Some had tears, others looked like death warmed over. There were few, if any, smiles. Everyone was told to leave the house immediately, to just get their coats and hats, and get out. The universal message was, "Do not talk to anyone. Do not discuss the interview with anyone. Don't call us, we'll call you to let you know the outcome. Good bye!"

Just waiting for my turn at crucifixion was getting to be unbearable. To add to my already nervous stomach, I had a deep sinking feeling inside. No, I was not leaving, hadn't even thought of leaving. But what was happening? A couple of days ago, everyone was nice, receptive, and seemingly interested in each of us. Today, they are cold-hearted, disconnected, and act like they could care less. The truth, I thought, must lie somewhere in between.

Then it was my turn. By now, several other guys had come to the house, and were likewise awaiting their respective turn for their interviews. I knew two of them, David H. Reid, III, my childhood friend, and Bruce Stewart, a D.C. guy whom I knew casually from high school days. Tyrone Mitchell and Julius S. McClain, III, also D.C. guys, were interviewed on a different night. McClain was the grandson of Julius S. McClain, Omega's 12th Grand Basileus (1926-1929). The eventual amassing of nine D.C. men for the 1964 Alpha Chapter pledge line would place a serious dent into Kappa's claim, now partly discredited, that D.C. was a "Kappa Town" and that very few D.C. guys would ever pledge anything else.

Climbing up the dimly lit staircase to the second floor, I immediately noticed how poor the lighting was. I could hardly see where I was going, and knew that this could not possibly be good for what was about to occur. I was literally led by the arm down a totally dark hallway, and into a likewise dark room. Directed into a straight back chair, and told to lean a little forward, I was startled when a single bright light came on, close to my face, which shocked my partially dilated pupils. Immediately, a series of questions were fired at me. "Tell us about yourself." "Why do you want to be an Omega?"

"What do you think you would bring to Omega, and why?" "Do you think that just because your father is an Omega, that you should be too?" "Do you think that because your dad and uncle are in Alpha Omega, that you can just walk into the fraternity?"

I could hardly answer one question before they barraged me with another or more than one at a time. It was truly "organized confusion," and they had and maintained the upper hand. After asking me what Omega-related activities I had participated in, they harassed me because I talked about having attended Grand Conclaves and meeting present and former grand basilei. That was surely the wrong, but a truthful, answer. The interview took a nasty turn at that point, because I was accused of name dropping, when, from my own perspective, I was just trying to honestly answer their rapid fire questions. It was a no win, no way to win, situation. But I tried to handle it as best as I could.

Next, I was asked which brothers in Alpha Chapter I already knew. I mentioned Bro. Frank Patterson first, as he and I had worked on the decks at the Library of Congress. He was in the room, and went to bat for me, I later learned, when it came time to vote. Next, I mentioned Bro. William "Hook" Hall, but was so flustered that I called him "Richard" Hall. That was it. I was beaten in the face and head with one sheet of newspaper – it did not hurt – and told to, "Get the hell out, and don't ever come back. This interview is over!" Someone grabbed my arm, the light was turned off, and I was gruffly escorted out. What just happened? I was not sure, but I was terribly upset. Still, there was nothing that I could do about it. I was warned, like the others, to not discuss the interview with anyone, to get my hat and coat, and to leave the frat house. As I left the room, someone said, "Don't call us, we'll call you, and it may not be anything that you want to hear."

I heard them laughing and talking as soon as the room door was closed. They were congratulating themselves and each other on the "game" that they had just played. It was from that moment that I realized that it was, indeed, nothing but a game, and that the interview's negative outcome, at least in my case, would probably play only a small role in the decision of whether I would be placed on

## INDUCTION INTO OMEGA PSI PHI FRATERNITY, APRIL 4, 1964

the 1964 Alpha Chapter pledge line. At least it was over, and there was nothing further to do but wait.

Despite the admonitions, I did discuss the interview with David Reid, III, my childhood friend, and learned that his interview was largely the same as mine, although less harassing and less stressful. Maybe I talked too much, and made it worse for myself. We'll never know!

When the interview cycle ended, the chapter voted and then submitted the names of those upon whom Alpha Chapter's favor rested. I do not know who, if anyone, was rejected who also had the minimum academic average of a 2.3 G.P.A. I always believed that this academic threshold was too low, given that Scholarship is a Cardinal Principle. But it was not my determination to make, as the university's minimum standards were the official threshold for qualification, at least from the academic perspective, of who met the criteria for membership. Of course the fraternity could deny membership to an individual based upon some other determination.

I received my letter of acceptance on about February 17, 1964, which letter congratulated me, and directed me to present myself at 2:00 p.m. on Saturday, February 22, 1964, at the fraternity house, for induction into the Lampados Club. David also received his letter of acceptance. We were both overjoyed. I only wish that I still had the letter, and surely would have included a copy of it in this publication. We were directed what to wear, and given other instructions concerning the financial obligations, which were not that demanding, compared to what the level of monetary consideration is today. A dark blue or black suit, white shirt, and dark solid tie was the required "uniform."

I presented myself at the appointed time, with money in hand, and was subsequently inducted into the 1964 Lampados Club. Of course I was nervous, having endured the mind shattering experience of just a few days prior. But things calmed down considerably. Initially, there were 25 of us.

## 50+ OMEGA INSPIRED YEARS

The list of 25 Lampados included (primarily, but not necessarily in height order):

Donald Royster, *Brooklyn, New York*
Rohulamin Quander *Washington, DC*
Solomon H. Smith, Jr. *Washington, DC*
David H. Reid III *Washington, DC*
Derek C. Brown *Baltimore, Maryland* (Omega Chapter)
Gilbert J. Brown *Bronx, New York*
Ernest David Caldwell *Concord, North Carolina*
Lenox S. Dingle, Jr. *New York*
Ralph M. Durham *Philadelphia, Pennsylvania,* **President** (Omega Chapter)
Tyrone D. Mitchell *Washington, DC*
Halvor Parris, Jr. *South Ozone Park, New York*
LaSalle Petty, Jr. *Roanoke, Virginia,* **Dog Captain**
Eldridge Harvey Pearsall *Greensboro, North Carolina*
Robert Allen Siegel *Staten Island, New York*
Willie Singleton, Jr., Massachusetts
Samuel L. Spears *Philadelphia, Pennsylvania*
Larry Edward Davis *St. Petersburg, Florida*
Bruce T. Stewart III *Washington, DC*
Haywood Patrick Swygert *Philadelphia, Pennsylvania*
David A. Felder, Jr. *Washington, DC*
George C. Garrison, Jr. *Montclair, New Jersey* (Omega Chapter)
    The following four men dropped the line:
Nehemiah Rucker, Washington, D.C.
Julius McClain, III, Washington, D.C.[30],
Michael Benoit, Washington, D.C.
One other – name not recalled

Our Dean of Pledgees was Taft Howard Broome, Jr. (10-62-A), assisted primarily by Bernie Leroy Bates (Alpha 1963), Assistant Dean. They impressed upon us that they were our saviors, and that if we listened to them, and followed their directions, everything would be alright. At that point, although I was somewhat confused about what was about to begin, I was likewise afraid to not give them my utmost, undivided attention. It would be quite a six week period from

---

[30] Grandson of Julius McClain, Sr., 12th Grand Basileus, 1926-29)

## INDUCTION INTO OMEGA PSI PHI FRATERNITY, APRIL 4, 1964

now – February 22nd, until April 4th, the date of our ultimate induction into the sacred ranks of Omega.

There were many things that had to be accomplished inside of six very short weeks. First, the emphasis had to be placed upon academics, although it was hard to concentrate when there were so many other things to get accomplished at the same time. Then there was the matter of the coronation of the Lampados queen, which included interviews towards assembling a queen's court. There was also the matter of marching practice, because Omegas were known for their marching skills, and we had to work to uphold that tradition.

And of course we had to covertly schedule and secretly execute two parties, one each with the Pyramids of Delta Sigma Theta and the Ivies of Alpha Kappa Alpha. These parties were both traditional and mandatory, and the Lamps were supposed to prove how cleaver they were by keeping the date, time, and place a secret from the big brothers, who had "officially" forbid us to party during the pledge period. It was a game, and we played it excellently. The women pledgees likewise knew that the joint party was supposed to be a secret, and were as closed mouthed about it as we. I am happy to report that both parties were successfully pulled of, and that the big brothers and big sisters, although suspicious as to when, where, and how we did it, did not find or invade us during either party.

My pledge line had an extra element in 1964, and it proved to be most beneficial. Kappa Psi had a pledge line of 12 lamps at the same time. It was a smaller line, perhaps 12 to 14, most all of whom were either in medical or law school. But they liked to party too. And besides, with AKA having initially 63 on their line (later known as "The Sassy 56"), a double line due a one year suspension and no line taken in 1963, we needed several extra men. I do not recall where that party was held.

### Omega Memories (Extracts)

*As I approach my fiftieth year as an Omega, I remember when my father introduced me to two of our founders: Love and Cooper. I clearly recall Doctor Oscar J. Cooper's smile as he reached down to shake my hand. I realized this was a special moment when I turned and watched my dad's expression. I decided that I wanted to become a physician like our founder.*

*Later, I had the pleasure of going to Coleman's house while on line with Kappa Psi. He was very attentive as he talked to us about our ambitions. .....*

*I will never forget walking across Howard University's campus and shaking hands with H Carl Moultrie. My father impressed upon me the important work he was doing with the fraternity. After completing my last two years of undergrad, I was able to join Kappa Psi. Brother Aubrey Dent helped me in medical school. As an older student, he mentored me by sharing his old notes on anatomy. He helped me to organize the details and understand the concepts. I formed a bond with the brothers of Alpha Chapter because we were on line at the same time. Brother Patrick Swygert, Brother Rho Quander, and I have maintained a fifty-year friendship. We shared unforgettable experiences on Howard's campus. .....*

*It has been rewarding for me to interact with brothers of all ages from all over the country. We have helped each other in many endeavors.*
*Que Psi Phi till the day I die! - Everett A. White, M. D., M.B.A., Kappa Psi, May 1964*

It was customary for the Lampados to have a party with both the Pyramids and Ivy pledgees during the annual pledge cycle. These were two separate fun events, and always garnered memoires of how the pledgees managed to steal away from campus and the watchful eyes of the big brothers and big sisters, who had expressly forbidden us to party during the pledge season. Of course they knew that we would do so, making it an annual test of wills, wit, and pledgee wisdom. Indeed, sneaking off to a secluded location to have a pledgee party was a part of the rigor of pledging. And 1964 was no exception.

The party with the Pyramids was at my Uncle Joe's house. He and my Aunt Algetha were open to having the Lamp-Pyramid party in their newly constructed recreation room. The large house was located at 1203 Hamlin Street, N.E. The back yard of their home was diagonally across from the rear yard of Founder Frank Coleman's home, located at 1232 Girard Street, N.E. I wonder if the Colemans

## INDUCTION INTO OMEGA PSI PHI FRATERNITY, APRIL 4, 1964

heard us on that raucous Saturday night in mid-March? If so, they did not complain. Nor did they report us to the big brothers and big sisters. Frank Coleman, an Omega Founder, was married to Edna Brown Coleman, one of the January 13, 1913 Founders of Delta Sigma Theta Sorority, Inc. They both had a stake in our event of that evening, and surely would have wanted it to be a great success, had they been advised that it was ongoing, just a couple of hundred feet from their own comfortable home, located in the Brookland section of Washington, D.C.

One particular event of that evening is still very clear in my mind. It was a great party, with plenty of good music, an agreeable assemblage of would be Omegas and Deltas, plus the big brothers and big sisters of the pledge staff. With the Lamps of Kappa Psi Chapter present too, it must have been close to 100 people in attendance. Kappa Psi chapter was founded in 1926 by Bro. Dr. Montague Cobb, a legendary Omega man who was a fixture of the Howard University College of Medicine staff for decades. In 1964, with our pledge lines being run at the same time, we shared many activities and became quite close to them too.

While the music and ambiance was good, one component of the party was lacking – something to eat. Potato chips and snacks did not fit the bill. It was a long day for everyone, with class, errands for the big brothers and big sisters, planning our coronation, and the like. Omega men are known for their "Purple Passion," a grain alcohol and red or purple wine combination. I had never tried it before, and was a bit skeptical about it, because of its high alcohol content and reputation for getting people stinking drunk if they imbibed too much. The Dean of Pledgees' staff and some of my line brothers seemed to know exactly what to do, and they concocted it well. Still, if there was no food to offset the effects of the alcohol, you can see that you are headed for trouble.

And trouble did come. As the night wore on, and we danced, talked, and generally felt so proud of ourselves because we had successfully "defied" the big brothers and big sisters who had officially forbade us to party during the pledge period, a couple of Pyramids showed signs of being quite drunk. They felt that they were about to throw up and desperately wanted to get some fresh air. Both of them managed to escape from the basement recreation room to the front yard, and vomited profusely in my aunt's flower bed.

Most all of us knew what was happening, and I think it was initially considered to be a laughable event. In retrospect, though, as I look back on the event these several years later, I realized that it could have been far more serious, even fatal, as alcohol poisoning is nothing to play with. Both of these ladies recovered without incident, although I know that their pride was damaged, and that they were greatly embarrassed at their loss of discretion, which is a key element that all Black Greeks are mandated to demonstrate and exercise. I would image that they were exposed to some admonishment from the Deltas after the event, when they were sober and able to fully understand what had happened.

We were fortunate that only two people got ill, although a number of us were quite high, and possibly even drunk. When the party ended, we were all pretty much wiped out. I wonder how we managed to safely get back to the dorms or home. By today's standards, many of the drivers should not have been on the road, since they were legally drunk, or at least had the strong presence of alcohol in their body systems.

We had arranged with my uncle and aunt to not clean up immediately after the party, but to send a cleanup crew the next afternoon. All went as planned in that respect, and we rendered the area as though no raucous party had occurred the night before. Upon arriving at their home, my aunt lit into me. She had already discovered vomit in her flower bed, and wondered what type of people they were, to come to someone's home, and behave in such a manner. She was furious, to say the very least. I tried as best as I could to explain exactly what happened, including poor planning that did not include food for the many of us who had not eaten properly before the party the night before. She was not having it.

When she realized that the culprits were two women, and pledgees at that, she questioned their integrity, and how they could put themselves into such a position where they did not know what they were doing, and might have befallen some tragedy or sexual misfortune. She ended the conversation by adding, that, "Thank God! They did not throw up on my recreation room floor, or in the

## INDUCTION INTO OMEGA PSI PHI FRATERNITY, APRIL 4, 1964

carpeted hallway." Although the recreation room was new and quite nice, it did not have a separate off-the-street entrance. Therefore, everyone had to enter via the front door of the house and walk down the hall, to get to the basement steps.

My uncle, on the other hand, took everything in stride, commenting that in his day, which was during Prohibition, they drank whatever they could get ahold of. Living in West Virginia at the time, moonshine was easily accessible. They were occasions when some of it was not good, and people got sick. He even heard of a few occasions where someone died from moonshine poisoning. To him, alcohol and drinking too much, was a part of growing up. Still, he could not agree with me too much, because Aunt Algetha would have let him have it too.

By the time the party was held, we were about half way through the pledge cycle. We had to plan our Lampados Queen coronation, including assembling a court of ladies from whom a queen would be chosen. We also had marching practice at least twice a week. There were only 24 hours in a day, and the dean and his staff found a way to squeeze activities into almost every hour. The marching practice was held on Beach Drive in Rock Creek Park. In 1964, several of the park's road were closed during the winter months, because they passed through water and the fjords were not considered safe for use in the winter months. Beach Drive, just outside of the National Zoo, was one of those roads.

But before we ventured to go there, generally assembling about 11:00 p.m., and staying for a couple of hours, it was necessary to get permission to use the public street. After all, with a crew of 20 young black men, one Caucasian, and their dean of pledgees staff of five to six present, jumping around, learning marching steps, singing Omega songs, and acting in unison at this late hour, to the unsuspecting, we might appear to be planning some type of guerilla activity. But good fortune was ours. Bro. Grant Wright, former basileus of Tau Upsilon Chapter, Washington, D.C., which merged with Alpha Omega in the mid-1950s, after a longstanding feud was resolved, had been selected as the first African American Chief of the National Capital Park Police.

## 50+ OMEGA INSPIRED YEARS

Mindful of his exalted position, Taft Broome, our dean, asked for permission to use Beach Drive for our training activities. Permission was given, but supplemented by a written document that specifically said that, by a grant in use and authority from the Chief of Police, the men of the Omega Psi Phi Fraternity have been given specific permission to use this space for their pledge-related activities, including marching and singing practice.

The letter was certainly necessary, because although the white subordinate officers were informed of our presence and that it was approved, they routinely came by to watch, witness, and wonder what this was all about. Most of them were probably not college educated, and for those who were and knew something about fraternities, they were totally unprepared for this "black experience" that witnessed us doing our thing, getting ready for an open probation demonstration on Howard University's campus. I am convinced that they were there just as much out of curiosity, as to assure that we were not doing anything that would be illegal. Indeed, I would not be surprised if Chief Wright had advised his officers to keep an eye on us, to assure that all was in order, so that if any complaints came, particularly about "strange noises" coming from the park late at night, the National Capital Park Police would be already fully aware, and able to explain what was going on.

It was during this marching practice cycle that my line number got changed. There were 21 of us, having lost four along the way. It was decided that we would do our open probation marching demonstration, set for April 3, 1964, in a double line. Going according to height, I was #3 on the line. When we lined up to learn the marches and steps, my line brother, Solomon Smith, a Panamanian whose family had migrated to the U.S. some years before, was having trouble getting the steps. Fraternities and many of their activities were still rather new to him, and he just could not catch on quickly. Originally assigned as #2 on the line, it would have put him in the very front. The odd numbered brothers were to march in the left column and the even numbered brothers in the right column.

The dean decided that he was not going to have Sol embarrass us and himself by being a guidon who could not get it straight. So he declared that I would switch places with Sol, making me now #2, and

## INDUCTION INTO OMEGA PSI PHI FRATERNITY, APRIL 4, 1964

Sol now #3. That way, at least, he could follow my initial steps, rather than be the one to initiate whatever was next, only to have it be incorrect. This was critically important, since many of our moves were sequential, the forerunner to what is now generically called, "the Rolling Que." So that is how I became "The Deuce" after having been a "Trey" for about two weeks. I find, though, that having been a Deuce for 50 years has not been bad. I am five feet, seven inches tall, not very big, and have met so many vertically challenged other Deuces, that it almost seems like we are a fraternity within the fraternity. In 2011, when we attended our Centennial Celebration in Washington, D.C. in 2011, I also attended a party convened by and for brothers who were Deuces. Can you imagine that? Others were there too, but we were the focus of the event – a party for Deuces.

The six week pledge period of 1964 was not easy. Given all the talk and hype associated with becoming an Omega, and particularly being inducted at the site of the fraternity's founding, I was not sure what to expect. The thought of having to endure a paddle, was more frightening and worrisome than the actual paddle itself. We had all heard horror stories about the "brutal triangle – Bloody Beta, Brutal Pi, and Horrible Alpha" but I can truthfully say that I came to believe, and maybe I was just fooling myself into believing, that much of what was being touted was really a big psychological effort to frighten us into the formation and brotherly attitudes that the big brothers and Omega as an organization wanted us to have.

Yes, there was some paddling, and I had some sore spots on my buttocks to prove it. Yes, there was also some chest action, and I likewise had the remnants of that too. But, on the whole, Taft Broome and Bernie Bates, our dean of pledgees and his assistant, were dedicated to protecting us, and making certain that whatever happened, that it stayed within the realm of reasonability. Of course by today's standards of zero tolerance for hazing, what occurred in 1964 would be considered too much by far, in the present day, 2014, my 50th year in the fraternity.

I was never a protégé of the concept that any form of violence was an integral part of making one into an Omega man, or that without it, one could not nor would not be a good and true brother. That was never my thing, and I can truthfully say that in all my years in the fraternity, I did not swing wood or hit any lamp in the chest, testing his "Perseverance," to see if he was true Omega material. To some Alpha Chapter brothers, I guess I was a "softie," but I simply never believed, and still don't, that physical violence is a necessary component towards earning and attaining membership in the fraternity.

The dean's staff had several jobs to do during this truncated six week period. Their most important task, by far, was to make us into one cohesive unit as quickly as possible, which was not an easy task. For the most part, we did not know one another before Saturday, February 22nd, 1964. We also came from different backgrounds too. Some of us were the sons of doctors and university professors. Others parents were government workers. Some of the line brothers were the first to attend college in their families, while others had family education and money of longer standing. A few of us came from single parent homes, where the economic challenge was greater than in other family units. As well, at least five of us, myself included, came from foreign family backgrounds, and were first generation Americans, on at least one side of our respective families.

Who were they? Bruce Stewart's mother was from Korea; Halvor Paris's family was from Barbados; Sol Smith was from Panama; the family of Robert Siegal, a Caucasian Russian Jew, were Russian immigrants; and my mother was of mixed East Indian-Irish-Scottish background, with a dash of Afro Caribbean, whose father (Mohammed Abdul Rohualamin, my grandfather) had migrated to the island from Calcutta, India in 1913. Then too, we had New England, the mid-Atlantic, and the Southern states all represented, with men who had never been exposed to overt racism, and others who lived it daily, migrating to Howard from the Carolinas, Florida, and other points south.

And then there was the issue of class, and the proverbial issue of color, both of which seemed to rear their ugly heads whenever African Americans of diverse backgrounds and exposures are assembled together for any period of time. Thank God, we did not spend much time on either of these components, but I heard it a few times, nonetheless. In all of my then 20 years, I never considered myself to be "light-skinned" until I went to Howard University.

## INDUCTION INTO OMEGA PSI PHI FRATERNITY, APRIL 4, 1964

Further, I did not even know the words "bourgeois" or "bougie" – a term that came later – until I was on the pledge line.

In retrospect, it was an issue of sorts, as my family background, genealogy, and stability were viewed by some in both the fraternity and on my pledge line as "problematic." With my given name, "Rohulamin" and East Indian background, I was labeled on occasion, as not being a "real Negro," the racial identity term by which African Americans were then known. As well, I had not come from a neglected, dysfunctional background, but rather a two-parent home of solidly middleclass people, who were devoted to one another and to their four children. My personal legacy as well as my Omega legacy were both well established. I had attended virtually all-white parochial schools in Washington, D.C., and travelled in a social circles that included house parties in upscale D.C. neighborhoods, attending the Girlfriends and Bachelor Benedict's annual cotillion balls, with me often serving as an escort for that year's group of debutants, summer activities at Highland Beach, and later, rented houses in resort towns.

What I considered to be an upwardly mobile asset, a few others viewed as a "liability," or if not a liability, then at least a point about which they could make some issue or comment. I think that I weathered that would-be-storm with my perseverance and overall attitude, but I do not believe that the sentiment ever went away, pursuing me into law school, also at Howard, and into some aspects of later life. But that's getting ahead of myself at this stage in my Omega life story.

By early March 1964, several chapters of the fraternity were in the process of conducting their annual initiation process. I have no record of which campuses were in the process, but I do recall that several of the chapters in Maryland and Virginia paid us a visit. Even Beta chapter came to D.C., especially to check me out. Assembled in the basement of the frat house, dressed for a rumble, and not knowing at all what to expect, I looked up and there was Chester Fortune, a neophyte Beta brother, who had very recently been inducted into Omega. Was he here to "beast" on me, or to offer words of advice?

Few words of "advice" were being offered that night, but thankfully, our dean's staff, ever vigilant and concerned that visiting brothers not take liberties and administer some hurt that was not part of our chapter's program, warned them that physical actions against us was strictly off limits. Of course, as lowly lamps, we did not know that this had been said, but learned of it shortly thereafter. Broome and Bates absolutely did not want us to get hurt, nor for Alpha Chapter to be cited for pledge-related injuries that might have been inflicted by a visiting brother(s), who, after doing his harm, then anonymously retreated back to his campus at Lincoln, Morgan, Virginia State, or elsewhere.

Our dean's staff pledged to protect us, provided that we listened and obeyed them without questioning their judgment. We could ask questions for clarification purposes, but not too many of them either, unless we wanted to face being called "stupid" or "dumb' for being too thick-headed to get it right the first time. These periodic "sessions," most often on Wednesday nights, gave both them and us ample opportunities to demonstrate that we were on the same page as far as this aspect of the total program was concerned. We soldiered through the process, although we did loose four from among our initial number of 25. I never knew why they dropped off line, but one of them, Nehemiah Rucker, pledged the following year or two, and was inducted into Omega through Kappa Psi chapter.

Omega made many great strides under the three year administration of Grand Basileus McClain (1926-1929). Inducted into Omega via Beta Chapter, he was a graduate of Lincoln University, Pennsylvania, class of 1922, and later a Trustee of the University. In 1927, during Bro. McClain's administration, and at the urging of fraternity member Carter G. Woodson, the fraternity made *National Negro Achievement Week* an annual observance, which continues today as Black History Month.

The balance of our pledge period was uneventful, and I quickly learned that this was a good thing. We held the usual Lampados Club Queen's Coronation on one evening in Rankin Chapel, crowning Betty Cave, of Philadelphia, as our queen.

As the pledging events came closer to conclusion, the pace picked up quite a bit, and for a while, it did not seem to me that it was possible to get everything that we needed to do, done on time. There was the continuing marching practice down in Rock Creek Park, which increased, both in frequency and the duration of each practice.

## INDUCTION INTO OMEGA PSI PHI FRATERNITY, APRIL 4, 1964

There was also the matter of putting together the purple and gold outfits that we were going to wear during the open probation marching demonstration, held annually on the long walk that also passed by the Omega sundial, a gift to Howard from the "Lampodos" Pledge Club of 1929. The project was specifically spearheaded by Leroy Clay, a pledgee from Baltimore, Maryland, and paid for by the Lampodos Club themselves.[31]

Clay was not only the brainchild of the sundial, colloquially called, "the dial," but he was also the follow through point man. In January 2012, I would be fortunate enough to obtain the records and photographs of his effort on behalf of the 1929 Lampodos Club, all of which have been donated to the Moorland Spingarn Research Center, Howard University, and will be discussed in more detail at a later time in this publication.

With the pledge period drawing to closure, we needed wood, lanterns, and bricks. The wood was for the Omega shields that we were going to make and carry during our campus open pro demonstration. The lanterns, we were to keep with us all week, as we traveled to class and other locations about campus during probation week. The bricks were to be painted purple and gold, and we were to guard with our lives, and not let a big brother take from us, no matter what. I could see that one hell of a time was rapidly approaching – literally.

Tyrone Mitchell, my line brother, was put in charge of much of this cooperative effort. He formed a committee and they set about the tasks. The wood and purple and gold paint were obtained from Hechinger's Lumber yard, a well-known retailer in D.C. I cannot recall who cut out the shields into the desired shape of the official Omega crest, but the outcome was perfect. Gilbert Brown and Solomon Smith, both of whom were good artists, made the stencils that we used to paint the shields into the desired patterns, featuring

---

[31] *The spelling for the pledge club as listed in the 1929 printed sundial donation programs was universally spelled "Lamp o dos," and not "Lamp a dos" as it later became known to be. I am unaware of why there is a spelling difference, but cannot assume it to be simply a spelling error.*

all of the requisite symbols, and making certain that the 20 Pearls, symbolic of what Omega truly means, were both appropriate in size and correctly spaced. The outcome was excellent, although the big brothers went to great lengths to criticize us, to make adverse comments about our supposedly not knowing what we were doing, and threatening us with bodily harm and otherwise, if we produced an end product that they would be ashamed of, and embarrassed to have presented to the campus on the upcoming open pro demonstration, set for Friday, April 3rd.

We were determined to make everything a great success, but a big issue and question remained. Where do we find the lanterns and the bricks? Time was increasingly short, and our funds were likewise greatly limited. But Tyrone, the innovator that he was, scheduled something that I had never heard of before – "A midnight requisition." What was that? Was I the only one who had no idea, and why it was limited by name to "midnight?" Several of my line brothers laughed and teased me unmercifully, calling me a "Catholic school boy, who didn't know anything," adding, "Fool, don't you know that a midnight requisition is when you go somewhere, locate what you need, and under the cover of darkness, when no one is looking or attending, just help yourself?"

I was surprised, maybe even shocked, to learn that the committee, having identified a nearby construction site, would simply visit the site after dark and help themselves to more than 25 bricks, and likewise, after extinguishing them, remove about 25 working lanterns, one for each of us, and a few more for the dean's staff. Stole! Yes! And yes again! I was a Catholic school boy, and the very idea that this is how they acquired the items that we needed was something that I had never imagined before. But what choice did I have? This action is certainly not one that we could be proud of. At the least, it was inconsistent with Uplift, a Cardinal Principle of Omega.

But we needed the items and there they were, all ready to be modified for our purposes. We set about to paint the bricks purple and gold, but none of them were the same. The big brothers told us that these would be our personal bricks to keep for life, and that we could modify them as we saw fit, to suit our wishes, provided they maintained the purple and gold theme. The lanterns were different.

## INDUCTION INTO OMEGA PSI PHI FRATERNITY, APRIL 4, 1964

All of them had to be painted gold, and they were. I kept my lantern for many years, and had it in the storage room at my parents' home.

After the excitement of the moment, including carrying the brick and lantern around the campus, after my induction into Omega, and with other fraternal and non-fraternal matters attracting my attention, I sort of forgot about both items. But some years later, as I refocused my Omega-related life, and wanted to reassemble myself into a better affiliation with the brotherhood, I went looking to retrieve both my lamp and my brick, recalling their symbolism and all that I had to go through to achieve the right to carry both of these treasures during the latter part of my pledge program. I knew exactly where the lantern was, or rather where I last saw it. The brick was also somewhere in that room, but underneath a number of items. But when I entered my parents' storage room, and moved several items around during my search, I could not readily locate either of them. I inquired of my mom regarding their whereabouts, to which she casually replied, "Those old things. What did you need them for? When I was clearing out the room a couple of years ago, I threw them out." Threw them out! And a vital part of me with it!

But I have no one to blame but myself. By then, several years later, I was married man, with a beautiful wife and three young children, and I had my family obligations, and indeed family was and remains my first priority. But I had also clouded my other values and the priority to be an ever-vigilant brother of Omega, someone that legendary brother Dr. Montague Cobb would be proud to know, and who would be a good example of demonstrating the lifelong journal that is Omega. The loss of my lantern, and likewise my brick, were both wakeup calls, reminding me that I had taken a sacred oath, blindfolded and on my knees on April 4, 1964, which had gotten a little ragged around the edges due to my neglect.

April 3, 1964, was a brilliantly sunny early April day. The weather at that time can be tricky, often still cool and even rainy. In my many years at Howard University, attending the annual open probation demonstrations of the Greek-letter organizations, there were some days that were quite cool, and on occasion even rainy. In the morning it did not look like it would be a good day to perform. But about 12:00 noon, the rain stopped, the sun came out, and we shouted, "Let the sun shine for Omega!" So fortunately we did not have to go through a weather anxiety for the "21 Titans," our line's name, during the open demonstration.

The night before was a non-stop marathon. It seemed as though we had accomplished little or nothing up to that point. The purple and gold outfits, particularly the capes that we were to wear, were not finished. Complaints were made that our capes were a little too red, not "purple enough" to satisfy some of the brothers. Several of us were still ragged about our marching, and we did not want to mess up in front of the entire campus. The finishing touches on painting the shields was almost done, but would they be sufficiently dry by the time we carried them. The head bands were still undone. My belated question now is, were they purple bands with one gold Omega letter or gold bands with one purple letter? At any rate, they too had to be completed. I asked myself, "What have we been doing for these last six weeks? Why aren't we ready?"

A large part of the answer to the "Why aren't we ready?" question lies in a breakdown that came towards the end of the pledge period, many of the details of which escape me now. But a couple of days just before "hell week," the term used for the last week of pledging, and just before induction into the fraternity, there was a serious breakdown in communication between the chapter and the Lampados Club. It seems that a number of the Alpha Chapter brothers were complaining that we were not being "made right," a term that I would later learn and interpret to mean, that the dean's staff was interfering with the brothers' access to the lamps. "Access!" What did that mean? Were they trying to haze us without our dean's staff supervision? We called it "beasting." Did they want to beast on us within their own discretion, and outside of the dean's structured plan of action? To this day, I am still not sure.

As we got wind of this controversy and rightfully became concerned about our fate, we also were apprehensive about being turned over to the youthful discretion of the actions of individual brothers in the chapter. What would happen if we fanned out into 21 different directions, some at this big brother's room, and others at that brother's apartment? Would this be a license for them to haze us and worse? Paddling was the prerogative of the dean's staff, and they

## INDUCTION INTO OMEGA PSI PHI FRATERNITY, APRIL 4, 1964

exercised that action sparingly. If left to their own devices, we were concerned that some of the brothers, especially the neophytes who had "scores to settle" might loose their obligation to be discrete when dealing with us. We did not want to get physically abused, and especially not injured. From my perspective, some 50 years later, it was obvious that Taft Broome and Bernie Bates, plus the rest of the pledging support staff, needed to remain in the picture.

In an effort to get to know the big brothers on a one-on-one basis, we were directed to make personal visits to them. We were instructed that while visiting, we should secure the signature of the big brothers in our composition books. We were directed to obtain a certain number of signatures by a specific date. While this plan of action sounds good in theory, there soon were reports of individual lamps visitation turning into some form of harassment, and even physical abuse. The dean's staff had previously told the brothers that such actions were strictly off limits outside of the confines of the formal pledge program and not allowed, if not under the dean's staff's supervision, generally in the basement of the fraternity house.

All of my line brothers had to carry these notebooks and protect them from being stolen or confiscated. Beyond obtaining signatures, we were supposed to also take notes, formulate written plans related to pledging, and treasure them as an artifact symbolic of our journey to becoming a proud Omega man. That did not work. Several of the lamps' notebooks were confiscated by the big brothers and never seen again. I do not recall what happened to mine, but assume that it was taken from me, because it did not last the six week pledge period still in my possession.

Well, the "dissatisfaction" with us boiled over about half-way through the fifth week, and we were thrown off line. If my memory is correct, and I think that it is, there was a sentiment in Alpha Chapter that they, or at least some significant portion of the chapter brothers, wanted to break the line, accept some of us and blackball the rest. When we got word of what they were thinking about doing, we said, "Hell no!" We started this together and we are going to finish it TOGETHER. We will not allow ourselves to be split into who will be an Omega within a few days and who will not. It was a very tense period, with only 10 or so days before scheduled induction, six of which days, March 29th to April 3rd, being hell week.

Rather than let Alpha Chapter do this to us, we quit! We quit! I did not want to quit, but my "LBs" (line brothers) voted and I went along. What's going to happen now? We were the future of Alpha Chapter. Did they really need or want us? Surely they could survive without us, but at what cost? The lifeblood of the undergraduate chapters is to do annual induction. It is not like the graduate chapters which have sustainability over time. Brothers come and go over the four year period, and the failure to induct a pledge line for one year will greatly inhibit the fraternity's presence and functionality for the ensuing year. Without an intake of new brothers, there will be no new blood to replace and succeed to positions of leadership and participation as the prophyte brothers graduate.

The adverse effect of such a course of action reaches beyond just the confines of the chapter. It also affects your leadership profile at the university level, when it comes to positions such as a class president, student council positions, editors of the yearbook and *Hilltop*, the student newspaper, etc. A skipped pledge cycle also adversely affects your ability to attract new brothers the following year as well, since your physical presence on campus would have been greatly reduced, and those brothers who were still present, would have transitioned from juniors to graduating seniors, focusing upon the next phases of their lives, and having little to less time to devote to inducting men who might be good members of Omega, and then taking some action to solicit their interest.

No, skipping a pledge line is never a good idea under most circumstances, and we did not believe that it was in Omega's best interest to do so at this time. But where do we go from here? When Alpha Chapter learned of our decision to quit and be unified, we were informed that we could not use the name "Lampados Club" anymore. So we had no name. Tyrone Mitchell, the LB of the famed "midnight requisition," came up with a new name, "Emanon," which is "No Name" spelled backwards. So for several days we were known as "The Emanons." The what?

It was not generally known that we had dropped line, and I think that the Alpha chapter brothers intentionally made it look like they

## INDUCTION INTO OMEGA PSI PHI FRATERNITY, APRIL 4, 1964

had put us off line. It was in their best public image to make it appear to be that way. To their thinking, or at least programmatically what they were telling others, was that we were "trifling, and many of us were not Omega material." That dismissive statement sounds very familiar in retrospect, for I have heard that statement many, many times during my 50 years, although it has generally been used with regard to specific individuals, but not to an entire line.

To this day, I do not know which of my LBs was deemed to be "unworthy" or "not Omega material," but we were determined that it would be ALL or NONE. It was a standoff for those few days. As well, Omega needed and wanted men who were destined to be somebody, and to go someplace in life. How many times do we take especial note of the achievement of several of our members and proudly beat our chests, shouting to all, "You know, he's an Omega man!" This determination and attitude is something that we want, celebrate, and magnify in later years.

So to expect so much humility from a lamp during the six week pledge cycle is somewhat unrealistic, given that the day after the initiation, everything changes and the new brother is expected to be "out there," and demonstrating just how cool, sharp, focused, and determined he could be and to be a leader on the campus. Was our alleged arrogance the main factor in why were we not "Omega material?" I honestly do not know. A few of us were considered to be arrogant, above it all, myself included. In the estimation of some chapter brothers, I guess that we were not humble enough, our eyes not cast down sufficiently. But I did not come from that slave mentality background.

The chapter brothers had no concept of what being of proud West Indian background meant, and being of Barbados descent made it even more so. Barbadians are always being accused of walking with their heads up in the air, to the point that they might trip over something on the ground which they did not see, because their noses were the highest points on their bodies. As to me, was that it? They also thought that H. Patrick Swygert, my LB, was particularly arrogant. He was a junior, while most of us were sophomores. He was a member of Alpha Phi Omega, the service fraternity, and was already familiar with much of what pledging entailed.

## 50+ OMEGA INSPIRED YEARS

Many of the big brothers considered that to him, the whole pledge process was a game. And in a great sense it was just that. Pat Swygert, arrogant? Perhaps so! But in retrospect, he was right, and he parlayed his smarts, focus, training, and determination into becoming the 15th president of Howard University in 1995, a position that he held for 13 years. And Omega brothers everywhere, and especially Alpha chapter and Alpha chapter alums, would beat their chests and proclaim, "He's one of us!"

All of that aside, the chapter brothers had a long, late night meeting, during which they decided to let us back on line. I thought and expected that this would happen, but did not want to take anything like this for granted during our Emanon hiatus. But the loss of this valuable time, so close to the start of hell week compromised our ability to get all of our final pledge tasks done. So, as noted above, we had many projects still far from complete. Somehow we managed, functioning in confusion, but finishing in style. A key element to this component of the pledge period was a change in pledge staff. At that time, as the final week of pledging approached, it was standard practice in Omega to change staff, to pick up the pace in the final week, which was not called "Hell Week" for nothing. It was hell, indeed.

When we were informed that we were back on the line, we were also directed to be at the frat house to meet with our new dean, the Dean of Probates. He was supposed to be a "Nasty Que," someone that we should be afraid of – very afraid. He was to be a no nonsense big brother who would test us thoroughly, to see if we had mastered what we had been taught over the preceding five weeks. And he was to take no prisoners, able to recommend to the chapter brothers whether each of us, evaluated as individuals, were ready, capable, and most importantly worthy, of becoming Omega men. Who was this Goliath? And was he as bad as promised? We had no idea, and speculated among ourselves just who it might be?

No, it would not be Bro. Robert Beale, the Alpha Chapter basileus. Maybe it would be a brother imported from another chapter. No, that cannot happen, because Howard University probably would not allow that to happen, due to liability questions. We speculated among ourselves, but did not get it right. Hold up in the kitchen, in total

## INDUCTION INTO OMEGA PSI PHI FRATERNITY, APRIL 4, 1964

darkness, there was singing and loud noises coming from the rest of the basement of the frat house. And the 21 of us, now officially "the 21 Titans" held each other in prayer, and in nervous anticipation.

We had no idea exactly what was to come, but we knew that whatever it was, it was also imminent. The door flew open and into the dark room burst Bro. Terry Reynolds, a transfer brother from Eta Sigma Chapter, Lincoln University, Missouri, and James Baker, another transfer student from Pi Chapter, Morgan State University, Baltimore, Maryland. They were our Dean of Probates and Vice Dean of Probates, respectively. Two transfer brothers, both of whom had enrolled at Howard only the semester before. None of us really knew either of them, so for us this was a very new venture, or should I say "adventure." But they proved not to be that bad, actually each a great inspiration.

My line brother, Robert Siegel, a first generation American of Russian Jewish parents, had rented a house, along with several of his fellow former Drew Hall residents, newly minted friends, who had pledged Omega the year before on the "Potent and Prolific 20," Alpha chapter's 1963 pledge line. Omega abandoned its "Negro only" racial policy in the late 1940s, in an attempt to send a message to the larger white community that it was time to put aside racial labels and become one American society.

Thus having a white Russian Jew on the pledge line in 1964, did not seem to pose any problem within Omega. And it was not a problem at all with his fellow LBs. We all had to endure the same "s- -t," as it was called, and he was not subjected to any harsher treatment than we, although references were occasionally made to "the white boy." Visiting brothers who came from other chapters, particularly from outside the local area, were especially curious and queried about, how did this "white boy" become attracted to the frat.

In later years, when Robert and I, joined by our wives, Colleen and Carmen, got together for lunch, I asked him the same question, i.e., "What attracted you to Omega." In his lengthy reply, he said, "My parents were Russian immigrant Jews. I am a first generation American, born and raised on Staten Island, New York. When I was looking for a college, to be the first in my immediate family to go to college, I saw something about Howard University located in

## 50+ OMEGA INSPIRED YEARS

Washington, D.C. Somehow it escaped our attention that Howard was a predominantly black school, and I never knew it before the day that I pulled up to Howard in a taxicab. I was quite surprised and called my mom, and said, 'Mom, I don't know how this is going to work. I've never been in a situation like this before.' She said, 'Robert, we are not like these white Americans, who have their prejudices against the colored people, right here in their own country. Give it a try, and if it does not work, you can always come back home or transfer to someplace else. I said, "OK, I'll try."

> *I was assigned to live in Drew Hall, the freshman dormitory, and met a few guys there who were friendly enough, and the next day several of us were in the registration line together. They quickly became my Howard friends, made me feel comfortable, both in Drew and at Howard. I felt at ease with them and in my new surroundings. As the semester progressed, several of them, particularly Calvin Trent, Teddy Powell, Teddy Stewart, and Milton Hatcher were talking about pledging a fraternity, Omega Psi Phi, by name. I had never heard of Omega before, although I had seen the guys dressed in purple and gold on the campus. They pledged and made the fraternity in 1963, on the Potent and Prolific 20, and urged me to pursue Omega in the following year as well. Attracted by their enthusiasm, and learning just a little about the prominence of Omega men, I stepped forward and followed through into the Lampados club and then into Omega. It was a good decision, which I have never regretted.*[32]

Bro. Siegal also related that the next year, he and some of the newly minted neophytes decided to live off campus and rented a large row house, located in the 1900 block of Kenyon Street, N.W., just a couple of blocks from the National Zoo. The lease was in his name, but he allowed several brothers to take up residence as his sub-tenants. Being college students, engrossed in their academic requirements and schedules, and not focused on cooking and housekeeping all that much, the house quickly became a pigsty,

---

[32] *Statement of Bro. Robert Siegel to me during our luncheon conversation, c 2009.*

## INDUCTION INTO OMEGA PSI PHI FRATERNITY, APRIL 4, 1964

which we jokingly referred to as the "Roach Ranch." Of course it had much more than its share of cockroaches, mice too, which were naturally attracted by the accumulated empty food containers that were left everywhere, except in the trash cans. Where there were trash cans, they never seemed to be emptied, left overflowing with accumulated trash spilling over onto the floor.

Having spent a year at Lincoln University from 1962-63, I learned a new term of art, i.e., "riding the zebras," which meant unchanged bed sheets, often to the point that the nasty sheets had been removed, were unlaundered, and the bedroom occupant slept on the bare mattress, which in those days, was most often covered by thinly striped in black and while material. Hence the term, reminiscent of the animal of the same name. "Riding the zebras" became *de rigueur* of the day. In retrospect, it was a pretty unsanitary situation, and looked unsightly too, since most of the beds remained unmade, visibly baring the circumstance of unclean bedroom laundry and bedrooms. Beyond being unclean, the Roach Ranch attracted a reputation for being a bawdy house too.

Many of the brothers had no place to bring their lady friends for some hours of private intimacy, and the Ranch seemed to be an ideal location. When I mentioned these many recollections to my wife, Carmen, she cringed at the very thought of being taken to such a place for a possible assignation, noting that she would have never gone there, and if she had, she would not have allowed herself to succumb in such an unsightly and unsanitary location, which was also being used by so many people.

I later learned that the neighbors were hardly pleased about the unseemly character and adverse reputation of this alternative "Omega house" location. While I never heard of any formal complaints being lodged with the Metropolitan Police Department, related to either noise or questionable activities, including comings and goings at odd hours, such may well have been the case. But to the brothers' credit, there was never any violence or drug-related activities ongoing, just a bunch of noisy, horny, and neglectful college students. So in retrospect, the activities of this Omega institution, "the Roach Ranch," contributed greatly to who we became as responsible adults, Omega men of accomplishment, who had to go through this portal as a component of learning how to be citizens of the world, work together in a cooperative manner, and be fully exposed to conditions and circumstances that were not always the most favorable or necessarily to our personal liking.

As far as drugs were concerned, in the spring of 1964, the drug culture as we know it today, was in its nascency. Many locations around the country, particularly at the historically black colleges and universities, had not yet been invaded by the avalanche of illegal drugs that would soon invade the country as we withdrew from Viet Nam and other Southeast Asia locales. Many of the returning veterans brought back to the American homeland several of the bad habits they had picked up overseas, including a taste for marijuana, which often led to a pursuit of a more diverse and stronger drug menu.

It would not be long, however, before the prevalence of marijuana, and to a much lesser extent, heroin and cocaine would present themselves in HBCU venues, including at Howard University. However, I do not believe that this culture, beyond smoking some occasional pot, managed to take hold within our academic community, and was especially not a problem within Alpha and Kappa Psi chapters, both of which were my affiliated chapters during my Howard University academic tenures, September 1961, to June 1969, except for one academic year at Lincoln University, Pa., September 1962, until June 1963.

Looking back now, I can still say that the Roach Ranch was a vital part of our Howard and Omega culture at the time. As noted above, it helped to build our character as individuals, beyond just being a great party house. Working at the Roach Ranch during our Omega Hell Week, March 29-April 3, 1964, we ceased to be members of the Lampados Club or Lamps, and became "Dogs."

In retrospect, our becoming "dogs" has become a misnomer and even poses a problem regarding Omega's seriousness of purpose. In most all of the Divine Nine pledge groups, the pledge club members take on a new status name during the final week that denotes that we are lowly individuals, yet preparing to rise, preparing to become a brother or a sister in the organization to which we are aspiring. Omega elected to call those Men Seeking Omega, "dogs" during the final week of pledging. That word is generally identified with being

## INDUCTION INTO OMEGA PSI PHI FRATERNITY, APRIL 4, 1964

something of a lower order, and although one might argue that the dog is man's best friend, to call someone a dog is truly not a term of endearment, but rather an insult. Thus, when Omega referred to its pledgees as "dogs," there was no endearment intended.

What bothers me the most now, 50 years after I was a dog for one week, the term has crept into Omega's common parlance, as if it were a term of endearment. It is quite common for one brother to call another, "My dog," or to say, "What's up dogs?" The canine reference, frequently noted as a bull dog, has even appeared on Omega paraphernalia, much to the chagrin of the Supreme Council. The fraternity has tried valiantly to get the brotherhood to stop using these words and terms, citing the adverse effect that it connotes. Many a time I have been told by a would be Omega man, "I still like Omega, and especially Omega's spirit, but I am not a dog and will not allow anyone to call me such. So no, I will not seek Omega."

Where does that leave us? Omega has lost far too many men who were initially attracted to us, but got turned off by some aspect of our behavior. Calling each other "dogs" is certainly not the least of what has driven some of the best away. The concept of being a dog, permanently, is completely different from what we were exposed to. Called a "dog" on Sunday night, as hell week began, we ascended to the Omega brotherhood on the following Saturday afternoon, less than a week later. The dog was then retired to the doghouse and was not seen or heard from until 51 weeks later. I think that was much better, as it gave us a true sense of perspective and a sense that we were striving for something of value and significance – to be an Omega Man.

During all of our probate week, we furiously worked to complete everything – cutting wood, painting, making capes and head bands, and off to the nearby Rock Creek Park woods for final runs through on our marching routines. By sun up each morning, we were dead tired, some of my LBs even mastering the art of sleeping while standing up. Samuel Spear and Eldridge "Rick" Pearsall come to mind in that department. But we soldiered on, and eventually the adrenaline of excitement took over and we were all revived each morning by the time that we should have been heading out to classes. But class time during Hell Week became a bit of a luxury during this frantic, fretful week, and a real challenge to Omega's Cardinal Principle of Scholarship.

# XII – An Omega Man At Last

But the "smell of Omega" was increasing by the day, as everyone knew that the university directed that all pledge lines must cross by Saturday, April 4th. This was the final week of pledging.

*All Hail Omega* **(aka, *Omega Men Draw Nigh*)**

*Omega men draw nigh
And lift a song of praise
Omega Psi Phi
Be with us all our days.
All hail, Omega hail!
Thy loyal sons are we,
O, may we never fail
In trust and loyalty.
All, Omega, hail!
We pledge our lives to thee
Long Live Omega, Psi Phi
Long live fraternity.*

*Omega men draw nigh
In fellowship and cheer,
Long live Omega Psi Phi,
Fraternity most dear.
And when we revere that name,
And strive with manly art,
To keep it free from shame.
All hail, Omega hail!
We pledge our lives to thee.
God bless Omega Psi and Phi,
Long live fraternity.*[33]

---

[33] *The fraternity's first official hymn, written in 1917, was All Hail Omega, aka, Omega Men Draw Nigh, written by Bro. Otto Bohannon (Alpha, 1913), during the administration of Bro. Clarence F. Holmes, Omega's Sixth Grand Basileus (1917-1918).*

## 50+ OMEGA INSPIRED YEARS

Friday, April 3, 1964, was a typical early April spring day. Classes were never suspended because the Greek-letter organizations were having their open pro demonstrations. But none of my line brothers went to class that day. There was too much to do – final touches, and we were not in a frame of mind to go to class. Again, where does that place Scholarship? There was a consequence, naturally, and when the semester ended, the adverse toll that pledging took upon our academic pursuits was greater than any of us wished to recognize or acknowledge. But there was still time for scholarship and academic catch-up, as manifested by the number of my LBs who subsequently were accepted into graduate and professional schools, and who later prospered in their respective chosen professions.

Thus, taken as a whole, when the physical demands and time challenges that were imposed upon us during the six week pledge period are viewed in total, the short cycle was just a bump downwards in our academic journey. And we still had another two months, in the then academic year, which ended in early June, to pull up our grades. And universally, we did just that. Eventually, from the line we had a future Howard University president (H. Patrick Swygert), a Phi Beta Kappa (Derek C. Brown), and several medical doctors, lawyers, and engineers. While still enrolled as undergraduates, several of us were respectively selected for membership in student division honor societies which recognized students who were majoring in certain disciplines, who had likewise distinguished themselves in their anticipated fields prior to graduating. I was one such student, awarded a certificate of merit from Phi Alpha Theta National History Honor Society during the 1965-66 academic year, based upon the recommendation of history department faculty. I was also selected for membership in Who's Who Among College and Universities for the same period.

Leaving the Roach Ranch at about 9:30 a.m., on that Friday morning, everyone was wiped out. We had been up all night tending to the final touches. Carrying all the materials that we needed for the day, we reassembled in Cook Hall at 12:00 p.m., to get dressed and go over final preparations. Since the pledge groups presented themselves to open probation demonstration in alphabetical order, Omega had the privilege of being the last Greek letter organization to appear on

## AN OMEGA MAN AT LAST

the long walk, located on the upper campus. We were set to depart from Cook at about 12:45 p.m.

The "Long Walk" is an institution location unto itself. It is the place where most all of Howard's important out of doors activities occurred, and still do. Commencements, special large convocations, political and civil rights rallies, and homecoming concerts and assemblies now take place "on the yard," as the current genre of students calls our "Long Walk." I have seen photos of very famous people who were assembled or received honorary degrees during out of doors convocations that were assembled at this location.

Beyond Howard's distinguished presidents, the Long Walk has been the hosting locale for many world leaders, including: Nelson Mandela, President of South Africa (1994); President Lyndon Johnson (1965); President Harry S. Truman (1952); Senator Hillary Rodham Clinton (1998); United Nationals Secretary General, Kofi Annan (1999); U.S. United Nations Ambassador, Susan Rice (2012); and Oprah Winfrey, television host and philanthropist.

And in the center of all this history is located the Omega sundial, a gift to Howard University from the "Lampodos Club of 1929."[34] Conceived by Bro. Leroy Clay, then a member of the 1929 pledge club, the young men on that line followed through with Clay's suggestion, and with the assistance of Bro. Ralph Vaughn, a staff architect at Howard, paid for both the architectural design and the commissioned granite product that is today an integral part of the University's history.

But my comments to my reading audience are retrospective, because none of use, mostly 19 and 20 years old at the time, fully appreciated the historical significance of the location where we were about to undertake our first and only public presentation to the

---

[34] *Take note that the spelling of the pledge club was "Lam o dos," which is a slight change from the later spelling of "Lamp a dos." At this time I do not know why the spelling is different. I would not attribute it to a simple spelling error, as the "o" spelling was used in both the invitation to the unveiling, as well as the printed program for the unveiling event and subsequent news articles about the gift from the pledge club to Howard University.*

Howard University community. But we knew this! We had better get it right, or else. None of us wanted to face the "or else," so it was incumbent upon the 21 of us to get it right the first time. There would not be a second opportunity to make a favorable first impression.

And we did not disappoint. As I had mentioned earlier in this publication, my initial place on the line was #3, placed according to height. I am five feet, seven inches tall, which placed me towards the front of the line. It was expected that the brothers at either end of the line would have the marching steps down to perfection, since we set the marching tone in both directions. Sol Smith and I were switched from #2 to #3, and #3 to #2 for a good reason. He was from Panama, and the culture of "marching" (now called "stepping") was totally alien to him, and just could not get it.

> *One of the things I remember about our pledge period is when the football players who were Ques from Morgan State University came to the ranch and want to kick our butts. We escaped but had to go back for one of us who was trapped. We got the person and ran for dear life. The best thing about being a member of Omega Psi Phi for me has been the feeling of brotherhood and friendship that developed over the years and continued after graduating. So much so that even if many years pass since I have seen a brother, when we meet it almost feels like I just saw him yesterday. A great feeling!* – William Singleton, the 21 Titans, Alpha Chapter, April 4, 1964

A pledgee's line number, i.e., place on line, is something of great significance, a fact that one is supposed to remember and cherish throughout his entire life and membership in Omega. As I previously noted, my place as #3 was truncated, as I was switched unceremoniously to #2. I think that with a little more time and practice, Sol Smith, the original #2, would have done fine, but the big brothers had neither to spare, and gave up trying to get him into line. And with a quick gesture of the hand and a tart comment, i.e., "Quander, you and Smith switch places!," he and I were permanently and forever locked into our fraternal identifications. In Omega parlance, I became a "Deuce" and he became a "Tray" on that cold

## AN OMEGA MAN AT LAST

night down in Rock Creek Park during one of our many midnight marching practices.

But today, April 3rd, after weeks of preparation, and my psychological longing and waiting for this day, the time has finally arrived. If not before, then at this very moment I now appreciated the favor that the brothers of Kappa Psi chapter had done for me, when they declined to accept me into the pledge club that they assembled in June-July 1963. Had I pledged into Omega then, I would not have ever had the great experience of pledging Omega via a fully programed undergraduate chapter, a valuable component that is indigenous to joining the fraternity as an undergraduate. As well, had Kappa Psi accepted me into the pledge club in June 1962, I would likewise have been denied the esteemed and unique honor of being inducted into Omega via the Mother Pearl, a distinct and lifelong honor.

Kappa Psi, one of the fraternity's most historic chapters, being then intermediate and populated by brothers from other campuses, did not have a parallel public open pro demonstration, which was deemed to be a centerpiece of pledging at the undergraduate level, with the girls screaming and squealing, and the guys, many of whom aspired to Omega, likewise gathered tightly around us, wanting to witness everything that we said and did during these highly anticipated and emotional moments. I would not trade it for anything.

Dressed in white shirts, black slacks and black shoes and socks, we were adorned with luminescent purple and gold capes. They were purple on the outside and identically matched gold on the inside. It was not a lining, but actually reversible, except that we only wore the purple side out. In the middle of the purple side, there was one gold Greek letter of "Omega," about six inches tall and about four inches wide. I cannot recall who made the capes, but I do think that we did it ourselves. We wore gold satin headbands, tied pirate style with the material training down our necks a couple in inches. In the middle of the headbands, which was also in the middle of our foreheads, a purple felt Greek Omega, about one inch tall, was glued on. I think that we also wore gold sashes around our waists, but time has dimmed my certainty on this point. I do know, however, that more than one line did wear those sashes, and I believe that we were among those who did.

We walked in lock step from Cook Hall to the steps of the Fines Arts Building, and from that location we began our lock step march down the Long Walk. Screams! Sighs! And statements – "Man, do they looked whipped, tired! I know that they're glad that this is almost over." We heard them all. But our biggest concern for keeping the crowd back a few feet was our performance routine that called for swinging our hardwood two-tiers shields in the air as a part of our marching. We did not want to hit anyone in the head with our shields, and that could easily happen. And if it can happened, it did happen. I do not remember to whom the accident was visited upon, but it was not one of the screaming audience members. A fellow LB was struck in the mouth by one of his own fellow probates, causing a small cut, drawing blood nonetheless.

But the show must go one, and we continued to march to the dial, arriving at that historic location, still without a clue as to the historical significance of who placed the dial there in 1929 and the underlying history that was associated with that effort.[35] As tradition dictated, the probates then put on what I call a "challenge program," delivering

---

[35] *During a brother only party for Bro. Albert C. "Butch" Hopkins, (Potent and Prolific 20, 1963, now Omega Chapter), Bro. James Baker, my line's assistant commandant during hell week, volunteered to me that he knew JoAnn Clay, whose dad, Bro. Leroy Clay, was the brainchild behind the installation of the Omega dial in 1929, when he was still a member of the Lampados Club. Baker added that she had the photographs and a file related to the creation of the dial. Knowing that the Moorland Spingarn Center was hungry for Omega-related archives, I jumped at the opportunity, contacted Ms. Clay, and traveled to Baltimore, where I secured more than 150 photos of Bro. Leroy Clay's Howard University days (1928-1931), including many Omega-related pictures taken incidental to the dial and other activities. Further, I secured an invitation to the February 1929 dedication of the dial, newspaper articles, and the dial dedication speech of Bro. Clay. This information is a valuable piece of Omega history, and now rests in Howard's archives for the education and enjoyment of future generations.*

## AN OMEGA MAN AT LAST

friendly insults to the big brothers, some of which were quite stinging and not so friendly after all. We saluted Betty Cave, our 1964 Lampados Queen, a native of Philadelphia, giving comment to her beauty and graciousness. It was a fairly short undertaking, since classes were still in session, and everyone, Lamps included, was expected to return to class as quickly as possible.

What was said about whom during the program, I can no longer recall after 50 years, but sex was the favorite topic. We took great liberties with the subject, often referring to a big brother's alleged deficiency in that department. Whether it referred to the size of his manhood, the lack of much Manhood (considered in the context as a Cardinal Principle), his inability to attract and keep a girlfriend, his poor skills with women or friends, his goofy look, his lack of style, or jokingly, referring even to his color, we said it all. It was one guffaw after the other. It was one gasping for breath after another. But it was all in fun – BIG FUN. There was not a serious word spoken, and everyone present knew it. So it was all in jest. Still, when my turn would come in later years, I would find myself "enjoying" the wrath of the probates, as they attempted to settle a score and level the playing field that had been anything but, for the prior six weeks.

Now, 50 years later, I have no clue as to the details of what we said at the dial on that bright sunny day, and there are no documents available to refresh my recollection. Sufficient enough is to say that we were instructed by Terry Reynolds, Dean of Probates, and James Baker, Vice Dean, and their support staff, to rag on the big brothers. This was our turn to "get even," for the prior six weeks, and to poke public fun at them – in front of the entire campus.

The program concluded, we marched back to Cook Hall, repeating the marching steps, and drawing just as enthusiastic crowd as before. By 2:15 p.m., it was all over, but not quite. Directed to report to the fraternity house later that evening, perhaps at 7:00 p.m., we were instructed to "come hungry," and to "dress warmly." Neither one of those directives could possibly be good. And I thought that the pledge program that we had endured for the past six weeks was over – well almost.

## 50+ OMEGA INSPIRED YEARS

*Reflecting back on my Alpha Chapter, Omega Psi Phi Fraternity, Inc., Line, the 21 Titans, Spring 1964, my line number was #19. Pledging Omega was a milestone in my life. I truly believe that "Friendship Is Essential To The Soul." Recalling incidents while on line: Remember get lost night? We were in the middle of nowhere, a mostly white community; we sent our white line brother Bob Segal to knock on doors to call for help and we were able to get help to get back to the yard.*

*During my career as a jazz trumpet player, I became a member of the Count Basis Band, found out that the Count was a brother. Also, I met and shook hands with Dr. Cosby, who is a brother. Omega Psi Phi is my family 'til the day I die. Que Psi. PEACE!* –Larry E. Davis, 19-A-64, the 21 Titans, Alpha Chapter

Reporting as instructed and dressed as directed, I said to myself before showing up, "What the heck? It can't be much more now, anyway." But it was. "Come hungry!" took on a new meaning that night. Bro. Frank B. Paterson, then a newly minted prophyte brother, was in his second year of preparing the "evening meal" for the probates, and for undertaking that task he would eventually become famously known as "Chef Boyar-P." It was not a meal fit for a king, and was never advertised as such. Rather, the brothers made it clear, "This was a meal fit for a dog!" Dog food! It was not clear what it was, but one thing was certain. They had plenty of it and served it to us in generous portions. It has been a long time, but I think that it actually was dog food, doctored up by Bro. Frankie P., who used his culinary skills to disguise this mystery meal.

Enduring the indignity, we all survived, asking among ourselves, what was that that we just ate? There was little consensus among us, except that we agreed that the "evening meal" was far, far from delectable. Thankfully, no one got sick from the menu, so whatever it was, it was not all that bad.

The next item on the agenda was to make us get lost. The big brothers loaded us up into vehicles, blindfolded us, and took us away. Where were we headed; what was the plan; how are we going to get back to wherever we were being taken? Before we left, we were

## AN OMEGA MAN AT LAST

carefully searched, allegedly to make certain that we had no money to hire a taxicab to bring us back to "civilization." And none of us had any money – or so it seemed. Of course, in April 1964, there were no cell phones, so the only respite would be to knock on someone's door – in the middle of the night – and ask to use their telephone to call for a rescue. Obviously this situation was a test – a test of our personal discretion, in addition to the exercising of the Cardinal Principles.

MANHOOD in the sense of what we, 20 young African American males and one Caucasian, dropped off late at night, about 11:00 p.m., in the middle of nowhere, going to do to get back to D.C.? SCHOLARSHIP in the context of giving our situation some thought, to figure out how to find our way, without scaring others who might be fearful of us, just to see 20 blacks outside of their door, and maybe even take some offensive action against us. This was still largely segregated times, after all.

PERSEVERENCE to measure our determination to overcome this temporary setback, and find a way to get home, despite the obstacles of not knowing where we were, and who and how to contact someone to come and get us. And UPLIFT, by not giving up in the face of this adversity, accepting it as only temporary, and focused on how we were going to help ourselves, both individually and collectively.

But it was not as bad as it might have been. The temperature was probably in the high 30s or low 40s, typical for an early April night. The sky was clear, and given that we were located in a very dark area, we could see countless stars and the plants. I recall one of my LBs commenting what a nice night it was, to which the universal reply was, "Hell, who gives a f--- about how nice it is out here. It's cold, it's dark, and we are lost with no money. Let's get the hell out of here." When they dropped us off, most of us had no idea where we were. So even if you had a rescue plan, how can we implement it if we did not know where we were, and had no money to place a telephone call, to get someone to come and get us?

Both David, III, and I knew approximately where we were, once the blindfolds came off. Both being Washingtonians, we realized that we were somewhere south of the city, most probably near Andrews Air Force base, in the Temple Hills-Camp Springs area of Prince George's County. We could see the top of the Washington Monument from a slightly elevated area near to where we were dumped out. As well, one of my LBs, and it might have been Eldridge "Rick" Pearsall, having gotten wind of what was about the play out, had solicited a few of his dorm buddies, and put them on alert to come and rescue us when called to do so.

In response to the "no money allowed" directive, he hid some coins in his shoe, which were not discovered during the body and clothing search before we left the frat house. Perhaps we should nominate him for sainthood. If he had gotten caught that evening, there is no telling what might have happened to him. I think, though, that they would have berated him, but still let him proceed. After all, this entire scenario was a test of our will against the big brothers, and our ingenuity and ability to adjust under adverse circumstances. Strength of character and determination were both assets that Omega was seeking and still cherishes.

Now, all we needed to do is find a defined landmark for reference and to aid in giving directions, and a telephone booth, in lieu of knocking on someone's door. Our first decision was in which direction to walk. We did not want to complicate the matter by going in the wrong direction. But with the Washington Monument slightly visible to the north, northwest, we figured that this was the direction in which to head back to Washington, D.C. Despite being "in the middle of nowhere," after we walked a mile or more through a residential neighborhood, and having decided not to knock on anyone's door at 12:00 midnight, we came to a more commercial area, that was reasonably well lighted, and which also had a pay telephone. We also saw someone who was able to pinpoint our location. Dropping the precious coins into the phone, our rescue team was contacted, and after verifying where we were, and with God's guiding hand, they showed up with four or five vehicles, and we were rescued.

Climbing into the warm vehicles, we felt safe, confident that we had passed whatever test was intended by the action of the big brothers. It was about 12: 00 a.m. at the time. I was still living at home, and did not learn until the afternoon of April 4th, of the big brouhaha immediately associated with the "dogs" relatively early return to their dormitories. They had caught the big brothers by surprise, many of whom had been out partying, feeling quite full of themselves about how they had "disposed" of us earlier that evening. They were shocked to discover, when they returned to their dorm rooms, that the probates got back to the dorms before the big brothers did and were comfortably resting in their beds, getting their first good night's sleep in a long time.

They woke up several of the probates, demanding to know, "How did this happen? What did you do to make yourselves so special?" Historically, some of the prior lines stayed lost for hours, well into the daylight of the following day. Some of those line members have even gotten separated from the others. But somehow all of you got back in one piece, in one group, and so quickly after having been discarded." It was a secret, and those LBs who lived in the dorm had agreed not to tell how they got back so fast. They made up all sorts of stories. "We hitchhiked," said some, as if it was credible that 21 hitchhikers would be picked up on a dark road after midnight. Of course we were still learning at that moment that the ability to keep a secret was a major component of Discretion, which is highly valued in Omega.

Much of what occurred next is Omega ritually-protected, and does not appear in this memoir. The Omega brothers and other Divine Nine members who are reading this document, know of what I speak. For non-Greek-letter readers, you can respect the fact that membership in Omega mandates that certain components are to be known and enjoyed by only those who have taken Omega's sacred oath of membership, and that adhering to those components, likewise dictates that we have discretion and not share them with anyone who is not a member of the sacred brotherhood.

However, by now, at about 12:00 p.m. on April 4, 1964, assembled on an upper floor of the Omega house, the 21 Titans had endured. We had shown that we were a single unit, ready for induction into the sacred realm that is the Omega Psi Phi Fraternity. At approximately

## 50+ OMEGA INSPIRED YEARS

2:00 p.m. that afternoon, the 21 Titans were re-assembled on the first floor of the fraternity house. Shortly before that hour, the Omega brotherhood, many from other chapters, were assembling for the induction ceremony. We could not see them, But it was a noisy bunch.

Brothers were coming in who had not seen each other for a while. Besides Alpha Chapter, Omega's Mother Pearl, there were brothers from Kappa Psi (the intermediate chapter), Omicron Gamma (D.C. Teachers College), and Alpha Omega (city-wide graduate chapter). As well, there were many other chapters represented by brothers that I had never seen before, and even today do not know who there were. But the most important milestone for me was that both my dad, James W. Quander, and my uncle/godfather, Joseph P. Quander, Sr., were in the house.

Directed to my knees, with our left hand on the Bible and our right hands raised, the 21 blindfolded Titans took the sacred oath of membership for induction into the Omega Psi Phi Fraternity, Inc. No truer or happier words were ever uttered, than "Arise my brothers!" And it was all over. No! It was not over, but just beginning. For when I took that oath, and pledged myself to faithfully execute the fraternal and community-at-large expectations as recited in Omega's sacred oath of membership, I also undertook to create and maintain a life-long allegiance to Omega's Four Cardinal Principles – Manhood, Scholarship, Perseverance, and Uplift, and to do whatever was required to uphold both these principles and Omega.

Years later, when Founder Oscar J. Cooper was asked if there was anything about the initial founding of Omega that he would have changed, now in retrospect, he replied that there should have been a fifth Cardinal Principle, to wit, "Service." But he concluded that Service is inherent in the other four Cardinal Principles, and that Omega men must be and remain committed to rendering Service to others. But on that day, April 4, 1964, I was just beginning my journey with Omega, and would have to develop an appreciation for all that Omega represented, including service to others. But, Let the Journey Begin!

# AN OMEGA MAN AT LAST

December 17, 1941

Mr. George A. Isabelle
138 Cadillac Square
Detroit, Michigan

Dear Bro. Isabelle:

You asked me to outline in a paragraph what I consider the purpose of our Fraternity. From my viewpoint, that is a very difficult thing to do; for my observation has been that the object of the Fraternity shifts with every decade, and that is as it should be in any wide awake, growing and progressive organization.

In the beginning, the Fraternity was built around four cardinal principles, Manhood, Scholarship, Perseverance and Uplift. To those we stuck very closely throughout the years, but as time went on, we found ourselves reaching out to broaden our scope of activities and to include in our program those who were not affiliated with the Fraternity. In so doing, of course, we were only developing the ramifications of the four cardinal principles, the ultimate manifestations of which are limitless.

And so we have come on down the years developing first one idea and then another, until today we stand on the threshold of developing into another phase of activity; for with the world changing as it is, with the possibility of a new order of things within a few years, it becomes necessary for Omega to prepare to meet the changed conditions in order to take her rightful place in the sun of the scheme of things.

I feel that we should be entirely unselfish in our future conduct and should develop some phase of activity from an economic standpoint that will meet the needs of many of our people. Surely, with the indomitable personnel which comprises our organization, we have the machinery to set in motion about anything that we might wish to effect. This is our big chance I feel and a grand opportunity for Omega to make her influence felt in a very material way, for the benefit of those whom we represent.

*In other words, to sum up what I mean; we should add one more cardinal principle, if not actually, we should make it a part of our future activities, "Service"; for it is the one thing that dominates all business and economic life of today. It is the key note of all living vital agencies which are set up in the interest of mankind, and it is the one thing that makes life in whatever sense we wish to consider, worth living.*

*Let it be said of Omega of the future that "We live to serve our fellow man." Trusting you can catch the essential thread of this rambling bit of thought, I am fraternally yours,*

*Oscar J. Cooper, M.D.*[36]

Managing to get to the going-over party, held at the Hotel Continental on North Capitol Street, across from Union Station and just blocks from the U.S. Capitol building, and lasting through the night, was a pure act of adrenalin. We were all bone tired, yet elated for now at last being proud Omega Men. That journey had been concentrated into six very short weeks, during which time we got a lot done – trying to keep up with the academics, remembering why we were at Howard University in the first place; visiting the big brothers and getting to know them more personally and having them sign our lamp notebooks; learning the marching steps and attending regular practices down in Rock Creek Park; stealing away to party with the Pyramids of Delta and the Ivys of AKA; planning and executing the Lampados Queen coronation, which required interviewing several young ladies and deciding who would be our queen; attending the Kappa Alpha Psi Scroller and Alpha Phi Alpha Sphinxmen pledge clubs' coronations; and making midnight

---

[36] *Letter of Founder Oscar J. Cooper to Bro. George A. Isabelle, Omega's 10th KRS, dated December 17, 1941, just days after the U.S. entered World War II, assessing the anticipated change in society that was to be forthcoming, as the different political powers of the world engaged in fierce military battles. Dr. Cooper's foresight correctly anticipated that "Service" and rendering same, would be the new watchword for the post-war era.*

## AN OMEGA MAN AT LAST

requisitions and other plans for our probate demonstration at the end of the pledge cycle.

It was really quite an undertaking, a lot to accomplish within a very short time. So it is fully understandable that we would just be worn out by the time that it was all over. Many of my LBs proclaimed that they were planning to sleep for a week after they were inducted. As for me, my agenda was completely different. As mentioned earlier, I had attended the Lincoln University, in Pennsylvania, for academic year 1962-63, and was still tied to Lincoln with many friendships that as of yesterday, became my new Omega brothers.

**50+ OMEGA INSPIRED YEARS**

# XIII – Beta Chapter, A 50th Anniversary Celebration

The weekend of my induction into Omega was the same weekend that Beta Chapter, second in Omega's birth, was observing its 50th anniversary. Having been appointed by the Alpha Chapter brothers to the newly created fraternity expansion committee, on February 2, 1914, brothers Oscar James Cooper, Omega Founder, and second grand basileus (1912-1913), John M. McMorries, Alpha Chapter 1913, and later the fifth Grand Basileus (1916-17), and William Griffith Brannon, Alpha Chapter 1912, traveled to Lincoln, where four days later, on February 6, 1914, they initiated the first 20 men from Lincoln, who became the charter members of Beta Chapter, the second chapter established within Omega.

The initiation conducted on the above-noted date and early Beta chapter activities were all conducted off campus, at the home of Charlotte T. (better known as "Sister Lottie B.") Wilson, reputedly the only woman who was ever inducted into the Omega Psi Phi Fraternity, Inc. The off-campus initiation and meetings were dictated by the university's refusal to allow the fraternity on campus, as hard fought efforts to gain access and recognition by the Lincoln administration was still a goal for the near future.

Several weeks before, I had noticed that my probable induction weekend would conflict with the Beta Chapter's grand Golden Anniversary celebration. Hoping to be a newly minted Omega man, I obtained the planned schedule of events, which reflected that Bro. Langston Hughes was the keynote speaker on Sunday, April 5, 1964, and determined that it was still possible for me to be present and participate on at least the last day, April 5th. But in order to do that, I would have to plan my schedule carefully, and leave D.C. on a Trailways bus that departed at 3:00 a.m. Three o'clock in the morning? That was a challenge, but maybe not.

## 50+ OMEGA INSPIRED YEARS
### *Cross,* A poem by Langston Hughes

*My old man's a white old man*
*And my old mother's black.*
*If ever I cursed my white old man*
*I take my curses back.*
*If ever I cursed my black old mother*
*And wished she were in hell,*
*I'm sorry for that evil wish*
*And now I wish her well*
*My old man died in a fine big house.*
*My ma died in a shack.*
*I wonder where I'm going to die,*
*Being neither white nor black?*

I figured that the going-over party would end about 2:00 a.m., and that a bus at 3:00 a.m. was possible. So I planned for that. Taking my overnight bag to the going over party, I parked it in a corner and celebrated my newly minted status. I did not have a date for that night, and danced with every woman I wanted to. I cannot recall if the newly inducted Deltas and AKAs stopped by, but probably not, since they were planning their own parties. Still, there were so many other young women there that night, that the absence or presence of these new sorors did not make a difference.

I was never much of a drinker, but that night I did have a couple of stiff ones, and left the party with a buzz, caused by one or two rums too many. Getting a ride to the Trailways bus station, I was in plenty time for my 3:00 a.m. departure. Lincoln is about 100 miles from Washington, D.C., and getting there was relatively easy by automobile. Located at Lincoln University, Pennsylvania, all you had to do was drive straight up Route One, until you arrived at the main gate. That was the old route to Lincoln, but now we had the newly opened Interstate Route 95, which made it quicker to get there, although there were more route changes to make from Route 95 to get to Route One.

The bus ride was a milk route, and stopped at every little way station along the way. The trip took about four hours, but I was able to get some rest, arriving at Lincoln's gate at about 7:00 a.m. Sunday morning. I had my suit rolled up in my overnight bag, and headed to

## BETA CHAPTER, A 50TH ANNIVERSARY CELEBRATION

Cresson Hall, where I had made arrangements to recoup before the 11:00 a.m. services at the Mary Dodd Brown Chapel, Lincoln's main religious center. Breakfast started at about 8:30 a.m., and it was in the refectory that I first presented myself – a newly inducted Omega man.

The Beta Chapter brothers welcomed me with open arms, very happy that I was now a member of the sacred brotherhood. Some of them had paid an earlier visit to D.C. during one of our evening sessions, anxious to "beast" upon my LBs, and me in particular, only to be denied access by Taft H. Broome, our dean of pledgees and his staff. His admonition – non Alpha Chapter brothers were to have restricted access to Alpha Chapter's lamps, and there was to be no physical contact with us. Among other concerns was the issue of potential liability.

Taft, whom we called "Chuck," for reasons that are unrecalled, was a very level-headed brother, someone whom we trusted and placed our confidence in. And he deserved this level of respect, because this was how he projected and carried himself in all things. So when he said, "The Lamps are off limits to any physical contact by visiting brothers," he meant it. Shortly thereafter, he would be elected as basileus of Alpha Chapter, and served his term with distinction. In later years, his academic achievements and professionalism would be recognized by his Howard University peers, who would elect him as president of the faculty senate.

Due to my final pledge-related activities, I missed Beta's Friday night jazz concert, featuring the Michael Lambert Quintet, and likewise all of the Saturday celebratory activities. Saturday was a full day, starting with a song fest at 1:30 p.m. in front of McCrary Hall. Beta Chapter had a reputation as one of Omega's premier singing chapters. Singing brothers was a long tradition at this chapter. They mastered many traditional Omega songs and were well-known for that particular characteristic. Alpha Chapter held its own too. Given that Lincoln had been for so many years an all-male institution, with female students being a recent addition to the campus, singing was one of the pastimes that occupied the brothers. In the absence of a female student population, the brothers diverted much of their youthful energy towards song.

## 50+ OMEGA INSPIRED YEARS

At 3:00 p.m. on Saturday, the chapter sponsored its 50th Anniversary Banquet, which featured Rev. Bro. Oliver Franklin, Sr., of Baltimore, as guest speaker. His son, Oliver, Jr., was a Beta Chapter undergraduate at that time. While I was not present to hear his remarks, I learned that Bro. Franklin, Sr. was both retrospective and prospective. Looking back over the past 50 years of Omega history at Lincoln, he drew upon what he knew of the Beta Chapter's illustrious past. He highlighted many of the events which shaped the character of the chapter to its present constitution. Central to that story of course, was the singular and unique input and role of Omega Sister Lottie B. Wilson, in whose home Beta Chapter was founded.

As the brothers related to me what has been stated on the day before, Rev. Bro. Franklin challenged the Beta brothers to remain on the forefront of achievement, both for Omega and the University's sake. He also reminded them that the responsibility was an individual one as well, as each brother and as Lincoln men, had to be true to himself and remember why he was in college – to get an education, and then use it for the betterment of mankind overall. The day's activities were closed out with a 50th Anniversary semi-formal dance in the campus auditorium, featuring the Donald Mosley Quintet, with the Fabulous Dials, a singing group. As is a traditional comment of longstanding with reference to Omega social events, "A grand time was had by all."

Having missed both the Friday and Saturday anniversary events, the extent of my direct enjoyment was limited to Sunday, April 5th. With breakfast in the refectory, and then 11:00 a.m. chapel service, I was in a great frame of mind, giving God the praise for the experiences that I had sustained during the pledge induction cycle. I had no fear of bodily injury or permanent harm during my pledging period, although there were rumors about dastardly events and even injuries, when the pledging activities had gotten out of hand. So this Sunday morning was a time for me to restate my thanks and appreciation for having completed the pledge period without me or any of my LBs sustaining any mishaps or injuries.

Lincoln University was found in 1854 as Ashmun Institute, and affiliated with the Presbyterian Church. The overlay and presence of the church was still very much felt by me during my 1962-63 academic year. Therefore, returning to the Mary Dodd Brown Memorial Chapel on that Sunday morning was a comfort. While I cannot recall the songs that we sang, I do remember that Bro. Charles Woodard, Jr., basileus of Beta Chapter, was the lead on-campus organizer for the 50th Anniversary Celebration. His message was one of praise and thanksgiving to the Almighty for having brought us, both the men of Omega and our race, this far, considering that we were just a few miles above the Mason-Dixon Line, and racial segregation was still the law of the land in many other parts of our country. We were likewise mindful that the Ku Klux Klan had a footing in Rising Sun, Maryland, just 10 or so miles to our south.

There were many Beta alumni brothers present from all over, many of them appearing to be at least in their seventies. The chapter had reached out to the alumni brothers and welcomed them home for this auspicious occasion. As well, there were many wives, lady friends, faculty members, and others in attendance, some for the Omega celebration and others, simply because it was the Lord's Day. The choir, directed by Professor Orrin Suthern, Director and Minister of Music, sang several meaningful songs, none of which can I recall at this moment. As well, there were several Omega men in the choir, characteristic of the brothers' longstanding tradition of singing at Lincoln.

When the Sunday service ended, somewhere around 1:00 p.m., it was lunch time. Since I was not enrolled at Lincoln any longer, it was expected that I would pay for the lunch. But several brothers offered food to me on their meal tickets, and I found myself with more than I could ever eat. Mrs. "Ma" Renwick, the director of food services was present, as always, and expressed kind words at seeing me back on campus. She congratulated me on my new ascendance to Omega. I imagine that she knew from where the bounty had come, since I had not been in the food line and likewise had not tendered any payment in exchange.

After shooting the breeze for a while, it was time to reassemble in the chapel for the final event of the Golden Anniversary Celebration. Bro. Langston Hughes, Beta Chapter, c 1929, was the keynote speaker for the final, but most significant anniversary program. His anticipated arrival had been touted for a couple of months, and several of the Beta brothers had encouraged me to come up for the event, based upon the assumption that I would be a brother by that time. The final anniversary event was open to the public, as the significance of having someone so famous as Langston Hughes on campus, even if it was for a fraternal event, was something that should be shared with the entire Lincoln community.

Once again, there were wives, sweethearts, and friends present on the campus and now assembled in the chapel. As well, Bro. Hughes' address and Beta's participation in the program that afternoon, was not a ritualistic event, which, by Omega's constitution and by-laws, must be a brothers-only activity. Several Omega dignitaries were present, including Rev. Bro. Jesse Jackson, then the Second Vice Grand Basileus, the highest ranking undergraduate in the fraternity, and Bro. George Meares, the First Vice Grand Basileus, who later that year, would ascend to the role as our 26th Grand Basileus (1964-67). The university glee club sang some verses from Langston Hughes' poetry that had been set to music, featuring several Omega men, including some soloists, whose singing capabilities were renowned.

Hughes' remarks, as captured in the April 15, 1964, edition of the *Lincolnian*, the student newspaper, were very poignant, demonstrating a true understanding of the plight of the Negro, his obstacles, spirit, and adversarial context of the present existence. I refer to the above-noted article from the student newspaper, which reported Hughes' remarks and presentation of that afternoon. Hughes recounted that the civil rights struggle that the nation was still enduring was bringing about a real moral change in society, and how proud he was that the Negro youth were focused and determined to make the nation come to grips and change the history of continuing indignities to its own sable citizens.

He likewise selected lines from several of his poems, commenting upon their relevance in the struggle for equality and the "moral atmosphere" in which we were then existing. As well, Bro. Calvin Morris, a 1963 Lincoln graduate, gave an outstanding rendition of Bro. Hughes' poem, "Freedom Land," accompanied on the piano by Bro. Michael Frank, whose musical abilities served to enhance Calvin's moving and dramatic reading of Bro Hughes' famous work.

## BETA CHAPTER, A 50TH ANNIVERSARY CELEBRATION

Bro. Hughes closed his remarks by fondly recalling both his college and Omega days at Lincoln. He expressed how proud he was to be both an Omega and Lincoln man, charging us, both male and female, to go forward and grab what is rightfully our due as citizens of this great nation. With that said, and in the fervor of the moment, Bro. Basileus Woodard stepped forward to bid all adieu, and requested all Omega brothers to "Hymn Up!," an expression that we use to form the Omega singing queues, whereby the brothers join in a circle. Depending upon the chapter and its location, we hold hands, hold thumbs, form crossed arms and then hold hands, or use others practices as well. I had only been a member of Omega for one day, so although I had seen the brothers form the queue at many locations and at different previous times, I cannot recall how they hooked themselves together at Beta for the fraternal hymn, *Omega Dear*, jointly written by Bro. Charles Drew and Bro. Mercer Cook, and officially adopted as "the Hymn" in 1931.

But one thing that I do recall, and recall it vividly, With more than 125 brothers present, Bro. Basileus Woodard placed Bro. Hughes in the center of the queue to be serenaded, and then turned and came to me and said, Brother Quander, welcome to Omega. We want to serenade you too. Omega's newest brother, along with our esteemed guest of honor, Bro. Hughes." We were directed to kneel, face each other and hold hands, just as the brotherhood was doing as they prepared to sing Omega's most sacred hymn.

And never have I heard *Omega Dear* sung that well. It was great! Truly great! Or maybe it just appeared that way to me. But at any rate, I knew that, just as the tune says, *Omega Dear we are thine own. Thou art our life, our love, our home ...*, I had truly found another home, one to whom I had, just 24 hours prior, pledged my loyalty to them for life.

Arising from my kneeing position, I had tears in my eyes – tears of joy. My thoughts were tracking in many directions at that moment. I thought of my uncle/godfather's journey to Omega, 33 years prior, 1931, through Theta Psi Chapter, West Virginia College (now University). I thought of my dad, James W. Quander, whose journey to Omega was delayed for several years, until July 9, 1958, but that his enthusiasm was no less dimmed by the years of not being exposed to the brotherhood. And I thought about the significance of what it meant to be inducted into the first chapter of Omega, known collectively as "the Mother Pearl."

It would not be long before I more fully realized the significance of being an Alpha Chapter initiate, and later an alum. When I visited other campuses, attended conclaves, district meetings, and community events, when it was mentioned that Alpha Chapter, or an Alpha Chapter brother was in the house, the other brothers often gave deference, sometime speaking in hushed or exalted tones, when referring to the Mother Pearl chapter, and the situs where our Four Beloved Founders walked. And I knew then, that this was something very, very special. To be a Beta brother is likewise of great significance, for it was the *Second of Our Birth*, a phrase that Beta brothers carry just as proudly and high as we Alpha Chapter brothers do when referring to being from the *Mother Pearl*. Beta has the unique distinction of being the chapter that represents the beginning of Omega as a national fraternal organization.

I came to a fuller realization and determination on that day – April 5, 1964 – just one day into Omegadom, that I was going to be a brother who took his sacred oath seriously. And that as I embarked upon this journey, a lifelong journey, that I would do my part to uphold Omega's name, the Four Cardinal Principles, and my own personal principles and values, so that when the final page is written on my life, that I should have nothing to regret or to be held accountable for having neglected. That was a tall order for a man of 20 years of age.

Life has tempered me somewhat, made me less idealistic. I have always taken my oath of allegiance to Omega seriously, and still do. As such, I am deeply troubled when I observe other brothers around me who seem not to place the proper emphasis upon the importance of those sacred word of fealty that they so willingly recited on the jubilant day of their respective inductions into the fraternity.

The events of Beta's Golden Anniversary Celebration having been completed, it was time to get on with the rest of life. Returning to D.C., I had many "catch up" items that had been neglected over the last six weeks, and among them was the finalization of my international student exchange travel plans. Pledging Omega was not a monolith, as Omega demands that her sons be strong, capable, and diverse men, able to face and answer several challenges, of which many may be posed at the same time.

# 50+ OMEGA INSPIRED YEARS

# XIV – Refocusing On The Academic Mission

Lucy E. Moten, M.D., (1851-1933) an alumna of Howard University (class of 1870 and 1887, Med.), was an outstanding educator who, upon an offer from Frederick Douglass, a member of the school's board, became principal of Miner Training School for Teachers. The school, initially known as the Normal School for Colored Girls, and founded in 1851, later became known as Miner Teachers College, and is now a component of the University of the District of Columbia. My dad, Bro. James W. Quander, was a 1940 graduate of that college.

The mission of Miner, named for Myrtilla Miner, a white teacher who was run out of Mississippi in 1851 for teaching colored girls, was the preparation of Negro teachers in the District of Columbia. Dr. Moten was a firm believer in the importance of offering black students fellowships, to enable undergraduate students at Howard in the College of Liberal Arts and Sciences to enrich their education with study abroad during the summer. She likewise hoped that a significant number of these fellows would eventually become teachers, and be able to share their undergraduate travel experiences with their young charges. Upon her death in 1933, Moten bequeathed $51,000.00 to Howard University, to provide scholarships to students in the arts and sciences for travel and study-abroad opportunities.

As a child of the Caribbean, and second generation back to Calcutta, India, I grew up knowing that I had many family members in places that I had never visited, but longed to. When, as a child, my mother would fix some food that I did not want to eat, she always said, "Just think of your poor cousins in India. They have nothing to eat, and would be only too happy to have this food." She told me that one day, after she had said the same thing several times, that I replied, "Well, why don't they catch a boat and just come over here and eat it." Funny! What did I know then, perhaps only three to four years old at the time?

When I discovered Howard's annual summer exchange program, which the university operated under the name "Broader Horizons," I was immediately interested, and determined to make application for a travel fellowship. Both the process and the timing were a great challenge for me, however, because the window of making application was fairly short, and the demands of pledging Omega during the same semester only added to the stress, and maybe even the impossibility of being accepted. But I was determined to try, just the same.

I secured an application, started the completion of same, and also had other work to do to make it complete. The grants were made available to students who were demonstrating sustained academic achievement. That meant providing two transcripts, one each from Howard and Lincoln universities. Next I had to obtain several letters of recommendation, which were expected to address components of my character, values, and stability. They wanted to know what extracurricular activities I was engaged in, including what I had done during my high school years.

I completed and filed the application in a timely manner, sometime around February 1, 1964, shortly before the pledge program was also scheduled to begin. I was poised for the interview, which was conducted by a panel of the university's faculty, administrators, and fellow students, many of the latter group having been Lucy E. Moten fellows in the prior year. The interview date was about the same week as the beginning of the Omega pledge period, and having been inducted into the Lampados Club, I arrived for my interview proudly donning by Lampados Club cap, which was required attire for the duration of the pledge period.

The interview started off well enough, with typical questions, like, "Why would you like to be selected as a Lucy E. Moten fellow?" "What advantage would you expect to receive from this experience, if you are privileged enough to be chosen?" "Have you ever travelled abroad before, and why, and where did you go?" "This is a competitive program, and only a limited few are selected each year. If you are not selected this time, what plans do you have for the summer that would render service to somebody else?" Indeed, they were rather thorough.

But then the interview took a different turn. One of the interviewers, a member of the Delta Sigma Theta Sorority, who I later learned had a bone to pick with Omegas on Howard's campus, asked me, "Why would you want to pledge Omega Psi Phi? That's a fraternity that is dying on this campus." I was absolutely shocked! That question was not relevant to this application and the process, and also, why would she pick this non-related interview to ask such a question?

I was only 20 years old, and newly inducted into the Lampados Club, perhaps less than a week. I asked myself, "What kind of answer should I give? If I say the wrong thing, she might speak out or vote against my application for a fellowship. I can't not respond, because I have come this far and for this long, determined to be am Omega man, and I am not going to let her knock me of base by trying to shoot me down in front of the others, including faculty and administrators."

While I cannot recall the details of my answer, I do know that I set her straight, talking about my Omega legacy of longstanding, mentioning some of the great Omega men that I knew, reminding her that, whatever she thought of the Omega men currently on Howard's campus, the fraternity was a national organization with members all over the world, including ambassadors. I think that I also mentioned Bro. Lawrence Oxley, 14th Grand Basileus (1932-35), and a member of President Franklin D. Roosevelt's "Kitchen Cabinet," whom I had had the privilege of meeting more than once, due to my father's connection with Oxley family members who had attended Miner Teachers College with him.

I tried to be diplomatic, but was very nervous about what she had done. And, as you see, I never forgot it. Conversely, Marsha Echols, an Alpha Kappa Alpha soror, who was always friendly and kindly disposed toward me, made some comments too, which I cannot recall, but were very encouraging. When I was ultimately selected and notified, Marsha later told me that I had placed second in the scoring of all the student applicants for 1964, and that she thought that I had handled myself very well under the circumstance. She noted too, that while others in the room did not dress down the adverse soror for her irrelevant question, that they felt that my composure and response was a positive, adding to my maturity and stability, in the face of unexpected and surprise adversity. In retrospect, that interview incident was a test of how I applied Omega's Four Cardinal Principles to an extreme situation, and came out on top.

There were about 10 or 12 successful applicants for the 1964 fellowship. We were called to a meeting and declared the countries we wanted to visit. I learned that by now, 1964, the money that Moten had bequeathed was long exhausted, and that Howard University had a line item in its budget to continue the program in her name. As well, there were additional sponsoring organizations. Howard had negotiated with them, selected its own Howard-based students, and then referred them on to the respective international organizations for follow up.

The reason was obvious. In 1964, the U.S. Congress considered and passed the Voting Rights Act, followed in 1965, by the implementation of the federally mandated law providing for public accommodations of African Americans in public facilities. Things were still very much segregated in this country. All one needed to do was cross into Prince George's County, Maryland, or the Fourteenth Street Bridge into Arlington, Virginia, where you would find a diminishing number of "White only," and "Colored entrance," signs. In an effort to address that issue, at least in part, several organizations determined that they must make efforts to open up the foreign exchange opportunity to Negroes. White students had been enjoying these opportunities since the 19th Century. Howard's Broader Horizon's program was a perfect fit for this effort. Howard did its internal qualifying, set funds aside for each successful applicant, and then the sponsoring organization took it from there. The format assured a ready-made annual pool of qualified applicants from the Capstone of Negro Education – Howard University.

The four organizations that Howard had made arrangements with were: Project Crossroads Africa, the Encampment for Citizenship (Latin America), Experiment in International Living (near and far Asia), and the American Friends Service Committee (AFSC)(Europe and near Asia). Being from an Islamic background, with a Muslim name, "Rohulamin," ("The spirit of the wise one"), I selected Turkey. Why Turkey and not India, where my family was from?

Maybe I should have gone to India, but at the time my thinking was to sail to Europe on a ship (the S.S. United States was the one

## REFOCUSING ON THE ACADEMIC MISSION

AFSC booked for me), travel across that continent via the Orient Express and the Balkan Express trains, and see as much as possible between Le Havre, France and Istanbul, Turkey. I then worked in an international work camp in Turkey for about five weeks, where I would be exposed to a Muslim society, and gain a greater appreciation for Islam and how people lived their lives, their culture, and practiced their religion in another part of the world. Turkey straddles both Europe and Asia. But my time there would be spend mostly on the Asian side, residing in a small village. However, before I could get there, there was still a lot of work to do.

With the planning cycle and pledge period running parallel, I was awake many nights, fretting about whether I could keep up my studies, keep up my end of the pledging requirements, meet mandatory ROTC requirements, obtain my first passport, and follow through with the AFSC's many supplemental requirements. AFSC had money to give to its successful applicants, but they required several things in order to qualify, including a tailored essay about why I wanted to go to Turkey, and what I hoped to accomplish there. The financial aid component also required that my parents and I financial forms to justify why AFSC should grant a supplemental travel award, beyond whatever Howard was committed to giving.

And of course, I cannot forget that there was a physical examination mandated, and several inoculations, which Howard offered complimentary through the university health service. I remember one day in particular. I reported to the intake desk as scheduled, and said to the receptionist, "I'm here to get my shots for the Broader Horizons program." From behind me an older woman, whom I did not yet know, replied in a bit of stilted and affected accent, which I later learned was called "American Continental." In her somewhat British-accented way of speaking, she said, "Young man. We do not shoot people here. We inoculate them."

I spun around. There she was, a distinguished woman in a white medical coat. She said to the receptionist, "I'll take him." Taking me into one of the medical areas, she proceeded to administer the inoculations. Looking at my medical chart, she asked me if I was related to Nellie Quander, First Supreme Basileus of Alpha Kappa Alpha. The answer was "Yes!" of course. Introducing herself as Dr.

## 50+ OMEGA INSPIRED YEARS

Dorothy Boulding Ferebee, Director of the Howard University Health Services Department, and former Supreme Basileus of AKA, she related some fond memories of her working with Nellie Quander on a number of projects.

Lamenting Nellie's death in September 1961, she added how much everyone in AKA appreciated cousin Nellie for rescuing the sorority in the "old days." I would later learn that this was a reference to the October 1912-January 1913 era, when the "renegades," who were later identified as the 22 AKA sorors who split off in October 1912, to found Delta Sigma Theta. The renegades refused to submit to Quander's directives, as she sought mutual cooperation from them in an effort to make internal changes, to assure that AKA survived and expanded.

Many years later, as one of Omega's historians, I learned and appreciated that Dr. Ferebee was a woman of great vision, which she utilized with distinction. She served as AKA's 10th Supreme Basileus (1939-41) and also succeeded Mary McLeod Bethune as the second President of the National Council of Negro Women (1949-1953). Beginning in the summer of 1935, Dr. Ferebee was appointed as the Director of the Mississippi Health Project.[37] She presided over the Project each summer from that year until 1942, eight years in total.

The Project brought primary medical care to the rural black population across the state for six summers. The program has been recognized as the first mobile health clinic in the United States, assisting approximately 15,000 people in the Mississippi Delta. The project was noted for helping to decrease cases of diphtheria and smallpox in the region and to improve nutritional and dental practices throughout rural Mississippi. Alpha Kappa Alpha members used the Mississippi Health Project to bring federal attention to the needs of African Americans in the rural South. They faced hostile, intimidating, and suspicious white plantation owners, who also saw an intentional effort by female doctors, black and white, to both perform the medical work, and to protect their Negro male counterparts by warning and urging them to stay out of the state.

---

[37] *Gleaned from several sources of the Internet, featuring the history of the Alpha Kappa Alpha Sorority.*

## REFOCUSING ON THE ACADEMIC MISSION

Dealing in ramshackle communities of black sharecroppers, they also tackled widespread malnutrition and venereal disease.[38]

Learning this valuable information helped to give me a broader perspective about what "Service" really meant, and how all of the black Greek-letter organizations have some form of the word "Service" in their cardinal principles or stated mission, dedicating themselves to rendering service to others who are in less fortunate circumstances. In 1941, when Founder Oscar J. Cooper was asked if there was anything that he would like to change or consider as something that should have been included in Omega from the outset, he replied that there should have been a fifth Cardinal principle, "Service," as this is what Omega is committed to rendering.[39] Founder Cooper goes on to say that, although Service is not a recited Cardinal Principle of Omega, it is strongly implied if a brother faithfully observes and executes upon the established Four Cardinal Principles of the fraternity.

Somehow, I managed to get through the international exchange application process, and was well on the way to dedicating myself to a work camp project in Turkey. One of my line brothers, Ralph M. Durham, from Philadelphia, also applied and was likewise accepted into the Broader Horizons program. He selected India as his destination. At the end of the academic year, early June 1964, I learned that he was unable to go, because he found the process for finally qualifying to be too demanding. He told me that he was electing to postpone his program for one year, until summer 1965. Some things should not be postposed, if at all possible. His one year postponement became a totally missed opportunity, and he never was able to take advantage of the travel abroad fellowship.

My first international experience was truly a "Turkish delight." I am focusing my memoirs primarily upon Omega, but find it necessary to give at least some consideration to other important aspects of my more expanded life as well. While Omega is an

---

[38] *Extracted from, "Dorothy Boulding Ferebee," a biographical statement found on the Internet.*

[39] *See Founder Oscar J. Cooper's letter to Bro. George Isabelle, dated December 17, 1941.*

important part of my life, the fraternity is but one component of my total being.

My family comes first. Still, I will stir in other components, especially the travel components, as I deem it relevant and necessary. For example, having been to Africa seven times, each time under different circumstances, it would be ill-advised to leave that out. To do so would paint a far different picture of who I am, what I have done, and where I did it. Likewise, travels to Russia and elsewhere in Europe, Dubai, Central and South America, and throughout the Caribbean, and another trip to Turkey, will also be mentioned.

In May 1964, Alpha Chapter held its annual elections. Robert Beale, the retiring basileus, was now focusing on graduation and entering medical school in the fall. Taft H. Broome, our dean of pledgees, and an engineering student, was elected as the new basileus. Frank B. Patterson, who would later become an Omega legend in due course, was completing his own elected term as Keeper of Records and Seal (KRS) for the period 1963-64. The position was foisted upon him when the prior KRS (1962-63) decided that the job was too time-consuming and abruptly resigned. Frankie, only months into the fraternity, and serving as the neophyte Assistant KRS, then became the heart and soul of Alpha Chapter.

I did not fully realize what that meant, but quickly learned. Frankie had become KRS while a neophyte, but grew, almost overnight, into the full expectations of the position. The KRS is the workhorse of any Omega chapter, charged with keeping the chapter's paperwork in good order, which requires extraordinary efforts to gather information, and complete and file documents, to assure that the chapter is in good financial and administrative standing with both the university and national/international headquarters, and the local district. Frankie not only rose to the occasion, but was exemplary in the process and in following through to the point that today, more than 50 years later, he is revered as the gold standard for getting things together and keeping them that way. He received his 50-year recognitions in 2013, awarded at the chapter (Alpha Omega), district (Third), and international levels (the 78$^{th}$ Grand Conclave, Minneapolis, Minnesota). He continues to serve with distinction.

## REFOCUSING ON THE ACADEMIC MISSION

A similar situation happened to me in late September 1964. We held chapter elections in May of each year. I was elected to the position of Assistant KRS at that time. Serving only four months as KRS, Bro. Edison Moore resigned. Basileus Broome turned to me and said, "It's your baby, now. Frankie will help you get into it." And I did. The academic year 1964-65 was a busy one, as expected. Having transferred from Howard to Lincoln, and then back to Howard, but with a changed major from zoology to political science, I was a hyphenated student, more than a sophomore, but not quite a junior. I needed to take many course in my new major, since I had not yet taken any.

As well, I was serving as an international pal, one of the students who hosts and counsels the many foreign students who were attending Howard, many of whom had never been to the United States before enrolling at Howard. I was also working on the homecoming steering committee and other extracurricular activities. Yet I managed, somehow, to execute the duties of KRS for two years, September 1964 to May 1966, earning Alpha Chapter's Man of the Year Award in November 1965, along the way.

Completing the academic year 1964-65, I worked as a cleaning inspector for the Summer at the National Aeronautics and Space Administration (NASA). It was a 12:00 a.m. to 8:00 a.m. job, the graveyard shift, and required me to verify that the cleaning crew had made the cleaning and maintenance rounds in various NASA buildings, then located in Greenbelt, Maryland. It was a difficult job for me, as it totally disrupted my life. I found it very difficult to sleep in the day time. My home was not air conditioned, so my sleep time during the day was also the hottest hours of the day. But I struggled through, largely with a positive thought of what the next and final year of undergraduate study would bring. I could not wait for the first of September and the Labor Day weekend. Good bye NASA. Thanks for the opportunity, but I hope to never have to work those hours again.

If I had stayed at Howard, without transferring to Lincoln, I would have graduated in June 1965, with the class that entered in September 1961. Most of my classmates did exit the university at that time. However, due to my change of both universities and majors, I still needed more qualifying course work, and did not complete my requirements until December 1965, but just one semester late. In actuality, I was not that late, as many students did not manage to graduate within four years. But since there was no graduation exercise at Howard in December of that year, I could not participate in a commencement activity until June 1966. Consequently, Howard University carries me on its roles as a member of the Class of 1966. I generally refer to myself as a graduate of the "Classes of 1965 and 1966," and have had to explain exactly what that means on several occasions.

But the extra time was a blessing still. It allowed me to be more active on campus, contributing to my being selected to Who's Who in American Colleges and Universities, 1966, and to enjoy campus life. Because I was finished and ready to go, for the winter semester, January-June 1966, I worked at the U.S. post office, and took seven hours of class work, just to keep my finger in the academic pie. I still managed to get to campus by 1:00 p.m. on most Fridays, to meet the brothers around the Omega sundial.

It was a traditional sundial, colloquially called "the dial." Both the column and the base were constructed and hewn from high quality white granite. It stood about 40 inches high, with a 15 inches diameter. Upon its flat top was a circular bronze plate, upon which was installed the time-telling edge of the gnomon, the thin straight edge which casts a shadow, indicating the time of day. Inscribed in the brass on the dial is the statement, "Grow Old Along With Me, The Best Is Yet To Be," a quote from Robert Browning, a famed 19th Century poet. Although the gnomon is now missing, presumed to have been stolen, Brown's words as inscribed on the brass plate sets a tone and imprints an indelible mark upon the psyche of all Omega men, underscoring that the Omega is a life-long journey, and a defined way of life.

The Omega sundial at Howard University is an icon, and consideration is being given to having it be declared as an historic fabric indicative of Greek life at Howard, the founding site (the Mother Pearl) of Omega, as well as four other Black Greek-letter organizations (AKA, Delta, Sigma, and Zeta). Although there are those brothers who feel that the dial is now "old and outdated," I feel

## REFOCUSING ON THE ACADEMIC MISSION

that they lack a sense of history and place. Rather than seeking to replace the dial with something "modern and new," their efforts should be focused upon protecting and restoring the current dial, thereby enhancing its historical significance and creating a greater appreciation for the history of both Alpha Chapter and Omega Psi Phi.

For continuity, allow me to recount the story again, a portion of which I mentioned earlier. I was at the frat house in January 2012, joined in a party for Bro. Albert C. "Butch" Hopkins, a member of the Potent and Prolific 20 (Alpha 1963), who was terminally suffering from pancreatic cancer. My former vice dean of probates, James Baker, came over from Baltimore for the party and in conversation stated that he knew JoAnn Clay, daughter of Leroy Clay. He advised that she had the full archives of the history of how the dial came to be and might be willing to donate it to Howard at this time. The mere mention of the dial and its history brought back many positive memories for me.

During my tenure at Howard (1961-1969), "the dial" was an institution and the centerpiece of Omegadom. It was where we assembled every Friday at 1:00 p.m., after every football game, and after important events, most typically just after commencement exercises. The then graduated brothers, adorned in their caps and gowns, and banners and academic ropes, reflecting their honors and colleges of the university, would convene. I took my place at the dial when my turn came in June 1966, and again in June 1969, fittingly adorned to represent that I had completed my academic work, first from the College of Liberal Arts, and later from the School of Law.

On that day in June 1966, several of my line brothers were with me, including Derek C. Brown (Phi Beta Kappa) and fellow legacy brother, David H. Reid, III. Several academic programs, such as Engineering, Architecture, and Pharmacy, were five year programs. As a consequence, many of my LBs were ultimately in the class of 1967.

Gathering around the dial, we shared many of our memories and recollections of the past several years, appreciating that this was the first time that we were assembled here as newly minted Howard alumni. As well, for some of us, this would also be the last time that we would ever be together, and likewise assemble at this historic Omega monument. We were from all over the U.S. Some of us planned to pursue further formal education, and would remain at Howard, entering medical-dental, law, or graduate programs. But the greater percentage of us would not be continuing our education at Howard. Some went to New England or New York universities, while others considered that their formal education was now complete, and made employment plans from this point forward.

Me, I had decided to seek application to go to law school. I was ambivalent about it, not fully knowing just what I wanted to do. But with a B.A. in Government (Howard had not yet changed the title of the major to Political Science), I knew that my options were limited at best. I had had a great time in undergraduate school, maintained a decent academic average, which increased to well above 3.0 as I progressed towards graduation. However, I felt that I needed to pursue a program that would enable me to be of service to someone, somewhere.

## Civil Rights Experiences While Attending Undergraduate School

It was the turbulent '60s, and the greatest social pressure and issue of the time was to be "relevant," especially to the downtrodden black communities that characterized the great underclass in all to many of our cities and rural areas. Since the 1930s, Howard students had supported and reinforced the Mississippi Health Project, which Dr. Dorothy Boulding Ferebee, noted above, had directed for eight summers, 1935-1942.

The program lagged for many years, but during my undergraduate tenure, the Freedom Rides and sit-in demonstrations took place all across the South. There was increased and sustained awareness about the plight of African Americans in the rural South. Consequently, there was a renewed interest in their circumstances, and several projects and programs were initiated, mostly sponsored by private sector entities, with the stated mission to lift up America's downtrodden blacks, who were still living in some form of slavery more than 100 years after the issuance of the Emancipation Proclamation.

## REFOCUSING ON THE ACADEMIC MISSION

Randall W. Maxey, a young Howard professor, and later recognized as an outstanding medical doctor, following through on his desire to make a visible and sustained difference, established in the late 1960s a program to provide social and medical services to the poorest counties in Mississippi. Known as the Howard University Mississippi Project (HUMP), the effort revived the interest in extending medical care and related programs in Mississippi. Many Howard students, supplemented by many students from historically black colleges and universities (HBCU), as well as Caucasian volunteers, wanted to be of service. While the greatest priority was for medical professional in all areas, there was also a need for support services and general educational efforts to encourage literacy and learning how to take better care of oneself.

Although I was not an active participant in the Civil Rights Movement, I realize in retrospect that I should have been. I was inspired by the Movement and its goals and objective, to pursue law school, intending to use my future service in some manner, yet to be determined, that would be of benefit to those whose rights had been denied or compromised. I applied to only two laws schools, Howard and Duke universities. My application to Duke received a rejection letter, which also contained a statement of best wishes.

My father was relieved, because he did not want me to go to a Southern law school, regardless of its stellar reputation. He was fearful about how I would be treated, in light of racial attitudes and the violence that was only beginning to settle down in North Carolina. The Civil Rights Act of 1964, which assured increased voting rights or black people, was complimented by the public accommodations law, assuring access to hotels, restaurants, and other places of public accommodation.[40] Still, as he reminded me, you

---

[40] *The Civil Rights Act of 1964 (Pub.L. 88-352, 78 Stat.241, enacted July 2, 1964) was a landmark piece of legislation in the United States that outlawed major forms of discrimination against racial, ethnic, national and religious minorities, and women. It ended unequal application of voter registration requirements and racial segregation in schools, at the workplace and by facilities that served the general public ("public accommodation").*

cannot legislate people's attitudes, and surely many of these "crackers" (one of his favorite words) would be bent upon doing harm and making it difficult for me if I were enrolled in this just recently all-white institution.

The issue of public accommodations reminds me of a life-learning experience that I had one night in Baltimore, Maryland, in the Fall of 1964. I had only been an Omega for a few months, 20 years old, when several of the Alpha Chapter brothers travelled to Morgan State University for a football game and then a fraternity party afterwards. Heading back to D.C., we were hungry and decided to stop at a local restaurant for a sandwich and a coke. There were perhaps six or eight of us. We were wearing Omega paraphernalia, and were quite obviously college students. Or at least we thought that we looked the part.

We entered the restaurant, which was almost totally empty. It was about 12:00 a.m. The proprietor came forward and told us to our faces, that he would not serve us, and to please leave. Please leave! This is America, and all of us are equal. But we had no choice but to leave, like or not. The newly enacted Civil Rights Act of 1964, forbade discriminating in public accommodations, but it was not due to take effect until January 1, 1965. The restaurant operators were determined to figuratively slap us in our faces, enforcing their racially "whites only" discriminatory policies until the last day.

Thinking back to that night, I recall some of the others who were in that group with me, including Brothers Sigmund "Jay'" Gullins, William "Hook" Hall, Derek C. Brown, and H. Patrick Swygert, a future president of Howard University. We were scholars and would become doctors, lawyers, engineers, a university president, and men of substance. There were no thugs among us. But the restaurateur saw nothing but the color of our skins, and made his judgment based solely upon that undeniable fact. Indeed, we were dressed better than several of the white patrons, and our appearance to that effect was readily apparent. As well, not one of us was under the influence of alcohol or any illegal substances. So there was not one legitimate reason to deny us service, but for our race. That is one memorable experience that will last me a lifetime. As my wise old dad, James, had said on several prior occasions, and nowhere was it more true than at that moment, "You can change the law, but you cannot legislate attitudes." And today, 2014, 50 years later, I still feel the sting, and the related humiliation that was heaped upon us that early morning in that Southern-focused big city.

Yes, the law was changing, and our rights were about to be guaranteed by the force of the federal government. And we, as the citizens of sable persuasion, will have to put ourselves on the line and exercise those newly achieved rights that were only attained upon a hard fight that included the death of several who came before us or stood with us in the Civil Rights Movement. We had to begin to make a difference somewhere, and on that morning we threw down the gauntlet to anyone who thought that they could maintain life as it had been, and to continue to refuse service in a place of public accommodation. Those days were limited, and within weeks, would be no more.

Just a couple of weeks later, the wisdom of what I am referring to was most succinctly underscored. I remember that November 1964 evening and event quite vividly when Bro. Walter E. Washington (Alpha Chapter 1935), then the Executive Director of the National Capital Housing Authority (the housing department of the then federally controlled District of Columbia) addressed the Washington, D.C. chapters' jointly-held Achievement Week banquet. Washington was appointed to that position by President John F. Kennedy, and in later years, 1967, would be appointed by President Lyndon Johnson as the city's first Mayor-Commissioner. Later still, 1974, he would be elected as the city's first African American mayor, which was a major milestone. No other city of Washington, D.C.'s significance had African American mayors at that time, although Richard Hatcher of Gary, Indiana, and Carl Stokes of Cleveland, Ohio, were both elected to their posts in 1967, the same year that Washington was appointed.

Some of the details of Bro. Washington's remarks that evening are still recalled, and for good reason. He focused upon the forthcoming implementation of federally mandate public accommodations.[41] He noted that he had been working in housing for the last several years, and that his Agency had encountered many instances of rampant discrimination throughout the country in many areas. He had expanded his personal horizon well beyond just the parameters of housing. As a presidentially appointed federal official, he had a wide platform from which he could observe and address the issues of racial discrimination on all levels. On some occasions when he would travel into the South, he was still unable to stay in certain hotels and eat in certain restaurants, because of historic practices that limited and denied members of his race full access and enjoyment of facilities. He added that we often believe that things are different in the North, but racial discrimination, including denial of access to "white only" places was also still the *de riguear* in certain corners in the North as well, although less well known.

His message on that November 1964 evening, in Baldwin Hall, Howard University, was simple and clear – in a few weeks, effective January 1, 1965, all of that is going to change. The Civil Rights Act of 1964 included a federally mandated public accommodations provision, directing that all persons, regardless of their race, must be served in places such as hotels, motels, restaurants, and places of entertainment.

---

[41] *Section 2000a of Title 42, Chapter 21 of the U.S. Code (42 USC 21) prohibits discrimination or segregation in places of public accommodation. Under this provision, all persons are entitled to full and equal enjoyment of the goods, services, facilities, privileges, advantages, and accommodations of any place of public accommodations without any discrimination or segregation based on race, color, religion, or national origin. Private establishments serving the public are considered places of public accommodation. Such private places include:*
*Inns, hotels, motels, or other organizations that provide accommodation to temporary visitors;*
*Restaurants, cafeteria, lunchrooms, lunch counters, soda fountains, or other facilities providing food for consumption; and*
*Motion picture houses, theaters, concert halls, sports arenas, stadiums or other places of exhibition or entertainment.*

## REFOCUSING ON THE ACADEMIC MISSION

He underscored to the brothers and their guests that no longer will we have to fear rejections and outright embarrassment at being turned away from a facility, just because of our sable composition, noting that it will be the federal law, won after a hard fight in the U.S. Congress, and we, the persons most benefitted and affected by the change, must now step up as our duty and responsibility by exercising our fully accorded civil rights in this area.

He urged the fraternity to look anew at holding conclaves, district meetings, and fraternal activities in Southern venues that were heretofore not available, to underscore that we too have the right to use and enjoy these facilities, and fully intended to do so. He urged the assemblage to be bold, take up the torch, and march back South to let the oppressor know that we are not fearful, and will not be intimidated by the history of past practices. In concluding, Bro. Washington entreated everyone to likewise spread the word to our families and friends, to promote public accommodation use among our church groups and other affiliated organizations, to fully expand ourselves into the newly available venues as quickly as possible, to let everyone know that we intended to use what was our right. He concluded his remarks by entreating us to show the doubters that we too knew how to behave.

"How to behave" might seem to be an inappropriate expression at this juncture, but not necessarily. When viewed in the historical context of why whites often so steadfastly denied blacks the use and access to these facilities, one of the big arguments, itself racially infused, was that we did not know how to behave, and that we would sully these places, being dirty, drunken, loud, and otherwise out of control. The fear that lustful Negro men, staying in a hotel and separated from white women by only a shared wall, would somehow be lustful towards her, and possibly compromise her virtue. This was a pejorative attitude among many whites.

Bro. Washington, therefore, charged us with understanding the importance of being personally and collectively responsible in how we conducted ourselves in these places, to underscore that we were always being viewed by the skeptics in a negative context. Therefore, we had both the duty and obligation to prove otherwise. Looking back on that bit of advice, many of us might feel that it was too paternalistic, possibly even insulting to think that Omega men would not know how to conduct themselves in these places. But when framed against the backdrop of Selma, Birmingham, Atlanta, Jackson, and many other places during the 1962-64 greatest efforts of the struggles of the Civil Rights Movement, Bro. Washington's words were right on.

Thus to me, Bro. Washington's remarks only served to underscore what we had just experienced at a location some 30 miles north of my Washington, D.C home, when we were refused service in Baltimore. If I never before appreciated that I lived in the South, that experience, and Bro. Washington's Achievement Week's remarks, underscored that fact.

**Fraternal Life at Howard**

Several traditional fraternal-related activities occurred during my tenure in Alpha Chapter (April 4, 1964 – June 1966 graduation). I will not try to enumerate them here, other than to say that homecoming was always a big event, with the Greek-letter organizations competing to see who could make the best float. Omega traditionally made a float, and under the supervision and direction of Taft H. Broome, initially my Dean of Pledgees and later Basileus of Alpha Chapter, the frat won first prize at least once in that time frame, and perhaps placed second in one of the other years. At any rate, the campus grew to anticipate that Omega would have a great parade entry, and we tried not to disappoint.

One year, and it was probably October 1964, I particularly remember that the night before homecoming was bitterly cold for October, adverse to any float-making plans and efforts. Bro. Basileus Broome was not having it. There were no cell phones in those days, so he had to send brothers out to find the others, and to "make" them show up. It took several hours to assemble the unwilling, but he did. By the time the real effort got underway, it was well past midnight. All of the equipment was in place, but the frame still had to be built. The devil is in the details, and a sane execution was still required.

With disagreement about what, and how, the effort was a struggle. As daylight approached, we were still hours away from completion. Our plan was to build the float in the frat house driveway

## REFOCUSING ON THE ACADEMIC MISSION

on 13th and Harvard Streets. Can you imagine all the noise associated with saws, drills, and hammers at 3:00 a.m.? But despite a few complaints from neighbors, we still persevered. Our initial intent was to tow the float to campus and take our assigned place in the parade queue. We did not make it.

When the parade started in front of Cramton Auditorium, officially at 10:00 a.m., but always late, we still had a lot more work to do. Everyone was dead tired, still cold, now hungry, but fully pumped up. We had totally missed the Friday night parties, which many of our errant brothers still managed to attend, by escaping the wrath and capture by the basileus. Our new plan – forget about the quarter mile parade route distance from Cramton to the Omega house, via Georgia Avenue and Columbia Road to 13th Street. Wait until the parade came to us, and then push ourselves into the parade from the frat house, as it proceeded down 13th Street onto Florida Avenue and then up Fourth Street to get back to campus.

It was a grueling parade route, long and very disruptive to the entire Howard University area. Since then, the route has been significantly modified, and is less invasive to the lower Georgia Avenue community. The fact that we entered the parade from the frat house, while known to many of our fellow contestants, and especially the Greek-letter organizations, was a subject of some discussion. Some organizations felt that we should have been disqualified from the competition. But there was no existing rule that forbade our competing, so we entered where we entered, and still won a prize. As well, it appears that the judges who evaluated the floats and awarded the prizes were likewise unaware of what we had done, until after they had awarded us. No further action was taken on that issue as a result of their belated knowledge.[42]

---

[42] *It is now about 50 years later after the fact, and the brothers cannot recall if we won first or second place that year.*

## The Meaning of Fraternity[43]

> *The College Fraternity has as its goal, in harmony with that of the college, to provide training and discipline of the individual, who is seeking an education and desires to make himself a useful member of society, possessing knowledge, trained skill and capacity for accomplishment. The College Fraternity as a group organization, seeks to teach men how to live together and work together, striving by precepts and examples of the personal development of the individual in the training of mind and body. It carries forward fundamental purposes of education, adding a fraternal influence for correct living and individual development...One of the basic assumptions of Alpha Chapter, Omega Psi Phi Fraternity is that 'Greek-letter organizations' contribute to and are a part of the total educational process of the University. On any university campus, a student leads two lives – an academic life and a social life. The 'Greek-letter organization' strives to blend those two lives in a healthy proportion for its members, plus inculcate a third influence of cultural awareness. The Greeks do this by giving its members a sense of belonging and by fostering a healthy competitive spirit towards other organizations.*

Another event that comes to mind is the annual Greek song fest. In the 1960s, the fest was an event of longstanding. It was conducted in the spring, about the middle of May, after the new inductees had gotten the opportunity to sing with their new chapter members, but before the outset of the final exam period. Between 1946 until about 1955, Omega enjoyed a unique status. Under the founding directorship of Bro. Valerian E. Smith (Alpha Chapter 1945), the chapter achieved a status that it had never had before, or since. The Omega Chorale Ensemble became so famous that it held its own concerts in Rankin Chapel, then the largest auditorium on the

---

[43] *Extracted from a letter dated October 27, 1964, written by Edwin Sapp, Alpha Chapter Editor and later basileus, to Carol Lawson, Feature Editor, the Hilltop, the Howard University school paper, after she penned an article questioning the relevancy, and criticizing the role and value of fraternities and sororities on university campuses.*

## REFOCUSING ON THE ACADEMIC MISSION

campus, and often had to schedule at least two concerts in order to accommodate the audience. They even travelled to other cities for Omega-related events, including at least one Grand Conclave and several annual district meetings.

### The Que Chorus

*Entering its fourth year of existence at Howard University is an Omega project which has gained such prominence that it has become an "Immortal Institution" on the campus and in the city. Wherever it goes it acquires a tremendous following. One has only to say, "The Que Chorus in concert," and the auditorium is full soon after seven for an eight o'clock concert. The idea of an Omega Chorus, here at Howard, grew out of a fraternity skit presented in the Delta Jabberwock in 1946. A group of brothers, merely a few with singing experience, but all with intense interest, were gathered together by Brother Valerian Smith. A musical background was needed for a skit adapted from Gershwin's "Porgy and Bess," so Brother Smith rehearsed them for the occasion. That night the Ques won first place and the singing was received with such explosive enthusiasm by the audience that the group decided to formally organize a Choral Ensemble. ... In their Spring concert of 1946, the chorus was received with resounding applause. At its conclusion there were eight encores. ... In 1948 the Chorus was invited to the Grand conclave in Columbus, Ohio. The Chorus has given concerts in the District of Columbia, Maryland, and West Virginia. They are in constant demand by many cities for concerts.* – the Oracle, Vol. 40, #1, March 1950, P. 3.

By the time of my induction into Alpha Chapter, those glory days had been largely forgotten. Still, there were some references to it in the Alpha Chapter records, which most of us had never seen, not even to this day. However, when we were pledging in 1964, the brothers of the chapter realized that there were several excellent voices among the 21 Titans. We competed in the 1965 song fest, but did not win first place. Determined to best everyone for 1966, my graduating year, we started our preparations earlier than the prior year.

## 50+ OMEGA INSPIRED YEARS

Several rehearsals were held at the frat hose, with Larry Caldwell, my line brother and a music major, taking the lead in arranging the music. Each organization was allowed to sing up to three songs. After much discussion about which songs we would sing, we settled on what Larry wanted from the outset. One three songs each had some special meaning, and we approached them with gusto. We sang, *I've Been 'Buked and I've Been Scorned,* an old Negro spiritual, *The Sweetheart Song,* sometimes called *Dear Omega Girl,* and *For Those in Peril on the Sea,* which is often associated with the last Sunday-onboard religious service prior to the sinking of the *Titanic* in 1912.

On the day of the competition, which began at about 4:00 p.m. on a Sunday afternoon, we scheduled a final rehearsal at the frat house. Arriving at about 1:00 p.m., we found the house locked tight, with no access possible. We hightailed it to my house, located on 13th Street, about 10 blocks north, and using my parent's' grand piano, which was in the living room, our Alpha Chapter chorale completed its final rehearsal. My parents were so impressed, Mom said, "You guys have got to win." My dad, who had an excellent voice, and sang in plays in both Dunbar and Miner, and later on the Lincoln Theatre stage, got so enthused that he joined the rehearsal. He knew all the songs. A couple of brothers said, "Bro. Quander, you should join us in the competition. We'll hide you in the back, so no one will see you and know that you are not a student at Howard." We all laughed at the suggestion. He declined, advising that we could win this competition on our own, and did not need his voice to make it so.

### Dedication of Omega's New National Headquarters

*We have gathered today for a momentous occasion in the life of Omega. The dedication of the national headquarters of Omega Psi Phi Fraternity, Inc., has great significance for the welfare and progress of our fraternity. It is a dream come true for several administrations. It is, therefore, a great pleasure for me to welcome you to this dedication. I appreciate the honor and privilege of presiding at these ceremonies. I am sure that everyone here is impressed by this beautiful setting and structure.* Words of George E. Meares, 26th Grand Basileus, the *Oracle,* Vol. 79, March 1965., P. 5.

# REFOCUSING ON THE ACADEMIC MISSION

Assembling shortly thereafter in Cramton, most of us sat in the front left section, closest to the steps onto the stage. When Omega was announced as the next competitor, we arose and ascended onto the stage, all dressed in white shirts, black ties, and black slacks. It was melodious, to say the least. The audience went crazy. Cramton seated about 1,500 people, and the place was packed. As the different sections of the chorale found their respective vocal niches, I knew that there was victory in the offering. I doubt if Bro. Smith's Omega Chorale Ensemble ever sounded better. But they had staying power and lasted for eight years before disbanding. Our group's highlight of the evening was basically a single time win, for the organizational efforts and results were not consistent enough to keep us in the first place column the following year. Still, that event and all of the associated memories were one of the great highlights of what it meant to me to be a member of Alpha Chapter, and to be identified with Omega's Mother Pearl.

### What is the Omega Psi Phi Fraternity?[44]

*Our Fraternity is not a church per se, yet it recognizes the Supreme Basileus of the Universe and the Creator and sustainer of all that is good. For our Fraternity aims to emphasize Judeo-Christian Manhood.*

*Our Fraternity is not a social organization per se, yet we believe that men of like attainment and similar ideals of fellowship should bind themselves together in order to approach these ideals.*

*Our Fraternity is not a foundation per se, yet through our Scholarship Commission we have made grants and awards to worthy Brothers each year that run in the thousands.*

---

[44] *Extracted from the keynote address delivered by Bro. Cary D. Jacobs, 25th Grand Basileus (1961-1964), during the Founders Banquet at the 48th Grand Conclave, Indianapolis, Indiana, December 1962.*

## 50+ OMEGA INSPIRED YEARS

*Our Fraternity is not a housing project per se, yet through our Housing Authority we have purchased, leased, rented and constructed chapter houses that would justify our existence if we had no other programs.*

*Our Fraternity is not a research organization per se, yet through our Achievement Program we have fostered, promoted and encourage our youth to delve into the history of our heroes, write about the accomplishments of our race, and become creative in their thinking on modern-day subjects.*

*Our Fraternity is not a promotional organization per se, yet through our Talent Hunt Program we have discovered and presented hundreds of our young people who are talented in music who perhaps never would have had an opportunity to demonstrate their worth in the musical world.*

*Our Fraternity is not a civil rights organization per se, yet through or Social Action Program we endeavor to lift the veil of ignorance and superstition from the American public and to stimulate all who believe that out of one blood God made all men to dwell upon the earth.*

# XV – Graduation And Entering Law School

In June 1966, I graduated from the College of Liberal Arts, with a major in Government (now renamed "Political Science") and a minor in History. I was accepted into Howard's School of Law, but still wonder how it might have been different had I gone to Duke instead. Duke had quietly integrated its law school in 1961, with the admission of two black students, David Robinson, Class of 1961, Howard University, and Walter Johnson, Class of 1961, North Carolina A&T University.[45] Duke also accepted at least two Howard grads in its fall 1966 class, Charles Becton and James Hatcher, both members of Kappa Alpha Psi Fraternity. Both of them did well academically, and meaningfully contributed to furthering the reputation of the quality of Howard University graduates, However, with two other Howard students accepted, my application did not result in an admission letter, at least not yet.

I found Howard Law to be a challenging academic experience. I took all of the first year classes, including contracts, civil procedure, and constitutional law, anticipating a traditional law school education that would lead to graduation and then into a life of public service, consistent with the law school's longstanding reputation. I make several new friends, and we quickly formed a study group to help us along with our studies. From the outset, we realized that learning and applying the law is quite different from the academic approaches that were the standard in undergraduate school. Reading and writing alone were not sufficient, as the issue of the day and the components of the various legal cases had to be discussed in terms of what did actually occur, how the occurrence might have been different if a singular fact was changed, and even how we would handle the issue in dispute, if we have been the legal counsel for one of the parties.

---

[45] *"The Pioneers" David Robinson, II, '64 (Howard University, '61) and Walter Johnson, Jr., '64 (North Carolina A&T, '61) recall integrating Duke Law School, Duke Law News, April 16, 2012.*

## 50+ OMEGA INSPIRED YEARS

Our break-out sessions quickly disclosed to us the importance of forming a study group, i.e., fellow students who would be dedicated to getting through, and serious enough to want to stick with it until the mission was accomplished. None of us had any appreciation at the outset that our group, which we named "The Group," would be a three-year fixture, starting in the first semester of our first year, and lasting until graduation, three years later. The group's members were all in my section, and by name: Algie R. Lewis, Harvey Latney, Jim Miller, Melvin Hughes, Joseph Gibson, Steven Zaben, and me. With such dedication and seriousness, we were able to approach several professors and ask them for tutoring sessions, which we often held on a Friday evening, most often in the professor's home, where we ate snacks and often drank adult beverages, while discussing certain aspects of civil procedure, or whatever the subject was for that evening.

In late April-early May 1967, towards the end of my first year in law school at Howard, a letter arrived from Duke University School of Law. What do they want with me? They had already said "No!," so why would they be sending me a letter? Perhaps they were asking me to contribute some money for their scholarship program? I was beyond curious. Tearing open the letter, my eyes got a wide as saucers. Duke apparently knew or assumed that my grades were at least decent, and offered to accept me as a second year transfer student, if I still wanted to come there in the fall of 1967.

My dad thought that this issue was over with, and so did I. But when I shared the letter's contents with both of my parents, I could see the worry immediately come across his brow. "I don't think that you should do this." he said. "Why not?," I replied. Sitting me down, he reviewed all of what he had said several months previously, recounting the many frustrations that he had had over the years in dealing with prejudiced white people right here in the District of Columbia. He recounted incidents that he was still having with certain people on the job, and concluded with sayings, "If they can be like that, say certain things, and just show their racists selves here in the federal government, in a nation that belongs to all of us, what makes you think that they wouldn't feel empowered to act up or take some action against you in the Old South? No, I don't want that for

## GRADUATION AND ENTERING LAW SCHOOL

you. But, I'll let you make up our own mind on that one. I'm finished."

My mother, on the other hand, took a much different approach. She was not American-born, having come from Barbados to New York in 1934. She was of mixed racial background, East Indian (Father from Calcutta), Irish, Scottish, and Afro Caribbean. She noted that there had been racial and color discrimination in Barbados, citing the Barbados Yacht Club as but one "whites only" example. Still, she felt that things were changing in the U.S., and that maybe I should consider transferring. She stated, "James (my dad) had many bitter racial experiences here in D.C. which I was not directly exposed to. Consider where he's coming from in his position against your transferring to Duke, but at the same time give realization to why he feels the way that he does."

After pondering the issue in my mind for several days, I decided to remain at Howard. In retrospect, now 47 years later, I still wonder if I made the right decision. This decision's effect and long term result is a classic example of the road not taken, based upon Carl Sandburg's famous 1916 poem by the same name, *The Road Not Taken*, for indeed, it made all the difference. I am a proud Howard University graduate – two times – and have benefited in innumerable ways as a result of it. But one cannot help but look back to where you came to a crossroad and a potentially life-altering situation, and question, asking yourself, "Did I make the right decision?" Should I have taken the turn, perhaps to the road less traveled, and gone to a new place? I have thought about this often, and know that I cannot alter the outcome now. But in retrospect, knowing what I know now, including the tumultuous times that were Howard's law school in the later 1960s, I should have followed my initial instincts and transferred.

I make no indictment against my beloved Howard, but a Duke Law School degree in 1969 would have taken me to many other and different places, and opened up opportunities in various legal disciplines that the Howard degree, and the overt discrimination against black law graduates at the time, could not. In reviewing the comments from some of the early African American Duke law graduates, and in discussing the matter with Charles Becton, my fellow contemporary classmate (1966), and who did go to Duke that year, it was apparent that the significant majority of white law firms and several businesses as well, were simply declining to hire "Negro lawyers" in 1969, when he graduated.

So just where I could have gone with my newly-minted Duke law degree remains uncertain. But, it would have been worth a try. I believe that I would have done no worse in the job market by declining to go to Duke, and staying at Howard, but the job and social affiliation opportunities that a Duke law degree would have, almost assuredly, been different from those available to Howard law grads at that time. Being in the mood of the 1960s, of always "being relevant to the needs of the black community," I too was interested in being of service. I anticipated working in a legal aid-related job upon my Howard graduation, which opportunity I most likely could have still gotten with a Duke degree, although making entrees into the corporate world was clearly Duke's focus for its graduates.

Conversely, given the focus of Duke's history, as a Southern-based virtually all-white corporate law firm-focused institution, it is not likely that legal aid work would appear on the law school's agenda as a viable goal for its graduates. I well might have been compromised, changed my focus and attention and traveled into still another direction. But that never happened, so there is no need to fret about it now.

**First Year – Unrest**

Law schools are certainly expected to be places of intellectual firmament, a location where issues, both academic and real, are to be hotly contested with wide disagreement, all designed to help minds that are learning the law, and how to use both the law and their minds to effectuate changes in our society. And during my three years at Howard law, the situation was no difference. There were many great minds in residence, great intellectual arguments, and strides made, both in understanding the law and how it has helped each and all of us, and in our own personal growth, towards becoming first rate lawyers.

However, I never anticipated that all three of my law school years would face major disruptions, events that I believe significantly interfered with our ability to remain focused upon both our

## GRADUATION AND ENTERING LAW SCHOOL

individual and collective goals, to learn the law, graduate, and become effective advocates for those in need. During the 1966-67 academic year, I was a first year student, and still idealistic about what it meant to have well known faculty members to be in the national limelight, bringing attention to our law school in the process. Only the attention, while beneficial on a national level, was also detrimental on the local and personal level.

The first incident occurred in January 1967, when the U.S. Congress's House Democratic Caucus stripped Congressman Adam Clayton Powell of the chairmanship of the powerful House Education and Labor Committee, based upon allegations that he had badly mismanaged his committee's budget, had taken trips abroad at public expense, and had consistently failed to attend important meetings of the committee. In response to the Caucus's action, on March 1, 1967, the full House refused to seat him, despite his reelection in November 1966, until completion of an investigation by the Judiciary Committee, the outcome of which confirmed that several of the allegations were in fact true.

Seeking legal counsel, Congressman Powell called upon several of his personal friends and legal colleagues, including Howard Law professors Herbert O. Reid and Frank Reeves, to help him fight the censorship and apparent loss of his Congressional seat. Both men were highly respected constitutional lawyers, and well connected to fellow legal specialists who likewise were of the opinion that Congress has overstepped its bounds. During this period both Reid and Reeves essentially abandoned the law school, as they travelled to Bimini Island in the Bahamas, and strategized with Powell and other lawyers, about what actions should be taken against the U.S. Congress for its censure. I still vividly recall the *Washington Post* photo of Powell, Reid, and Reeves leaning on the rail over the side of a fishing boat, with the caption to the effect that, "Howard University School of Law professors, Herbert O. Reid and Frank Reeves, join Congressman Adam Clayton Powell, and take a break during their strategizing session, on how to counter Congress's action of excluding the Congressman from his elected seat in the House of

Representatives.[46] As well, when the two faculty members were in town, they often neglected to keep class, further exacerbating an already critical situation of causing their students, including me, to miss contact hours.

This legal battle raged for more than two years, and was eventually decided on June 16, 1969 by the U.S. Supreme Court in the landmark case, *Powell v. McCormack*, 395 U.S. 486, (1969). I had graduated the prior week. The ultimate decision was in Congressman Powell's favor, holding that Congress did not have the power to deny someone from serving in that body, who had been duly elected by their constituency, who meets the requirements of the U.S. Constitution for serving in the Congress.[47] Although the Supreme Court's decision was not until June 1969, our legal education was punctuated at various times in both 1967 and 1968, by Reid and Reeves' absence for pending court actions.

But what we were facing during this tumult, while operating under the guise of being one of those great moments in our personal legal journey, was perceived as such by some, but resented as a waste of time and loss of focus by others. The academic year, 1967-68 came to an end, but without any resolution of what would eventually prevail.

**Second Year – Another Year of Unrest**

During my second year of law school, burning questions and cross arguments about relevance came to a head. Students were asking whether we, both as a law school with an historic mission, and each of us as individuals, were fulfilling our mission of service. In the Spring of 1968, a sizable faction of the law student body, primarily drawn from the first and second year students, shut down the law school's operations, expressing frustration over the seeming

---

[46] *Although I could not locate the exact news media document for attribution, the above statement reflects the general sentiment as expressed by The Washington Post, The Washington Star, and several other print and video media, some of which questioned whether the sessions in Bimini were more of a frolic, than legal strategy sessions.*

[47] *See also, Powell At The Supreme Court, Will Haygood, APF Fellow, The Alicia Paterson Foundation, 1988.*

## GRADUATION AND ENTERING LAW SCHOOL

irrelevance of some of the school's curriculum, and the claimed "Ivory Tower" attitude of certain faculty members.

Although there were certainly militant factors among my fellow students, a majority of them were not in that camp. The action imposed a divide within our ranks. While they were not unsympathetic to the plight of the less fortunate, the majority's focus remained on getting their academic work completed, graduating and passing the bar, and getting on with their lives. Several were married, had children, and jobs, and were hardly interested in protesting or making waves. Actually, the majority was clearly turned off by the militant minority. Still, the accumulated complaints from among the protest forces had the desired effect of interfering with everyone else's opportunity to attend classes. It was a most difficult time indeed.

With graduation close at hand for the Class of 1968, the third year students wanted no part of this disruption. They still felt the sting of the Powell-Reid-Reeves verses the U.S. Congress scenario of the prior year. For them, two consecutive years of disruption, with this one in 1968 being based in the law school, was more than they wanted to give any consideration to. William "Buddy" Blakey, president of the SBA, and my good Omega brother, wanted to put as much distance between himself and the protest as possible. Yet at the same time, as president, he needed to be in the mix, to demonstrate leadership and a sincere interest in the students' concerns.

Since I was the elected SBA vice president, at his direction, I assembled the student body, creating a forum for letting them air their grievances, to see how best we, their elected leaders, could serve them. Since the disruption of the prior year, many felt that important changes needed to be made in the school's operations. Faculty absences, due to professors' other non-academic involvements, was of major concern. Students were also questioning the academic credentials and preparations of certain faculty members, and whether the commitment to social activism, a benchmark for the Howard University School of Law, was still a component of our mission.

The SBA's efforts to serve its constituents were hampered by the militant attitudes of the striking students and their declaration that the SBA was a part of the problem. They attacked the elected leadership, including President Blakey and me, alleging the that student government was not "down with the people." In as much as we, the elected leadership, had convened the forum to air grievances, it was painful to be accused in those same assemblies of being "the irrelevant bourgeoisie."

It was believed by many of us that, once we got back into class, the militant lot would continue to pursue their agenda, and that maybe they would be able to see their mission through and realize some changes that would benefit all of us. I believe that they were committed to doing so, but their intentions were interrupted by still another major jolt, the second in this academic year 1967-68. The forums accomplished nothing by way of a resolution, thus creating more problems and hard feelings between the militant faction and the rest of us. Still, they did serve the purpose of rallying "the irrelevant bourgeoisie" to get back into class, and try to keep the academic wheels moving. While we all felt the sting of being called "irrelevant" and "unconcerned," the true measure of our circumstance, and how all of us were in a similar situation as people of color, was painstakingly brought to the fore on the evening of Thursday, April 4, 1968.

I was scheduled to present my appellate oral argument in Moot Court on Saturday, April 6, 1968. This was an oral argument class taught by Luke C. Moore, U.S. Marshall for D.C, and later associate judge in the Superior Court of D.C., and Judge Barrington Parker, a federal judge in the U.S. Court for the District of Columbia. Both men were Omega brothers who volunteered their time to help law students prepare for court appearances.

Judge Parker's wife, Marjorie Holloman Parker, was the founder of Beta Lambda Chapter of AKA at Miner Teacher's College in the mid-1930s, and later the Supreme Basileus. Moot court was a standard part of the law school curriculum, and the stipend that Moore and Parker received for their services was quite miniscule, compared with the amount of time and true dedication that they each gave towards helping us prepare to meet the legal world of the court room.

I was in the stacks of the A. Mercer Daniel Law Library, preparing for my oral argument. I had several books piled up on the table, furiously taking notes from court cases that I had read and intended to cite and emphasize in my forthcoming oral presentation argument.

## GRADUATION AND ENTERING LAW SCHOOL

I intended to assert before the fictional court of appeals that the lower court had committed several reversible errors when it ruled against my imaginary client.

Suddenly, there was a commotion out in the main library area. I heard someone cry out, "Oh no! Oh no!. That can't be true! Oh no!" Then I heard a shrill female voice cry out, "Tell me it's not true! Dr. King can't be dead." I was dumbstruck. The quiet that was characteristic of this place of study, where I had spent many an hour past midnight, pouring over books and documents, was quickly in turmoil. Everyone was on his feet. "What happened?" "When?" "Who did this to Dr. King?" "Why? Everyone was talking at once. A television was quickly set up on the front counter. We were all standing around, unable to speak coherently. Grown men and women, adults, in tears.

This was a very painful moment in all of our lives. It was 1968. The Civil Rights Act of 1964 was the law of the land, and with it voting rights and public accommodations were likewise the law of the land. Although my dad always said that you cannot legislate peoples' attitudes, surely their disagreement should not be carried out to the point where they kill one another. But, if you know American history, you also know that this is surely not the case. There have been racially-motivated crimes in America from the first day this country was established. Now, there was the force of law to officially remove certain racially discriminatory actions that previously were universally imposed by certain states. But this was not the time to wax philosophical. All of us were both upset and angry. We were fearful too, not knowing what the immediate outcome would be or what would happen next.

Someone in our group referred to the Watts riots in Californian in 1965, and wondered aloud whether such a thing could happen here in the national's capital city. We did not know how the anger of the local residents would play out, many of whom were resentful of the white-owned businesses still located in the neighborhood. Several of these small businesses were family owned, but still refused to hire black employees. Many of them were located along 14th Street, close to U Street, N.W., where burning and looting would soon occur. Dr. King's assassination brought the rage of the black community to the surface.

That rage was about to take an even more violent form, including mass burning of business and buildings, and would also result in the deaths of many people.

Looking towards the west, with no obstructions in my sight from the law library windows clearly to at least 11th Street, I could see smoke, the beginnings of the many arson fires that would be set before the long night ahead. Although the media would claim that the fires did not start until April 5th, the next day, some of my friends, including my cousin Kenneth A. Brown, who would later serve as Omega's Grand Keeper of Finance, were adamant about the April 4th late evening torching of the Safeway store then located at 14th and Clifton Streets, N.W. Kenny told me that when driving home from work, just hours after the assassination, he was frightened by what he saw at the Safeway site, including a young man getting seriously cut by falling glass. He fled home in his vehicle, terribly concerned about what was about to unfold.

Living at 13and U Streets, right in the midst of both the U Street and 14th Street corridors, by the next morning his entire family felt under siege, afraid to venture out, with military convoys setting up in every street. They heard occasional gunfire. Smoke and fires were very close by. There was no escaping the acrid smell of tear gas. Told to stay in the house, the closed doors and windows were not match for the wafting aroma of tear gas, nor the burn that it inflicted upon the eyes and nostrils of those who were in essence prisoners in their own homes.

All of us in the law library knew on that fateful evening of April 4, 1968, that it would be a long night. We were unsure whether the law school would even be open the next day. Gathering my belongings, I headed home. My family lived at 3714 13th Street, N.W. The core of the fire and disruption was only one block over, and concentrated just a few blocks down, from about the 3200 block of 14th Street and lower, down toward U Street.

By the time I arrived home, it was already past midnight and the new day, April 5th, had begun. I could not sleep. The day before was the fourth anniversary of my induction into Omega. I had thought about that point the day before, but in light of recent events, Omega seemed to be insignificant by comparison. In retrospect though, I now

## GRADUATION AND ENTERING LAW SCHOOL

know otherwise, because it was through the sustained efforts and devoted service of several men of Omega, coupled with other like-minded friends, that our society has gotten to this point. Because of these forebears' efforts, we have legally assured rights, liberties, and protections, even when some deranged mind, whether acting alone or in concert, decided to take the law into his own hands, and commit an act of murder.

Who were some of these Omega men who rendered these services, some of whom remain relatively unsung? First, I give recognition to Luke C. Moore and Judge Barrington Parker, both Omega men, who were devoted to us as Howard University law students, helping to prepare us to go forth and challenge the many injustices of the world. Next, I give credit to Omega men who have made sustained contributions to our American society through the years, too many men to name here, when it comes to the point of explaining how they served us. But a few of them should be noted, and given their proper due.

I start with Ernest E. Just, Founder, who proved time and again, and against all odds, that black men are men of science too. He was faced with repeated insults to both himself and his family, as some of the other scientists, men and women of otherwise great intelligence, refused to accredit to him his intellectual capacity, preferring to ignore or question his strides in science, or to attribute it to the fact that he was a mulatto, a man of white ancestry.

Then there was Bro. Lawrence Oxley, 14th Grand Basileus (1932-35), who served in President Franklin D. Roosevelt's "Kitchen Cabinet," along with some of the greatest African American leaders of the 20th Century, including Mary McLeod Bethune. There was also Bro. Grant Reynolds, 21st Grand Basileus (1951-53), whose professionalism and devotion to equalizing opportunities in the U.S. military, is majorly credited for President Harry S. Truman's decision to issue Executive order #9981, on June 26, 1948, which committed the federal government to desegregating the U.S. military. It still took another three years, July 1951, with the Korean Conflict in full swing, before the full effect of integrated fighting units was realized.

More contemporary to our present time, I mention Bro. Jesse Jackson, one of Dr. Martin Luther King, Jr.'s right hands, who served as the fraternity's Second Vice Grand Basileus in the 1960s, the highest position that can be held by an undergraduate student, and Bro. Charles Bolden, former astronaut, and director of the National Aeronautics and Space Administration (NASA). Both of these brothers have proven to be effective and sustained American leaders, and not just limited to exercising that quality among the African American community.

I must also accredit the sustained presence of Bro. Mayor Walter E. Washington, my fellow Alpha Chapter (1935) Mother Pearl initiate. At the time of Washington, D.C.'s greatest crisis, i.e., during the riots of 1968, he did his absolute best to keep the peace. He worked to calm down the city, and sent the strongest message to local and national black communities that, despite the tragedy associated with the tragic death of Dr. King, with the proper exercise and use of the law, peace would return and there would be a much brighter day.

While some might malign him, even call him an "Uncle Tom" for not being more aggressive in responding to the threats from the inserted military forces, those same critics need to also factor in that it was his calm, cool, and collective demeanor, that prevented the savagery that J. Edgar Hoover, the Director of the FBI, and who was extremely hostile to Dr. King in particular and African Americans in general, sought to visit upon the black residents of D.C. His efforts to inflict a "shoot to kill" order upon the looters and arsonists failed at Mayor Washington's doorstep. As mayor of this city, the Capital City of the United States, Washington steadfastly stood in Hoover's way, and refused to issue such an order. Reminiscent of those same tactics that were used in civil rights actions in the early 1960s, Washington refused to shoot down his fellow black brothers and sisters.

His professionalism in the face of the most trying circumstances, should always be regarded as one of the most significant actions ever taken in the Civil Rights Movement. Washington demonstrated that he could successfully stand up to the directive of a very high person in the federal government who only saw protection of property, most all of which belonged to absentee white owners who daily fled to the suburbs at sunset, as the paramount concern. Said forces, as represented by Hoover's thinking, gave little consideration to the underlying reasons and causes why the black citizens of Washington,

## GRADUATION AND ENTERING LAW SCHOOL

D.C., and elsewhere were reacting to the death of Dr. King in the manner in which they did.

It is to these members of Omega Psi Phi that I give a fitting tribute and recognition. Each of them, individually and collectively, paved the way for us today. To me, each of their acts was significant and worthy of recognition for the benefit that was delivered to us as a race. Taken together, they were huge milestones, and made a sustained difference that we are privileged to enjoy today. I fear that many of our younger African Americans have little understanding and no appreciation for the struggles that their forebears, even 20 to 30 ago, endured.

By this memoir, I hope to encourage younger citizens, Omega or not, to better understand, appreciate, and inquire further into the individual acts and sacrifices that were made by the above-referred men of Omega. And while I am so noting, there were many, many others who likewise served – too numerous to mention here. Still, some names of course come to mind beyond just Dr. King (Alpha), Thurgood Marshall (Alpha), Robert Weaver (Omega), Mary McLeod Bethune (Delta), Mary Church Terrell (Delta), Dorothy I. Height (Delta), Roy Wilkins (Omega), Lucy Diggs Slowe (AKA), James Nabrit (Omega), George E.C. Hayes (Kappa), Benjamin Hooks (Omega), Anna Julia Cooper (AKA), Oliver Hill (Omega), and Nellie Quander (AKA).

### Third Year – Still More Unrest

Clarence Clyde Ferguson, a brilliant *Cum Laude* Harvard graduate, became the dean of the law school in 1963. Coming to us with stellar credentials and a well-respected reputation, he served us well until his departure in early 1969, when President Richard M. Nixon named him ambassador-at-large to the United Nations, and later, the U.S. Ambassador to Uganda (1970), and later still as Deputy Assistant Secretary of State for African Affairs (1973). While at Howard, he was a teaching dean, and taught constitutional law.

Effective February 1, 1969, Patricia Roberts Harris, the first female African American head of a U.S. law school, was installed by the Howard University Board of Trustees as Ferguson's successor. Harris was a *Summa Cum Laude* graduate from Howard's undergraduate division, Class of 1945, and a member of the Delta Sigma Theta Sorority. Among other occupational positions of significance, Harris served as the sorority's National Executive Director and was the Dean of Women at Howard, a position that was first occupied by Lucy Diggs Slowe, a Founder of the Alpha Kappa Alpha Sorority.

While there was no question about whether Professor Harris was qualified or capable of serving as the new dean of Howard's School of Law, her appointment created a firestorm among several members of the faculty, who made it clear that from their perspective, her selection as the dean was not made in consistence with the ABA's guidelines for the purpose of vetting and appointing a law school dean. The many vocal dissenters asserted that there had been neither faculty consultation nor input prior to her selection as the new law school dean. They felt greatly disrespected by the manner in which she had been chosen, regardless of whether she was qualified, which many faculty members readily acknowledged her to be.

When Harris decided to pursue the law as a profession, she entered the George Washington University School of Law, graduating first in the Class of 1960. Being well connected, upon law school graduation, she worked for the criminal division of the U.S. Department of Justice, before joining the Howard law faculty in 1962. She held several high profile positions, being appointed by President John F. Kennedy as chairperson of the National Women's Committee for Civil Rights, and later as the first African American female, appointed by President Lyndon B. Johnson, to be ambassador to Luxembourg.

When the new dean appointment was announced, the law faculty convened their own private meeting to discuss the matter. The details were shared with the student body in a follow-up session with the faculty and students assembled by the student bar association in the moot court room. I recall vividly when Professor Elmwood Chisholm, who had taught me civil procedure in my first year, thunderously declared that the first time that he learned about Dean Harris being selected ("crowned" was the term that he and some of the faculty used) as the new dean, was when he read the news in the *Washington Post*. I am convinced that there was a certain amount of professional jealously, and likewise some resistance to the fact that they were to be supervised by a woman. From what we students were hearing, the faculty meetings were bastions of disrespectability, as claimed by many of my female student counterparts. As well, there were no other presidentially appointed former ambassadors on the faculty, who had also seconded the nomination of a U.S. president (Johnson) at that time.

An unrelated crisis developed in February 1969, the same month that Harris assumed her position. A professor, whose credentials many students had already been questioning, administered an examination which about 25% of the class failed. As I later came to understand the matter, there was grumbling during the exam about certain questions and issues that were raised under the applicable law. And when the exam was graded and the test scores distributed, there was an explosion, which shortly degenerated into a protest and then another law school disruption.

Many of the same issues that SBA President Blakey (Class of 1968) faced during the prior year, were raised anew in 1969, and I, now serving as the elected SBA president, found myself in his shoes. By now my focus was upon graduation, having taken my photo and submitted my under photo narrative for the yearbook. Already I was interviewing for jobs, including just returning from travel to Chicago for an interview. I hardly wanted to be at the helm of another crisis, this one, unlike the prior two school disruptions in 1968, being strictly an in-house matter.

Harris initially gave some consideration to the students' grievances about the examination, but did not conclude that she should intervene and readjust the test scores. She told me that the administering of the test and grading was a faculty prerogative. Therefore, the handling of the matter was best left for the professor and his students to negotiate further and try to work out the details and settle the dispute. I do not know whether there was a side bar conference, that included her bringing the professor into her office for consultations about how the dean thought that they matter should be addressed and resolved.

From the students' perspective, her response was insufficient and represented a refusal to give their grievances some legitimate consideration. As well, the faculty was watching closely, to see if the then newly installed dean – then in place for only a couple of weeks at the time of the crises – would play a heavy student-favorable hand, which faculty could interpret as an inappropriate interference into faculty academic prerogative. On the whole, as the number of protest days increased, both sides became further indignant towards each other, despite the fact that only one faculty member's action was at issue. Negotiations quickly came to an impasse.

### Quander Posits Reasons for End of Law Boycott[48]

*The Student Bar Association President, Rohulamin Quander, answered some major questions concerning the accomplishments of the law school boycott.*

*Question – What was the rationalization of the law student's capitulation?*
*Answer – To begin with, the word "capitulation" is inappropriate and conveys a meaning inconsistent with what, in fact, happened. The law students did not capitulate, but decided that the boycotting of classes ceased to be an effective tactic as a means of realizing our goal of meaningful student participation in the final decision-making process. ... The law student body met and voted to end the boycott as a tactic and to instead seek other means and tactics to force the faculty and administration to the conference table with the intent to accede to our demands.*

*Question – What are you doing now?*
*Answer – Consistent with the idea of seeking to focus additional attention upon the plight of the law school, we decided that we would have to expand our total area of involvement, reorganize our steering committee and decentralize the lines of thinking into various committees. ...*

---

[48] *Extracts from the interview of Rohulamin Quander, Student Bar Association President, Howard University School of Law, by Romona Jones, as appeared in the Hilltop the university newspaper, on March 14, 1969, as the 21 day law student boycott finally came to an end.*

## GRADUATION AND ENTERING LAW SCHOOL

*[W]e are further agitating to testify before the house of Representatives Committee investigating the problems of student unrest and the causes of same, with alternative remedies. It should be noted here that we are in contact with certain Black Congressmen who are extremely concerned with the problems of Howard University.*

*Question – To what extent have your demands been met?*
*Answer – We feel that if the student interest is to be fairly and adequately represented in these [law school] committees, then it is incumbent that students be represented in all areas that substantially affect students. Similarly, we are not seeking to control these various committees, but only that our participation be meaningful, that it that we also be vested with power (votes) to see that the recommendations of the committee be adopted as posed, rather than suffer a demise at the hands of insensitive faculty members. ...*

And once again, the SBA was thrown into a situation where we were outside of the realm for which we were created. The SBA's role is to deal with student-related issues, but from a position of governance and formulating policies. It is not equipped to be getting into disputes over test scores. I said as much to those who wanted the SBA to take a more activist role. Caught between a rock and a hard place, I scheduled an appointment with Dean Harris, and was graciously received by her in her office on short notice.

At the outset of the meeting on that cold blustery February afternoon, she threw down a gauntlet, and said to me, "I will not negotiate anything with your colleagues (referring to my fellow law students) until they return to class. Then we can sit down, like reasonable and responsible adults, and talk this thing out." I replied, "I too would like that to happen, but my colleagues are so angry, that they want to negotiate from a position of strength, and feel that maintaining that position requires them to remain out of class until some meaningful progress on the issue is made." The meeting was short, and went nowhere. She offered me a cup of tea and some cookies, both of which I enjoyed, and I said adieu. I did not realize as that moment that our first meeting on that subject, would likewise be our last.

With the crisis at impasse, and Harris seemingly unwilling to negotiate with students who were not in class, and disruptive to the orderly function of the law school, this activist cadre of students took their protest to another level. Despite supposed assurances having been given by the university administration that the president's office would not entertain an end run around the dean's authority, the opposite occurred. While the details of the resolution are fuzzy after 45 years, sufficient is to say that the students came away from a meeting with President James Nabrit and his staff, satisfied that they had "won."

A satisfactory resolution had occurred. Some of the grades were adjusted, although I cannot recall just how they were adjusted, and the continuation of the student protest came to an end. Of course it did not sit well with me, as I felt that the university central administration had caved in to student demands. I must give consideration to several salient elements which influenced Nabrit's decision.

First, the entire university community was still on edge, including the prior law school student protest in 1968. Second, the assassination of Dr. King on April 4, 1968, totally disrupted the entire national capital city. Third, there were nation-wide student protests, and in 1969, Howard was simmering, as students protested the relevance of the university, the supposed intransigence of the black middle class who were not "down with the people," and the actions of anyone over 30 years of age. I concluded then, and reaffirm my beliefs now, that President Nabrit and his administration did not want to draw greater attention to the state of unrest at Howard University, which had already piqued national awareness.

Then too, the issue of whether the law school's accreditation could be affected by the accumulation of so much unrest and so many protests coming in such a close sequence, was uppermost in the minds of the entire Howard law community. Despite the longstanding reputation and respect for the role of the law school and its graduates in the area of civil rights, Howard students were not enjoying a stellar pass rate on the various bar examinations.

## GRADUATION AND ENTERING LAW SCHOOL

Therefore, we did not want to inject anything into that equation which might call our competence or the possible compromising of the accreditation into question.

Furious with how this entire episode had been handled, Dean Harris resigned her deanship immediately, within about a month of her appointment. She determined that, as a matter of principle, she could not remain as dean, having been placed into such an untenable position. Without question, and she made it clear in her resignation, there was an open conflict with President Nabrit, himself the former dean of the law school until his elevation as president of the university. She publically accused him of undercutting her authority by negotiating directly with law students engaged in what they titled "a civil rights protest" which included a demand that she remove a faculty member who had given failing grades to 14 of about 56 students in a course.[49]

At the time, students across the nation, including at Howard, were demanding a meaningful role in both the university and the law school's governance. While I have little intention to examine that issue much further at this point, it is worthy of noting that in the post-1960s decade, a comprehensive study of student participation in law school governance was conducted by George P. Smith, II, Associate Professor of Law, the University of Pittsburgh, and published in the *Washington University Law Review*. He published his findings in 1976 in an article titled, *Student Participation in University and Law School Governance*. The article did not mention Howard's law school, but cited Columbia University's law school as a typical case study. He noted that participatory democracy in an academic surrounding often descended into violence as a means of expressing one's political expressions, which circumstance was antithetical to any successful academic environment.[50]

Although Harris resigned from the deanship, she remained as a tenured professor on the law faculty for the balance of the academic

---

[49] *See J. Clay Smith, Patricia Roberts Harris: A Champion in Pursuit of Excellence, 29 Howard Law Journal, 437, 449-50 (1986).*

[50] *"Student Participation in University and Law School Governance," Washington University School of Law Review, Volume 1976, P. 38.*

year. She then left to pursue several of her other interests, including private practice, civil rights work, high profile activities in the national Democratic party, and membership on the corporate boards of IBM, Chase Manhattan Bank, and the Scott Paper Company, all Fortune 500 companies. This accumulated involvement kept her profile very high.

Several years later, after her tenure at Howard, and upon two nominations from President Jimmy Carter, she would hold two Cabinet Secretary positions, initially at Housing and Urban Development (1977-1979), and later, at Health, Education and Welfare (later renamed Health and Human Services, 1979-1980). Continuing in her accumulated status of "firsts," she was also the first African American woman to be appointed to a U.S. Cabinet position, and distinguished herself further, by being appointed a second time by the same president, to serve in a different cabinet position.

With the huge dustup over faculty governance, students' rights, and questions concerning the relevancy of the law school curriculum to the needs of the African American community having all been aired, the matter sort of came to an end. Not really, though! With the end of the school year approaching, and my class contemplating both graduation and taking bar exams, there was a need for everyone to buckle down and turn attention towards completing the academic year.

Perhaps this reality played as much a part in the quieting down of the protest activity as Nabrit's capitulation. His capitulation did not ultimately serve him that well. Sensing vulnerability in having caved in to law student demands, and operating in the highly tense political atmosphere that Howard was in during the spring of 1969, student demands for his resignation intensified and were realized later that same year, when he announced his retirement.

Having endured and persevered, one of Omega's Cardinal Principles, and likewise culminating a profession that had met with much success, especially for the benefit of discriminated against African Americans, I found it to be highly disrespectful for him to be repeatedly called an "Uncle Tom," by those who had neither knowledge nor appreciation for what he had done for so many for a sustained period. Regretfully, it is not inaccurate to say that President

## GRADUATION AND ENTERING LAW SCHOOL

James M. Nabrit, president of Howard from 1960 until 1969, resigned from the presidency in an atmosphere of disgrace.

I never agreed with this immature assessment. Nabrit was a civil rights giant. Alongside Thurgood Marshall and several others, he successfully pursued the granting of our civil rights as African Americans through many courts, some of which were outright hostile to him, both because of his race and the efforts to upset the apartheid apple cart. Still, begrudgingly in some instances, the courts were forced to agree with his logic and interpretation of the federal laws to the advantage of African Americans.

Slow in his speaking pattern, and very "Georgia" in his drawl, his demeanor disarmed many a hostile white person, who otherwise might have thought that this was a simple Negro, not a man of great knowledge, intelligence, and skill. I am proud to say that I was one of his mentees. While I did not have a personal relationship with him, I met him on many occasions, and visited his presidential office a few times, incidental to my position as a student government leader or organizational representative on campus.

As well, he was another outstanding Man of Omega, and always kept the image of what an Omega man should be before all of us. We (the Alpha and Kappa Psi Chapter brothers) greatly respected and admired Bro. Nabrit, and appreciate what he had done for our race, and the indignities that he suffered at the hands of the white establishment, in the process of pursing and assuring our constitutional rights. For him to be so pushed out of the university, resigning at a time when he had much more service to give, was not a good thing.

But he lived to be 97 years of age (1900-1997), and rendered sustained and appreciated service to the Washington, D.C. community during his almost 30 years of retirement. Fortunately, he lived long enough to witness that the university that he had served from 1936 until 1969, was still at the forefront of American leadership, and that time and events were both kind to him. As the protest generation of the 1960s matured, many of them gained an appreciation for the sustained efforts that Nabrit extended on their and their parents' and grandparents' collective behalf.

## 50+ OMEGA INSPIRED YEARS

Things calmed down considerably after the 1968 riots and renewed protests of 1969. We had witnessed student take overs around the country in 1968, with Howard students shutting down the administration building and thus effectively closing the university in the Spring of 1968. This action related to the issue regarding the claimed irrelevancy of much of what Howard was pursing as its mission. As well, we had sustained the assignation of Dr. King on April 4, 1968, and the subsequent riots across the nation. Then again, in 1969, we had the law school fray that resulted in further tumult and daily unrest from February until graduation day.

By now, I was ready for a much deserved rest. I had been an SBA leader for all three years. First year as Class Representative, second year as SBA Vice President, and finally, SBA President in my third and final year. I had had more than enough. Beyond graduation, my concentration was on passing the bar examination, and getting into a career of legal service.

It was an atmosphere where many African American law school graduates, especially at Howard, were caught up in the focus and demand of "being relevant to the needs of the black community," as if that was a sing word. Many of us were truly dedicated to becoming foot soldiers in the War on Poverty, a concept and social action program against poverty in the U.S. This objective was imbedded into our daily consciousness by President Lyndon B. Johnson, who made the "War" as a centerpiece of his presidential administration. It was also the time when the war in Vietnam was grabbing our daily attention, as several of our classmates from high school, college, and even law school were drafted and given a uniform and a rifle, and directed to the rice field of South East Asia. A few of them never returned alive.

I too was bitten by that atmosphere, determined to make a difference, as I interviewed for a number of social service jobs, before accepting an offer from the D.C. Neighborhood Legal Services program (NLSP), and being assigned to Law Office #1, then located at Ninth and P Streets, N.W. The pay was agonizingly low, $10,000 per year, typical of poverty program salaries. The running joke was that we too, as poverty program employees, would have to likewise suffer some, in order to better understand the plight of those who we

## GRADUATION AND ENTERING LAW SCHOOL

served. At $10,000 per year, even in 1969 dollars, it was very difficult to make ends meet. And if I had had a wife and children at that time, it would not have been possible to work for such a little bit of money, unless my spouse had a larger salary than I did at that time.

I got along well with everyone at the office. We represented clients in landlord and tenant matters, domestic relations, qualification for benefits in social service programs, and generally served their needs, which were often not of a legal nature. That was always another concern. Critics of the concept of free legal services were watchdogs, looking to criticize and threatened to remove or restrict our funding on the accusation that these type of programs were "meddling" in the affairs of the free enterprise system. They deprived "legitimate lawyers" from being able to earn their living.

"Legitimate lawyers!" What did they think that we were doing? With the exception of occasional *pro bono* legal services donated by some of the major law firms, but then only for short periods of time, no law firm was going to take on representing clients who had no money. That is where we came into play. Funded by the federal government and with grants from the private sector, the legal services programs throughout the U.S. were largely restricted to representing clients who met income guidelines, which also meant that they could not afford an attorney when a problem arose.

As well, the central office of the D.C. program had a small staff that specialized in taking on larger issues, or suing on behalf of groups (class actions), i.e. individuals who, for example, might have a building-wide housing problem with a deep pockets landlord who was focused on getting his rent, but giving little in return. Such situations were beyond what we could generally handle in a small neighborhood office of two or three attorneys.

It was during this period that I met Geraldo Rivera, attorney, journalist, author, reporter, and later talk show host. He was then a recent 1969 graduate from Brooklyn Law School. Beyond the NLSP program, there was the Reginald Heber Smith Program, a grant-funded program, which targeted special needs legal services, and provided funds for certain programs to add a few additional attorneys to an office or city program as needed. Rivera was one of those selected law fellows, as was Willie Cooke, one of the attorneys in my office.

They were both activist-focused, and had many issues that they were working on to increase national attention and focus upon the needs of the poor. Rivera, who was claiming his place as an activist on behalf of Puerto Rican causes, travelled to D.C. routinely to meet with Willie and other fellows. Together, they held several of their meetings in Willie's second floor office in our lowly digs at Ninth and P Streets, N.W. I first met Geraldo in the early Fall of 1969, standing on the sidewalk in front of the building. Willie introduced him by saying, "He's going places!" I had no idea at that time who Geraldo Rivera was, but I quickly came to know otherwise as both his visibility and credibility arose, not just for Puerto Ricans, but as a universal drum major for the poor and deprived.

With the passage of time, however, many have soured on him. Several of his viewing audience have noted that he has morphed over time from political activist on behalf of the poor and underrepresented, to a politically conservative Republican. He had been accused of grabbing headlines at the expense of others, his acidic tongue focused upon the work of his fellow journalists, and his sustained identity as a component of the conservative Fox News network.

I worked at Law Office #1 of NSLP for about one year, and not having yet passed the D.C. bar examination, I elected to pursue a masters in labor law through the Urban Law Institute program, founded by law professors Dr. Edgar S. Cahn and his wife, Jean Camper Cahn. The program was based at George Washington University, and our classes were held thee. The idea was to learn to use the law effectively to fight poverty, and to assure that the poor were well represented in the pursuit of their constitutional rights.

I did not care for the program, which seemed to be more the personal project of the Cahns, than what I initially anticipated. Therefore, I left after a few months. Shortly thereafter, the relationship between the Cahns and the university ended, allegedly on a sour note. However, the Cahns, resilient as ever, managed to create the Antioch School of Law (now the Dave Clarke School of Law,

## GRADUATION AND ENTERING LAW SCHOOL

University of the District of Columbia) out of the ashes of that experience.

# XVI – Starting Over, Continuing With My Legal Career

At this point in my life, early 1971, I was at a crossroads. Having been in school since 1949, not including nursery school (I never went to Kindergarten), for the first time in over 20 years, I was not in school. Now it was time to grow up and make something of myself. "The party is over!" And I realized that for me, it was time to refocus and to start over. It was a good thing, though, for I needed to make some adjustments. Having completed law school, been involved in two successive social action programs at both the Neighborhood Legal Services and the Urban Law Institute (both an academic program and social action in the law), I felt that my offered services were not being fully developed or appreciated.

What had been billed as providing services that were relevant to the needs of black people, had morphed into my own personal poverty, which was increasing by the day. I asked myself, is this what we've been talking about all these last several years, about being "relevant to the needs of the black community?" If so then poverty stinks, and I will not get to go much further if I restricted myself to this personal poverty that was only going to be worse if I did not change courses, and quickly. I was determined to never abandon the needs of those less fortunate, but still felt that I needed to be in a different position, one from which I could really lift as I climbed. And to date, what I had seen and was experiencing was in no way going to get me there.

I had taken the D.C. bar twice, and had not passed. I wondered whether the failure was in any way due, at least in part, to the three truly tumultuous years that I spent at Howard's law school? But I cannot "blame" Howard for that, as others in my class were passing the bar exams and being admitted to practice law in Washington, D.C. and elsewhere. I was determined to buckle down, give it a third, and hopefully final try. In the interim, I worked a few temporary jobs, including at a marketing development company. Looking back, I was drifting, but had not lost sight of my intended goal – to pass the exam and get into the legal profession, possibly into private practice. Upon my third attempt, I passed the exams of both the District of Columbia and Pennsylvania during the same examination cycle. Indeed, my focus and hard work paid off, and I earned two prizes as a result of a singular coordinated effort.

I was sworn into both bars in February 1974, and immediately took a term appointment with the U.S. Presidential Clemency Board, which was created under President Gerald Ford to assess the issue of whether to grant presidential pardons to many of the Vietnam era service men who received less than honorable discharges from the military for offences and actions that they committed while in the U.S. military services. It felt good to be working directly back in the law, although the job was term, and offered no opportunity for promotion or career status.

In 1971, which was earlier in this same general period, my dad experienced a major milestone in his life, one that forever will be recognized for its lasting significance. For about 800 years, the Catholic Church did not have permanent deacons, having abolished the permanent diaconate service in about the year 1,1000. The abolition of permanent deacons was politically motivated by the feeling of many in the church hierarchy that the deacons, who were both more personable and accessible and who worked more closely with the faithful, were usurping the roles and purpose of the sacred priesthood. It was then decided to abandon the *permanent* diaconate, but to leave in place the *temporary* diaconate positions of "sub deacon" and "deacon" as two intermediate steps towards the final step of ordination into the priesthood.

With the increased shortage of priests worldwide, it was decided in the late 20th Century that the position of permanent deacons, most of whom were married men with families, needed to be brought back into service. Recruited in 1968, my father was ordained a permanent deacon by the Archdiocese of Washington on September 11, 1971, after a three-year intense training cycle. History was made that day, as he was one of the original 16 permanent deacons to be ordained in the United States, upon the permanent diaconate's revival. It was an important honor to be included in the *Very First Class* of the revived program, an honor and recognition which he cherished for the rest of his life.

## STARTING OVER, CONTINUING WITH MY LEGAL CAREER

As he grew older, may people asked him questions about his being recognized for his diabetic longevity (recognized since 1921) and his experiences as a member of the first class of Catholic permanent deacons ordained in the United States. After frequently sharing his many stories, whether in small groups, or as a CVS pharmacy invitee to discuss the challenges of being a diabetic to members of the local community, he was exhorted to reduce his story to writing, and to share it with others for longevity purposes. Although it would be years before he did so, after sharing his stories with many others, beginning mostly in the 1970s, and later, he and I co-wrote the story of his life. *The Quander Quality – The True Story Of A Black Trailblazing Diabetic*,[51] was widely acclaimed for both its historical content and upbeat approach to getting diabetics and their families to understand that diabetes is a challenge, but not a death sentence. He would often say. "Diabetes is not a death sentence, but rather challenge to live!"

After my 1974-75 term appointment with the U.S. Presidential Clemency Board ended, I entered the private practice of law upon the invitation of Ernest C. Dickson, a 1920 graduate of the Howard School of Law. His office was located at 913 U Street, N.W., an historically significant address for Omega, which I did not know at the time. As my much older associate, he provided me with a great opportunity to get into the field of private law practice, where I quickly came to appreciate that a sole or small office practitioner's work is never done. With only myself working, as he was past 85 years of age, and not doing much in the profession, everything fell up my shoulders. He had earned his retirement time, and mostly came into the office to oversee his real estate holdings and to just get out of the house for a few hours.

Don't miss a deadline. Don't miss a court date. Get in touch with a witness and prepare for trial, or gather the information needed to support a personal injury claim. And not the least – be certain to keep track of the client's money, so as not to co-mingle them and other

---

[51] *Co-authored by James W. Quander and Rohulamin Quander, Robert D. Reed Publishers, Bandon, Oregon, 2006.*

funds or to mishandle. That will surely get you before the bar committee upon a client complaint. No one wants that.

Then too, was the issue of just how far I could spread my professional wings, without expanding myself into an area of law where my professional knowledge and competence might be questioned. I learned early that the issue of professional competence is always a matter of concern in small office practice. In a larger office, there are systems and individuals who keep track of schedules, dates when filings must be made, and how much time the attorney spends on each case or components of a case. They also handle the client's funds, which removes some of the opportunities where an otherwise competent attorney might run afoul by mishandling a client's estate or money.

In a small law office, especially where you are the sole attorney, you have to do it all. Even if you hire a secretary or paralegal, the buck stops with you. If your staff misbehaves, the complaint, if there is one, will be lodged against you, calling both your legal competence and professionalism into question. Looking back and having vacated a full-time private practice (1975-1982), I was never subject to any complaint about mishandling or misappropriation of a client's funds.

When I moved into the 913 U Street, N.W., building, Mr. Dickson mentioned to me that the site used to be the local operations office of the *Pittsburgh Courier* newspaper. Although he had owned the building for several years, he did not add to the conversation, and perhaps was unaware, that the local editor for the Washington, D.C. office was an Omega brother, and that for several years, the *Oracle*, our fraternity's national publication, was published from that same office.

I discovered this latter point years later in 2010, when I was working on an Omega history project for the Third District (Washington, D.C. and Virginia). I noticed, printed on the publication information page of a 1920s *Oracle that* "913 U Street, N.W., Washington, D.C." was the operational location for the periodic publication. It makes sense though, because Murray Brothers Printers, then located directly across the street, was listed as the printer for the periodical. I contacted Murray Brothers and inquired whether they still had an Omega-related materials left over from the 1920s. They

## STARTING OVER, CONTINUING WITH MY LEGAL CAREER

did not, advising that the archival materials that they once had from that era had been long ago disposed of.

I am comfortable in knowing, however, that I did not abandon or overlook any Omega archival documents when I vacated the building for another location in 1981. Although still unaware of the site's connection to Omega and the *Oracle* at that time, I examined the building carefully before I moved. There was nothing there of historical significance. But if those walls could talk, what would they have said? I am certain that they would have much to say. Bro. Stephen Douglas, the first editor in the 1919 initial edition of the *Oracle* was still on the scene. William Stuart Nelson, editor for the sole 1920 issue, a man who I knew and greatly respected, would likewise have his view and say.

### Rekindling An Old Relationship

Overlapping is this time cycle of the early 1970s, I was living in New York working for a marketing company. I rekindled my long-established relationship with Carmen, my high school sweetheart. Despite our having gone our separate ways over the years, she was always there. When she came down from New York to D.C., we would often get together, go dancing or to a party. Our families also saw each other at mass on some Sundays at Sacred Heart. And the question was always, "How is Carmen?" or "How is Ro? Tell him I asked about him."

Well, she would undoubtedly say that she was not necessarily my high school "sweetheart." Because I had so many of them. "Sweethearts" is probably more of an accurate term. I previously mentioned a couple of them, but elected not to delve into too much detail about any of them, except for Carmen, whom I eventually would marry. We met in August 1950 at the birthday party of Richard Washington, our lifelong friend.

She was just five years old, and I was six. What we did not know at that moment, was that she and I, along with Richard, and Carmen's brother, Ramberto, would literally integrate the Sacred Heart Elementary School the following month, September 1950, which is when the parochial schools of the Archdiocese of Washington integrated and accepted their first children from the African Diaspora.

## 50+ OMEGA INSPIRED YEARS

Carmen, Richard, and Ramberto (we call him "Ramsey") were first generation Americans from mothers who migrated from the Dominican Republic. Carmen and Ramsey's father was Puerto Rican, considered as "foreign" by many Americans who did not want anyone who was not white. Richard's mother was also Dominican, while I was first generation American on my mother's side as well, she having immigrated from Barbados, then part of the British West Indies. Together, the four of us constituted the "colored" enrollment at the elementary school level. Little did Carmen and realize that fate would shine upon us, and the later, in the 1970s, we would marry and be the proud parents of Iliana, Rohulamin, and Fatima.

## XVII – The Middle Period, The 1980's, My Second Omega Jubilee

It is all too typical for many of Omega's sons to migrate away from the central core of what Omega stands for, once they get involved with the demands of marriage, a young family, and efforts to get ahead in their careers. My situation was not any different in that respect. Having then recently joined into a small two-person private practice of law, and the attending responsibilities of a family (a wife at home with three small children), my focus turned in a different direction. With these responsibilities, neither Carmen nor I was idle.

Still, I managed to get away from D.C. for the 57th Grand Conclave, convened in August 1976 in Atlanta, Georgia. Carmen stayed home, while I hitched a ride with Bro. Gilbert Colwell. We took along a young neophyte, David Garza, an Hispanic brother from Milwaukee, Wisconsin. This was his first conclave and, like most neophytes, he was basking in his new-found status as a proud Omega man. He met this comely AKA neophyte on the first day of arrival, and we hardly ever saw him afterwards. We all had a great time. For me it was especially refreshing, since I had not attended a grand conclave since 1968 in Charlotte, North Carolina, where I first met Bro. Jesse Jackson, who was then a recent Second Vice Grand Basileus. Although he and I were present at the Beta Chapter's 50th anniversary program on April 5, 1964, I did not have the opportunity then to meet him. My recess from Omega was not so much a loss of interest, but rather a great demand upon my time, as my interest and devotion to Omega has never waned during my 50 years of brotherhood.

I secured a legal position with the D.C. Department of Consumer and Regulatory Affairs (DCRA) in 1986, and remained there for 16 years, rising to the level of administrative law judge. While there, I came into legal prominence from an unexpected source. In February 1998, I was appointed as the Mayor's Agent for Historic Preservation for the District of Columbia. This appointment came as a surprise, on the tail end of a controversy of which I was initially unaware. By way of background, someone else, who was a contract employee of DCRA, had been serving as Mayor's Agent for about two years.

The District was experiencing a financial crisis and budget cuts were being implemented, seeking to save governmental expenditures. The general consensus was that the deputy supervisor of our office did not hold any of us, all African Americans, in particular regard. Steadfastly and, for a few years, he successfully insisted that a certain Caucasian female must be continued on contract, because there was no one on staff in the Office of Adjudication who was "capable" of conducting the Mayor's Agent hearings and rendering credible, legally sufficient decisions. These decisions would have to be able to withstand the inevitable appeals that would be made to the D.C. Court of Appeals, if the ruling against the property owner was adverse to their desired result. How insulting to each of us, most all of whom had membership in the D.C. bar, and were fully capable of applying the historic preservation law, should we be assigned to this new undertaking.

When the latest round of budget cuts took effect, I was called into the office of the agency director, and informed that I had been appointed as the new Mayor's Agent, and that I would work with the director of the Historic Preservation Office to be introduced to the governing law and underlying circumstances of several cases that were waiting to be heard by the Mayor's Agent. Thus, the deputy director of my office had been overturned by the agency director and Mayor Marion Barry. The contract employee was soon terminated and I took on this new role, in addition to the full case load that was ongoing from my other area of jurisdiction.

I was likewise informed that this new assignment would fit under the "other duties as assigned" component of my job description, and therefore, there would be no additional compensation for my undertaking. The director then added, "You were selected because we are aware of your interest in history and how much you have been doing with regard to Washington, D.C., history and the Quander Family. I think that this new assignment will be a good fit for you, and interesting too." And with that statement, my new found tenured status began.

## THE MIDDLE PERIOD, THE 1980's, MY SECOND OMEGA JUBILEE

Under the preservation law of the District of Columbia, if a real property has been designated as historic or the collective properties in a particular quadrant of the city have been designated as contributing to the historic fabric of the neighborhood, the property owners cannot demolish, alter, partition, or add new exterior construction without first obtaining the approval of the Historic preservation Review Board (HPRB). Obtaining that approval can be very tricky and difficult, depending upon the scope of what the property owner is seeking to do.

The preservation law provides that, in the event that the HPRB denies the sought after relief, the affected property owner can take exception and file for an administrative hearing before the Mayor's Agent for Historic Preservation, who literally serves in place of the mayor of the District of Columbia. The decision that is rendered by the Mayor's Agent is the final decision of the mayor, but can still be appealed to the District of Columbia Court of Appeals.

I undertook the new assignment with both gusto and uncertainty, never thinking for one moment that I would still be serving in that capacity until 2010, 12 years later, when I decided that it was time to let the reins go. Yet, in that 12-year period, I played a major role in preserving the historical fabric of Washington, D.C. buildings, and in shaping the skyline of the National Capital City for generations to come. My role as Mayor's Agent was not full time. The law only called for the Mayor's Agent to serve as a hearing officer when the applicant and the District could not agree on how or what the applicant wanted to change on an historic building or make some modifications in an historic district.

Still, it was a most important role, considering both the immediate and long term effects of modifying an historic site, which pursuant to the historic preservation laws, was intended to be enjoyed and appreciated by both present and future generations. I rendered more than 80 decisions, some of which were obviously more significant than others. Among the most important decisions, I allowed subdivision (which also included joining two or more sites into one), alternation, new construction, and on rare occasion, even demolition.

# 50+ OMEGA INSPIRED YEARS

## XVIII – Coming Into My Own, A Diversity Of Experiences

At this time, I elect to drift back, reaching across the decades, tying together certain experiences that I have over time that underscore the diversity that has been my life. Some of the time frames noted have already been visited, but hopefully this time the reader will be further enlightened by fresh approaches, as I seek to draw a line from then to now.

As I noted previously, I entered Howard University as a freshman in September 1961, the same month that Nellie May Quander died, at the age of 81. Although I do not recall ever meeting her, my dad knew her for many years and made a practice of staying in contact with her. She never taught him during his brief enrollment at Shaw Junior High School (September – October 1930), before he was transferred to Garnett-Paterson by his doctor, so that he could be closer to home for medical reasons. But still he felt a continued closeness to her, because of her befriending him during his brief several week enrollment at Shaw, taking him around and introducing him as "my young cousin." This was the opposite behavior of her sister, Susie R. Quander, who taught Civics at Garnett-Patterson. For three years, October 1930 until his June 1933 graduation, Susie ignored my dad, although she certainly knew who he was.

In later years, my dad rekindled his contact with Nellie, and would see her out at luncheons and other daytime social activities, always cordial and later continuing telephone contact with her. So when she died, it was only natural that he would make plans to attend her funeral. However, things developed somewhat differently. On the morning of the wake, he got a telephone call from Kitty Bruce, Nellie's cousin on the other side of the family.

Kitty said to my dad, James, "I know that you were always fond of Cousin Nellie, and you probably know of the certain estrangements within the family.[52] I am not certain who among the Quanders will be

---

[52] *Nellie Quander and he sister, Susie, had a fractured relationship that endured for decades. The underlying reason for the rupture is not*

at the wake, and available to stand at the casket. It would be so embarrassing if no Quander family member stood by her casket. I do not want to take a chance of that happening. Are you available?" Kitty, whom I knew, although she was an age contemporary to Cousin Nellie, went on the say, "The wake will be at the Lincoln Temple Congregational Church, and we expect a large number of visitors, who must be greeted, especially the leadership and membership of the Alpha Kappa Alpha Sorority."

Honored at the request, my dad immediately agreed and made plans to be present for the entire multi-hour wake and for the funeral on the next day. After he had been present for quite some time, greeting the many guests, some of whom he knew as fellow Washingtonians, Susie Quander, Nellie's sister, and several other Quander family members arrived at the wake, which had been ongoing for well more than an hour. As Kitty anticipated, their prior conspicuous absence underscored that all was not well within that sector of the family. She later told my dad that she was very relieved that he was available, and made his presence known to visitors who did not readily know that he was a Quander. Later, well after the funeral, dad related that while many of the visitors already knew that he was a Quander family member, they did not necessarily know that the sanguine relationship was quite distant.

As Susie stepped up to the casket, and seeing and likewise knowing full well who my father was, she, in her typical brusque manner, inquired, "And just who are you?", to which my dad replied, "My name is Quander, the same as yours, and after all these years, for you to pretend that you don't know who I am, then shame on you." He then withdrew from the casket area and took a seat in the

---

*certain, but is thought to have something to do with the long time separation of third parents, John Pierson Quander and Hannah Bruce Ford Quander, who never divorced. The daughters are said to have sided with different parents. As well, Susie, who was two years younger, made efforts to separate herself from Nellie's social circle, which some say contributed to why Susie joined the 1920-founded Zeta Phi Beta Sorority, rather than to be in Nellie's Alpha Kappa Alpha shadow. In their late years, some reconciliation occurred, but the relationship was said to be still strained.*

sanctuary. The incident occurred in the presence of many who both heard and saw, and some people came to him afterwards and said, "James, don't worry about her. She's been like that for as long as we have known her. You did the right thing for Nellie, and no apologies or explanations are needed at this point."

Thus it was into this atmosphere of Nellie's immediate death that I was enrolled at Howard University. Her death in late Summer 1961, coincided with my finding my way around campus, getting to know a few new people, and making some new friends. At 17 years of age, I was not particularly aware of who Nellie M. Quander was. However, as soon as a couple of the campus pals, the organization that helped freshmen and transfer students get oriented to Howard, learned of my name and that I was "a Quander," they immediately were interested in me and asked questions of me that I could not yet answer. Both of these ladies were also members of AKA.

Typical of the questions asked were, How are you related to Nellie Quander? Was she your grandmother? What was she like as a person? Did you know that she was AKA's First Supreme Basileus? Did you know that she was the one who rescued our sorority when those "other women" broke away in 1912? Well No! I did not know that answer to any of those questions, and was likewise unaware of Nellie's role as related to those various activities. One thing for sure though, she was not my grandmother, although she and my grandparents most probably knew each other, since Nellie lived at 15th and T Streets, N.W., a few doors away from Howard and Jennie Quander, and visited them regularly, as did my grandparents, John Edward and Maude Pearson Quander, who lived at 17th and T Streets, N.W.

But it was from that time to the present that my interest in Nellie Quander and her historical significance on several fronts was piqued. Over time I would research her life, her contributions and significance, and eventually write her biography, *Nellie Quander, Alpha Kappa Alpha Pearl*, subtitled, *The Story of the Woman Who Saved an International Organization*, published in 2008, to coincide with AKA's Centennial Celebration.

## 50+ OMEGA INSPIRED YEARS

All too often many of us who belong to Black Greek Letter Organizations (BGLO) drift away from our fraternities and sororities, overtaken by many of life's demands, including family obligations. And keeping current with our BGLO obligations is often relegated to the second tier. Sometimes, and all too frequently, we never put out fraternal affiliations back into a place of prominence or priority.

On the same day when we were inducted into Omega, April 4, 1964, others likewise took a scared oath to always uphold "Noble Kappa Alpha Psi," "Sweet AKA," or "Dynamic Delta." But then reality set in, and we drifted in other directions. What about the pledge that we made on that most significant day? Did we forget the sacrifices that we made in order to get through the process? And now what? Does it still mean anything to us after all of these years? These are soul searching questions, one that each inductee must ask him or herself, and likewise come up with a recent answer.

In my case, I was no exception. Having graduated from Howard Law School in 1969, I entered private practice in 1974, after a series of further legal study and law-related jobs for nonprofits and temporary appointments in the federal government. With a wife who worked periodically for the government in a number of term appointments, but made us all proud with her school, church, and community involvements, bringing home the bacon fell mostly upon my shoulders. That was fine, but required a carefully monitored expenditure of the limited resources.

It was in this same general time frame that I was invited by my cousin, Norbert King, to join the Pigskin Club of Washington, Inc., a men's sport club, which initially focused upon following football, and honoring African Americans who were making a mark in that sport. The club was chartered in 1938 by Dr. Charles Fisher, partly in direct response to the refusal of the Touchdown Club of Washington, Inc., to admit Negro members or honor our race's athletes. Dr. Fisher contacted a group of local prominent men who became the club's charter members. The theme of the club, "Democracy in Sports" was adopted shortly after its founding. Dr. Fisher stated in his initial letter of invitation to the first meeting, the following:

## COMING INTO MY OWN, A DIVERSITY OF EXPERIENCES

*That there be an ever improving relationship between persons interested in the game of football; that there may be given encouragement for good clean sport; that there may be a more perfect understanding among such persons; and that there may be mutual benefits and pleasures derived from such association.*[53]

Although, to the best of my knowledge, Dr. Fisher was not a member of Omega, his central theme for the club's Purpose was certainly one of Uplift, which is one of Omega's four Cardinal Principles. Further, as a member of the club since the mid-1980s, I have been impressed by the club's commitment to brotherhood among its membership, not unlike Omega's commitment to same. Until I was writing this memoir, I never compared the list of Alpha Omega Chapter charter members of 1922, with the Pigskin Club's first meeting invitees or charter members of 1938.

While my list is not comprehensive, and surely I missed a few, the following names appear on both lists: Edwin Bancroft Henderson (the Pigskin Club's first vice president), Campbell C. Johnson, Alfred Kiger Savoy, Garnet Crummel Wilkerson, Charles Herbert Marshall, Jr., and Robert Nicholas Mattingly. As well, several other Omega men, some of whom were also the charter members of Alpha Omega Chapter, joined the Pigskin Club within a few months of its founding. In 2013, the Pigskin Club of Washington, Inc., observed its 75th anniversary, and commemorated that milestone with a series of sports, service, and cultural activities befitting the occasion. As well, the club elected to admit women about 10 years ago, and as of this writing, Lucille Hester, a well-known sports figure in her own right, serves as the club's first female president.

My active participation in the Pigskin Club for about 30 years also mandates a commitment of specific time, certain efforts, and the production of some visible gains each year. The dues are reasonable. I am still wrapped up with the club, although not as much as before. As I have gotten older, I find that the demands upon my time have not

---

[53] *From the Pigskin Club's "Statement of Purpose," as recited in the club's 72nd Annual Awards Dinner program, based upon the initial July 1938 letter of invitation from Charles Fisher, M.D., Organizer.*

decreased to the extent that I anticipated. Working with my wife in pursuit of her art career, my continued focus upon Omega, and engaging in various community activities, with a focus upon youth, has caused me to cut back on some other activities, including the Pigskin Club. And, at the age of 70 years, I have become a licensed tour guide in the District of Columbia and escort tour groups around Washington, D.C, often walking significant distances between sites.

Still, I remain devoted to the club and the principles upon which Dr. Fisher based his decision to reach out to the men in the community, and try his best to right the wrong that was visited upon us because of the complexion of our skin. And to that extent, the club has been most successful, as it has expanded itself to all forms of sports, and into recognition of men and women who have made a great difference in the quality of life in Washington, D.C. and beyond. In many cases, those contributions have been in areas other than the sports arena.

I was never too far away from Omega's fold, but for several years between 1990 and 2000, I drifted into many other endeavors. During that decade I continued to build my law career, including becoming an administrative law judge for the District of Columbia, a position that demanded much of my time. I retired as a senior ALJ on May 1, 2011. As well, during a portion of that time, I maintained a small private law practice focused upon probate matters. I continued and expanded my international travels to Barbados, my mother's birthplace, and my historical and genealogical research and writing. I found myself in demand by more than one museum component of the Smithsonian locally, plus many history-focused organizations. Beyond the usual lectures in D.C., Maryland, and Virginia, I lectured at Temple University, Philadelphia, the main library facility in Chicago, Morehouse College, Atlanta, and several annual historical conferences or Black history Month programs in North Carolina, Pennsylvania, Utah, Wisconsin, and Georgia.

Along the way I encountered several interesting people, including Etta Moten, the beautiful well-known African American movie actress from the old days. She was about 90 years old at the time. Carmen and I were attending an annual meeting of the Carter G. Woodson's Association for the Study of Afro-American Life and History

## COMING INTO MY OWN, A DIVERSITY OF EXPERIENCES

(ASALH), held in Durham, North Carolina. We were at a reception, when someone mentioned that my last name was Quander. Etta who was a member of Alpha Kappa Alpha, lit up, saying, "Quander! Are you related to Nellie Quander?" The answer of course, was "Yes!", at which time she took my arm and escorted me over to meet Dr. Lorraine Richardson Green, who I immediately learned was the second national president of AKA, succeeding Nellie Quander in 1919, when Nellie voluntarily stepped down in Green's favor.

Dr. Green, who was also at least 90 years old at the time, had driven her Sedan De Ville, a full sized Cadillac, by herself from Chicago to Durham for the ASALH meeting, and was fascinated to meet Carmen and me. She extolled how great Nellie was, and how, but for her determination and drive, there would no longer be an Alpha Kappa Alpha. Several years later, in 2008, when I was completing the then untitled biography of Nellie M. Quander, I thought back about what Dr. Green had said about Nellie, and elected to title the book, *Nellie Quander, Alpha Kappa Alpha Pearl,* subtitled, *The Story of the Woman Who Saved an International Organization.*

## 50+ OMEGA INSPIRED YEARS

## XIX – Just Beneath The Surface, An Unique Interaction With AKA

The final events of Alpha Kappa Alpha's Diamond Jubilee Celebration unfolded in Washington, D.C., AKA's birthplace, during the summer of 1984 at the sorority's 51st Boule. The sorority was founded at Howard University in 1908, with its 75th anniversary year actually being 1983. The sorority decided to celebrate certain events in 1983, but waited until the summer of 1984, the established biennial boule cycle, to have its Diamond Jubilee culmination. More than 10,000 sorors and guests attended the power-packed workshop sessions and festivities at the then recently opened Washington Convention Center. Howard University's campus, as an historical site, was visited by thousands of sorors and guests during the event. It took three years of planning, and the mutual cooperation of 12 chapters – graduate and undergraduate, from both the North Atlantic and Mid-Atlantic Regions, with a resounding and successful end result, driven by 36 host committees.[54]

The program included several prominent history makers and speakers from the political arena, including Maxine Waters and SCLC president, Rev. Joseph Lowery, all speaking to the essence of "power." AKA member and newly-installed Miss America, Suzette Charles, the second black Miss America, made one of her first public appearances at the Diamond Jubilee. Vanessa Williams, the first black Miss America, was forced to step down when it came to light that she had posed in several nude photographs. What a unique year that was. Both the winner and first runner up, Williams and Charles, were African American, and from the neighboring states of New York and New Jersey.

As well, Elizabeth Dole, the Secretary of Transportation and later a U.S. Senator, and Geraldine Ferraro, the Democratic vice presidential candidate for 1984, each addressed the convened

---

[54] *This information was extracted from the Alpha Kappa Alpha, Inc., official Centennial Celebration 1908-2008, Service to All Mankind web site.*

attendees. Gladys Knight and the Pips performed to high acclamation, after which Ms. Knight was delighted to accept the invitation to become an honorary member of AKA. The 75th anniversary theme was *Energizing for the Twenty-first Century,* with the recited organizational goals to always keep moving forward, to cement AKA's footprints in areas of international concern, operating under the moniker, "Service with a Global Perspective."[55]

Among the highlight events of the Diamond Jubilee boule was the formal establishment of the Nellie M. Quander Memorial Scholarship Fund, which had been initiated in late 1982/early 1983 by Esther Garland Pollard, the AKA Regional Director, with the help of several other sorors, most notably Zelma Chaney. Several Quander family members, upon learning of the creation of the scholarship, stepped forward and also made significant contributions. Honoring Nellie Quander's memory at that time, 1983, was also reminiscent of the fact that 70 years prior, in 1913, Nellie Quander, using her own money, created the first endowed organizational named academic prize at Howard University. The "Alpha Kappa Alpha Prize" was to be awarded to the graduating female senior with the highest academic average in the College of Liberal Arts.

By merit of her academic prowess, Eva Dykes, A.B. 1914, *Summa Cum Laude,* and one of the original pledged inductees into the 1913-established Delta Sigma Theta Sorority, was the winner of the first AKA prize, a $10.00 gold piece. It does not take too much imagination to figure out how the rebounding membership of AKA must have felt on that commencement day, to see the prize that their Supreme Basileus had established on behalf of AKA and in the sorority's name, be awarded to "an enemy." Of course Dykes was not really an enemy, and had deservedly earned the prize. Still, with enmity between the two organizations, and the wounds of a tumultuous separation still festering, I would imagine that there were some AKA sorors, had they

---

[55] *This information was extracted from the Alpha Kappa Alpha, Inc., official Centennial Celebration 1908-2008, Service to All Mankind web site.*

been given a choice in the matter, who would have refused to award to a Delta soror this valuable initial prize.[56]

Eva Dykes would later bring greater honor to both Delta and the African American race, when, in 1921, she became the first African American woman to earn a PhD. degree. Interesting though, 1921 was a banner year for African American women to each PhD. degrees, as two other African American woman also earned their degrees that same year.

The AKA prize, noted above, is still extant, now bearing the name, "The Nellie M. Quander Memorial Alpha Kappa Alpha Scholarship Fund," and funded by multiple resources, including Howard University, the AKA sorority, and donations from the public, including members of the Quander Family. While I do not have a quote or specific response from Nellie Quander, to reflect her reaction to learning that a Delta was being awarded the first AKA prize, knowing what I do of Nellie, I believe that she took and stayed on the high road, encouraging her young sorors to strive on, to try harder, and to prove, as she was known to say on frequent occasions, "that the Alpha Kappa Alpha woman must always create a memorable presence."

---

[56] *Still, it must have been a sour experience to have this academic prize, the first of its kind, be awarded to a "renegade," as the sorors of Delta were colloquially called on Howard's campus at the time. Not only did this award embarrass AKA, it underscored that the new sorors of Delta were credible, here to stay, and likewise were striving to maintain high academic standards, just as their "step-sisters" of AKA were focused on doing. In 1921, Dykes co-shared the honor of being the first African American woman to earn a PhD. (English), when she graduated from Radcliff College. Oddly enough, Dykes shared this 1921 honor with two other African American women. Sadie Tanner Mossell Alexander, a Found of Delta and niece of Henry Ossawa Tanner, acclaimed artist, earned her PhD. in economics from the University of Pennsylvania. Georgiana R. Simpson, an AKA, earned her PhD. in German from the University of Chicago. Both Dykes and Simpson would later teach at the famed Paul Laurence Dunbar High School in Washington, D.C.*

> *I announce to you this morning the forthcoming book, "Nellie Quander, Alpha Kappa Alpha Pearl," which will be available shortly. The book chronicles her life of service, and her dedication to others. Dr. Martin Luther King, Jr., said, "The ultimate measure of a woman is not where she stands in moments of comfort and convenience, but where she stands at times of challenge and controversy." In January 1913, Nellie Quander faced both a challenge and controversy. She took a stand, ... and made Alpha Kappa Alpha and all of us the better for it.*[57]

Nellie Quander is an historical icon within African American Greek letter organization circles. Known for her forcefulness in times of adversity, she led the fight in October 1912 to persuade the young, recently initiated sorors of AKS to not separate themselves from AKA's purpose and ideals, but instead to work within those circles to see what changes could be made to accommodate their wishes. Alas, it would not be so, and the 22 sorors elected to vacate the ranks of AKA and to charter another sorority, Delta Sigma Theta, in January 1913.

Since that time there has been a raging controversy about whether the sorors of AKA joined the March in the Women's Suffrage Procession, convened on Pennsylvania Avenue in downtown Washington, D.C. on March 3, 1913, the day before Woodrow Wilson as inaugurated at the 28th President of the United States. For well-nigh a century, Deltas have touted that they were the only black sorority that marched on that day, citing the assertion that appeared in a news article and buttressed by a group photo that included a banner on which was printed, "Delta Sigma Theta Sorority."

However, on March 1, 2013, as the women of Delta assembled in Washington, D.C., for the Centennial reenactment of the 1913 March, an article appeared on the Opinion Page of the *Washington Post*, "The Day the Deltas Marched Into History." The article was written by Mary Walton, the author of *A Woman's Crusade: Alice Paul and the*

---

[57] *Extract from Rohulamin Quander's prepared Centennial Remarks for the Alpha Kappa Alpha assembly, Andrew Rankin Chapel, Howard University, January 15, 2008.*

## JUST BENEATH SURFACE, AN UNIQUE INTERACTION WITH AKA

*Battle for the Ballot.* During her research, Walton uncovered two February 1913 letters written on Alpha Kappa Alpha Sorority letterhead, by Nellie Quander to Alice Paul, a principal person in the National American Woman Suffrage Association. In the initial letter, dated February 15, 1913, Quander requested that Negro women be included in the March, and that they be allowed to march with groups from their respective geographic areas, not subject to a "Negro section" placed at some other location.

```
NELLIE M. QUANDER, A. B.           Alpha Kappa Alpha Sorority           MINNIE B. SMITH, A. B.
       President                                                              Recording Sec'y
ETHEL G. JONES, A. B.                      Howard University              NORMA E. BOYD, A. B.
     Vice President                                                         Corresponding Sec'y
NELLIE M. PRATT, A. B.                                                   JULIA E. BROOKS, A. B.
  Second Vice President                                                         Treasurer

                                        Washington, D. C.

                                        February 15, 1913.


              Miss Alice Paul,
                    Chairman, Equal Suffrage Parade.
              Dear Madam.
                          There are a number of college women
              of Howard University who would like to partici-
              pate in the woman suffrage procession on Monday,
              March the third. We do not wish to enter if we
              must meet with discrimination on account of race
              affiliation. Can you assign us to a desirable
              place in the college women's section?


                                        Yours truly,

                                        Nellie M. Quander
                                        Pres. Alpha Kappa Alpha Sorority,
                                                Howard University.
```

**Nellie Quander letter demanding a place of respect in 1913 Suffragist March**

The tone of the second letter, also directed to Alice Paul, dated February 17, 1913, was stronger in determination and attitude. This discovery clearly and unequivocally refutes any assertion by Delta, in claiming to be the sole African American sorority that joined the

March. The newly rediscovered information reinforced AKA's long asserted claim that they too were present in significant numbers, and that the fact that they were not carrying a banner proclaiming the name "Alpha Kappa Alpha," did not mean that they were not present or concerned about the rights of women and others who were subjected to daily discrimination in their lives.

> *There are a number of college women of Howard University who would like to participate in the woman suffrage procession on Monday, March the third. We do not wish to enter if we must meet with discrimination on account of race affiliation. Can you assign us a desirable place in the college women's section?[58]*

While I have no definitive proof that Nellie and the other AKAs showed up on March 3, 1913, to participate in the March, surely they were present, and claimed places of physical prominence in the event as well. Why would Nellie work so hard, put her reputation on the line, and even possibly face physical danger for daring to insist on a proper place in the sun for Negro women, and then elect to stay home on the day that her hard won efforts were to be recognized and rewarded? It would make no sense to do that at all. Further, throughout their history, the AKA historians have repeatedly referred to the presence of Alpha Kappa Alpha women at the 1913 Suffrage March. No, AKA did not stay home. Yes, Nellie May Quander was surely at the forefront of everything that occurred on that day. Let the matter finally rest!

To Nellie Quander, AKA represented a way of life, a high-minded approach to what it meant to be an educated Negro woman at a time when most people in our society did not value women in a manner similar to what we do today. At that time, women were viewed largely as child bearers, who stayed home and cooked and took care of their husbands. The multi-faceted talents that women had to offer were squandered for the most part. There were a few exceptions, and

---

[58] *Extract from the letter of Nellie May Quander, President, Alpha Kappa Alpha Sorority, to Alice Paul, National American Woman Suffrage Association, dated February 17, 1913. No response by Paul to either of Nellie Quander's two letters has been found.*

those exceptions were most notable. Among those outstanding women, women of sustained achievement, Nellie Quander's presence was noted on many levels by distinguished men and women in authority, people who recognized that she was truly a woman of distinction, and through her sustained efforts, they likewise came to the realization that there were many more like her.

> *I am Rohulamin Quander, representing my family and Nellie May Quander, your lead national incorporator. Indeed, she is with us this morning, and I hope that I am worthy as her humble servant and voice, to tell you have absolutely ecstatic and proud she is at what God and Alpha Kappa Alpha have wrought over this past 100 years. Her vision, foresight, and determination stretched from the day she took her oath of allegiance in the Spring of 1910, and then served as Basileus at Howard University, 1911-1912, and then reorganizer, preserver, and the one who refocused the sorority, serving as your First Supreme Basileus, 1913-1919.*[59]

All of the above information that I have stated serves as a backdrop for a major event that occurred in the Spring of 1984. As well, in 1984, the Quander Family observed and celebrated its Tricentennial (1684-1984), the documented presence of the family in the New World, with a highlight celebration in the Blackburn Center at Howard University. One month later, it was AKA's turn, and, as a result of some careful planning and maneuvering, I returned to Blackburn as a part of that Boulé-related event.

A little background. In early February 1984, my home telephone rang. The caller was an AKA soror who, after introducing herself as one of the Diamond Jubilee organizers and a committee woman, asked me if I was available to bring greetings on behalf of Nellie Quander and the Quander Family at the Alpha Chapter alumni luncheon, scheduled for a Saturday afternoon. My reference to the July 1984 calendar indicates that the luncheon was held on either

---

[59] *Extract from Rohulamin Quander's prepared Centennial Remarks for the Alpha Kappa Alpha assembly, Andrew Rankin Chapel, Howard University, January 15, 2008.*

Saturday July 21st or 28th of that month. I was honored to accept, and immediately began to organize in my mind what my message should be.

Though allotted five minutes to speak, I felt that I could adequately convey a few words that would be reminiscent of Nellie, and likewise underscore to the assemblage that she believed very strongly in values and setting goals. Further, she was always focused on doing the right thing. "Yes," I said to myself, "I got this!"

A couple of days later, but still in February, I received a different kind of telephone call, this one from Dr. Dolores E. Cummings, a close childhood friend of mine, who was like a sister to me. A member of Xi Omega chapter of AKA, she was both furious and upset because Sheila Mitchell, her goddaughter and an outstanding student at Howard University, had been rejected by the sorority as a candidate for the 1984 Ivy Leaf pledge club. Dolores noted that Sheila was attending Howard on partial AKA and NAACP scholarships, and was quite brilliant. Initially, I tried to console Dolores, reminding her that the sorority still has discretion to not accept every applicant, and perhaps there was a sound reason why Sheila was not accepted. I also noted that it is possible that they might accept her next year, should she still be interested in pursuing membership.

Dolores was not having it. She assured me that she had been doing her homework, having previously established a rapport with a number of the undergraduate Alpha Chapter sorors, and they advised "Dolo," as I usually called her, that the sole reason for Sheila's rejection was that she was blind, and had a seeing eye dog. Blind? That is not a "reason." We both recalled that our dear friend, Freddie Lilly, had pledged Alpha Chapter in 1964, the same year as my induction into Omega. Freddie too is blind, but was widely sought after by AKA and Delta, and was very popular with everyone on campus. We agreed that we have never heard of such foolishness, when being blind would be an impediment to induction into the sorority.

Dolo asked me if I would initiate an appropriate inquiry to Esther Garland Pollard, who was then the Regional Director of the North Atlantic Region. Time was of the essence, as the lines were just about to begin, late February being the traditional start of the pledge period

## JUST BENEATH SURFACE, AN UNIQUE INTERACTION WITH AKA

at Howard. Together, and with input from my wife, Carmen, we crafted a carefully worded letter, outlining Sheila's sterling credentials, her interest in AKA from the time that she was in high school, and culminated by asking several pointed questions that were intended to prevent a generic reply.

Within a couple of days I received a call from Soror Pollard, who initiated the conversation about how much she loved Nellie Quander and what a godsend she had been to save the sorority back in 1912-13. Getting past the small talk, Esther then raised the issue of Sheila not being accepted into the Ivy Leaf club, noting that the selection process is discretionary, and that not everyone who wants to be an AKA can, should, or will be. To this I retorted, "I am fully aware of this. I belong to a Greek letter fraternity, and appreciate the membership selection process. In Omega, whenever we elect not to invite someone into the Lampados Club, it is always for a reason, a sound reason we trust, because it is a serious matter and must be treated as such. I would hope that Alpha Kappa Alpha gives likewise consideration to the significance of the action that they are undertaking, should they elect not to accept someone into the pledge club."

Soror Pollard assured me that the sorority had its reasons, which are both private and discretionary, and that she was leaving it up to the leadership of Alpha Chapter to make the decision on whom to invite into the Ivy Leaf club. That response served only one purpose – it made me very angry. I responded and said, "Mrs. Pollard, you are right about exercising discretion, as that is a universal principle of all of our black Greek letter organizations, but we have here a huge abuse of discretion. There is absolutely no valid reason why Sheila was rejected. The sole reason as stated in the Alpha Chapter meeting is that she is blind, and that that would be too much trouble for the chapter." How do you know so much about what is going on in the chapter meeting?" she asked. My reply was, "There are some sane heads in the chapter, but they feel intimidated by what is going on. They don't like it, but are apprehensive about the consequences or possible retaliation if they speak up. But they have been speaking to outside parties, including us."

There was a pregnant pause, and a deep breath taken, after which Mrs. Pollard retorted, "Well, it's still their decision, and I do not intend to interfere." The conversation ended, but it was far from the end of the matter. Rather, it was the beginning of a series of express mail communications between my law office and Dr. Faye Bryant, Supreme Basileus and an Alpha Chapter alumna. With letters literally flying back and forth between Houston, Texas and Washington, D.C., Dr. Bryant was initially unfazed by the dust up, again leaving it to the discretion of the local chapter.

However, she began to receive calls from other graduate sorors who had gotten wind of what had happened, and did not think that it was consistent with AKA's stated principles and objectives. They wanted the issue to be addressed and satisfactorily resolved immediately. As well, someone had called the *Washington Post*, which is always hungry for news related to hazing, and a reporter called me more than once, seeking information or at least a statement. I declined to say anything, and likewise was not certain what he already knew.

One thing continued to occur, however. Sheila was receiving nasty telephone calls from a small cadre of Alpha Chapter sorors, telling her that she would never be an AKA, and threatening to push her and that "flea-bitten dog of yours, down the steps." Although Sheila had never physically seen any of these sorors, due to her sight disability, she knew who each of them was by voice recognition. After a couple of calls, and when she identified the caller by name, indicating that she knew exactly who was calling, a couple of the sorors became frightened about what might happen to them if she reported them to the authorities. They stopped calling. Still, the sting of the words, "You will never be an AKA!" deeply hurt her. But it also made her more determined than ever to be accepted into AKA by way of Alpha Chapter, its Mother Pearl.

Appreciating that this matter was not going away, and after conducting their own investigation, both Dr. Bryant and Mrs. Pollard came to the logical conclusion and their good senses. They realized that Sheila had been grossly discriminated against, and that truly there was no legitimate reason for her rejection. And blindness was certainly not a reason for an application for membership to be turned down.

By now, it was about three weeks into the six week pledge period. Indeed, based upon my long experience with black Greek–letter

## JUST BENEATH SURFACE, AN UNIQUE INTERACTION WITH AKA

organizations, it is most unusual, and almost never heard of, for someone to be added to the pledge line at such a late date. But in Sheila's case, an exception was made. While I never saw a written directive from Dr. Bryant, and perhaps there was none, Dolo called me and advised that Mrs. Pollard had contacted Sheila and informed her that she was to be added to the Ivy Leaf club immediately. The next day, I saw Sheila on line, and knew that the matter had been resolved. Or had it?

Her line sisters had already bonded, and the sudden addition of a blind girl with Banner, her seeing-eye dog, was a surprise to them. I do not know what, if anything, they had previously heard about the entire mess that developed surrounding Sheila and her application to AKA. Sheila later told me that for the most part, the Ivy Leaf club girls were surprised, but acted better, in most cases, than the sorors in the chapter. After getting over the initial shock of getting a new line sister so late in the program, and having to take her and her dog along with them everywhere, a certain maturity set in quickly, especially once her line sisters got the details of the huge dust up that was made in an effort to deny her membership.

Upon learning the details, several of her line sisters became angry, feeling that this attitude was not what they expected from AKA, and that the entire concept of "Finer womanhood" certainly should accommodate taking qualified people as you find them. They believed that a physical challenge should not be a basis for rejecting an otherwise qualified applicant. Although there were a couple of reservations among some of her line sisters, who kept themselves in a reserved state of mind, the others were generally warm, open-minded, and welcoming.

And when the pledge lines were eventually inducted in April 1984, Sheila found herself among those who were called to sisterhood. But there was still some ill will. While the majority of the chapter sorors were welcoming, and likewise the visiting sorors quite open and accepting, there was still a cadre of sorors who were holding a grudge, making it clear that they did not appreciate being forced to take someone into the chapter that they did not want.

While I do not sit in judgment on Alpha Chapter's behavior toward Sheila, there were some individuals who refused to buckle to authority, even when the authority had made the right decision on behalf of the organization. Such was the case here. Now, 30 years later, I do hope that those sorors who were nasty and harbored the resentments that they so openly manifested, have come to realize that their attitudes and actions were grossly immature and very inconsistent with what the Founders of AKA had in mind in 1908, and likewise inconsistent with the values that were continuously expressed by Nellie M. Quander, about what it meant to be an AKA.

For me personally, Sheila's induction into the sorority represented a great personal success. But the matter was not finished. Far from it! A few days later, my telephone rang again. The lady on the line was the same soror who had called in February to invite me to speak on behalf of Nellie Quander and the Alpha Chapter Alumnae 75th Anniversary Boule luncheon. Only this time the tone was quite different. The graciousness was missing from her voice. It was as if someone had sent her on an errand to do their dirty work. I could tell, even before she got to the main reason for her call, that something was up.

Bro. Quander at Nellie Quander's gravesite, Lincoln Cemetery Suitland, Maryland

She then proceeded to tell me that my invitation to address the luncheon was being withdrawn, adding, "Thank you for being so gracious to AKA, but others have decided that your remarks will not be necessary." Not be necessary? Now that is a mild way of putting it. Still, I inquired as to why I was being dis-invited, but she held steadfast in her assertion that she really did not know. I cannot say at

## JUST BENEATH SURFACE, AN UNIQUE INTERACTION WITH AKA

this removed date, 30 years later, whether she really did not know, or was just good at covering up the truth. We finished the conversation, a bit stilted, to say the least, and bid adieu. I turned to Carmen and said, "Well, I've heard about people getting a dis-invitation, but me, I've never had one before now. I have just been disinvited from addressing AKA during their 75th Anniversary Boule in July."

Carmen was shocked too. She could not believe that such a thing had happened, adding, "You know it's all about Sheila, and how you handled the matter to assure that the right thing was done in the outcome." I replied, "Yes, I know that this is in reply, or maybe I should use the word 'retaliation,' but I will not. I don't know the level from which the decision to withdraw the invitation came, so I won't form an opinion on that now." Further angered, Carmen said, "That's your problem, always giving the benefit of the doubt to someone, You're too damn nice, but you aren't going to let those b------ get away with this. No, this is far from over. In fact, it's just beginning – all over again. They think that they can sweep this under the rug and all will be fine. Not while I live and breathe. We're going to do something, and it will be big. Just what, I don't know yet. But it will be big!"

For the next couple of days, we wondered about how to handle the matter. The Boule was not until late July, and it was now just early May, so we had some time to think about what we should do and how we should respond. And besides, we were also very busy with the planning of the Quander Family Tricentennial Celebration (1684-1984), scheduled for the third weekend in June, to be held at Howard University. As president of the Quanders United, Inc., the family corporation, the task of seeing to the proper execution of all the planned events was resting primarily upon my shoulders. I hardly had much spare time, as we were already generating national level interest in the family's 300 years of documented presence in America. Media interviews from all disciplines were occurring. Calls were coming in from overseas as the international media – print, audio, video - picked up the press releases that we were issuing, announcing that an African American family in Washington, D.C. was planning this big 300-year celebration, reminiscent of Alex Haley's *Roots*, which had been a bestselling book, and later a highly successful miniseries on national television.

But we could not let the Quander planning overshadow the need for a timely response to AKA in light of what had just happened. Asking my dad and a few other family members to take the reins of Tricentennial Celebration planning and hold them for a while, I refocused on AKA. I called Dolo and told her what had happened. She was furious, to say the least, and did not bite her tongue. Sheila was her goddaughter, and we had pulled out all the stops to make sure that AKA, to which both Dolo and Ivaline Maxwell Cummings, her mother, belonged would make the right decisions in the end.

Dolo commented to me that she understood how immature the young sorors of Alpha Chapter had been throughout this entire episode, and that sometimes the younger sorors need the guidance of the more mature sorors, who are older and have life experiences, in order to assure the proper outcome in their collective behavior. But this, this disinvitation from mature sorors was beyond the pale. She asked me, "Do they expect you would come to the luncheon and act up? Do they think that you would disrespect Alpha Kappa Alpha and the memory of Nellie Quander at the sorority's own forum? Then they certainly don't know you."

Dolo indicated that she wanted to come by the house and sit at the dining room table, so that we could strategize how we might respond to this insult. We set the time for the forthcoming Friday evening about 7:00 p.m. When Friday came, Dolo arrived as scheduled, and brought Charlotte Jarvis, a lifelong friend and fellow soror with her. Around tea and cake, Dolo, Charlotte, Carmen, and I discussed what had happened, and how the four of us, aided by the concerns and inquiries of several other mature sorors, had worked to get this matter corrected, and then the most recent challenge – the disinvitation.

Carmen is an professional artist. She studied at some of the top art programs in the United States, including the Corcoran in Washington, D.C., and Pratt Institute, the Art Students League, and New York University in New York. In later years, after this AKA incident had blown over, she would be invited to study and paint at the Repin Academy of Fine Arts in St. Petersburg, Russia. Indeed, her art credentials are well established.

## JUST BENEATH SURFACE, AN UNIQUE INTERACTION WITH AKA

Dolo commented that we do not see many pictures of Nellie Quander, although she is legendary in the sorority. She then added, "Carmen, why don't you make a painting of Nellie Quander, which can be presented to AKA at the luncheon? They can't possibly say 'No!' if you just show up with a gift." "What a brilliant idea," I added. "Yes! That's a great idea, although if the Trojans had time to do it over, I doubt if they would have accepted the Greeks bearing gifts. You know what happened the last time." (Laughter) Carmen, a little apprehensive at first, then began to react favorably to the idea. Yes, she would make a painting or drawing, and I could show up at the Alpha Chapter Alumnae luncheon, uninvited, and make a surprise presentation. She added, "They can't possibly say no to that, although I know that they will be scared to death about what you might say or do."

I replied, "Don't worry about that. Nellie taught us to take the high road and to stay there. My presence will be frightening enough for them, so I don't need to say or do anything other than stay on the congratulatory path. They know what they did, and they also fixed it. I will respect that and leave that old issue completely alone. Now Carmen, you've got work to do."

I looked into my Quander historical archives for a photo of Nellie, but none of them was particularly good. However, one photo which Henry Robinson, my cousin and former history professor at both Howard and Morgan State Universities, had retrieved when doing family history research, was quite appropriate. It was a full face of Nellie, an older woman, perhaps about 65 years old. Because the background and her complexion were close by comparison, Carmen decided that a pencil drawing would be better than a watercolor, and she undertook to render such.

The outcome was very successful, a full facial drawing, about 20 inches high and 15 inches wide. The keys to the success of the drawing, however, were the matting and the frame. When we took the drawing to the framer and asked to see what color options she had in pink, the framer was surprised but understood, once we explained the significance of the colors, salmon pink and apple blossom green. However, despite her significant frame inventory, she had neither color in stock, and the time constraints incidental to make a special order would not accommodate our needs.

So we settled upon a different shade of pink frame, complimented by a light enough green and a more traditional pink for the double matting. The outcome was very impressive, a fitting portrait for a queen, or at least a First Supreme Basileus. Picking up the finished product on Saturday morning, Carmen and I headed to Howard's Blackburn center for the luncheon. So as not to tip anyone off that we were attending, Dolo had purchased a group of tickets under her own name, distributing them to other sorors who knew what we planned, but kept their counsel.

Of course by this time, the Diamond Jubilee Boule was well underway, with activities ongoing at the Washington, D.C. Convention Center and various hotels. Several chapters had planned reunions, so that sorors who were made in said chapter as undergraduates could get together in a planned venue. Such was likewise the case for the Alpha Chapter alums, who were gathered at their *alma mater* to remember the good old days.

Checking in at the reception desk, which included giving my name, I did not discern any particular concern among those sorors who were at the table, as they welcomed us as Nellie Quander's family members. No one got up and rushed off, to alert the senior committee members that we were present and likewise had a presentation to make. I had planned ahead, and consequently brought a written note, addressed to Esther Pollard, Regional Director, informing her that I was present (she had already observed me seated at a guest table and wished to make a presentation to Alpha Kappa Alpha on behalf of the Quander Family. Watching her closely, I could see that she was agitated, and probably nervous as well.

Having been informed of both my presence and of my desire to make a presentation how could she say "No!"? I am certain that she asked herself, "Will he be gracious? Will he insult us? Does he have an agenda to unload upon this assemblage? What should I do?" I think that she took a page from the Nellie Quander's book on personal behavior. And the answer came forth. Invite him to make his presentation, despite his presence and potential remarks being both unplanned. And ask him to keep his remarks as brief as possible.

## JUST BENEATH SURFACE, AN UNIQUE INTERACTION WITH AKA

The official program begun, with greetings from several AKA national and district leaders, including Dr. Faye Bryant, an Alpha Chapter alumna, who was then also serving as AKA's Supreme Basileus. Although she and I had communicated several times by express mail related to the "Sheila incident," Dr. Bryant and I had not met before that afternoon. She related how pleased and honored she was to be serving as the Supreme Basileus and also an Alpha Chapter inductee, which made the occasion extra special since she was standing in the grand ballroom of one of the University's most hallowed sites, delivering a Diamond Jubilee message to her sorors and their guests.

Mrs. Pollard also served as a trustee of Howard University. When her turn at the dais came, she announced the formal establishment of the Nellie May Quander Memorial Scholarship endowment in Quander's honor. The total amount of the initial scholarship was $125,000.00 at that time. It was to be awarded to female Howard University junior and senior women students. During Mrs. Pollard's time at the dais, she recognized another soror, an Alpha Chapter Alumna, who on behalf of the chapter, presented an additional $10,000.00 check for the endowed fund.

Relinquishing the platform to Dr. Bryant, the latter then yielded the floor to the event chair, whose name I cannot recall at this time. The chair then advised that Rohulamin Quander of the Quander family was present today, and on behalf of the Quander family, he would make a presentation and give a few "brief" remarks. I put the word "brief" in quotation marks because the manner in which the word was used was also a strong hint. By then I had moved to the front of the ballroom, and was waiting at the end of the head table, ready to ascend the few steps that would put me on level with the head table guests. Standing next to me on my right was Mrs. Pollard. I could tell that she was a bit apprehensive about my being invited to speak, but likewise, and being a lady, she felt obligated to respect and honor Nellie's memory.

Just as I was about to mount the stairs, having been introduced, Esther said to me, "You're not going to be mean to us, are you?" A bit surprised at her asking such a directed and pointed question, which she had obviously reserved until the final seconds before I was to speak, I replied, "No! Not any meaner than you were to Sheila." Startled at my retort, Esther looked extremely agitated as I departed her presence and headed to the dais, carrying my carefully wrapped surprise presentation,. No one had any idea what the presentation gift was, and for the moment, I relished keeping it that way.

My remarks were simple and straightforward. First, I thanked the ladies of Alpha Kappa Alpha for accommodating me on such short notice. I next paid a special tribute to Nellie Quander, who 74 years prior (March 1910) had been inducted into the sacred sisterhood that is Alpha Kappa Alpha. I urged all of the assembled members of AKA to keep striving to attain and maintain the characteristics of finer womanhood and to continue in service to those in need. That was it.

Although I could not see either Faye Bryant or Esther Pollard's faces at the moment, I am certain they both breathed a sigh of relief, appreciating that what had recently happened to Sheila was a bygone. Although I certainly had not forgotten what raged between February and April 1984, as Sheila pursued membership in AKA, I knew when, where, and how to pick my battles. They appreciated that I was a gentleman, at least on that occasion, and saw no need to either embarrass or insult the sorority on this joyous, celebratory occasion.

Next, I pulled the one piece of tape that was holding the gift enclosed. The brown wrapping fell away and the full head shot of Soror Nellie M. Quander was unveiled, to the collective comment, "Oh, how beautiful!", and a thunderous applause. At last, the Sheila event was finally closed, as the sorority leadership came to appreciate that I knew how and when to separate issues. I never intended to raise the ugly side of what had recently occurred with the spring pledge line and Sheila's application to AKA. To have done otherwise would not only embarrass AKA but, more importantly from my personal perspective, would also have created a negative impression of the entire Quander family. To think that I would elect such a public forum, and issue an insult to AKA, would have compromised me for life.

## JUST BENEATH SURFACE, AN UNIQUE INTERACTION WITH AKA

Instead, I gained the respect of Dr. Bryant, who realized that I was not such a bad egg after all. She was probably thinking, "He really could have hurt us, tarnished our image in the presence of our own sorors, but instead he was a perfect gentlemen, and never raised the specter of what had occurred earlier. I'll remember that." And remember it she has. I have seen Dr. Bryant on several occasions since that fateful day in 1984, including during AKA's Centennial Celebration year. Anyone who did not know otherwise, would have thought her to be a long lost friend to me. And indeed she was. A big hug, kind greetings to Carmen, Faye was most pleasant. As she stepped away the first time, Carmen said, "Do you think she's forgotten?" I replied, "Not a chance! She knows who she was dealing with, and has come full circle with that long ago matter. I'm sure that she appreciated that I could have made if bad for them, but elected not to do so, in part out of respect for Nellie." And that issue and matter has never since been raised, except for now being penned in this memoir.

Fatima, Rohulamin, II, and Iliana Quander vend with Bro. Quander at AKA Centenial Boule, July 2008

**50+ OMEGA INSPIRED YEARS**

A couple of years later, in 1986, Carmen and I attended the Chicago wedding of Dr. David H. Reid, III, my lifelong friend and 1964 line brother. We had never been to Chicago and decided to look around. One of the sites that we visited, unannounced, was the AKA international headquarters, located at 5656 South Stony Island Avenue. Staff was most gracious to us, and one of them gave us an escorted tour of the building. The highlight of the tour occurred as we ascended the stairs to the second floor, and immediately observed Carmen's portrait of Nellie Quander and the Sorority's original 1913 charter hanging side by side. It was an impressive site, to say the least.

OMEGA'S CENTENNIAL, MY THRID OMEGA JUBILEE, 2011
# XX – People, Places, & Things
# The World Abroad

Bro. Quander with President William Clinton and others in the White House Oval Office

Bro. Quander with Henry Louis Gates, Martha's Vineyard, 2013

## 50+ OMEGA INSPIRED YEARS
### People That I Have Met

Over the course of these years, I have travelled to many historically significant and interesting places, and met and interacted with many people of renown in addition to those previously mentioned above. While historically I am not a name dropper, I thought it significant to mention the below movers and shakers, as indicative of some of the activities and events that I have been involved with for these past 70 years.

As to places, my lasting impressions include: 1) Just off the coast of Alexandria, Egypt, where Cleopatra VII and Marc Anthony departed Egypt for Actium, Sea of Ionia, for a famous sea battle against Rome, which spelled the defeat of the Egyptian empire in 31 B.C.; 2) Troy (Turkey) where Helen of Sparta (aka Helen of Troy) fled to her lover, Paris, sparking the Trojan War in 1250 B.C.; 3) Gallipoli (Turkey) where the great naval battle occurred in 1915, with the loss of many lives which also sealed the decline of the Ottoman Empire; and 4) Cape Coast and Elmina Castles (Ghana), where millions of enslaved African were forced into involuntary servitude and removed from their homeland against their will.

Additional sites visited were: 5) Dachau (Munich, German), where hundreds of thousands of Jews and others were persecuted and then killed by the Nazis; 6) Victoria Falls (Zimbabwe and Zambia), one of the world's most well-known geological faults, which rupture results in water falling on the Zambezi River with such great and roaring force that it can be heard and felt for miles; 7) Sterkfontein (South Africa), a World Heritage Site where humankind had been documented for at least 2,000,000 years; and 8) the stature of Christ the Redeemer (Rio de Janeiro, Brazil), a monument located on the top of a steep mountain, and a testament to the faith of a Christian people.

In addition to the names of the people that I mentioned above as having met and intersected with, I also list the following individuals. In some instances I interacted with them on boards, committees, projects, or event planning. In other instances, I was simply introduced to them. As well, I have included the place or event where I met them:

## OMEGA'S CENTENNIAL, MY THRID OMEGA JUBILEE, 2011

1. President William Jefferson Clinton – 42nd President of the United States; the Oval Office.
2. Vice President Albert Gore – 45th Vice President of the United States; the Oval Office.
3. Senator Charles "Chuck" Robb – U.S. Senator, Virginia; the oval Office
4. Bro. Gov. L. Douglas Wilder – Governor of Virginia; 79th District Meeting, Omega Psi Phi, April 2012, Roanoke, Virginia.
5. Chief Justice Warren E. Burger – Chief Justice, United States Supreme Court; Georgetown reception; Washington, D.C.
6. Mr. Justice Samuel A. Alito – Justice, U.S. Supreme Court; Mount Vernon Estate and Gardens.
7. Grand Basilei of Omega Psi Phi, Inc., whom I met and sometimes interacted with – Founder Edgar Amos Love, 1st and 3rd; Founder Oscar J. Cooper, 2nd; Lawrence A. Oxley, 14th; Herbert E. Tucker, Jr., 23rd; I. Gregory Newton, 24th; Cary D. Jacobs, 25th; George E. Meares, 26th; Ellis F. Corbett, 27th; James Avery, 28th; Edward Braynon, Jr., 30th; Burnel E. Coulon, 31st; Moses C. Norman, 33rd; Dorsey E. Miller, 35th; Lloyd Jordan, 36th; Warren G. Lee, 38th; and Andrew A. Ray, 39th.
8. All of the elected mayors of the District of Columbia – Including Bro. Walter E. Washington, Marion S. Barry, Sharon Pratt, Anthony Williams, Adrian Fenty, and Vincent Gray; Washington, D.C
9. Bro. Robert Weaver – First African American to serve in a U.S. presidential cabinet, Alpha Omega Chapter; Washington, D.C.
10. Bro. George L.P. Weaver – Under Secretary of Labor, Alpha Omega Chapter; Washington, D.C.
11. Founders of Omega Psi Phi – Frank Coleman, Oscar J. Cooper, and Edgar A. Love.
12. Bro. H. Carl Moultrie, first international Executive Director, Omega Psi Phi Fraternity.
13. Outstanding civil rights attorneys – Thurgood Marshall, Member, U.S. Supreme Court; Bro. James Nabrit, George E.C. Hayes, Bro. Oliver Hill, and Bro. Wiley Branton, all involved in some aspect of *Brown vs. the Board of Education* school desegregation cases.
14. Rosa Parks – Civil rights leader, Howard University School of Law; Washington, D.C.
15. Caesar Chavez – political activist, Kennedy Center, 1992, live broadcast to the Americas to commemorate the 500th anniversary of Christopher Columbus's arrival in the New World; Washington, D.C.

## 50+ OMEGA INSPIRED YEARS

16. Malcolm X – Civil rights activist, Nation of Islam minister; Lincoln University, Pennsylvania.
17. Ralph David Abernathy – civil rights leader.
18. Coretta Scott King – Widow of Dr. Martin Luther King, MLK Jr. Holiday Commission; Washington, D.C.
19. Dr. Dorothy I. Height – National Council of Negro Women, worked with her on the first Black Family Reunion celebration; Washington, D.C.
20. Benjamin T. Jealous – 17th President and CEO, NAACP, the Humanities Council of Washington, D.C.; Washington, D.C.
21. Stokely Carmichael – Fellow Howard University classmate, including taking one class together; Washington, D.C.
22. Julian Bond – Civil rights leader, Howard University School of Law; Washington, D.C.
23. Senator Edward Brooke – U.S. Senator, Massachusetts; classmate of James W. Quander, Dunbar High School, Class of 1936, Washington, D.C.
24. Rudy Giuliani – Former mayor of New York City; Washington, D.C.
25. Bro. Kent Amos – National philanthropist, educator, outstanding mentor and community servant, Omega National Citizen of the Year, 1988; Alpha Omega Chapter.
26. Cokie Roberts – Journalist; fellow board member, U.S. Capitol Historical Society.
27. Hon. Richard "Dick" Fazio – fellow board member, U.S. Capitol Historical Society.
28. Lynda Johnson Robb – fellow board member, U.S. Capitol Historical Society.
29. Gale King – Journalist; Martha's Vineyard, Massachusetts.
30. Henry Louis Gates – Professor and historian; Martha's Vineyard, Massachusetts.
31. Charles Ogletree – Law professor, Harvard University, legal scholar; Martha's Vineyard, Massachusetts.
32. Debbie Allen – Howard University classmate, dancer; Washington, D.C.
33. Felicia Ayers Allen Rashard – Howard University classmate, actress; Washington, D.C.
34. Jessye Norman – Howard University classmate, world class singer.
35. Celia Cruz – entertainer, Kennedy Center, 1992, live broadcast to the Americas to commemorate the 500th anniversary of Christopher Columbus's arrival in the New World; Washington, D.C.

## OMEGA'S CENTENNIAL, MY THRID OMEGA JUBILEE, 2011

36. Madame Lillian Evanti – World class opera singer who came to our home on occasion and sang; Washington, D.C.
37. Tito Puente – Internationally famed Latin orchestra leader, Spanish American festival, Washington, D.C.
38. Byron Lee – Internationally renowned Calypsonian extraordinaire; Port of Spain, Trinidad.
39. Shemar Moore – Actor; Miami Beach, Florida.
40. Bro. Langston Hughes – Internationally recognized poet; Lincoln University, Pennsylvania.
41. Maya Angelou – Poet, author; Washington, D.C
42. Norma Boyd – Founder, Alpha Kappa Alpha Sorority, teacher of James W. Quander; Washington, D.C.
43. Dr. Lorraine R. Green, 2nd Supreme Basileus, Alpha Kappa Alpha Sorority; Durham, North Carolina.
44. Dr. Marjorie Parker – 15th Supreme Basileus, Alpha Kappa Alpha Sorority and historian; Washington, D.C.
45. Dr. Faye Bryant – 21st Supreme Basileus, Alpha Kappa Alpha Sorority, AKA Diamond Jubilee Celebration, July 1984; Washington, D.C.
46. Dr. Barbara McKinzie – 27th Supreme Basileus, Alpha Kappa Alpha Sorority, AKA Centennial Celebration, January and July 2008; Washington, D.C.
47. Bro. Bobby Mitchell – First African American to play for the Washington Redskins, Football Hall of Fame, Pigskin Club of Washington; Washington, D.C.
48. The Generals Brooks – Leo, Sr., Leo, Jr., and Vincent – first African American family of three generals, members of the Quander Family; Washington, D.C.
49. Gen. Chappie James – Father of childhood friends Denise and Daniel James; Washington, D.C.
50. Gen. Benjamin O. Davis, Jr., Tuskegee Airman; Washington, D.C.
51. Rear Admiral Michelle J. Howard – First female African American Rear Admiral; Mount Vernon Estate and Gardens, Virginia.
52. David Driskell - Internationally renowned artist; Martha's Vineyard and Washington, D.C.
53. Simmie Knox – Internationally renowned artist; Washington, D.C.
54. Richard Dempsy – Internationally renowned artist; Washington, D.C.
55. Lois Mailou Jones – internationally renowned artist and Brookland, D.C. neighbor; Washington, D.C.

## 50+ OMEGA INSPIRED YEARS

56. Lonnie Bunch – Founding Director, the Smithsonian Museum of African American History and Culture; Washington, D.C.
57. Joe Louis – Heavyweight boxing champion, caddied for him in D.C. golf tournament; Washington, D.C.
58. Sean Cardinal O'Malley – Archbishop of Boston, formerly a parish priest then posted to Sacred Heart Church, personal family friend; Washington, D.C.
59. Johnetta B. Cole, PhD. – President, Spelman and Bennett Colleges, National Director, Museum of African Art, Smithsonian Institution; Atlanta and Washington, D.C.
60. Bro. William Stuart Nelson – Vice President, Howard University; second editor of the *Oracle*; Washington, D.C.
61. Bro. H. Patrick Swygert – President, Howard University, my line brother, Omega Psi Phi; Washington, D.C.
62. Ralph E. McGill – Pulitzer Prize winning anti segregation editor and publisher, the *Atlanta Journal and Constitution,* civil rights pioneer, Top of the Mart; Atlanta, Georgia, 1963.
63. Charlene Hunter Gault – international news correspondent and journalist; Martha's Vineyard, Massachusetts.
64. Monica Lewinsky - Student intern and associate of President Clinton, Mardi Gras party; Alexandria, Virginia.
65. Patricia Roberts Harris – First African American woman to serve in a presidential cabinet; dean of Howard University's School of Law; Washington, D.C.
66. Chester Bowles - Former governor of Connecticut, Undersecretary of State, U.S. ambassador to India and Nepal; Lincoln University, Pennsylvania.
67. Hon. Thomas R. Pickering – International consultant, former ambassador to several countries, including Kenya, Israel, and India; Chair, the Accountability and Review Board; Mount Vernon Estate and Gardens, Virginia.
68. Frank Gehry – World renowned architect; Washington, D.C.

On three occasions I served as a baccalaureate or commencement exercises speaker. The first was in the early 1980s at the invitation of the Maharishi International University of Fairfield, Iowa. My address was delivered to an international audience on a worldwide closed circuit television broadcast. The second occasion was in 2001. I was invited to Beloit College for the black history month program in February 2001. After delivering my remarks at that time, the audience

## OMEGA'S CENTENNIAL, MY THRID OMEGA JUBILEE, 2011

was so pleased that I was invited back to deliver the baccalaureate address during the following May. My daughter, Fatima, was a member of that class.

Despite those two college level addresses, I consider the highlight of my commencement activities to have occurred on May 26, 2011, when I was invited to address the John Carroll High School Class of 2011, which was also the occasion of my 50$^{th}$ anniversary graduation from Carroll. My remarks were simple, but direct, and hopefully made a lasting impression upon the well more than 1,000 people in the audience, including about 150 graduates. The essence of my remarks were the following:

> *LEGACY – How will you be remembered in 50 years? In 1961, I never thought, not even for a minute, that I would be invited back to Carroll 50 years hence, and asked to address this graduating class. Nor did I entertain then that, God sparing life, I would be joining with my classmates of that year in our reunion celebration this September. But I followed through, developed a work ethic, pursued and maintained a moral standard that was already well formed, and dedicated myself to being a good Christian family man, responsible citizen, and giving back as I selected and pursued my life's paths. Would those members of the Carroll Class of 1961 who are present, please stand.*
>
> *It's all about **PERSEVERANCE**. It's about remembering who you are and whose you are. We are all your Carroll family. Enduring friendships were created here, and now must be nurtured and maintained. Each of us has a purpose. Dedicate yourselves in pursuit of finding your purpose. As you step into the unknown, it need not be fearful. Your Faith, Hope, and Love will see you through.*

## 50+ OMEGA INSPIRED YEARS

*Have **FAITH** in God and in yourselves and your ability, and indeed be gratified in the outcome. Be mindful that you must always help yourself too. Sitting back having "Faith" will not get it, as the Lord helps those who help themselves.[60]*

### Places That I Have Visited

To date I have been out of the United States at least 31 times, and visited at least 34 countries, some of them more than once. In keeping with the mode of this chapter, in tooting my own horn, I believe it necessary to list those countries, followed by an enumeration of some of the more important places that I have visited.

Quander Family Reunion at George Washington's Mount Vernon Plantation, 2010

Some of them are more well-known than others, particularly those places that have been designated as World Heritage Sites (WHS) by the United Nations Education, Scientific and Cultural Organization (UNESCO). A World Heritage Site is a place (such as a forest, mountain, lake, island, desert, monument, building, complex, or city) that is listed by UNESCO as of special cultural or physical significance.

### Out of The Country Trips: 1964 To Present

1. 1964 - Europe (France, Germany, Austria, Yugoslavia, Bulgaria, Greece, Italy, Spain, Netherlands, Luxembourg) and Turkey (European and Asian sides).
2. 1966 – Canada (Quebec City, Quebec).
3. 1966-67 - Jamaica (Christmas).
4. 1968 – Barbados (ancestral homeland).
5. 1969 – Barbados, Dominica, and U.S. Virgin Islands.
6. 1970 – Puerto Rico, Dominica, and Barbados.
7. 1971 – Barbados.

---

[60] *Extract from Commencement Remarks delivered by Rohulamin Quander, Class of 1961, to the Class of 2011, John Carroll High School, Washington, D.C., National Shrine of the Immaculate Conception, May 26, 2011,*

## OMEGA'S CENTENNIAL, MY THRID OMEGA JUBILEE, 2011

8. 1974 – Mexico (bus trip, including Mexico City, Morelia, Guanajuato, San Miguel Allende, the silver and gold mines).
9. 1975 – Trinidad and Tobago (Carnival), and Guyana.
10. 1975 – Canada (Caribana Festival, Toronto).
11. 1976 – Trinidad and Tobago (Carnival).
12. 1977 – Trinidad and Tobago (wedding) and Barbados.
13. 1977 – Cape Verde Island and Senegal (Dakar, first trip to Africa).
14. 1981 – Dominican Republic (Carmen's family).
15. 1981 – Great Britain and France (Educational Institution Licensure Commission).
16. 1986 – Egypt (EILC, 2nd Africa).
17. 1991 – Egypt (EILC, Cairo, Alexandria, Luxor, Edfu, Comombo, Aswan, 3rd Africa).
18. 1991 – Ghana (Quander United reunion with Amkwandoh ancestral families, 4th Africa).
19. 1994 – South Africa (Johannesburg, business expo, 5th Africa).
20. 1996 – Barbados.
21. 2002 – Cayman Islands (with Dad).
22. 2003 – Jamaica and Dominican Republic.
23. 2003 - Dubai (EILC), plus three other Emirates, and Oman.
24. 2004 - Barbados (family reunion).
25. 2004 Brazil (Tuskegee alumni).
26. 2006 - Egypt (Cairo, Luxor, Aswan, Abu Simbel, African Genesis Institute, 6th Africa).
27. 2006 – South Africa, Zimbabwe, and Zambia (Tuskegee alumni).
28. 2007 – Turkey.
29. 2007 – Panama, Belize, and Costa Rica (Tuskegee alumni).
30. 2010 – Russia (Repin Academy of Fine Arts, St. Petersburg).
31. 2011 – Cuba (Tuskegee alumni).

The below listing includes UNESCO World Heritage Sites that I have visited.[61] Some of these sites were so designated after I had already visited them. As well, I might have overlooked listing certain ones. Only the World Heritage Sites are designated as "WHS." Many other sites of interest are also listed, but lack the WHS status.

---

[61] *The list of designated sites is maintained by the international World Heritage Program administered by UNESCO World Heritage Committee, composed of 21 states participants, which are elected by their General Assembly. It is headquartered in Paris, France.*

## 50+ OMEGA INSPIRED YEARS

### The Orient Express, 1964

Traveled on the Orient Express from Paris to Istanbul, Turkey, to my summer internship in Turkey in 1964, getting on and off throughout European countries.

## AFRICA
### Egypt
- Ancient Thebes with its necropolis, Luxor, Egypt (WHS).
- Historic Cairo, Egypt (WHS).
- Memphis and its Necropolis – the Pyramid Fields from Giza to Dahshur, Egypt (WHS).
- The Tomb of the Aga Kahn, Egypt.

### Senegal
- Goree Island slave castle, including the Door of No Return (WHS)

### Ghana
- Slave castles, including Cape Coast and Elmina, and the Doors of No Return (WHS).
- The home and burial site of W.E.B. DuBois, Accra, Ghana.

### South Africa
- Sterkfonte in Caves, Pliocene and Pleistocene epochs, dating pre-human existence back 3.3 million years, Gauteng province, South Africa (WHS).
- Inside the former home of Nelson Mandela, Soweto.
- Outside the home of Winnie Mandela.
- Outside the home of Archbishop Desmond Tutu, Johannesburg.
- Regina Caeli Roman Catholic Church, site of major anti-apartheid demonstrations, Soweto.
- Table Top Mountain, Cape Town,; District Six, Cape Town.

### Zambia and Zimbabwe
- Victoria Falls National Park, Zimbabwe (WHS).
- The National Park, Zambia (WHS).

## EUROPE
### Russia
- Saint Petersburg monuments, 18$^{th}$ and 19$^{th}$ Century architecture (WHS).
- The Hermitage, St. Petersburg.
- Ballet theatre (name written in Russian only) and saw *Swan Lake* performed by the Jacobson Ballet Company, St. Petersburg.

## OMEGA'S CENTENNIAL, MY THRID OMEGA JUBILEE, 2011

### United Kingdom (Great Britain)
- Historic Town of St. George and Related Fortifications, 17th to 20th Centuries, Bermuda (WHS).
- Royal Botanical Gardens, Kew, 18th to 20 Centuries, Greater London (WHS).
- Westminster Palace, Westminster Abbey, and Saint Margaret's Church, Greater London (WHS).
- Tower of London, Tower Hamlets, Greater London, England (WHS).

### France
- Banks of the Seine, including Notre Dame Cathedral, Ile-de-France, Paris, France (WHS).
- Palace and Park of Versailles, Versailles, France (WHS).
- The Louvre, Paris.
- The Eifel tower.

### Luxembourg
- City of Luxembourg, its Old Quarters and Fortifications, Luxembourg (WHS).

### Austria
- Historic Center of Vienna, Vienna, Austria (WHS).
- Palace and Gardens of Schonbrunn, Austria (WHS).
- Historic Centre of Salzburg, Austria.

### Turkey (Europe and Asia)
- Goreme National Park and the Rock Sites of Cappadocia, Nevsehir Province, Turkey (WHS).
- Historic areas of Istanbul, Istanbul Province, Turkey (WHS).
- Hierapolis-Pumukkale, Denzil Province, Turkey (WHS).
- Archaeological site of Troy, Canakklale Province, Turkey (WHS).
- The Grand Bazaar, Istanbul.
- Topkapi Gardens, Istanbul.
- St. Euphemia, Cathedral of Chalcedon, 5th Century, Istanbul.
- The Blue Mosque. 17th Century, Istanbul.
- Hagia Sophia (Church of the Holy Wisdom), Sixth Century, Christian cathedral, mosque, and now national museum, Istanbul.

# 50+ OMEGA INSPIRED YEARS

**Greece**
- The Parthenon, Acropolis, 5th Century B.C., Athens, Greece (WHS).
- Paleochristian and Byzantine monuments of Thessalonika, 315 B.C., Central Macedonia, Greece (WHS).

**Italy**
- Historic Center of Rome, including the Coliseum, Pantheon, Via Apia, and Trevi Fountain (WHS).
- The Properties of the Holy See, the Vatican, Italy (WHS).
- Historic Center of Florence, Florence, Italy (WHS).
- Venice and its Lagoon, Venice, Italy (WHS).
- The Rialto, Venice.
- Saint Mark's Square, Venice.
- David in Academia, Florence.

## THE CARIBBEAN

**Cuba**
- Old Havana City Scape and El More Fortification, 16th to 19th Centuries, Cuba (WHS).
- The National Schools of Art, Cabanacan, Cuba (WHS).
- Plaza do la Revolucion, Havana, Cuba.
- Hotel Nacional, home of the Buena Vista Social Club, Havana, Cuba.
- Ernest Hemingway Farm, Havana, Cuba.

**Dominican Republic**
- Tomb of Christopher Columbus, Santo Domingo, Dominican Republic.
- Colonial City of Santo Domingo, Distrito Nacional, Dominican Republic (WHS).

**Barbados**
- Historic Bridgetown and its Garrison, Bridgetown, Barbados (WHS).

OMEGA'S CENTENNIAL, MY THRID OMEGA JUBILEE, 2011

# NORTH AMERICA
## United States
- Independence Hall, Philadelphia, Pennsylvania (WHS).
- La Fortaleza and San Juan National Historic Site, Old San Juan, Puerto Rico (WHS).
- Statue of Liberty, New York, New York (WHS).
- Monticello and the University of Virginia, Albemarle County and Charlottesville, Virginia (WHS).
- Everglades National Park, Florida (WHS).

## Mexico
- Historic Center of Mexico City and Xochimilco, Mexico City, Mexico (WHS).
- Historic Center of Morelia, Michoacán, Mexico (WHS).
- Historic Town of Guanajuato and Adjacent Mines, Mexico (WHS).
- Pyramid of the Sun and Pyramid of the Moon, Avenue of the Dead, Teotihuacan.

## Canada
- Historic District of Old Quebec, Quebec City, Quebec (WHS).

# SOUTH AMERICA
## Brazil
- Carioca Landscapes Between the Mountain and the Sea, including Christ the Redeemer, Rio de Janeiro, Brazil (WHS).
- Historic Center of Salvador do Bahia city and the Orixa, Bahia State, Brazil (WHS).
- Town of Cachoeira, 16th to 18 Century buildings, Bahia State, Brazil.
- Slave Markets, Salvador de Bahia city, Bahia, Brazil.

## Guyana
Historic Georgetown, capital city, Guyana.

# 50+ OMEGA INSPIRED YEARS

# XXI – Planning Omega's Centennial, My Third Omega Jubilee, 2011

## In Pursuit of Omega's History

### Omega – In the Last Quarter Century, 1986 – 2011

*As the Diamond Jubilee Celebration drew to a close in August 1986, the euphoria that settled over the membership was not long to last. While many of the brothers viewed this time as an occasion for self-congratulation and elected to rest on their laurels, several pressing issues clouded the clarity of the moment. Not the least of them was the continued plague imposed by hazing and brutality. Despite the fraternity's officially adopted policies and efforts to address the issue, and discipline imposed against those brothers who continued to violate Omega's adopted policies, recalcitrant brothers have made it difficult for the rest of us. Operating under the guise of "making a new brother in the right way," the issue, while less serious than in past eras, has caused the fraternity to face liability suits and other challenges which undermines us as a brotherhood as well as an organization of professional men.*

*As we look back over these last 100 years, the Omega Psi Phi Fraternity, Inc., has much to be proud of. But there is still room for improvement. As we reflect over the many things, both good and bad, which have had an impact on the current state of the brotherhood, we can link much of the behavior and traditions that we exhibit back to several common foundations.*[62]

For most of my adult life, I have pursued major history projects. Being the main historian for the Quander Family, and the individual most responsible for uncovering, documenting, preserving, and now

---

[62] *"Omega - In the Last Quarter Century, 1986-2011, Centennial Souvenir Journal Statement, authored by Rohulamin Quander, Chairman, Third District History and Archives Committee, June 2011.*

sharing that history, and its direct connection to George Washington and many other national level American luminaries, I have transcended my interests in history into several other historical pursuits. As previously noted, I was the Mayor's Agent for Historic Preservation for 12 years (1998-2010), serving under Mayors Marion Barry, Alexander Williams, and Adrian Fenty, and resigned from that uncompensated position only when I was close to retirement.

But monetary compensation has never been my objective or guide. Rather, it was always the love of history, the feeling that we need to know what was done in the past, in order to shape our future correctly, that has led me down this path all these years. As Mayor's Agent, I rendered more than 80 decisions, the effects of which molded the historic fabric and skyline of many D.C. buildings, and designated historic districts in D.C., thus prese rving or reshaping the skyline for the benefit and enjoyment of generations yet unborn.

Along the way, I have published two books to date, both of which are heavily ladened with historic information about life in Washington, D.C. in the late 19th and most all of the 20th Centuries. In *The Quander Quality: The True Story of a Black Trailblazing Diabetic*

(2006), I traced the life of James W. Quander, my dad, that addressed issues of racial and health discrimination, the segregated public school system that was pervasive in the nation's capital, inter-racial marriage, and becoming one of the first permanent deacons in the Roman Catholic Church, after an 800-year hiatus. The church, during an internal political feud of longstanding, abolished the permanent diaconate. Now, after an eight century absence, and with the critical shortage of priests, the church revived the permanent diaconate. My dad was privileged to be one of the initial 16 in the United States, when he was ordained on September 11, 1971.

In 2008, I published *Nellie Quander, An Alpha Kappa Alpha Pearl, the Story of the Woman Who Saved an International Organization*. The title says it all, and details the life of this outstanding woman who was involved in much more than just her sorority, which she served as its first Supreme Basileus.

Being a product of history, and one who has lectured to many august organizations about African American history subjects, beyond just the Quander family, it was only natural that I should be sought out by the executive committee of Omega's Third District, and asked to chair a project that would result in the creation of the first published history of the District. Although there have been comprehensive statements written in the past, most notably by Bro. Vernon Johnson (Omega Chapter) and Bro. Joseph McKinney (Delta Omega Chapter), no effort to date has culminated in the publication of a hard cover written history of our District.

Completing such an effort should be of great interest and importance, as this is the District of Omega's birth, cradle, and early nurture, for it was on Howard University's campus where Omega was born on November 17, 1911. As well, it was just a few blocks south of the campus where the first Omega fraternity houses were established. It was realized that Omega's year-long Centennial Celebration was fast approaching, and that the history of the Third District should be a prime instrument to both market and enlighten others concerning what this District represents. Thus in October 2009,

## 50+ OMEGA INSPIRED YEARS

I was appointed by Bro. Anthony Knight, the District Representative for the Third District, and asked to chair the district's History and Archives Committee.

The charge from Bro. D.R. Anthony Knight was to draw upon the known available resources, primarily created by Bro. Johnson and Bro. McKinney, and use the collective knowledge of several other brothers of Omega, to write the district's first publishable history book. Although the task was monumental, both in content and time frame, I was fully up to the task, anticipating the able assistance of Omega men from across the District, which included both Washington, D.C., and throughout the state of Virginia. I accepted the challenge, reached out to all of the chapters in the District, and recruited dedicated brothers, those imbued with a serious purpose, to help me undertake and complete the project.

While attending one of the District wide organizational planning meetings for the Celebration, I was requested to expand the role of the H&A Committee to also include writing the official Statement for the Centennial Souvenir Journal that would reflect Omega over the last 25 years, since the Diamond Jubilee Celebration of 1986, but also leading into the fraternity's Second Century. Although that would add another layer to our duties, I felt comfortable with taking this extra assignment, as I was familiar with the process, and had done exactly that for the 1986 gathering. That time, the effort was done by four Alpha Omega brothers – William Clement, the Grand Marshal, Herbert Dixon, the Basileus and wearer of many hats, Kenneth Brown, the Deputy Grand Marshal and member of the Supreme council, and me.

In 1986, they had the credentials, and I had the time. My wife, Carmen, a professional artist, created the official cover for the Souvenir Journal. Taking the crafted words of my fellow committee members, drawn from many available Omega history sources, I added major sections of my own, edited the entire document, and rendered the final Diamond Jubilee product, *The Statement of Omega History*. No brother's name was attributed to the effort at that time.

## OMEGA'S CENTENNIAL, MY THRID OMEGA JUBILEE, 2011

*As the Fraternity traversed through the 1990s towards the present, more than 725 Chapters and 5,000 Life Members were registered as active. As well, there was a renewed interest in re-establishing undergraduate chapters in Canada, and in overseas locations, as the brothers of the worldwide-based 13th District became more assertive, despite the challenges imposed by geographic distances between far-flung locations. In 1990, Omega, as an accredited member organization of the National Pan Hellenic Council, joined in the Council's unanimous agreement to disband the traditional pledging program, replacing it with a Membership Selection Process (MSP), as the new process for admission into one of the nine member organization. Although it took far more years than it should have, the organizations finally acknowledged that the misapplication of the pledging program as we knew it, bore no relevance to the mission of the fraternity, the intent and meaning of the Cardinal Principles, and whether Omega men would continue to achieve and make us proud.*[63]

I understood the necessity for structure in an undertaking of this magnitude. Further, we were challenged by the short time frame – appointed in late October 2009, and requested to have a completed book product by Founders Day 2010, November 17, 2010, if possible, or at least by early spring 2011. One of my first tasks was to craft a mission statement. Discussing the mission with several local brothers, I crafted a document which they commented on, and took it to the first District-wide H&A meeting, convened on the campus of Virginia Union University on December 5, 2009. There were 11 brothers in attendance, all focused and enthusiastic. Based upon our instructions from the D.R., I presented a rough draft of the Mission Statement, as I understood it. With some minor editing, the committee adopted the following statement:

---

[63] *"Omega - In the Last Quarter Century, 1986-2011, Centennial Souvenir Journal Statement, authored by Rohulamin Quander, Chairman, Third District History and Archives Committee, June 2011.*

## 50+ OMEGA INSPIRED YEARS
**Mission Statement: For 3rd District History and Archives Committee**
1. To oversee an update to currency of the 3rd District's historical statement that appears on the District's web page.
2. To chair, coordinate, and publish the first comprehensive history book of the 3rd District.
3. To chair, coordinate, and publish a history statement from the 3rd District, divided by decades, to be submitted to the Centennial Souvenir Journal Committee for inclusion in the Journal.[64]
4. To complete the above-noted items by Founders Day, November 17, 2010.[65]

At the initial outset of the undertaking, there was a lot of enthusiasm for the entire project. You could feel the excitement in the room, as the brothers discussed how the book should be structured, what the book should contain, which brothers should be featured as a component of Omega's stellar history. We also discussed who in the various chapters might have some documents to share, and likewise who should be interviewed, both to gather information for the book, and further, to capture their fraternity life stories before they went on to Omega Chapter. We adopted a proposed conventional working title, *The History of the 3rd District of the Omega Psi Phi Fraternity*, which conveyed exactly what we were about, but deferred making a final title determination, as this was the prerogative of the D.R.

The organizational structure and sections of the district's first published history book were to be essentially as follows:

---

[64] *This statement was never created. The Centennial Souvenir Journal Committee, Bro Bernel Coulon, 31st Grand Basileus and Chair of the Committee, modified this initially anticipated format, and requested Bro. Rohulamin Quander, Alpha Omega Chapter, to write a more general statement on behalf of the entire fraternity. Bro. Quander, as sole author, but with editorial and content review from his 3rd District H&A Committee members, submitted, Omega –In the Last Quarter Century, 1986 – 2011, which statement also looked forward to the fraternity's next 25 years.*

[65] *Extracted from the minutes of the meeting, prepared by Bro. Ivory G. Cooper, Alpha Omega chapter.*

### OMEGA'S CENTENNIAL, MY THRID OMEGA JUBILEE, 2011

1. Introduction – a global statement to relate Omega's history in broad strokes for the period from 1911 to the late 1920s.
2. A biographical statement about each of our Founders, but with the intent to make the statements more personalized, since each of them lived in the District and two of them, Founder Just and Founder Coleman, had sustained ties to Howard University.
3. Late 1920s/early 1930s – creation of the concept of defined districts, including establishment of the 3rd District in 1934, to include Maryland until circa 1945.
4. Narrating the 3rd District history, divided by periods (tied to both decades and programs).
5. The District's adoption of nationally mandated and 3rd District-specific programs (SASE, Project Give Back, etc.) and the involvement of brothers individually and by chapters.
6. Leadership Profile I – biographical feature on every brother who has served as 3rd District DR, plus a statement of what was accomplished during his tenure.
7. Leadership Profile II – biographical feature on approximately 125 prominent brothers, both living and in Omega Chapter, who significantly contributed to the District. [66]
8. Leadership Profile III – We will have to decide whether to include in this section any national leaders who emerged from the 3rd District, beginning from about 1933.
9. Chapter histories – 500 to 2,000 word statements from each chapter in the District, both active and inactive.
10. Photo gallery – The photo might be situated next to the biographical statement of a featured brother, or located into a single photo gallery, depending upon cost and the challenge in laying photos throughout the document.

---

[66] *This group of brothers would be drawn from several professional disciplines, subdivided to include their respective professions. Law, medicine, education, military, religious, political service, community service, and science were several of the subject areas to be utilized as headings, with a biographical statement on each featured brother and a suitable photograph if possible.*

## 50+ OMEGA INSPIRED YEARS

The more we discussed, the more we appreciated that the magnitude and scope of the undertaking was beyond the existing 11 H&A committee members present, and that in order to succeed, we needed to locate and involve many additional brothers, men with skills, to benefit this effort. This would include photographers; historians and history minded brothers, to both write and to interview those brothers for whom no biographical information was immediately available; certain IT and technical services, to include computer and programmatic literacies and other related skills; and a design and layout and team.

One brother suggested that we not limit ourselves to just recruiting Omega men for this effort, noting that there are many people beyond Omega who might have valuable skills to donate. He asked that they too should be considered. We agreed. No ritualistic secrets will be divulged during this process, so there is no need to protect what is already mostly in the public domain. Not a small bit of concern was expressed about this undertaking being a volunteer effort, and that the scope of the undertaking might be more time-consuming than we can accomplish in such a short time. Still, it was worth a try, and even if we did not make the initially suggested publication date of November 17, 2010, we would be on track to create the first published history book of any District in Omega, whenever it was published.

As chair, I asked Bro. Victor Taylor, (Psi Nu Chapter) and Bro. Charles Pleasants (Lambda Omega), to serve as my Vice Co-Chairs. Both brothers would prove to be most reliable, knowledgeable, and committed to Omega and the project. Over the next several months the H&A committee held regular meetings. It became readily apparent that travelling around the district was impractical, since everyone was busy with other matters that were not related to Omega. Therefore, telephone conference calls proved to be the best option.

The more than 150 back issues of the *Oracle* that I obtained from Bro. Charles Harry (Zeta Psi Chapter), proved to be a treasure trove. His dad, Bro. Charles Harry, Jr. (Alpha Chapter 1918), had been collecting and retained many *Oracles,* beginning from 1925. They contained so much relevant information that addressed what was occurring in Omega in Washington, D.C., Virginia, and Maryland (which was formerly a part of the district). Brothers were assigned a certain group of *Oracles*, provided a format to follow, and directed to extract certain information that documented events that had occurred in the relevant geographic area.

After completing that task, all but one brother returned his set of *Oracles*, with the requested information properly documented on the forms. He claimed to have returned them in the self-addressed, stamped envelope that I provided, but would not confirm whether he mailed them at a U.S. Post Office, which by law he was mandated to do, or simply dropped the heavy envelope into a local mailbox, where it was confiscated and sent to a dead letter office, and then destroyed. For security reasons, postal regulations forbid mailing any item that weighs more than 13 ounces from a mailbox.

Although we lost those eight *Oracles*, we were able to replace some of them. These issues were from the 1970s, and their significance to us was not of the same level of rarity as pre-1940s issues. For those older issues, I made the decision not to mail any of them. Rather, they were given to local brothers who were directed to return them to me in person. I retained all of the 1919 -1930 issues, and evaluated them myself.

From these vintage *Oracles*, we learned invaluable information about brothers, chapters, and events that occurred in prior decades, all of which lend valuable insight into what Omega was all about in the early days, and various sentiments and attitudes that helped to shape who we are today. The old documents also gave insight that helped the H&A committee to discover and determine who among those heretofore unknown brothers, should be included in the Leadership Profiles component of the book. As well, valuable information was gleaned about several of the prior District Representatives, some of whom were only names to us.

Omega's mandated programs evolved over time. The *Oracles* contained several stories or references to the establishment of Negro History Week (now Black History Month), the Charles Drew Scholarship Program, the National Talent Hunt, Voter Registration drives, Achievement Week, Social Action, and Membership (Reclamation and Retention). Omega has its own treasure trove of historical data, information compiled by the men of Omega who were intellectual giants in their day, and created and left great legacies for us to follow, if only we will.

> Over the past 25 years Omega men have continued to be in the fore front of several endeavors. For example, Omega has led the way in space exploration with astronauts: Robert H. Lawrence, Jr. (First African American astronaut, Omega chapter); Dr. Guion Bluford, aerospace engineer, Col. USAF (Retired), first African American in space; Dr. Ronald E. McNair, physicist, (Omega Chapter); Frederick Gregory, engineer, former Deputy NASA Administrator, first African American to command a space flight; and Charles F. Bolden, engineer, Major General, U.S. Marine Corps (Retired). On May 23, 2009, President Barack Obama, nominated Bro. Bolden to become the first African American to head NASA. His nomination was confirmed by the U.S. Senate.[67]

Beginning with *The Challenge*, as stated by Founder Ernest E. Just in the First Issue of the *Oracle* in 1919, to *Members vs. Men*, crafted by Bro. Walter Mazyck in the March 1925 issue, to the many statements from Bro. Montague Cobb, that addressed the issue of the importance of Scholarship, one of our Four Cardinal Principles, the *Oracles* led the way. Further, the publication always had a statement from the Grand Basileus, which statements clearly reflect that Omega has had some great men at the helm. Each one was different in his right, but each still had Omega's best interest at heart, even if political considerations and competing interests prevented some of them from more fully realizing their initial objectives.

The lack of a defined location where we could securely store and access the *Oracles* was an immediate issue. However, Bro. Kent Amos (Alpha Omega) stepped forward and made space available in one of his Community Academy Public Charter School (CAPCS) buildings. He operates several charter schools in Washington, D.C., including

---

[67] "Omega - In the Last Quarter Century, 1986-2011, Centennial Souvenir Journal Statement, authored by Rohulamin Quander, Chairman, Third District History and Archives Committee, June 2011.

one in the old Armstrong High School building, located at First and P Streets, N.W. Armstrong was founded in about 1902, to provide a more generalized and manual training alternative to the famed Paul Dunbar High School. Together, these two schools educated most every African American who entered high school. The business division of Dunbar was extracted in about 1928, with the creation of the Cardozo High School. The provided space in the CAPCS building included internet access, telephone, and a secure place to store and maintain our growing archival files.

Bro. Amos and I have known each other for more than 50 years. Our dads were in Alpha Omega, and we have maintained our personal contact through the years. His generosity was most appreciated, and contributed mightily to the progress that we made. Having a central location from which to operate was essential, as information began to be uncovered from a variety of sources in addition to the *Oracles*. I still had a full-time job, so the best that I could do was to render my services to Omega in the evening and on Saturdays. I did both. I would drive to CAPCS several days a week, park my car on the school lot, and then take the bus to work. After work, I would take the bus back to the school, and work with the gleaned information until the night cleaning crew left at 10:00 p.m.

I followed this schedule religiously, and convened sub-committee meetings, telephone conference calls, and did some writing in the location. Meaningful progress was being made, but with it came the further realization that this was not a small project by any means. The call out for more volunteers went largely ignored. As well, several of the committee members began to wane in their interest, advising me that this project was too time consuming for the limited resources available. Still, I was not deterred.

The more we researched, the more we realized that we could not accurately tell the District's story if we did not likewise insert into our efforts and work product several pieces of extracted information from past *Oracles*. As chair, I recommended to the committee that we identify much of this extracted information and insert it into the text of what we are writing. These inserts are called "bump outs" and, properly inserted, are a valuable reference back to another time, but which are still relevant to the present. These bump outs would be a sentence or two, perhaps even a full paragraph, discussing civil rights, national projects, other things brothers were doing to respond to changing times. I talked to Tom Henderson, a good Kappa friend of mine, who referred me to the author of the then already completed Kappa Alpha Psi centennial book. He gave good suggestions on writing, emphasizing that the actual writing should be limited to a small group. That was a great suggestion, for at this point, I had already reached the same conclusion and was the only one doing the historical writing thus far.

Much of what I was doing at the time consisted of editing and expanding what Bro. Vernon Johnson and Bro. Joseph McKinney had already done,. However, the big difference was that much more information had been uncovered as well as some details that were heretofore not known or not included in what the prior two brothers had found. We intended to make the end product as exciting as possible, and deemed it necessary to include much of what was now known, but not previously mentioned or explored, since this was to be the first official history book to narrate the Third District from 1934 to the present.

I wrote to all 40 or so chapters in the District, requesting each to submit a written history statement, as well as to suggest from their chapter or knowledge, the names of brothers to be considered for Leadership Profiles. I even provided a detailed outline for them to follow, both for writing their chapter histories and for creating the leadership profiles. I regret that the response was far, far less than I wished for. Although some few chapters or brothers responded with the requested information, for the most part they did not respond initially, leaving me to call and call, and be accused in some instances of "harassing" them. Most of the brothers were polite about it, advising that they just had not done it, or that no history has ever been written about their respective chapter, and they simply did not know where to begin.

At this point, I was not about to take no for an answer, and had to take it to the DR level, entreating Anthony Knight to intervene and direct the chapters to cooperate. That was the essence of what was needed. Although several chapters still did not follow my written guidelines, so that the end product would be uniform, only then did I

## OMEGA'S CENTENNIAL, MY THRID OMEGA JUBILEE, 2011

receive a history from most chapters. Getting the statements from the undergraduate chapters was particularly challenging. All of them were students, and most of them had only been in the fraternity for less than two years. They simply did not have the institutional knowledge to write their chapter history.

I reached out to find alumni brothers of those chapters, and found greater, although greatly delayed, success. Still, as of this date, well past the initial time frames considered, I have never received history statements from certain chapters. Thus you know how and why this chapter is titled, "In Search of Omega's History." Far too many brothers of great note and accomplishment remain unsung, because those who followed them never learned who their chapter predecessors were and about what they did in life. One of the H&A committee's main objectives was to change that. Omega has brought, and still does, bring the best men home. But what good is it if no one knows about it.

We celebrate the achievements of our four Beloved Founders. We bask in the glory of reciting that Charles Drew, Benjamin Mays, L. Douglas Wilder, and Jesse Jackson are to be found in Omega's fold. But there were and are others, many, many others, who have made great individual and collective strides, furthering not only their personal selves, but benefitting us collectively as a group. My personal hero was James W. Quander, my dad, Alpha Omega, 1958. His was a life well lived, and I have done much to let others know of his personal trials, tribulations, joys, and triumphs.

> *In politics the accomplishments of L. Douglas Wilder (former governor of Virginia), Congressman James Clyburn (House of Representatives Whip), and Congressman Kendrick Meek (Democratic candidate for the U.S. Senate in 2011), validated that men who seek Omega are also those who are at the level of top achievers in every field of endeavor. Eight Omega brothers have graced a U.S. postage stamp, while 21 Omega men, beginning with Founder Ernest E. Just (First Awardee in 1915) have won the coveted Spingarn Medal, awarded by the NAACP for outstanding service. Six Omega brothers have earned the Medal since our 1986 Diamond Jubilee – Benjamin Hooks*

(1986); Jesse Jackson (1989); L. Douglas Wilder (1990); Earl G. Graves (1999); Vernon Jordan (2001); and Oliver Hill (2005). As well, Bro. Benjamin Mays and Bro. William Cosby each won the medal in 1982 and 1985, respectively. No other Black Greek-letter organization can claim such a distinction. In 2008 the keel of T-AKE 10 was laid and in 2010, the USNS Charles Drew was christened as a US Navy cargo ship, named after Dr. Charles R. Drew, the famed surgeon and hematologist. Bro. Drew was the uncle of astronaut Bro. Frederick Gregory.[68]

He and many other "ordinary" Omega men have done well, proving that they were not "ordinary" in the literal sense. They set a high tone for what an Omega man is supposed to be, and that realizing that higher plane, and making the sacrifices that are required to get there and to stay there, became the "ordinary" for them. Ordinary in this sense simply means that a high level of achievement and attainment is expected, and once there, dwelling among other men of like mind and similar attainment, becomes the expected, the "ordinary," if you will. That my brothers is the context within which I am pursuing writing this personal memoir.

When I was preparing to write the Third District's first published history book, the natural question was, what information might be in the history files of International Headquarters (IHQ)? None of us knew what was there. Nor was the staff in Decatur able to answer our questions. There was no one on staff who was specifically devoted to knowing and maintaining that history. Therefore, a trip to IHQ was necessary. As chair, I had to go, and asked around if there was anyone available to go with me. I did not want just "anyone," but rather someone who was history and research minded. No one stepped forward. Everyone that I talked to was committed one way or the other.

But then I realized that the person who was the most qualified and likewise available was my wife. A trained museum curator, with

---

[68] *"Omega - In the Last Quarter Century, 1986-2011, Centennial Souvenir Journal Statement,* authored by Rohulamin Quander, Chairman, Third District History and Archives Committee, June 2011.

both New York and Washington, D.C. museum curatorial experience, she was a natural to serve as my assistant and to help me expedite the effort to review the archives and make copies of whatever relevant documents might be located. We made plans to go to Atlanta in early November 2010. Searching for the best airfare and the most reasonably priced hotel and rental car, we took a very modesty priced trip to IHQ, and spent two and one half days in the archives.

The effort and the outcome were both quite enlightening. First, this was the initial expenditure that I made from the $15,000.00 that the District had allocated for the book project. Before the Centennial Celebration was concluded, it would become apparent that this figure was far too miserly, considering the scope of several extra requirements that the Supreme Council, IHQ, and others placed on the shoulders of the District and its H&A committee. My first inkling of a possible difficulty came when I got wind of some officials in the District questioning why I took my wife with me to IHQ at the fraternity's expense.

The cost to Omega, to include air fare, hotel, food, and archival supplies, was about $900.00. The cost to me was the use of three days of annual leave taken from my job and duties as a Senior Administrative Law Judge for the District of Columbia. The cost to Carmen was being away from her job as a professional artist and operating her studio and art gallery. Still, we lodged no complaint because we knew that the assignment had to be done, and that Omega would be all the better for it when completed.

While her curatorial credentials might not have been well known to certain brothers, her skills as an organizer were. She had organized several events for Omega, locally on the District level. Further, in her capacity as a professional artist, she created the 1986 Diamond Jubilee Souvenir Journal Cover, and other covers for fraternity events. Her adherence to meticulous detail has placed Omega in several favorable lights, and this journey to IHQ was no exception. As we worked side by side, under the direction of IHQ staff, Carmen and I located several significant documents that helped to shape both Omega's and the District's history.

Together, we found statements written by Founders Cooper and Love, but none from Founder Coleman. In his statement, Bro. Cooper said that in retrospect, Omega should have adopted Service as the fifth Cardinal Principle, but that Service could be implied in the purpose and proper execution of the other Four Cardinal Principles, for living with by those Principles, mandates that we as Omega men be of service to others.[69] We found a letter from Bro. Carter G. Woodson expressing consternation with the fraternity about setting up its own Achievement Week, and more than 10 years after Negro History Week had been established, declining to be guest speaker at Achievement Week events for 1938. We found an original copy of "Omega Dear," with a hand written note at the bottom from Bro. Mercer Cook directed to Bro. Charles Drew, admonishing him to not loose the enclosed copy, this time. But worst of all, we found that Omega's archives are in horrible disarray.

The file cabinets are so tightly packed, often with irrelevant or no longer significant information, that it is almost impossible to find anything. As well, there is no reasonable way to catalogue anything, because the documents are simply not accessible. Much of what is in the files need not be kept any longer. For example, a 1937 letter to the Grand KRS indicating that a check is enclosed representing chapter dues to the national body. It says nothing beyond that, but, multiplied 10,000 times over the decades, takes up space and renders nothing in return.

Carmen's initial main objective was to locate photographs of the Founders as much younger men. That effort was an exercise in frustration. We found nothing. There were thousands of photographs, taken by myriad photographers over the decades, but little was identified as to place, persons, or events. It was not possible to do any photographic research of any value, given the way that things were scattered about, sometimes stacked on top of cabinets, and wads of photos several inches deep. That was no way to store anything, and is likewise incompatible with any effort to research, identify, and evaluate. This component of our history search effort was a complete failure.

---

[69] *See Founder Cooper's letter to Bro. George A. Isabel, December 17, 1941, previously referenced.*

## OMEGA'S CENTENNIAL, MY THRID OMEGA JUBILEE, 2011

Distressed, I met with Bro. George A. Smith, then the Executive Director at IHQ, and told him that we were both disappointed and frustrated at the state of Omega's archives, which were not accessible for historical research. I added that with the fraternity's Centennial year almost here, it was inconceivable to me that nothing had been done to date to vastly improve what we have. There are very important documents in this building, but who can find anything, much less put the historical significance of anything to good use for all to be aware of and share.

While on site, I noted a trailer and asked what that was. To my horror, I was told that this is a "storage trailer" where other historically significant documents are stored, some older documents in fact, but that no one is allowed to go into the trailer, except for Lewis Anderson, Grand Keeper of Records and Seal. However, by this time, November 2010, Anderson had been removed from his position by the Supreme Council for dereliction of duty. Further, he is alleged to have removed many of Omega's original archival documents, supposedly for "safe keeping" and has refused to return them. He had the keys to the trailer, and knew well what was in it. Entering the trailer was deemed to be unsafe, as mold had accumulated in some of the documents, and many of the documents were scattered, even on the floor. We understood that access to the trailer and its contents was not to be granted to us. Nor would we want to enter it under the circumstances explained.

Bro. Smith assured Carmen and me that IHQ was aware of the problem, and the need to protect and preserve Omega's archives, but that the funds to really do a first class job were simply not available. I suggested that it be done in stages, with the first stage being to thin out the documents, and discard those that are determined to not have historical significance. Volunteers, perhaps brothers from the area, could be trained to discard useless paper. Otherwise, it is too costly to pay professionals to come in, have them go through and evaluate each piece of paper, at our expense, only to then discard useless documents and scan the rest. I told Bro. Smith that this would be paying a high price to have our trash taken out. He fully understood my point, and was polite to a fault. Our meeting ended with his assuring me that the Supreme Council hoped to get the archival project underway, but no time frame has been determined.

This was my first visit to IHQ. It is a beautiful building, reasonably well maintained, but located in the wrong place. Decatur, Georgia is a bit of a no-mans-land. There are no restaurants in close proximity other than fast food places. The neighborhood is not at all upscale, and my first impression was one of apprehension about how and why we managed to put ourselves into such a place. I believe that the building was previously a higher education site for the State of Georgia, and have been told that it was constructed at that location many years ago, with the hope that the state's presence would spark some economic development. Well, from what I have been told, the experiment did not work.

And eventually the state decided to unload the building. Enter, Omega Psi Phi! I heard that the building was mostly occupied when we purchased it in about 1994-95, but shortly after we took ownership, several tenants vacated, including the higher education tenant. When researching, I asked the Omega staff what percentage of the building was occupied. The answer – about 30% of the rentable space was occupied. Omega was not included in that percentage, since the fraternity was the building owner. No one wanted to say anything further about the area where IHQ was located, other than to express belief and hope that things will improve "in the near future."

Back in Washington, I reported to my H&A committee the results of what we learned. First, although there is much to be found at IHQ, we were not that successful in locating anything particularly historical or significant about the Third District. Not that there was nothing there, but the status of what was there was so poorly handled, or not handled at all, that it was virtually impossible to find anything. Still we were fortunate to find those significant documents that I previously mentioned, such as a copy of the original *Omega Dear,* and statements from Founders Cooper and Love. We were not discouraged though, because the trip to IHQ was a great incentive to make a difference where we could, and the Third District was our calling.

The brothers researched and submitted more Leadership Profiles, more photos were located, and a few of the older brothers were

## OMEGA'S CENTENNIAL, MY THRID OMEGA JUBILEE, 2011

interviewed about their life as members of the fraternity. I conducted three interviews of very senior brothers, i.e. Bro. Dr. David H. Reid, Jr., then age 101 (Upsilon 1927); Frank P. Bolden, then age 93 (Upsilon 1937); and Benjamin Spaulding, then age 99 (Alpha 1931). All of them were still very enthusiastic about Omega, having remained active and financial throughout their years of loyal and faithful membership. With a respective fraternal affiliation of 83, 73, and 79 years, these brothers had 235 years of Omega membership.

All three brothers, Bro. David H. Reid, Jr., Bro. Bolden and Bro, Spaulding are now enshrined in Omega Chapter, at the time that I was writing this Memoir. Bro. Reid lived to be 104 years old, and remained quite lucid, and still in love with Omega until the very end. Earlier, in November 2012, Dr. Reid was awarded Omega's first 85-year membership recognition, presented to him twice. The first presentation was at the Alpha Omega 90th anniversary dinner, held on November 2, 2012. Dr. Reid Jr., was not present, but his son, Bro. Dr. Reid, III, accepted the recognition on his father's behalf. Two weeks later, the recognition was re-presented to Bro. Reid, Jr., at the Founders Day convocation, held on November 17, 2012, at Howard University. This time he was present, feisty, and full of enthusiasm.

Cramton Auditorium was packed for this annual event. Having been lifted up on the stage in his wheelchair, so that Omega's sons could see who he was, and likewise enjoy his words of wisdom, Bro. Reid counseled us to always adhere to Omega's Four Cardinal Principles and to do nothing that would show disrespect or bring shame upon the fraternity, adding that he took a sacred oath on November 17, 1927, in the subbasement of the home of Bro. Col. Charles Young, located just off the campus of Wilberforce University. And in that oath, he swore to uphold Omega's meaning and to be a brother and friend to many, and especially those who shared the brotherhood. At this brothers-only convocation, the crowd went crazy, as you could observe tears in the eyes of several men who were emotionally taken back, just to be in the presence of a brother who met all of our Four Founders and was most likely Omega's oldest son, both in terms of years and length of fraternal affiliation.

In November 2010, one week after my research at IHQ. I interviewed Bro. Reid at his home in Fairfax County, Virginia. He had been looking forward to the interview and wanted to share some little known information about his life as an Omega man, and particularly events related to his pledge period and initiation. During the course of the interview, I was so impressed with Bro. Reid's words, that I deemed it essential that they be reproduced in the *Oracle*. Working with Bro. Reid, III, we wrote and submitted an article to the *Oracle*, which appeared in the Winter 2011 edition. Below, I state the essence of what he said, although a more full account can be gleaned from referring to the above-noted *Oracle*:

> *I, David H. Reid, Jr., was born in Raleigh, N.C. on May 17, 1909 and was first introduced to the Omega Psi Phi Fraternity at Shaw University located in that city. At that time there were no high schools in Raleigh that African-Americans could attend. However, both Shaw and St. Augustine, the other predominantly black college in Raleigh, offered high school courses. I was impressed with the Omega brotherhood and after my graduation from Shaw's high school curriculum in the spring of 1926, I entered Wilberforce University of Ohio, and in the fall of that year was inducted into the Lampados Club.*
>
> *A year later, on a cold and dreary day in mid-November [November 17] 1927, I, along with my other two line brothers, was taken from the campus blindfolded and walked a distance to what we assumed was a house. With assistance, the three of us entered the house and were immediately led down a staircase to the basement. To my surprise we were led down another staircase to a sub-basement with a dirt floor, where the induction rights of the Omega Psi Phi Fraternity were administered. Along with my two line brothers, I arose as Brother Reid. We were three new and proud members of the Upsilon Chapter of Omega Psi Phi. My Omega brand, though faded, is still identifiable on my chest. Later that month, I returned to Raleigh for Thanksgiving as "Brother Reid," so proud of my Omega pin, and wore it almost constantly.*

## OMEGA'S CENTENNIAL, MY THRID OMEGA JUBILEE, 2011

*During the initiation, it was revealed that the sub-basement was a station on the Underground Railroad. The house was owned by "Mother Young," wife of the deceased Omega Brother Colonel Charles Young, the highest ranking black officer (Lt. Colonel) in the United States Army until his death in 1922. The Colonel Charles Young house is a National Historic Landmark in Wilberforce, Ohio. In the fraternity, I, along with other chapter brothers, tutored young men in mathematics, science and English, many of whom later became Omegas. I recollect that there were not many members of the Fraternity at Wilberforce at that time. The academic and character standards of the Fraternity were so strict that few were eligible and even fewer were chosen.*[70]

---

[70] *Brother Dr. David Reid, Jr., Celebrates his 101st Birthday and 83 years in Omega Psi Phi Fraternity, Inc. Submitted by Br. David H. Reid, III, and Bro. Rohulamin Quander. The Oracle, Winter 2011 Edition, P. 32.*

# 50+ OMEGA INSPIRED YEARS

# XXII – Centennial Countdown

*Omega Psi Phi Fraternity has progressed from a simple organization composed of four men to take on the administrative character and complexity of the modern business corporation. It has caused more than 100,000 men to be guided in their lives by its Cardinal Principles – MANHOOD, SCHOLARSHIP, PERSEVERANCE, and UPIFT. May the light of the beacon continue to shine and send forth rays of life indicative of FRIENDSHIP and FRATERNITY.[71]*

On November 17, 2010, Omega Psi Phi convened a press conference on the steps of Science (Thirkield) Hall, Howard University, to formally announce the fraternity's centennial. This convocation represented the official countdown to the day, one year hence, on which our beloved fraternity was born. Gathered on those steps to commemorate what our Founders believed in and established were several members of the Supreme Council, supplemented by several brothers who had converged from the local area, anxious to be present and included in an event of history in the making.

Bro. Dr. Andrew A. Ray, 39th Grand Basileus, had been present in Washington, D.C. for the Supreme Council's meeting, but was called away due to a death in the family. However, his prepared remarks were delivered by Bro. Dr. Moses C. Norman, 33rd Grand Basileus, an extract of which appears below.

*Today is in all respects an historic and memorable day in the life of the Omega Psi Phi Fraternity, Inc. We gather here at Howard University on the steps of Thirkield Hall to kick off a year-long celebration of the upcoming Centennial Celebration of this brotherhood. It was here at Howard University on November 17,*

---

[71] *Extracted from the 75th Anniversary Diamond Jubilee 68th Conclave, Washington, D.C., "Omega Psi Phi Fraternity, An Historical perspective," unnumbered page, co- authored by Bro. William Clement, Grand Marshal, Bro. Kenneth A. Brown, Deputy Grand Marshal, Bro. Herber B. Dixon, and Bro. Rohulamin Quander.*

## 50+ OMEGA INSPIRED YEARS

*1911, that Omega was founded by three undergraduates under the guidance of their biology professor.*

*I doubt that Edgar A. Love, Oscar J. Cooper, and Frank Coleman could have envisioned this day when they convinced Professor Ernest E. Just to help them give birth to such an outstanding Greek later fraternity that would expand exponentially from Alpha Chapter, "the Mother Pearl" chapter, to more than 700 chapters worldwide. Yet today we stand here to bear witness to this fact.*[72]

As the Centennial Celebration was approaching, the Third District's host chapters, primarily located in the Washington, D.C., picked up the pace of making final preparations. Bro. Kenneth A. Brown, Grand Marshal, seemed to be on track and on schedule, but pulling together and executing an event of this magnitude and diversity was surely not easy. Many logistical assignments were given out, from "A" to "Z. Laughingly, we called it from Alpha Zeta. No detail was to be considered insignificant. No assignment was to be looked at as of little worth or value. And the questions came a mile a minute. Frequent Steering Committee meetings were held at the Omega house, while sub-committees convened in smaller groups or via telephone conference.

*But the foregoing is evidence of an extreme dichotomy, as all is not well within our African American communities. Within the last 25 years, there has been a marked increase of attention into the plight of African American males. Often referred to as "an endangered species" or "at risk," the negative blight of slavery, and the legacies of lack of freedom, equality, access to a quality education, employment opportunities, and health care, have all contributed to high crime and frustration within our communities.*

*What is the role of Omega when facing such a seemingly insurmountable problem? There is neither a single nor a simple answer. But Omega, both collectively and as a community of*

---

[72] *Extract from the Official Press conference Statement of Dr. Andrew A. Ray, 39th Grand Basileus, Howard University, November 17, 2010.*

## CENTENNIAL COUNTDOWN

*individual brothers, has already stepped forward and been nationally and locally identified on two particularly essential points, i.e., The Fatherhood Initiative and the Stop the Violence Campaign. Under the leadership of Bro. Robert Fairchild, former Grand KRS, Alpha Omega Chapter, and a stalwart cluster of other devoted Omegas, the fraternity's profile in both efforts has captured national attention and interest at the highest levels of government. Noting that he did not have the presence of his own father when he was growing up, President Obama has expressed gratitude that educated African American men have taken the lead in promoting the importance of fathers being a key and lasting component of their children's lives. Further, increasingly, more chapters are engaging in activities designed to elevate the prospects for the members of our own race by encouraging young men to step up and assume their fatherhood and domestic responsibilities, and likewise, to eliminate any physical acts of violence in their personal conduct.*[73]

I will not go into too much detail, on matters incidental to printing programs and tickets, menus for meals and particularly the Founders' Centennial Banquet, and the successful execution of the traditional public meeting are all a matter of the public record. And of course, if anything could go wrong, it sometimes did. Missed printing instructions, cold food, and generally miscommunication will and did happen. These are the foibles that we are confronted with in life, and which patience-testing incidents make us stronger as Omega men. From my perspective, however, only one significant subject area was amiss, but I do not hold the Grand Marshal to too high a level of accountability, as the call, that resulted in a mishap, came from another corner.

Referring to my personal calendar for 2011, I am amazed at how much time I devoted to promoting Omega and helping to shape the final plans for the Centennial Celebration. Averaging about two

---

[73] *"Omega - In the Last Quarter Century, 1986-2011, Centennial Souvenir Journal Statement, authored by Rohulamin Quander, Chairman, Third District History and Archives Committee, June 2011.*

evenings a week and most Saturdays, I devoted my time to working on the history book project. Well aware that the book would not be completed in time for the Conclave, still the H&A Committee was focused and determined to keep working to make the end product one that we could all be proud of. It was imperative, therefore, that we take our time and get it right. Bro. Emmanuel "Manny" McRae was doing an excellent job as our official photographer. Bro. Jamal Parker, Beta 1996, the District's photographer, continued to provide important photos as time progressed.

Chapter histories continued to slowly come in, as well as Leadership Profiles for Omega men from all walks of life. We were clearly on focus, and with my leadership, victory would eventually be ours. As a member of my committee commented during one of our frequent, and sometimes bi-weekly meetings, "Bro. Quander, the history of the frat reflects a Dreer history book in 1940, and the Gill history book in 1961, and not much since. So we really have to get this book right, because it is the only shot that we are going to have at this effort. And you know, after this, there will probably not be another history book on the Third District for another 100 years. So, let's get this book right!" That was our charge. But how do you do that? What is your resource base? And then there is the question of money.

In January 2011, six months before the brothers came to town, our mission was very much evident, even though we did not see how we could get a book completed by the July Centennial Conclave. But work towards completing a quality product we did. However, by May, much of our objective would be compromised by some short-notice directives that were issued by Omega's International Headquarters in Decatur Georgia that complicated our efforts. But before I get to that, it is necessary to address the issue of monetary resources.

In 2010, the Third District appropriated $15,000 for the history project, which was anticipated to be for a unilateral result, i.e. the history book. It is traditional to add a surcharge onto the District dues to underwrite or supplement expenses incidental to hosting a Grand Conclave. This time it was no different. However, since there had not been a conclave in the Third District since 1986, there were questions, and even grumbling in some circles, about the extra added expenses that the brothers would be incurring. Not a few complained that not only were they being assessed an extra fee to support the conclave, they were also facing significant conclave activity participation fees, such as registration, hotel rooms, extra tickets, parking, etc. Yes, it proved to be a costly undertaking, but something that only occurs on rare occasion. All things being equal, there will probably not be another Grand Conclave in Washington, D.C. until 2036, out 125th anniversary.

Although $15,000 had been placed in the budget for the District's history project, that line item did not consider anything else that would come up. Admittedly, at the time that the money was put into the budget, the diversity and magnitude of the additional matters that we would soon face, was not known. Begging the brotherhood to please step forward and alert us to where our Third District archival documents might be located, we got no more than one or two responses. Most inquiries led to a similar response – travel to IHQ and inspect their archives, for surely they have something.

As our research progressed, many of the results revealed an emerging pattern of sustained achievement that simply could not be ignored. With the Centennial Celebration fast approaching, I discovered that more Omega men than I ever realized had won the coveted Spingarn Medal, since the first was awarded to Founder Just in 1915. As well, eight Omega men have appeared on U.S. postage stamps. These were historical facts of such significance that they could not be ignored. When I mentioned these two points to Dr. Andrew A. Ray, 39th Grand Basileus, during one of the Washington, D.C. planning meetings, he replied, "I have been trying to get some movement with the NAACP, to get authority to list the names and publish a short bio of our Omega brothers who are Spingarn Medal winners. Can you take that on and get it completed for me?" What was I to say, other than "Sure, Bro. Grand?" And so I inherited another major assignment, one that would prove to be both a mammoth undertaking, and likewise a great success.

Contacting the NAACP in New York, and talking with Mrs. Roxborough, a volunteer, she proffered that although the NAACP did have photographs of all of its winners, plus a bio of each, perhaps it would be much easier and quicker to extract all of the needed information from the Internet. She added that it was not her intent to send us away, as the NAACP welcomes all inquiries and is only too happy to be of assistance, when possible. However, the nature of my request, and the shortness of time within which to complete the request and assignment augured for the quickest solution possible. During the conversation, I also discovered that she was the stepmother of Bro. Claude Roxborough, who was inducted into Omega via Kappa Psi chapter, and John Roxborough, both of Washington, D.C.

If one is going to undertake this Spingarn Medal documentation, it is likewise both obvious and necessary to parallel it with publishing the list of the eight Omega men who have appeared on U.S. postage stamps. Contacting my line brother, Dr. David Reid, III, M.D., National Director of the U.S. Postal Medical Program, I was directed to Carlos Rudas and Roy Betts, both of whom worked in the public outreach office of the U.S. Postal Service national headquarters, located on L'Enfant Plaza in Washington, D.C. After writing a detailed proposal that included the request to have the eight Omega men featured in a history display at the Centennial, I was requested to come to the office for a face to face meeting.

There I laid out the highlights of my prior communications, underscoring that Omega was a national organization that included men of stellar credentials, and that ours was a glorious and illustrious history that the USPS would surely want to sponsor, by donating eight posters, one for each of Omega's famed sons. After a brief hiatus of perhaps 10 days, Mr. Rudas called me and advised that the USPS would gladly provide the eight requested posters at their own expense, and would further make an additional poster that listed all of the 22 Omega men who were Spingarn Medal winners.[74] I was

---

[74] *This list includes: Ernest R. Just (1915), Col. Charles Young (1916), Roland T. Hayes (1924), Carter G. Woodson (1926), William Hastie ( 1943), Charles R. Drew (1944), Percy Julian (1947), Ernest Green (1959), Langston Hughes (1960), Robert C. Weaver (1962), Roy Wilkins (1964), Clarence M. Mitchell, Jr., (1969), Wilson C. Riles (1973), Benjamin Mays (1982), Bill Cosby (1985), Benjamin Hooks (1986), Jesse Jackson (1989), L. Douglas Wilder (1990), A. Leon*

## CENTENNIAL COUNTDOWN

elated. My hard work, including face-to face meetings and several written communications to several high up administrators in the USPS, had paid off. But the amount of personal time and energy, including incidental costs related to parking, gasoline, photocopying, and postage, were all taking their financial toll. Although I did submit several receipts to the fraternity for reimbursement from the H&A budget, I also elected to absorb some of the costs, as my devotion to the fraternity dictated to me that I should shoulder some of the expenses.

At about this same time, early March 2011, I had the distinct honor of being invited to join the Supreme Council and other designated brothers to conduct a one day pilgrimage to the grave sites of all four of the fraternity's Founders. This activity was a planned Centennial event, and was anticipated with much excitement. The invited guests joined the Supreme Council at the Grand Hyatt Hotel, located in Crystal City, Virginia, on Saturday, March 12, 2011, at about 8:00 a.m. The group consisted of one full bus, plus several other brothers who followed by automobile in caravan.

Our first stop was Lincoln Memorial Cemetery, located in Suitland, Maryland, just across the D.C. line in Southeast. On the way from the hotel to the first stop, several brothers on the bus, including First Vice Grand Basileus, Antonio F. Knox, Sr., and other members of the Supreme Council, made remarks that reflected upon the significance of what we were about to do – to pay tribute to our Founders by making a respectful visit to their respective final resting places. Upon arrival, we were greeted by a large gathering of other brothers, mostly from the local D.C.-Virginia chapters, who elected to join the entourage at the gravesite.

---

*Higginbotham, Jr. (1996), Earl G. Graves (1999), Vernon Jordan (2001), and Oliver W. Hill (2005). Source - Spingarn Medal Winners, 1915 to June 1, 2011. This honor is awarded to "American Negroes who perform acts of distinguished merit and achievement." Created by NAACP President Joel Elias Spingarn in 1914, to date, at least 22 of the Medal winner are members of Omega Psi Phi Fraternity, Inc., beginning with Founder Ernest E. Just, the first Medal winner in 1915.*

## 50+ OMEGA INSPIRED YEARS

Entering Lincoln Cemetery is like taking a major historical trip. There are so many famous Washington, D.C. luminaries buried there, that one cannot help but feel that you have not only entered very sacred ground, but are also in the midst of lasting greatness. Just as you turn into the main entrance of the cemetery and travel around the circle, you are viewing the final resting places of Bro. Carter G. Woodson, Mary Church Terrell's family, and the beloved Nellie May Quander. As well, there are many others of like status who are interred at that location. As I have said to friends who have visited the area and commented on the location of so many historical luminaries there, this is *very special ground.*

Not far from these three luminaries, and just up the hill, is the gravesite of Founder Frank Coleman and other members of his family. The Coleman gravesite was the first of the four that we visited. The brothers assembled in a reverential manner, removed their hats on this cold, windy day, and stood in silence. Bro. Knox, standing in for Grand Basileus Ray, delivered prepared remarks which noted the role that Founder Coleman played in the birth and early nurture of Omega. Bro. Knox then led the placing of a purple and gold floral wreath at the site. Also interred in the family plot was Edna Brown Coleman, wife of our Founder. She was one of the 22 Founders of Delta Sigma Theta in January 1913, after the young sorors broke away from AKA in October 1912. There were no Coleman or Brown family members present at the memorial wreath laying.

The prepared remarks, first delivered at the Coleman gravesite, were the same for each of our Four Founders, with only the name differences and years of the births and deaths inserted, as follows (using Founder Just as the stand-in for all):

> Founder Ernest E. Just – *Brothers, 100 years have passed, and we are assembled here today to pay reverence and admiration to our dearly departed Founder, Dr. Ernest E. Just. As all life must perish, and ever as we must come to the crossing of the Great Divide, so did this Founder reach that stage in 1941. Let us continue to avail ourselves to the will of the Supreme Basileus of the Universe. Brothers, on August 14, 1883, Founder Just entered a world that was dark and full of want. On November 17, 1911, along with Founders Bishop Edgar A. Love, Dr. Oscar*

## CENTENNIAL COUNTDOWN

*J. Cooper, and Professor Frank Coleman, they decided to organize an institution that would reflect God's original intentions of: Manhood, Scholarship, Perseverance, and Uplift.*

*Founder Just was, and will always be, a shining light in the bright crown of Omega. The radiance of his star has furnished a guiding ray to many who have come after him to seek the light of Omega. We are Brothers, bound inseparably by a chain of Friendship and Brotherhood that makes the joys of one, the joys of all. As a fraternity, we share the burdens, toils, cares, happiness, pleasures, hope, dreams and even our very life with each other. Our comradeship, my brothers, extends even to, and yet beyond the grave. No height, depth, or wall is high, wide or strong enough to separate us from each other; regardless of the state or station we find ourselves in. So Brothers, give head to our Grand Chaplain, who will now speak.*[75]

After the chaplain delivered a short but very poignant prayer of thanksgiving for the life and contributions of Bro. Coleman to Omega and the world, we traversed down a hill, perhaps 100 feet away, and came to the final resting site of Founder Ernest E. Just. How fitting that they were brothers in life, and remain physically close to one another in their final resting places. Once again, Bro. Knox fulfilled his role, and delivered remarks reminiscent of the contributions of Founder Just to the creation of Omega. Only this time, Kathy Just Robinson, granddaughter of the Founder, was present and welcomed the brotherhood to the site. She noted that she was pleased to be present and that the family appreciated that her grandfather, Ernest E. Just, was still so well remembered and respected by his fraternity. She is a Howard University graduate and a member of Delta Sigma Theta.

Next, we re-boarded the bus and travelled to the Mt. Auburn Cemetery, a United Methodist cemetery that contains mostly African Americans. The cemetery is located in Mt. Auburn, Maryland, just on the edge of south Baltimore. Founder Love and Mrs. Love are interred

---

[75] *Remarks delivered by Bro. Antonio Knox, First Vice Grand Basileus, representing Grand Basileus Dr. Andrew A. Ray, and the Men of the Omega Psi Phi Fraternity, March 12, 2011.*

in a location along the fence that is just to the left, perhaps 40 feet from entrance. Upon arrival, we were greeted by several Baltimore-based brothers, mostly from Pi Omega chapter. Like Their D.C.-Virginia counterparts, these brothers had come out to greet us and to support the pilgrimage, but I doubt if many of them continued on to Founder Oscar J. Cooper's burial site in Philadelphia.

Once again, Bro. Know delivered his message, recognizing Founder Love for his vision that helped to make Omega the mainstay that it has become. Founder Love was represented by his son, Bro. Jon Love, his wife, Jon's son, and other Love family members. Jon Love thanked us for coming and for remembering his father, who loved Omega so very much.[76]

Several members of the fraternity commented upon how poorly maintained the cemetery was, asserting that although Founder and Mrs. Love appear to have the best maintained site in the cemetery, the cemetery was clearly suffering from neglect. The weeds were already

---

[76] *Bro. Jon Love was inducted into Omega as an honorary brother in 2012 upon the decision of the Supreme Council. He was sponsored by Bro. Adam McKee, former First Vice Grand Basileus. At the time of his induction, Bro. Love took his sacred oath upon Founder Love's bible, and was pinned with Founder Love's Omega pin, which he, now Bro. Jon Love, deeply treasures. As the author of this Memoir, I had been suggesting to the brotherhood that Jon Love should be inducted into Omega. From what I understand, some brothers maintained that Bro. Love allegedly did not initially qualify for membership because he lacked a college degree.*

*However, Omega has through the years inducted other men into the fraternity, conveying honorary status upon them, despite the fact that some of them lacked a college degree. The response with regard to this group has mostly been, "But they made some stellar achievement in their professional field, but Jon Love is an 'ordinary man' who has not so distinguished himself." My response then, and still, has been, "Omega can do what it wants, and Jon Love has been there with us for all these years. It is time that we accord him this honor and I am stoutly in favor of doing so." Apparently, at long last, someone in a position of authority agreed with me and took the necessary steps to make it happen.*

tall, implying that there had been no mower through the site since last year. As well, several of the grave markers were leaning, and a disproportionate number of them were lying flat on the ground. We could not help but be disappointed at the lack of care that Mt. Auburn Cemetery was receiving, although Founder Love's site and stone marker were very clean and upright. A comment was made, and I will assume that it is true, that the brothers of the Baltimore area keep an eye on the site, to assure that it does not fall into the appearance of neglect that so characterized the other sites in the immediate area.

That would stand to reason, because Founder Love was Omega's longest serving visionary, and it would be most fitting for the brothers to commit themselves to assuring that his final resting place is up to par. Still, it is somewhat discouraging to work to maintain a standard, but to be likewise surrounded by such an indication of neglect. I do not know why the cemetery is not better maintained, and I would prefer not to believe that the basis is not due to the location in a poor, predominantly black neighborhood.

Back on the bus for the longer ride, to Whitemarsh Memorial Park, the suburban Philadelphia area cemetery where Founder Oscar J. Cooper and Willa Cooper, his wife, are interred. This site was a totally different place. Set in a peaceful, beautifully maintained site, Founder Cooper is resting is a very high class and well maintained site. Although Founder Cooper and his wife had no children, upon arrival we were greeted by several of the late Mrs. Cooper's family members. There were at least three generations present, to include older people and their grandchildren. After introducing myself to one of Mrs. Cooper's nieces, she retorted that "Uncle Oscar was like a father, and grandfather to all of us. So today this is the least that we could do to honor his memory." Later, I would observe some of the same individuals at the July 2011 Centennial Conclave celebration, likewise giving recognition and tribute to the memory of Founder Cooper.

Several brothers from Mu Omega and other Philadelphia area chapters were also in attendance, and listened attentively as Bro Knox delivered his fourth and final message of the day, thus bringing the Omega pilgrimage to all Four Founders' gravesites to a close. I do not think that there was a scribe to record the remarks, or to capture the impressions of the brothers and family members as we made all four stops on our journey. Suffice it is to say that the entire event was sacred, much appreciated and timely. As we were preparing to observe Omega's One Hundredth anniversary, it was fitting that we should pause, to see where we came from, how we got to where we are, and to commemorate the roles that each of our four beloved Founders played, respectively, in allowing these great days to now be upon us.

This one day pilgrimage was a true eye opener. As a loyal son of Omega since 1964, I increasingly see many things differently from yesteryear. I was never solely a "rah, rah" brother, as I always understood, even from my early teen years, that Omega was a serious organization, comprised of men of high ideals and like attainment. Still, to be in the presence of such men, to watch them humble themselves in the face of the greatness of our Founders, was a unique experience. And this experience likewise strengthened me in my resolve and increased dedication to upholding all that is dear to Omega Psi Phi.

As we concluded the four site pilgrimage to our Founders' resting places, I was infused with an even greater desire to be a better son of Omega, an example to others who will follow in my footsteps, and to create a path for them to follow. As well, to see the many well connected Omega men who were on the bus to humble themselves in the shadow of the greatness that was our four Founders, I was likewise inspired. This was a time for self-examination, reflection, and to come to realization that Omega is only as great as its membership acting in concert. Being men of like interest and like attainment is a good place from which to start, but these ideals have to be put into practice in order to make the fraternity continue to be a living entity.

I left the pilgrimage basking in the bright light emanating from Omega's beacon. But the bright light only reaches so far. There was much work to do between now and the upcoming Celebration in July. The Supreme Council had been meeting throughout this same period. And the outcome of many of those meetings were some new directives, instructions about how to make the Centennial Celebration better, how to accommodate more people, and logistical issues that seemed to keep popping up. For a while it seemed as though this was the first time that the brothers had ever planned a Grand Conclave. I could not help but wonder whether some of the uncertainty was due to the fact that we had been under the meandering helm of Warren G. Lee, Jr., 38th Grand Basileus, about whom there continues to be much discontent, despite his having left office.

Although Bro. Lee came up through Omega's ranks, and held many positions of fraternal leadership, including First Vice Grand Basileus, once he was elected as Grand Basileus in 2006, Omega seemed to become a rudderless ship. Some brothers maintain that the drift began before then, but became extremely obvious during his watch. Not until 2010, when he was succeeded by Andrew A. Ray, 39th Grand Basileus, did the drift in high waters begin to really change. During Lee's tenure, my impression is, and it is likewise the view of many other brothers as well, that Omega lacked someone at the helm with a firm guiding hand, to assure where we were headed. Sparing you the details, I believe that during Bro. Lee's four year tenure, Omega lost much of her focus.

Still, we had good leadership in the presence of many who had previously served as Grand Basilei, and others who were former Supreme Council members. Without them stepping forward, Omega might never have observed its Centennial, or the events could have been so poorly planned and executed as to make us the laughing stock of the other members of the Divine Nine and beyond. Although the brothers managed to pull the Centennial Conclave together, it was not without some scary moments, when it appeared that "little to not much" might be the end result.

As an "ordinary" brother, without national level credentials, and not privy to what was going on internally, I do know that several of the living former grand basilei banned together, and essentially took away from Grand Basileus Lee the responsibility of assuring that the 100 Anniversary celebration would be properly executed. It appears that Lee was toying with one thing, and then another. But in the interim, the months between then and the outset of the Centennial were growing shorter, and the time to assure success was likewise being compromised. These former grand basilei, each of whom has worked to assure that there would be no cause to find Omega wanting in any significant respect, were faced with the possibility that

## 50+ OMEGA INSPIRED YEARS

Omega would be found wanting when it came to noting her Centennial Celebration. And that just could not be!

All of the living former grand basilei stepped forward to right the drifting ship, although some assumed more involvement than others. The weight of the planning fell on the shoulders of former grand basilei Burnel Coulon (31st), Moses C. Norman (33rd), C. Tyrone Gilmore (34th), Dorsey Miller (35th), and Lloyd Jordon (36th). As well, former grand basilei Bro. Edward Braynon (30th) and George H. Grace (37th) did lend their involvement and support, although apparently not at the same level of personal involvement. Determined to execute a workable plan for our Centennial Celebration, the leaders got to work, seeking to close the reduced time gap issue, while still making the event as grand as we wanted it to be.

With the request for volunteers to step up and help pull off this once-a-century celebration, I sat in many organizational meetings. Some planning sessions convened at the local chapter house on Harvard Street in D.C., while others were held at the Hyatt Hotel in Crystal City, Virginia. These were two separate sets of meetings, each with a different, although overlapping focus. The D.C.-based meetings were primarily dealing with local issues. Logistics, transportation, Omega Wives/Quette activities, inquiry about the Third District history project, and who do we need to meet with for various reasons, were all on the local table. However, nothing was ever said about the need to set up a Third District history exhibit, an oversight that would later prove to be most unsettling.

On the national table, the issues were on a grander scale, i.e., typically how many hotel rooms do we need and the status of incoming reservations, how much space will we occupy in the Bro. Walter E. Washington Convention Center, getting fraternal content and advertisements for the hard cover Centennial Souvenir Journal, and then securing a printing contract, life membership activities, the status of confirming noted brother and other guest speakers for certain events, details related to planned breakfasts, luncheons, and banquets, including to whom and how membership plaques would be awarded to qualifying brothers. Everything appeared to be well organized, and for the most part, it was.

## CENTENNIAL COUNTDOWN

Bro. Kenneth A. Brown (Delta Theta 1971) was selected by the Supreme Council to serve as the Centennial Grand Marshal. However, from some accounts it appears that this appointment was reluctantly bestowed by Grand Basileus Lee, based upon a personal animus. Bro. Brown, a former Grand Keeper of Finance, had twice contested Bro. Lee for the position of 38th Grand Basileus. The first contest was during the 74th Grand Conclave, held July 2006 in Little Rock, Arkansas. It was a hard fought battle, and some personal animosity seemed to be lingering between the two men, particularly from Lee towards Brown.

During his first two-year term as Grand Basileus, there was some discontent expressed against Bro. Lee's leadership shortcomings. Many brothers, mostly from the rank and file, regretted having elevated him to Omega's highest office, and some expressed that they should have elected Bro. Brown as a more than fitting candidate to serve Omega at a time when some components of our national level programs needed updated attention from within some of the 12 regional districts.

As the time drew near for the 75th Grand Conclave, held in July 2008 in Birmingham, Alabama, several key brothers approached Bro. Brown and asked him if he would please run again for the position of Grand Basileus. Having been burned the prior time by brothers who gave their verbal support for his earlier effort in 2006, but then block-voted for Lee as a result of a decision that was made by their respective districts, Bro. Brown was hesitant about subjecting himself to a possible second humiliation at the hands of an incumbent Grand Basileus who some were claiming was not up to the job.

Kenny Brown declined to mount another campaign, but agreed to accept a nomination from the floor. He consented to stand for election, to let the brotherhood decide if they really wanted to make a change at the Grand Basileus level. That said, when the elections were held, as expected, Bro. Brown was nominated from the floor and stepped forward to accept the nomination. However, the entrenched Lee forces, anticipating the move, proved to be too much.

Although some of these same forces had been muttering that they were not pleased with the current Grand Basileus, a sufficient percentage of them determined to keep Lee in place. The outcome allowed those forces, despite their criticism of Lee, more freedom in running their respective districts' activities. Knowing the task master that Bro. Kenneth A. Brown is, and likewise his reputation for getting things done, I suppose that the feeling was that certain components did not want to be held to the level of accountability that Brown surely would have demanded. Subsequently, many of this disaffected group held firm and reelected Warren G. Lee, Jr., to a second term as 38th Grand Basileus.

Under these circumstances, it is easy to see why Bro. Lee did not wish to appoint Bro. Brown to be the Centennial Celebration Grand Marshal, despite the obvious correct nature of the choice. Several well placed brothers felt otherwise. For example, Adam McKee, former First Vice Grand Basileus, contacted Bro. Lee, and strongly urged him to bury any hatchets of animosity that he might be bearing, and to do the right thing for Omega. McKee reminded the Grand Basileus that Bro. Brown was a great organizer, someone who inspired others to work with and follow him.

Further, Brown had served as the Deputy Grand Marshal for the 1986 Diamond Jubilee Grand Conclave, also convened in Washington, D.C., and over the years had maintained ties to hotels, key people, and key organizations, all of which would be needed to make our celebration the success that we wanted it to be. Beyond having served as a Grand Officer, and District Marshal, time was getting shorter by the day. Given the lack of prior planning and execution to date, this was no time for bringing in an inexperienced neophyte to make a 100-year anniversary celebration and related events the success that was required.

Whether influenced by McKee's words or those of other sagacious voices, the Grand Basileus notified Bro. Brown of his selection. Much of the ground work had already been laid, as it was unrealistic to just sit in equipoise while nothing was happening. Thus Bro. Brown had some semblance of an organization, eager brothers who wanted to work, but were just waiting to be notified that their services were officially needed, and then given an assignment or two, that they could start to work on. Still, up to this time, little to no reference was ever made to showcasing Omega's history during the Centennial Celebration.

# XXIII- Planning A Centennial History Exhibit

On Friday, May 20, 2011, about 65 days before the 100 Anniversary celebration was to begin, I learned that each District of the fraternity was expected to install a display depicting the history of their respective District. This newly minted information came as a total surprise to me, and, apparently to most all of the other 12 districts' H&A chairmen. When I advised Bro. D.R. Anthony Knight of the directive that had come from Bro. Carl Blunt, international H&A Chairmen, Bro. Knight was surprised as well. He advised me that having been engaged in several national level conversations about various aspects of the planning, the only history exhibit that had ever been referred to was the one that international headquarters out of Decatur was planning. According to him, nothing had ever been said previously about having the individual districts also showcase themselves.

I was near panic at the thought of having to take on another major responsibility on such short notice. This is the Third District, birthplace, cradle, and early nurturer of Omega Psi Phi. No matter what any other district was planning as its exhibit, ours had to be the best, the most historically complete and accurate, as well as the most memorable. This new information was received and taken as a charge to make the entire district proud. By now, it was already late May, and the task of completing the history book had to be put on indefinite hold, as there were far too many other matters that claimed priority status.

What did the H&A sub-committee, and ever dwindling number of active brothers, still have to do? Several things. First, this new exhibit was going to be both costly and time consuming, if it was to be done correctly. What should be included in the exhibit that was also inclusive of the entire district, not just the Washington, D.C. area? What artifacts could be identified and borrowed for the display? We needed small signs that explained everything, and bigger signs to state historically significant information. Historic photographs that depicted our fraternal life had to be likewise located, duplicated and included. As an historian, I appreciate that "history" is not last year's picnic. It is not last year's Mardi Gras, either. Those are still current events. We needed to dig deeply, find something truly unique, and put that on display.

Second, there was the Centennial Statement to craft for the Souvenir Journal, with the request from the planning committee that the statement be an overview of Omega in the last 25 years, since 1986, but to also include a prospective looking forward to the next 25 years, i.e., 2036, when the fraternity will celebrate its 125th anniversary. Third and Fourth, the completion of the Spingarn Medal winners and U.S. postage stamp projects were still in the works. Although this effort was progressing well, as chairman of the committee, I had to keep a firm hand on the project, to make certain that the end result was to our satisfaction. Despite the signs and all of the copy and artwork being donated by the postal service, the H&A committee still had to supply the copy of what we wanted, to assure that nothing of great significance was left out.

In my mind, this was an opportunity for Omega to showcase how great a fraternity of men we truly were. Having grown up in Omega since the 1950s, I met the "giants" and other great men who served Omega as Grand Basilei and in other positions of influence. I firmly believed that this was Omega, and that this greatness was still dwelling within us. Now was the appropriate time to bring it out and showcase it to the world. And we would do it by putting our history of stellar achievement on display. That expectation would prove to be very naïve, as the fraternity had not yet placed enough emphasis upon creating, preserving, and sharing its illustrious history. I had two great models of what had gone before us, and was subsequently disappointed when we failed to come even close to either of them.

In the summer of 2006, Alpha Phi Alpha observed its Centennial Celebration here in Washington, D.C. It is my understanding that their planning steering committee set their sights and structured their plan at least five years prior to the celebration. Whether that is the case or not, I am not sure, but one thing is for certain. They appreciated that they were first, and determined that no one who came after them should be able to top them in their historical display.

## PLANNING A CENTENNIAL HISTORY EXHIBIT

Omega is a different fraternity, and was by no means bound by what Alpha did for its Centennial Celebration. From my perspective, we put a stronger emphasis upon brotherhood and friendship, while Alpha, in doing likewise, seems to place more emphasis upon getting themselves into high places in the overall society. And that difference showed up in their history display. They created "The Gold Room," an exquisite display of Alpha's glorious First 100 Years. It was a site to behold. They showcased Alpha's written and photographic history, including photos of great men of the fraternity.

The brothers reached out to all living, and some deceased, Alpha men who had served as college presidents, judges, and in places of national prominence. They showcased these brothers, and even had their judicial and academic robes on display, some hanging, some on mannequins, others in display racks. They obtained books written by Alpha men, and put them on display, to underscore the level of intellectual achievement that Alpha men had, and continue to achieve.

The following year, 2007, as Alpha Kappa Alpha was preparing for its 2008 100th anniversary, the sorority contacted me and inquired if I had any items of memorabilia from Nellie Quander, AKA's First Supreme Basileus. If so, they wanted to put the items on display. I had no memorabilia, but had previously placed some of her photographs at Howard's Moorland Spingarn Research Center. As well, I referred them to comments that she had made about Greek life and AKA, in particular. Their intent was to showcase all of the former Supreme Basilei in a manner befitting their station, and Nellie would, naturally, be the cornerstone of what they were planning. The end result was glorious, nonetheless, with several of Nellie's remarks captured in signs, and photographs, some of which I provided, being incorporated into their truly grant historical exhibit.

It was my great sin, then, to expect no less of Omega. One Hundred Years! One Hundred Years! You should not go half stepping at such an auspicious time. The gauntlet has been cast down. Omega was facing a challenge to pick it up and show that we were both worthy and up to the challenge.

We failed!

## 50+ OMEGA INSPIRED YEARS

The heavy lifting to get these entire tasks done fell predominantly upon seven people (six brothers and my wife). Although we had a committee, most of them drifted away as we got closer to the celebration. The remaining core consisted of Bro. Victor Taylor, Bro. Charles Pleasants, both my co-vice chairs, Bro. Emmanuel McRae, our primary photographer, Bro. Carroll Green, who helped by editing copy, including the Souvenir Journal Statement that I wrote, and me. I have purposefully not listed those brothers who helped with portions of the history book, as that project had been temporarily put on hiatus, as we raced to finish everything else.

As well, Carmen, the seventh person, who is a professional artist, museum curator, and artistic advisor to many, designed what she thought the history exhibit should look like. There were several options, always tiered, always with several shades of purple and gold. Royal purple and old gold were to be central, but the artistic appeal directed that a different intensity of purple and gold would be far more dramatic than just the two basic colors. Examining Omega's shield, she asked me which icons were the most dramatic. Responding that the Lamp, the Helmet, and the Gauntlet were such, in my estimation, she set out to find life size originals of each. The task was not an easy one, but with a dogged perseverance that would have made our four Founders proud, she found each on the Internet. She and I discussed a possible title and theme, and came up with, *IN THE BEGINNING – The Third District, Birthplace and Cradle of Omega.*

The cost of securing this exhibit was not yet determined, in significant part due to the need to locate, restore, and enlarge certain photographs, create appropriate signage and accreditation, and to retain professional services on such short notice. While IHQ was spending approximately $18,000 on its exhibit, which had eight components, they had the advantage of spreading the total costs (and savings) across several projects. Conversely, although we had just one exhibit, to accomplish what was required and on such short notice was also labor intensive.

I initially anticipated that the cost of our exhibit would be in the range of approximately $3,000.00, with the primary costs being invested in photography and personnel services. Fortunately, the 3rd District was blessed by having the services of the Torruella Quander

## PLANNING A CENTENNIAL HISTORY EXHIBIT

Gallery placed at the full disposal of Omega. The gallery is experienced, and has assembled prior exhibits for events sponsored by Omega, Delta, AKA, Zeta, the Links, the National Urban League, and several museums. Both my wife and daughter, Iliana, are professionals in this field. They determined that the design would be "Olde School" and reminiscent of the Omega of yesterday, while looking forward to the present and tomorrow.

Before we even knew about the call to set up a district history exhibit, Carmen began working on a series of four Omega history-related paintings.[77] As a licensed Omega vendor, it was my intention to display these original paintings in my licensed vending booth in the conclave exhibit area. However, Carmen felt that we should make copies of the paintings, and likewise showcase them in the history exhibit. At no cost to the fraternity, copies were made and exhibited in both places.

One lingering question was where to place the history exhibit? We had been told that a room of sufficient size had been set aside on the second floor of the convention center, and that the exhibit would be housed there. Already familiar with the building's layout, including the isolation of the rooms on the second floor, I was one of those few voices who protested that this was a poor location. It was way too far from the vending area which is always the heart of our conclave activity. As well, I questioned the wisdom of expecting a large numbers of brothers and guests coming into the area for a forum and staying to visit the history displays. The generic reply was, "No! We are placing the exhibit in a secure location, in the area where the forums will be held." I communicated my discomfort with this arrangement to both Bro. Carl Blunt, international H&A chair, and his assistant, Bro. Jarvis Green.

---

[77] *The four paintings are: 1) In the Beginning, November 17, 1911, depicted in the office of Founder Just with all four Founders present; 2) Omega - The First 100 Years, featuring icons; 3) The Lamp of Knowledge, which also included the 20 Pearls; and 4) Tribute to Omega's Founders, the Memorial at Howard University, with Science (Thirkield) Hall and Just Hall in the background.*

## 50+ OMEGA INSPIRED YEARS

Receiving my comments and warning, in at least one of our conversations Bro. Blunt spoke of possibly having the exhibit be relocated to the area outside of the exhibit hall, as an attraction for those walking down the hallway towards the exhibit area. I replied that the best area for the exhibit was outside of the Great Hall at the top of the escalator cascade. This is where many of the national convention exhibits are usually placed, including where AKA set up a most beautiful centennial exhibit in 2008. It is also where the National Urban League, among other organizations, always places some portion of their convention exhibits. The area features natural light, having a literal glass ceiling and glass walls on both sides. The area includes 24 hour security, if retained, to guard against theft, which was particularly reassuring to my wife, who for at least the last 16 years has curated the art show for the League's national convention when held in Washington, D.C. But the decision on where to locate Omega's history exhibit had already been made, and no change was forthcoming. It would prove to be a disaster in the end.

Undaunted by the looming prospect of not having an overall history exhibit that I considered to be up to par, I was determined that at least the Third District's H&A exhibit would be of true museum quality. Therefore, an excellent history display was planned. The photographs were carefully culled from available archival documents, including the Smithsonian Institution, the Scurlock Collection, the Moorland Spingarn Research Center, and other personal archives. Perhaps the photo of Alpha Chapter in 1912 created the biggest stir. Life size artifacts, including a helmet, gauntlet, and lamp of knowledge were located and placed on display in the designated history exhibit area. The entire exhibit was draped in different shades of purple and gold, and received the accolades of everyone who attended.

Interpretive signs were made, and posters created reflecting the honors that Omega men of the 3rd District have earned, including the prestigious Spingarn Medal, and being featured on U.S. postage stamps, and elsewhere. Kathy Just, granddaughter of Founder Dr. Ernest E. Just, lent his 1907 Dartmouth College commencement program, which reflected numerous awards that Brother Just earned in his graduating year. Also included among the artifacts was the

## PLANNING A CENTENNIAL HISTORY EXHIBIT

tunic of Bro. Dr. David H. Reid, Jr. (Upsilon Chapter 1927), a fully financial member of Alpha Omega, who at 104 years old (born May 1909), is most probably Omega's oldest living son. As referenced above, Carmen created four paintings, each a distinct depiction of a scene or moment that is relevant to and reminiscent of the history of Omega's first 100 years.

Iliana, my older daughter, who is a fashion designer in New York, created a giant "Omega," 15 feet wide, and nine feet tall, shaped into the traditional Greek letter. She painted it with a luminous gold paint, and framed it out with purple braiding. It was spectacular, and literally took your breath away upon entering the exhibit area. The figure was a fabulous attraction and likewise, an instant success. Compliments were both effusive and plentiful, including, "Bro. Quander, you have done us all proud," and "You have really captured the spirit of Omega's birthplace and early life, and we really do appreciate your efforts." Several members of the District's executive committee came through, Bro. D.R. Knight included, and to the man, they too were very impressed and most appreciative.

All of the districts, plus International Headquarters, created exhibits. While I have no agenda or axe to grind with any of the other district and their respective displays, it is sufficient to note that, in my opinion, not one of them put forth a museum quality history exhibit, something that was befitting a 100-year anniversary event. As well, the quality of the exhibits was uneven. The results were reflected in the efforts and experience of the brother-planners, with some presentations being reflective of greater experience in planning, plus forethought and proper execution, while others lacked what I considered to be proper historical content and context. Photographs depicting last year's picnic, or Omega men throwing up "hooks," with their tongues hanging out, were highly inappropriate and clearly not reflective of the positive messages of both Omega and Omega men's accomplishments at 100 years. Yet, there were a few of such photos on display, passing as "history."

Previously, I asked several questions of my Alpha friends about how they planned and executed their centennial history exhibit in 2006, when they observed their celebration, also here in Washington, D.C. One answer was that the national office of the fraternity considered the centennial history and its proper presentation to be too important a matter to be left to the local regions to execute. Instead, they elected to create their exhibit under the explicit direction of their national office, and did not request the regions to put up individual exhibits. Otherwise, like the result Omega garnered, the end product would be too inconsistent from region to region. Further, there was no uniform way to determine that the ultimate portrayal of a more localized Alpha history would be satisfactorily achieved.

We were prepared to open the display at 10:00 a.m. on Thursday, July 28, 2011. I was full of anticipation of great support from the brotherhood and much success. The announced time for the arrival of the truck from IHQ was adjusted several times. Although initially requested to be on site and ready to set up by about 2:00 p.m. on Wednesday, numerous e mail updates advised that the arrival was behind schedule, and adjusted our report time to later in the day. My crew got antsy, knowing how much we had to do to get our exhibit's components properly in place. With evening already upon us, we elected to report by 7:30 p.m., and just wait for the truck to arrive. And we were the first of the exhibit teams to arrive. Little did we know at the time that we would still be on site, preparing and installing the exhibits until about 2:45 a.m. the next morning. The primary element that created the delay was the non-availability of the display cases for the exhibited items. These cases were on the truck. Finally, everything was in place.

The exhibit was in place, ready to be the Third District's contribution to the Omega showcase of history. My son brought our van closer so that we could load up and carry away our building supplies and empty boxes which we would not need during the exhibit. At such an hour, I was surprised to hear and see a strong chorus of singing and stepping Omega men, mostly undergraduates, collected on the sidewalk in front of the convention center. It was now almost 3:00 a.m., and they were so full of enthusiasm that they could not contain themselves. My hope is that this enthusiasm and spirit, this love for Omega, will continue and characterize their efforts 25 and 50 years into the future, to assure that Omega will not only survive, but prosper.

## PLANNING A CENTENNIAL HISTORY EXHIBIT

Arriving home, I was so excited about the Centennial Celebration and the exhibit in particular that I could not sleep. I mostly lay in the bed and looked at the ceiling. As well, Bro. Carl Blunt, the International H&A Chairman, asked everyone to be back on site by 9:30 a.m., to receive our first visitors. We expected a substantial crowd, and we needed to be present to lend credibility and a sense of history to what we had to showcase. I arrived, wearing a suit, white shirt, and purple and gold tie. I was as tired as I could be, but already running on adrenalin at that early hour.

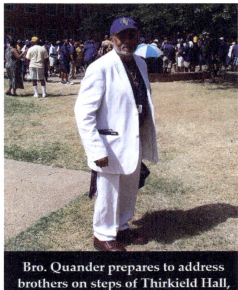

Bro. Quander prepares to address brothers on steps of Thirkield Hall, Howard University

As a licensed vendor for Omega, my wife and adult children were also operating a vending booth in the exhibit hall. Beyond vending my Omega wares, they encouraged everyone who visited our booth to likewise pay a visit to the history exhibit. As they continuously recounted where the exhibit was located, and encouraged attendance, they became frustrated by the often negative responses to their urging. Some brothers replied that the exhibit was too far away. Others stopped back by the vending booth and advised that they could not find the exhibit. Very few mentioned that they had seen the exhibit at all.

Meanwhile, my three days spent at the history exhibit were disturbing and disappointing. The lack of attendance was indicative of the non-support that all of our efforts received. Despite everyone's hard work and dedication to make the history exhibits a success, something properly befitting recognition of centennial achievement, attendance was extremely poor. I have previously commented that the quality of the exhibits was uneven between the 12 districts, and likewise stated that IHQ could have done much better in setting up the national exhibit, still the meager results that we did receive were both an insult and an embarrassment. As H&A committee members from all 12 districts and our respective chapters throughout Omega, we did not garner the attention, support and attendance from the brotherhood that we had worked hard to obtain and truly deserved.

From those who did visit the history exhibits, there was much praise, most particularly focused upon the Third District's exhibit. The brothers of the Third District were exceptionally proud of the work product that we produced, They had no idea, and did not really need to know, that the exhibit was not completed until 3:00 a.m. on the morning of July 28, 2011, because the display cases, where certain valuable items for the exhibits were to be secured, did not arrive until well after midnight. Nor were they interested in the amount of on-site construction mandated to erect the exhibits and place them to achieve the best, esthetically. They came to see the results.

Bro. Carl Blunt, immediate past First Vice Grand Basileus, and now International H&A Chairman, worked hard to raise awareness of Omega's history among the membership, but without the full support of the Supreme Council and the appropriate resources, monetary and otherwise, to increase and maintain that awareness, Blunt's best efforts were doomed to be well less than successful.

Although there were occasional announcements requesting the brothers to stop by the history exhibit, there were no professionally printed signs indicating where the exhibit was located, nor instructions in any of the souvenir programs directing brothers and guests where the exhibit was and how to reach our location. As I feared from the outset, our being set up on the second floor of the convention center, where very few conclave activities were ongoing, and at a significant distance from the exhibit halls and other activities, contributed to the confusion. As a consequence, only a miniscule numbers of the brothers and their guests knew where the exhibit was or how to get there. There was not even one professionally printed sign placed at the bottom of the long escalator, to indicate that the exhibit was "This Way!"

This Centennial Celebration Grand Conclave had several celebratory components which required that programs be printed for each such event. I consulted all of the programs – the General

## PLANNING A CENTENNIAL HISTORY EXHIBIT

Agenda; Service Recognition Awards; Centennial Worship Celebration; Public Program; Salute to Military; Salute to Business, Civic/Civil Rights and Political Involvement; Salute to Sports and Entertainment; Salute to Education, Scholarship, Undergraduate Leadership, and Religion; Salute to Science and Medicine; and Founders Walkway Dedication – and found NOT ONE WORD about the Centennial History Exhibit. It was simply not enough to say, "Exhibits Open, 10 AM – 7 PM," without also noting in writing that the history display was located in a different place. As a result, I feel comfortable in saying that we had less than 100 visitors to the exhibit on Thursday, July 28, 2011, the first day of the display. What a shame, and utterly unbefitting for Omega and the touted 20,000 plus attendees that IHQ claims were in attendance.[78]

> *The geographic focus of the conclave did not include the general use of the smaller conference area on the second floor, where the history exhibit was placed. As well, there were no other significant activities in that immediate area that could serve to help draw visitors and spread the word as to our location. As a consequence, very few of the brothers and their guests knew where the exhibit was or how to get there.*
>
> *Attendance on the first of the three days was embarrassingly meager. It increased on the second and third days of the display, but, in comparison with the total number of brothers and guests present, the visitation remained miniscule. Omega, by most counts, has done a poor job in preserving, protecting, and sharing its great history. The Centennial Conclave, our chance to showcase what Omega Men have done and are doing, was a*

---

[78] *It remains highly speculative regarding the number of Omega men and others who were in formal attendance at the Centennial Celebration. While the fraternity's promoters tout the higher figures, reality indicates a significantly smaller number, since so many of those present never registered. The numbers who were hanging out in the convention center or going to parties does not reflect an accurate number of how many were in fact present during the Centennial Grand Conclave.*

*great opportunity to underscore those accomplishments, and to place them in the historical context of what Omega Man have been doing for the past 100 years. Regretfully, this was a great opportunity that was almost totally missed. Efforts to improve "next time" will be too little, too late, as the Centennial Celebration will have passed. Still, we must begin anew, and now is the time, at the outset of Omega's Second Century of Greatness.* - Report of the History and Archives Committee for the Third District Fall 2011 Council Meeting, November 1, 2011, Rohulamin Quander, Chairman.

Once the Centennial Grand Conclave was completed, I returned the borrowed items to their rightful owners. Kathy Just Robinson was most thankful that her grandfather's commencement program from Dartmouth College, Class of 1907, was returned safely. Dr. David Reid was delighted to receive back his tunic, which he has proudly worn for about 50 years. As H&A Chairman, I put several items back into their boxes, and used them again for showcasing Omega at the next appropriate times. Those additional events would be not too far in the making.

## XXIV – Reflecting On The Centennial History Effort

I cannot leave the subject of the Centennial history exhibit without drawing an extensive picture of events that occurred behind the scenes, as they give context to the challenges that we faced in making the exhibit happen. I have already noted that nowhere in my charge or directive as Third District H&A Chairman was I told or requested at the outset of the 2010-2011 time frames, to plan for and create a Third District history exhibit for the Centennial Celebration. This exhibit issue was a much later development, and not a budgeted item within the planning cycle. The belated notice was inordinately short, given the nature of what a centennial exhibit for an organization of Omega's significance, should look like.

My personal history and background reflect that I have long been accustomed to doing things in a professional manner, making every effort to get the plan of action correct on the first attempt. I am of the firm belief if you cannot do something correctly, then perhaps you should not undertake the assignment. To my mind, "History Display" conveys a certain image, including who we are as Omega men at 100 years. As well, we are the oldest black fraternity to be founded at a black university. With both Alpha and AKA as examples of how to do a history exhibit, in my mind, "Nothing but the best for Omega!" was my expectation. And we fell very far short.

Despite our very best efforts, the final outcome was a double-edged sword. On one edge, it was a rousing success, with compliments still forthcoming on a regular basis. And for this I am most proud and appreciative. On the other edge, the Centennial Exhibit was a failure, not at all successful. Why? There was no audience. Insufficient effort was invested on audience development and proper notification, resulting in our labors not being appropriately recognized and appreciated. I restate again for the record, that not one professional sign was printed to reflect where the exhibit was located.

I detailed the above-referred activities for a reason. Each of them required an inordinate amount of time – personal efforts on my part, planning, execution, and additional out of pocket expenses (for which no additional reimbursements were received). Still, all of these activities were H&A Committee-input activities, and largely the result of highly focused effort. Whenever I called upon my two vice co-chairs, Bro. Charles Pleasants and Bro. Victor Taylor, they readily stepped up and rendered help as needed. Other H&A Committee members also gathered Leadership Profile information and edited. But it took my singular, consistent presence to assure continuity in what was being sought and completed.

While none of these above-referenced additionally directed activities related to the initial directive to write the history of the District, they were necessary extra-curricular activities, within the scope of what a dedicated H&A chairman should do. Everything that was undertaken was required, requested by key national-level Omega men, and forces whose requests could not be ignored. D.R. Knight was well aware of my efforts on behalf of each request, and likewise cognizant of my efforts related to creating the history exhibit. Yet, on March 31, 2012, he sent me an e mail disposing of my service, dedication, and hard work on behalf of Omega as a "frivolity."

He never provided any specifics addressing how, when, what, on in what way my efforts were frivolous. In response, when I tendered my epistle-length letter of resignation, dated April 3, 2012, detailing every service on behalf of Omega that I had rendered, both in planning for the history book, and in the many additional assignments I received, in pursuit of a grand Centennial celebration, he summarily dismissed me in a second e mail with a few terse words to the effect – Thank you for your service to Omega. Turn over your computer to the incoming D.R. That was it.

While my efforts were supposed to be voluntary, Omega took over my entire life for a while. Today I go on record as objecting to being treated so shabbily and with such disrespect. As well, I firmly reject any assertion that my work product, of which I am most proud, was an insignificant folly.

## REFLECTING ON THE CENTENNIAL HISTORY EFFORT
**Writing the History of the Third District Book - A Dormant Status**

Refocusing on our original mission, the structure of the planned Third District history book consisted of: a) An historical overview of Omega, 1911 to 1933; b) The creation of the district structures, beginning in 1934, to about 1961; c) the district's Omega history c1961 to the present; d) Leadership Profiles to include all of the DRs, and about 125-150 key brothers whose contributions are extraordinary; e) Chapter histories; and f) Extracts from prior Omega eras, inserted as a component of the total story. While significant progress towards completing the assignment and reaching the goal has been made, there is still a very long way to go.

The D.R. clearly did not have a full understanding or appreciation for how much time and effort I was putting into this project. For months, I would leave my office, and go to the Omega work site, remaining until the building was closed (about 10:00 p.m.). Saturdays were many times an all-day effort.

Both Bro. Vernon Johnson's and Bro. Joseph McKinney's respective prophesies have each proven to be right on the mark. This entire project encountered many delays, largely due to the consistent failure of pockets of the brotherhood to cooperate, including Bro. D.R. Knight and some of the former DRs, who simply ignored me, and never submitted their Leadership Profiles and Tenure Statements. My repeated telephone calls, letters, and e mails to them were to no avail. This was time wasted. In some instances, when there were eventual responses, the written guideline directions were ignored, rendering these documents unusable in the submitted format.

In my letter of resignation, I proffered that now that the Centennial Celebration events are done, so am I, adding that the incoming DR will have a clean and clear slate, free to select his new H&A Chairman without regard to any prior allegiances, personal, political, or otherwise. I concluded my letter by noting that it is apparent that a significant quadrant of the men of Omega do not have a sufficient enough appreciation for our history. To many, "Rah! Rah!" is enough. To me it is not.

As a Legacy Brother, with more than 50 years in the fraternity (April 4, 1964), I have a viewpoint that is not shared by a segment of the brotherhood. Some pay lip service to the need to identify, preserve, protect, and then share our history. Still, many of that same group look in other directions when their cooperation is sought and needed. I was not able to recruit a single professional editor or IT brother to help. Every time the request was made, there was mumbling about how much time was required, and that there is no offer of monetary compensation for what they knew would be a time-consuming effort of longstanding. Therefore, no stepping up to the plate. I got tired of this unending symphony.

**Frivolous Effort/Expense vs. Serious Dedication to Achieve Goal**

Noting that unbudgeted money was spent on Centennial Celebration projects and efforts other than the book, DR Knight admitted to me that he was not initially aware of the mandate to create a District history exhibit, nor of the requirement that we send a representative to International Headquarters in June 2011 for a planning session on the history exhibit. These were typical expenses that arose outside of the anticipated budget, which skewed the planned resources significantly. Of the $15,000.00 appropriated for H&A for FY 2011, we used about $8,100.00, that included the above-noted expenditures, plus materials and professional services, as previously referenced. I see nothing frivolous in these expenditures.

It is certainly true that no other district incurred such an expense. Again I remind my readers that Washington, D.C., which is located in the Third District, is the birthplace, cradle, and early nurture of Omega. We had to have an exhibit befitting that hallowed status. In order to achieve that result, existing resources had to be rededicated to create a quality end product. It is now apparent, if not so previously, that the unanticipated demand upon our history-related resources highlighted that the book could not be completed inside of just one budget cycle, and that perhaps a three-year budget cycle was required, in order to assure that the Third District's history book would be completed. If the project ever does get fully revived, I recommend that this approach be taken by the district's budget committee and the DR.

Needless to say, the relationship between Bro. DR Knight and me did not culminate on good terms, and remains estranged. While he has never attempted to explain to me why he referred to my sustained

## REFLECTING ON THE CENTENNIAL HISTORY EFFORT

efforts as "frivolous," I take great pride in the many continuing accolades that come my way with regard to the success of the District's centennial history exhibit. Although I have taken the brothers to task for not sufficiently supporting our efforts, I do see many pockets of appreciation for the dedication and hard work of our committee. Likewise, many brothers are aware of how I was treated by DR Knight, even if unaware of the underlying details.

Perhaps my redemption, if one can call it such, is that DR Robert Warren, the succeeding district representative, asked me to reconsider my resignation, and to continue serving as H&A Chairman. Although I declined, I advised him that I would gladly continue to serve on the committee at his request, and continue to do so at this time. With no disrespect intended or aimed towards the present H&A Chairman, I am confident in saying that had I not been so unceremoniously brought down, which resulted in my decision to resign, the Third District effort would have resulted by now in a published history book about which we would all be proud.

**50+ OMEGA INSPIRED YEARS**

# XXV – Founders Day, November 17, 1911 To November 17, 2011

### Members Verses Men

*When previously confronted with the issue of increasing the size of the membership, particularly in light of the other fraternities' efforts to become significantly larger than Omega, Bro. Walter H. Mazyck (Alpha Chapter 1913), former Grand Keeper of Records and Seal, and one of Omega's most stall worth early members, addressed the issue of "Members vs. Men." While editing the first issue of the 1925 ORACLE, he wrote that "The value of our Fraternity is not in numbers, but in men, in real brotherhood. Eight men thoroughly immersed in the true Omega spirit are far greater assets than eighty with lukewarm enthusiasm." His comments were clearly a rejection of mediocrity, the byproduct of a mad race to increase our numbers, and a call for Omega to retain its higher standards and to bring only the best men home. Mazyck's words were relevant then and remain ever more so today.[79]*

Every year in Washington, D.C. we observe Founders Day on November 17th, the date that Omega was initiated in the Office of Founder Just. November 17, 2011, was no exception. Indeed, it was a Special Occasion. Bro. Kenny Brown, still in the mode as Centennial Grand Marshal, and Bro. Steve Johnson, Director of Protocol at Howard, asked me to set up a smaller exhibit to be on display during the rededication program of 100 years of Omega Psi Phi. They advised that several thousand brothers were expected for the Centennial Rededication Program, many busing in from as far north as Connecticut, to as far south as North Carolina, and perhaps even further.

---

[79] "Omega - In the Last Quarter Century, 1986-2011, Centennial Souvenir Journal Statement, authored by Rohulamin Quander, Chairman, Third District History and Archives Committee, June 2011.

## 50+ OMEGA INSPIRED YEARS

About a month before the convocation, Carmen and I met with Bro. Johnson to survey the logistics and to consider different options for placing the icons. Two options were to place the icons either on the lower level of Cramton, in the lounge, or in the Blackburn Center. After some discussion, it was decided that it was most appropriate to place the three icons - the Lamp of Knowledge, the Helmut, and the Gauntlet – on the stage in Cramton Auditorium, as most brothers had never seen these life-size items, not having attended the history exhibit the prior July, where the icons had initially been displayed.

Arriving at 5:30 p.m. on November 17th, and aided by Carmen, we set up the history exhibit in the Cramton lounge, minus the three icons – the helmet, the gauntlet, and the lamp of knowledge. Always esthetically minded, Carmen selected different shades of purple and gold fabric for the draping, and then placed the three icons on the stage at Cramton on separate portable pedestals that my son made some years ago to support the portability of her art shows. Set up just to the left of the speakers' podium, capturing spotlights from the projection room in the rear of the auditorium, the icons were the perfect addition to the evening program.

As the brothers gathered in Cramton, they were truly taken aback by these three life size symbols of Omega. They came up on the stage in droves, touching the items, taking pictures for posterity, sending the images to other brothers and friends via cell phone, and expressing their excitement at the significance of today and the unique opportunities that each had by reason of their presence on this august occasion. I stayed close as "the guardian," and asked the brothers, despite their enthusiasm, not to touch anything. My entreaties were all for naught.

Cramton seats about 1,500 people, and was not large enough for the more than 3000 Omega men who converged on the campus for this once in a lifetime event. Bro. Johnson had anticipated a large spillover crowd, and set up the Ira Aldridge Theatre and Blackburn Center, as well as the lower level lounge of Cramton, to accommodate the men who could not obtain a seat in Cramton. They too, enjoyed Dr. Andrew A. Ray, the 39th Grand Basileus, and all of the invited brothers and Michael Stratmanus, a White House deputy assistant for

## FOUNDERS DAY, NOVEMBER 17, 1911 TO NOVEMBER 17, 2011

public affairs, who delivered and read a letter from President Barack H. Obama.

In the post-Grand Conclave planning for the November 17th Centennial Observance, I requested that a transcriber be hired to capture the many words of inspiration and values that were to be said on that evening. I noted that this was a once in a lifetime event, and that we owed it to those who will come after, to capture *verbatim* every word that will be said. As well, we do transcribe the proceedings of our conclaves, and to me, this was no different. I was not requesting that we transcribe anything that was ritualistically protected, such as taking the oath of rededication. I underscored that there would be many prominent brothers who will deliver special remarks, that several brothers would be recognized for their achievements, and likewise some discussion of Omega's history. During my request, I had no idea that Michael Stratmanus would be there to bring special greetings from President Obama, the first African American president of the United States.

My suggestion and strong request was not honored for that evening. It still is not exactly clear why not. A couple of brothers noted that the expense of a transcriber would be too much, especially since the fraternity was already obligated to pay a penalty to the hotels for our not meeting the guaranteed commitment for a specific number of rooms and nights stayed during the Celebration. That obligation was a fact, and we all knew it. Conversely, when I was asked to chair a forum on the next day, November 18th, *Omega, The Next 100 Years*, sponsored by the Third District, my request for a transcriber to document the proceedings for posterity, was met with approval. The only distinction that I can see is that the November 17th convocation was sponsored by IHQ, while the cost incurred for the follow up forum on the next day was borne by the Third District.

But all was not lost. As an historian, I have always been focused on preserving those elements of the past that might prove to be beneficial to us in the future. One such area of preservation should certainly be Omega's history. While it is not possible to capture in writing every word that has ever been said, still there are certain events and activities that are central to our history. All efforts should be made to document those activities. Brothers will come forth 50 and

## 50+ OMEGA INSPIRED YEARS

100 years from now, and hopefully beyond those time frames as well, and ask, "What was said, and by whom, when Omega celebrated her 100th anniversary?" Given the situation, the most probable answer would be, "No one knows!" Fortunately, I did not let that happen. But first, a quick review of what was done in 1961.

In 1961, on the occasion of the 50th Anniversary Grand Conclave, the brotherhood had the foresight to collect the speeches and remarks of as many brothers and guest speakers as possible. Then after the conclave, they printed and distributed those remarks in a booklet, *Golden Anniversary Grand Conclave, Omega Psi Phi Fraternity, August 14-18, 1961.* Capturing and preserving the words of several famous people, not all of whom were Omegas, also lent great credibility to Omega. The publication underscored that we were men of achievement who had great influence beyond just our numbers. As well, many of the brother-speakers had influential lives beyond Omega, and to present them to their fraternal body at that time, was reflective of the known fact, that *Omega Brings The Best Men Home.*

Beyond the three living Founders – Love, Cooper, and Coleman - Supreme Council, former grand basilei, and District Representatives, who were some of those speakers? Robert F. Kennedy, Attorney General of the United States. Carl T. Rowan, Assistant Secretary of State. Bro. Robert C. Weaver, Director of the Federal Housing Administration, and later the first African American to serve in a presidential Cabinet as HUD Secretary (Omega Man). Bro. Otto McClarrin Information Officer, U.S. Civil Rights Commission. Woody Hayes, Football Coach, Ohio State University. Bro. Oliver W. Hill, civil rights attorney, Presidential Medal of Freedom and Spingarn Medal honoree. Carl F. Hansen, Superintendent, D.C. Public Schools. Frank Reeves, civil rights attorney and Democratic National Committee. Bro. George L.P Weaver, Undersecretary of Labor. Bro. Spotswood W. Robinson, III, Dean, Howard University School of Law. Several ambassadors representing African nations, including Ghana, Sierra Leone, and Nigeria.

Not having the services of a transcriber for the Centennial convocation, 50 years later, I took matters into my own hands and made the decision to capture the words of all of the speakers for that evening. As H&A Chair for the Third District, I cordoned off two

**FOUNDERS DAY, NOVEMBER 17, 1911 TO NOVEMBER 17, 2011**

seats on the second row, left, in Cramton Auditorium, and from there I staged my plan of action. Carmen had already set up the three icons earlier that afternoon, so my sitting in front of them also served to keep an eye on them, to protect them from the enthusiasm of the brothers, which might result in breakage, but hopefully not theft.

The Centennial Rededication program, restricted to brothers only, began a few minutes after 7:15 p.m., with the initial words of welcome extended by Bro. Kenneth A. Brown, Centennial Grand Marshal, noting that the house was overflowing, and included several busloads of brothers from points north, south, east, and west, and those who had flown into Washington, D.C. for this occasion as well.

Kenny then introduced Bro. Dr. Bernard L. Richardson, Dean of the Chapel, Howard University, who delivered the prayers of invocation. And from that point forward, the program of the evening was delightful, with the highlight of the evening being the Centennial Message from Dr. Andrew A. Ray, 39th Grand Basileus. Rather than restate the words of the more than 10 brothers who spoke, and reiterate the letter of greeting from President Barack H. Obama, I have included the entire statement as an Appendix to this publication.[80] That way, the brothers can read, savor, enjoy, and reflect upon the goodness that was Omega in 2011, and use the same contemplation for engendering the success of the fraternity at the present and well into the future.

The intensely moving program did not end until 9:40 p.m., after the Men of Omega recited anew the sacred oath that each of us took on the day of our initial induction into the sacred brotherhood. With brothers of Alpha Chapter, Omega's Mother Pearl, leading the way and holding purple and gold lit lanterns that I provided, we then adjourned to the Monument to Our Founders in the lower valley, in front of Ernest E. Just Hall, for the singing of the hymn, *Omega Dear*.

The next day, November 18th, belonged to the Third District. Previously, as we were making plans for the Centennial Rededication Program, I, along with some other brothers, suggested to Bro.

---

[80] *See Historical Extracts, Parts I and II, the Centennial Rededication Program, November 17, 2011 (Rededication), and July 31, 2011 (Centennial Ecumenical Service).*

Anthony Knight, our district representative, that there should be more to the official rededication than just the program to be held in Cramton. We felt that, given the gravity and importance of what we were planning, that we should also continue and extend the observance with a forum examining Omega's perspective and plans for the future.

Bro. Knight was enthusiastic about the idea, and factored that event into our planning. He left the coordination of the event up to me, but requested that I contact brothers whose Omega credentials are well known, preferably of national repute, and ask them to serve on the panel. Several names were suggested, and contacts were made. Every brother contacted said "Yes!," and expressed that they were honored at having been asked to serve Omega in such a reputable manner.

As the program moderator, I delivered short remarks underscoring the purpose of this gathering, noting that Omega has served us well for the past 100 years, but now we are at a crossroads, and must make decisions on how best to proceed from this point, to assure that our future is just as bright, or even brighter, than has been our past. I then introduced Bro. Anthony Knight, Third District Representative, who in his welcoming remarks reemphasized that Omega has completed 100 very successful years, but that it was not without some strife through that time. But our mission is to move forward, to make Omega better and better understood. He charged the panel to share its wisdom and vision for Omega, and charged the audience to give close heed and to follow whatever advice emerges from this auspicious panel's presentations.

I then introduced the five panelists, giving some background information on who each of them was, and noted a few of their respective contributions to Omega. The panelists were: Bro. Dr. Moses C. Norman, 33rd Grand Basileus; Bro. Ernest J. Robinson, current Second Vice Third District Representative; Bro. Richard L. Taylor, 20th Second Vice Grand Basileus; Bro. Ademuyiwa Bamiduro, Esq., 37th Second Vice Grand Basileus; and Bro. Dr. E. Newton Jackson, Undergraduate Advisor to Alpha Theta Mu, University of North Florida.

## FOUNDERS DAY, NOVEMBER 17, 1911 TO NOVEMBER 17, 2011

As I had planned it, the remarks of each panelist are not captured in this Memoir. Rather, they are stated in detail in the transcribed document that emerged from this panel. Their sagacious remarks were captured in full, and I charge Omega to give heed to what each panelist said about Omega's strengths, but more particularly what needs to be addressed and corrected by Omega as we retool for our second century. Often we do not want to hear what is wrong with ourselves or the organizations to which we belong. There is a natural tendency to think that all is well, even when we know that just the opposite is the fact.

Omega is no different, an imperfect organization made up of imperfect human beings, men who have goals and dreams, but who likewise fall short of their stated objectives. This is nothing to be ashamed of, but simply human nature. However, at a time such as this, it was more than appropriate that Omega, both as a fraternity and in the capacity of its individual membership, should pause, do a self-assessment, then refocus towards its goals and purpose. We are then better equipped to move forward to a greater self-realization.

**50+ OMEGA INSPIRED YEARS**

# XXVI – Alpha Chapter Celebrates Its Centennial, December 15, 2011

Omega has never been a monolith. Rather, it is made up of fraternity brothers divided into geographical areas that we call "the 12 Districts." Those districts are subdivided into areas for ease and facility in unifying us into consistency in thought and plans of action. In 1911, there was no need for as much organization and subdivision, but since it was always the intent of our beloved Four Founders to make Omega a national brotherhood, there was the immediate need to create a chapter of the fraternity at several key locations. Hence Beta chapter, at Lincoln University, Pennsylvania, was established in 1914, an indication of Omega's initial move to expand beyond the bounds of Howard University. This was an action, taken over the objection of the Howard University Board of Trustees, but necessary if Omega was going to make the impact that it subsequently has.

Now more than 700 chapters worldwide, a mighty oak tree has grown from the initial acorn, which those of us who were inducted at the "acorn" lovingly called "the Mother Pearl." Yes Alpha Chapter! For without Alpha, there would be no Beta, Gamma (Boston citywide intermediate chapter, 1916), and Delta (Meharry Medical College, Nashville, Tennessee, 1919). Now, as each of these first four chapters reaches its respective centennial year, each will likewise execute a plan to celebrate and observe the milestone. Alpha chapter naturally started the trend with its own celebration.

The Founders realized from the outset that they needed to create fraternity chapters as a separately functioning body from the fraternity as a planned national organization. Thus on December 15, 1911, approximately one month after Omega was itself established, Brothers Cooper, Coleman, and Love convened a group of 14 young men, the charter members, from Howard University that they had been evaluating for some time. These were men whom the Founders believed were of like mind, had a serious purpose, and would serve to spread the message of Omega over time to those who would be influenced by the fraternity, and likewise wish to become a part of the sacred brotherhood.

## 50+ OMEGA INSPIRED YEARS

One hundred years later, Thursday, December 15, 2011, I joined my fellow Alpha chapter alumni brothers in the Howard University Blackburn Center for the Centennial Charter Day Ceremony, and to observe and celebrate the legacy of the Mother Pearl. On that occasion we paused to examine Alpha Chapter's history and glorious past, and how the chapter influenced the founding, growth, and development of Omega into the strong organization that it is today. Just as the Centennial Celebration did not get planned and executed overnight, the process by which Alpha Chapter came to celebrate its 100th anniversary was something that also emerged over time, and included the collective and individual effort of many Omega men and friends, to assure that the celebration was an event of lasting memory and significance. And indeed it was.

While I elect not to dwell too much on the details, of which there were many, I must note a few highlights. First, the Alpha Chapter Centennial Celebration Chairman was Jonathan "Flash" Matthews (7-83, Alpha Chapter). I give him all the praise, for it was phenomenal how he pulled this grand celebration together, while living several hundred miles away, in Atlanta. His zeal, leadership, and encouragement were such that many Alpha Chapter alumni brothers stepped forward and asked him, "What can I do to help make this a memorable celebration?" And he accepted their many offers, which resulted in a series of events which have made us proud.

I set the tone for what is to follow by noting that the back cover of the *Alpha Chapter Centennial Program Guide* stated, "1,700 brothers; 1,437 initiates; 118 lines; 14 charter members; 4 Founders; 1 Alpha Chapter." That sums it up in terms of the central core of who we, as Alpha Chapter inductees, are. We are many, but we are also ONE. My role in planning Alpha Chapter's Centennial Celebration was minimal, as my entire focus as Third District H&A Chairman had consumed virtually all of my time. However, at Flash's request, I provided one of the many history exhibits that were set up, first for the Centennial Charter Day Celebration banquet, held on Thursday, December 15, 2011, in the ballroom at the Blackburn Center, and then

**ALPHA CHAPTER CELBRATES CENTENNIAL, DECEMBER 15, 2011**
again at the Centennial Legacy Ball, held on Saturday, December 17, 2011, at the Westin Hotel, 1400 M Street, N.W., Washington, D.C.[81]

> *Centennial Charter Day Ceremony – Origin*
>
> *Alpha Chapter, the Mother Pearl, was chartered on December 15, 1911 on the campus of Howard University with 14 charter members. In an effort to honor the history and legacy of the Mother Pearl, Bro. Gernerique "G." Truly Stewart (6-95-A) organized the first formal Alpha Chapter Charter Day celebration in 1996. The purpose of the Celebration was to recognize Alpha Chapter's chartering while highlighting the achievements, accolades, and awards of the chapter and its history. The aim was for the brothers of various eras to fellowship, display visual mementos (scrapbooks, collages, videos, etc.), and to share their experiences as a member of Alpha Chapter with one another. ...*
>
> *Alpha Chapter holds a special place in the hearts and minds of her Sons. The Chapter's rich history, solid traditions, and noteworthy contributions to society have stood the test of time and remain unwavering. The impact of Alpha Chapter in the local area as well as on the global community through service, leadership and a commitment to excellence is second to none. We are the standard bearers. We are the beacons of light in the darkness to show the way. We are the Mother Pearl. May her legacy forever continue.*[82]

On Friday, December 16, 2011, we convened the Alpha Chapter Summit, having adopted the theme, "Redefining Ourselves Through Our History." The summit was held in the Blackburn auditorium, and accommodated all thoughts, suggestions, and included brothers who were inducted in the Mother Pearl from the 1950s, to the recent past. Several issues were discussed within the adopted theme, "Omega –

---

[81] *The location of the Centennial Ball was changed to the Westin Hotel, as the Blackburn Ballroom, as initially planned, was not available.*

[82] *Extracted from The Mother Pearl Centennial Celebration Program Guide, December 15-18, 2011.*

## 50+ OMEGA INSPIRED YEARS

The Next 100 Years," not unlike the agenda and items featured in the November panel discussion. The consensus was that the Alpha Chapter alumni should organize ourselves for the purpose of dedicating our energy, support, and finances to assure the continued health of the Mother Pearl.

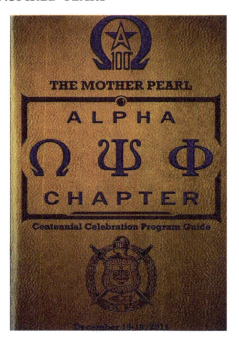

As well, there was some discussion about establishing an alumni club of Omega men who were inducted into the fraternity by way of Alpha Chapter. The latter group would function pretty much the same as the current alumni clubs, typically the Los Angeles Howard Alumni, or the Atlanta Howard alumni. Responses to subsequent inquiries at the university about the feasibility of creating such a support organization have been slow in coming, with certain university staff indicting that to date there are no Greek letter alumni clubs that have established or maintain a recognized relationship with the university.

When the response first came to my attention, I retorted, "Just because it has not been done heretofore, does not mean that it cannot be done now. This is a new source of establishing an ongoing relationship between Howard and its alumni. If we do this, we must start somewhere, and perhaps we can persuade the sororities and other fraternities' Howard alumni to do likewise." As well, the creation of these types of entities could prove to be a revenue source for the university, as well as create and foster alumni relationships that would encourage new students to select Howard as their university of choice. However, at the time of my penning these Memoirs, no follow up action appears to be in the making.

Continuing on Omega's mission to be of service to others, we sponsored *Project Aspiration* on the morning of Saturday, December

## ALPHA CHAPTER CELBRATES CENTENNIAL, DECEMBER 15, 2011

17. Aimed at teenaged boys and young men, the summit was operated under the theme, "Uplifting Our Young Men – Forging A Path For Future Achievement." Although the level of participation was not as great as we were hoping for, we still attracted a significant number of brother/mentors and young men and boys from the metropolitan area.

### Project Aspiration – Purpose

*The Project Aspiration initiative is designed to expose young black males to a variety of careers and life skills rooted in the cardinal principles of Manhood, Scholarship, Perseverance, and Uplift. The event includes a panel discussion on careers in Science, Technology, Engineering and Mathematics (STEM) and ways to prepare for success in those fields, as well as dialogue regarding personal responsibility and accountability.*

*Launched during Omega's Centennial Celebration in July 2011, the current module will target males, 13 to 18 years of age and feature four interactive sessions on financial literacy, health and wellness, professionalism and community involvement. ... The inspiration for Project Aspiration is from our 28th Grand Basileus, Bro. James Avery, who established this program Fraternity-wide in 1973, "to move young black students up the ladder of aspiration, encouraging them to stay in school and to improve their scholastic achievement."*[83]

This *Project Aspiration* event was a companion to one of Omega's current national projects, *The Fatherhood Initiative*, which has given Omega enhanced credulity and higher visibility over the last two to three years, including being invited to the White House for meetings with some of President Obama's staff and frequent visits to the U.S. Congress, where Omega men have conducted panels during the annual Congressional Black Caucus Legislative Weekend and on other relevant occasions. Bro. Robert Fairchild of Alpha Omega

---

[83] *Extracted from the Alpha Chapter Centennial Celebration Program Guide, P. 10.*

Chapter, has been our local spokesperson in this effort and enjoys the full support of the Grand Basileus and the Supreme Council.

On Saturday evening, we convened the Centennial Legacy Ball, a black tie event, at the Westin Hotel, 1400 M St., N.W. The original site for the ball was to have been the Blackburn Center, but due to a schedule mix up, their ballroom was not available. The Legacy Ball was very much the capstone of the four day celebration (December 15-18, 2011), and did not disappoint in the least. First, the Alpha Chapter history exhibit was something to behold, and underscores what one can accomplish, given sufficient early notice, available resources, and a committee of dedicated brothers who can put in the time to research and review documents and photographs for showcasing. Following Flash's lead, and primarily as a result of his own personal research, photographs and documents were culled primarily from the Moorland Spingarn Research Center, Howard University, and the Schomburg Collection, New York Public Library. Several other smaller historical repositories, as well as brothers who were in possession of artifacts and photographs, also lent to the celebration and displayed for all to enjoy.

Of particular note, beginning with academic year 1912, and then from 1915 onward, a number of annual group photographs of Alpha Chapter members were displayed, along with copies of historic *Oracles*, including original documents beginning from 1925, and reproductions from 1919 (the first edition of the *Oracle*). As the District's H&A chairman, my historical research and inquiries on behalf of Omega uncovered that Tulane University's Amistad Collection, holds most of the papers of Bro. Stanley Douglas (Alpha, 1915), first editor to the *Oracle*. Among those holdings is one of the few extant copies of the first edition of the *Oracle*.

It was from this collection that we obtained a reproduction copy of the original publication. The highlight of the issue is *The Challenge*, a statement from Founder Just, commenting upon the role of the Negro in the post-World War I world, in which many changes will be forthcoming and the need to both prepare ourselves and to step forward and claim our rightfully earned place in American society. The reproduced issue of this first *Oracle* proved to be a major highlight of the Alpha Chapter history display.

## ALPHA CHAPTER CELBRATES CENTENNIAL, DECEMBER 15, 2011

The intent of the program was to provide an opportunity for current and past members of the Chapter to celebrate the legacy of the Fraternity's Founders and the numerous men who have shaped the history of Omega's birthplace and the fraternity.[84] The program of the evening featured remarks from the Honorable Bro. James E. Clyburn, member, U.S. House of Representatives, the Sixth District of South Carolina. His remarks focused on how proud Omega's Founders would be to know from whence we came, but ended with a call for an even greater Omega, a fraternity that still upholds the Four Cardinal principles, but that also lifts others as we ourselves climb further up the ladder of success.

In addition to Bro. Clyburn's remarks, the ball was also an opportunity to give a special award and recognition to Bro. Frank B. Patterson, who to many Alpha Chapter alumni is "Bro. Alpha Chapter," a living legacy of what it means to be a member of the fraternity who has also been inducted into the sacred brotherhood by way of the Mother Pearl.

"Frankie P.," as he is affectionately known by all men of Omega, was both truly surprised and emotionally overcome. He choked up, with tears running down his cheeks, as he humbly accepted the award and recognition that the brothers bestowed upon him on this most auspicious occasion. We concluded the evening with good food, good fellowship, great music, and taking an Alpha Chapter Centennial Alumni Celebration official photograph.

Befitting the commitment of all good Omega men to the spiritual, and in recognition that there is a higher power that has always guided us since our founding on November 17, 1911, we closed out the Alpha Chapter Centennial Celebration with a commemorative church service, singing and giving praise for Omega, our friendship and fraternity, our lives, and with hopes for a blessed future. Our final event, on Sunday, December 18th, convened at the Macedonia Baptist Church, Arlington, Virginia, pastored by Bro. Rev. Leonard Hamlin, Jr., one of the Sons of Alpha Chapter. To assure unity and continuity, the brothers were requested to wear black suits, white shirts, and purple ties. After the service, we took an Alpha Chapter alumni photo

---

[84] *See the Alpha Chapter Centennial Celebration Program Guide, P.12.*

on the steps of Macedonia, and with the conclusion of such, we bid our brothers and friends farewell – until we meet again in due season.

The events of that celebratory weekend will long live in the hearts and minds of all Alpha Chapter alumni brothers. These four days were not just a party, nor a series of meetings at which fellowship was exchanged. Rather, it was a golden opportunity for men of like mind and similar levels of attainment, to pause and reflect from whence did come our strengths over these last 100 years. Further, we gathered together to seek God's continued blessing upon our beloved Omega and Alpha Chapter in particular.

It is always good to stop and reflect, to give heed to those hills from which we gather our personal and collective fraternal strength, and to bear witness to one another, in recognition that we have come from a special place, and were put here to do a special set of tasks. And when our days are done and the book of accomplishments is written to give an account of our lives, both individually and fraternally, we will not be found wanting. Indeed, this was a time for such reflection, and I am confident that the time was well spent, and that each of us went away from this place with a greatly renewed and enhanced spirit of what it means to be an Omega man, and of our obligation to lift others as we climb and seek to live by our four Cardinal Principles.

# XXVII – Omega, A Continuum Of Service

President Barack Obama meets with Omega leaders during the July 2011 Centennial Celebration

While December 18, 2011, ended my observance of Omega's Centennial Celebration, it did not interfere with the continuity of my service to the fraternity. As noted earlier, the fraternity's year-long celebration began on the steps of Thirkield Hall, where Omega was founded, on November 17, 2010. We noted at that time that the Men of Omega would be observing events for the succeeding 12 months, which extended to 13 months for those of us who were inducted into Omega by way of Alpha Chapter.

While the rah, rah has subsided, the work of Omega continues. The "Lift As You Climb" obligation and mentality are as relevant today as it ever was. We must now put away some of the clanging cymbals and the well beaten drums that we have used to announce and showcase Omega's centennial presence, to highlight who we are and what we have done, and in that place, adopt new standards, become refocused, engage in self-sacrifice, and renew our commitment to all mankind and one another.

## 50+ OMEGA INSPIRED YEARS

*Criticism about Omega being too social and not sufficiently social action oriented is not new. But we must be ever mindful that our Founders chose four words as Cardinal Principles - Manhood, Scholarship, Perseverance, and Uplift - and that social service to the less fortunate is how we, as Omega men, demonstrate our belief in these principles and live by them in our daily lives. It is upon this base that Omega was built, and upon this base we will continue to grow and serve. Otherwise, we might as well declare ourselves as dead, and cease to function. Dr. Andrew A. Ray, 39th Grand Basileus, in his recent message to the brotherhood, as reflected in the Winter 2011 edition of the ORACLE, stated, "The existence and success of Omega has been and continues to be a result of dedication, tradition, pride, and enthusiasm. I am constantly reminded of the many sacrifices our Founders made as they created this great organization. They built a solid foundation and remained active to assure that like-minded men would represent Omega well, while uplifting their communities. As I reflect on the time I met Founders Cooper and Love, they said, ' ... young brothers, we gave birth to Omega, but it is up to you to keep Omega alive.' I will never forget those words and the spirit and passion in which they were shared. To that end, it is our obligation to take the necessary steps to make sure Omega thrives for future generations."*[85]

When the fraternity was founded in 1911, the stated objective was for friendship and fraternity among men of like mind, men who were committed to attainment, and always had high aspirations. Those were worthy and relevant goals then, and are still such. However, over time and with a fuller realization that the struggles for African Americans (then called "Negroes" or "Colored") to get ahead, to close the racial divide and to keep pace with the majority population, it is necessary for the Men of Omega to close ranks. Further, we must also

---

[85] *"Omega - In the Last Quarter Century, 1986-2011, Centennial Souvenir Journal Statement, P. 33, authored by Rohulamin Quander, Chairman, Third District History and Archives Committee, June 2011.*

join with others who have the same or similar goals, and move forward in unison for the benefit of our people.

Great leaps forward came as a result of these collective efforts, and in significant measure due to structured outreach from many organizations like the NAACP (founded 1909), the Urban League (1910), the Association for the Study of Negro Life and History (1915), the National Pan-Hellenic Council (1930), the National Negro Congress (1935), and the National Council of Negro Women (1935). As well, there are many more such organizations, all of which shared one particular mission- *Service*. Whether primarily focused upon basic human and civil rights, economic and educational opportunities, or razing the consciousness of the many downtrodden in America, particularly among those of African ancestry, each organization couched its mission in terms of rendering needed service to an underserved population that was likewise the victim of ribald racial discrimination in every walk of American life.

As I read through many articles that appeared in the Oracle in the 1930s, I observed a changing attitude within the ranks of the fraternity. Omega men have always been known for their ability to have a good time, their celebratory attitudes that were coupled with sustained academic achievement. However, as Omega men continued to make their mark in the professions, as well as what the society at large would permit of our race at that time, there was also an emergence of a new attitude about the role and relevancy of Greek-letter organizations.

In 1936, the fraternity was approaching its 25th year. Brothers who were in a position to make a difference within Omega, began to speak out in louder voices, putting their sentiments into written form. The direction and intended focus of Omega's *Oracle* has been challenged from time to time, with some brothers questioning, particularly in the 1930s and 1940s, whether our fraternal magazine had gotten too political, and "too intellectual," perhaps more focused on the societal ills of the day, than might be in the best interest of the fraternity.

I find the latter assertion made during that era to be particularly disturbing, because Omega was founded as a fraternity of educated men, for educated men, and being "too intellectual" is an accusation that cries out for dumbing down the level and focus of what we are all about. Those forces would seem to be calling for a prior day when Omega was more "rah rah," than recognizing that times had changed and there was a great need for Omega to change with the times, if we were going to be both relevant and survive. African Americans had had enough. Slavery ended on January 1, 1863, with the issuance of the Emancipation Proclamation, yet in 1938, some 75 odd years later, very little had changed, with only limited progress made to ensure our rights as citizens.

Therefore, it would take the effort by everyone who was concerned to force society at large to reassess itself, and make the needed changes that we, as the sable citizens, were entitled to. In simple terms, we had to learn to be of greater service to our causes and to one another. Founder Oscar J. Cooper recognized the importance of service to our fraternal value system, and recited such in the previously mentioned letter he penned to Bro. George A. Isabelle, Omega's 10th Grand Keeper of Records and Seal (1937-1940) dated December 17, 1941, written in response to Isabelle's earlier inquiry about Omega's original purpose.

Responding to Isabelle's query, Founder Cooper wrote, "From my viewpoint, that is a very difficult thing to do; for my observation has been that the object of the Fraternity shifts with every decade, and that is as it should be in any wide awake, growing and progressive organization."[86] Bro. Cooper then expounded on the role of the fraternity, built around its four cardinal principles, but noting that we found ourselves reaching out to broaden our scope of activities to include in our program activities that were not affiliated with Omega, the manifestations of which are limitless.

The above referred-to letter was dated just 10 days after the U.S. was attacked by Japan at Pearl Harbor. Already a new world order was taking place, and Bro. Cooper wished to make certain that Omega remained at the forefront of these monumental changes. Further, he went on to say:

---

[86] *See Founder Cooper's letter to Bro. George A. Isabelle, December 17, 1941.*

## OMEGA, A CONTINUUM OF SERVICE

*And so we have come on down the years developing first one idea and then another, until today we stand on the threshold of developing into another phase of activity; for with the world changing as it is, with the possibility of a new order of things within a few years, it becomes necessary for Omega to prepare to meet the changed conditions in order to take her rightful place in the sun of the scheme of things.*

*I feel that we should be entirely unselfish in our future conduct and should develop some phase of activity from an economic standpoint that will meet the needs of many of our people, Surely with the indomitable personnel which comprises our organization, we have the machinery to set in motion about anything that we might wish to effect. This is our big chance I feel and a grand opportunity for Omega to make her influence felt in a very material way, for the benefit of those whom we represent.*

*In other words, to sum up what I mean; we should add one more cardinal principle, if not actually, we should make it a part of our future activities, "Service"; for it is the one thing that dominates all business and economic life of today. It is the key note of all living vital agencies which are set up in the interest of mankind, and it is the one thing that makes life in whatever sense we wish to consider it, worthwhile.*

*Let it be said of Omega of the future that "We live to serve our fellow man."* [87]

This powerful sentiment expressed so ably by Founder Cooper in 1941, was reiterated by him in another letter, dated November 4, 1968, directed to Bro. William C. Jason, Jr., of Mu Omega Chapter of Philadelphia. Brother Jason later became Chairman of the Recommendations Committee and served in that capacity with distinction. Extracting from that letter, I noted that Founder Cooper,

---

[87] *See Founder Cooper's letter to Bro. George A. Isabelle, December 17, 1941.*

in explaining why the Four Cardinal principles were selected, and most superficially why they were chosen in that order, states:

> *With these three Cardinal Principles [referring to Manhood, Scholarship, and Perseverance] found to be present, we naturally develop a high spirit of altruism and Uplift, devoid of any selfishness and with a natural spirit and tendency to be of service to others in proportion as we have developed the three previous principles and should make ourselves felt as an entity in any community in which we exist: for strong character and ambitions are developed not just to ingratiate the ones amplifying them, but should naturally spread beyond the narrow confines of the person or the organization represented by the person.*[88]

Shortly before his death in 1974, Founder Edgar A. Love addressed a group of Omega men on the subject, *The History of Omega Psi Phi Fraternity*. The address was subsequently transcribed by Bro. Lewis Anderson, former Grand Keeper of Records and Seal. Among the many remarks concerning the history of the fraternity, Founder Love, as did Founder Cooper before him, stated, " ... And finally, Uplift; which puts man in connection with the community in which he lives and lets him realize that he has a responsibility to those who are less fortunate than himself; that he must also do what he does with the idea of service to the community and to the nation. Bring all these together, we have the true Omega Man."

Founder Just, in issuing *The Challenge* in the 1919 first edition of the *Oracle*, stated,

> *These times demand clean men, of clear vision, of straight thinking, of unselfish doing. And every Omega man must accept this challenge. Out of groups like ours, men who know and feel to the utmost Fidelity, Liberty and Fraternity, must come to the world absolution.*

---

[88] *See Founder Cooper's letter to Bro. William C. Jason, Jr., November 4, 1968.*

## OMEGA, A CONTINUUM OF SERVICE

Perhaps the most complete statement about the obligation of Omega to be an organization of service comes from Founder Frank Coleman. Written in the shadow of the just ended Great War (aka World War I), his article, "The Negro Greek-Letter Men's Opportunity for Service" appeared in the 1920 issue of the *Oracle*, the only issue of the publication edited by Bro. William Stuart Nelson. Bro. Coleman said, in part:

> *The world is turned upside down, the voice of the iconoclast is raised and many pause to listen and ponder upon his merciless words; at no time in the history of the world were existing things more closely examined or project subjected to a more severe incredulity than at the present time. The only excuse for existence, the only raison d'etre of any public institution is the service it can render society. An institution which fails to render its mead of service to society must lead a tortuous and uncertain existence if indeed it continues to exist at all.*
>
> *High ideals and good intentions alone never did, and as long as human nature remains as it is, never will bring about one great reform, win a single battle or conquer a single dread disease. Great schemes, born in the minds of individuals never become potent until translated into action.*
>
> *Active service must be the slogan of every Greek-letter fraternity, and I make no apologies for the use of the Negro in the caption of this note. . . . It is very necessary for us to remember that we are living in an age in which great events occur quickly, that the opportunities for service are legion, but that to be effective we must as organizations concentrate on some few means of making ourselves effective, and our organizations felt. If we do this we shall realize that which must be the basic compelling motive of every national Greek-letter organization, the gospel of helpfulness and the brotherhood of man.*[89]

---

[89] *Founder Coleman's statement is significantly longer than appears here. He is assessing the negative racial climate that characterized the United States in post-World War I, noting the obligation of the educated Negro to take a bold stand to oppose further denigration of*

### 50+ OMEGA INSPIRED YEARS

My brothers, these too are words calling Omega's sons to serve. My charge then, is for all Omega Men to heed the words of our beloved Founders in every respect. Thus, all four of Omega's Founders went on record underscoring the need for Omega Men to be men of service; to be men who render to those less fortunate.

---

*our people, and to help uplift the plight of our race, emphasizing that the time is now, as a valuable opportunity is at hand, and we must rise to the occasion. For a full text, I refer you to the 1920 issue of the Oracle, the sole issue published by Bro. William Stuart Nelson, or The History of the Omega Psi Phi Fraternity, by Bro. Herman Dreer, Pp. 99-100. Bro. Dreer's extract appears to be shorter that Founder Coleman's full text.*

## XXVIII- Omega, In Its Second Century, 2012 And Beyond

As I wind this Memoir down, and look forward to receiving my 50 year membership recognition at the 79th Grand conclave in Philadelphia in July 2014, I am naturally drawn to reflection, drawn to looking at Omega in a context of overview. Neither my interest in nor involvement with Omega-related activities has waned. When the Centennial Celebration drew to a close on December 18, 2011, with the culmination of Alpha Chapter's own centenary observance, some might think that it was now a time for relaxation as well. Not me!

> *The survival of Omega as a unit of high achieving men and a solid brotherhood demands that we carefully and comprehensively reassess ourselves, and then focus on restoring and preserving our legacy of greatness. The reclamation of the brothers who have fallen asleep, as well as the retention of continuing interest from among the active membership, are integral parts of whatever plans and efforts are put forth. We cannot wait any longer, drifting from one uncertainty to another, before we decide what we must do, and how to do it. In addition to seeking men who already demonstrate their leadership and determination to achieve, to address and stem the inflow of mediocrity, the fraternity should create an internal program designed to teach its own members how to become tomorrow's leaders, men who will take up the Founders' and early members' mantles, and carry them forth into all of tomorrows many endeavors.*[90]

In my book, *Nellie Quander, An Alpha Kappa Alpha Pearl*, published to coincide with AKA's own centennial observance, I concluded my biographical study of cousin Nellie with the Spanish word, "Adelante," which means Forward or Go Forward. And with the

---

[90] "*Omega - In the Last Quarter Century, 1986-2011, Centennial Souvenir Journal Statement, P. 33,* authored by Rohulamin Quander, Chairman, Third District History and Archives Committee, June 2011.

conclusion on this publication drawing nigh, I likewise say, "ADELANTE!" This is my time to pick up a new helm for Omega, to be a wider known and appreciated spokesman on behalf of Omega's many causes, good deeds, and accomplishments, so that others might come to better know, or learn for the first time what Omega is all about.

When we say, "Friendship is Essential to the Soul," I want that phrase to be much more than just words. The Founders surely intended that it would be so. But all too often the brotherhood has not acted in sufficient unison to convey to itself and others, the true and deeper meaning of what it takes to be a friend, a really true friend. Each of us in life has had at least one experience in which someone that we thought was our friend, has proven otherwise. Further, I am convinced that this breakdown in relationship is often not the result of some deliberate or intentional act on the part of the other person, but often just carelessness, a failure to appreciate what friendship means and how we must be cognizant of the feelings and worth of the other person, in order to maintain that friendship.

Bro. Quander and Rev. Bro. Jesse Jackson at 78th Grand Conclave, Minneapolis, Minnesota, July 2012

Friendship should not be an unbearable task, but like marriage, it does require some work and should not be taken for granted. I am no different from you. Like you, I have people with whom I have been closely identified, but with whom I later disagreed. Depending upon the attitude of each of us, the disagreement did not part our friendship, but rather underscored our differences. It tested our mettle, as we worked through our differences, respected the other's opinion, but did not let the differences get in the way of our friendship and love for each other. The best example of this is with my wife. Carmen and I are as different as day from night on certain issues, but we never go to bed angry. We fully realize and appreciate that life is both unpredictable and short, and we would never want the day to end, or our respective lives to come to an end on a bad or unhappy note.

Through the years, I have been affiliated with many organizations in addition to Omega. The Howard University Alumni Club, The Pigskin Club of Washington, The Bachelor Benedicts Club, and the Association for the Study of African American Life and History (ASALH) have all found my name listed on their membership rolls. As well, I have taken on several projects for the schools that my children have attended. At a time when many people our age are cutting back, thinking smaller, and "winding up their affairs," Carmen and I are in search of new horizons. Obtaining a new art studio in September 2013, was a part of that new horizon, according the opportunity to expand her artistic reach, to create new works, and to satisfy ourselves in attaining goals not yet reached.

With Omega approaching her second century in the 2010-2011 timeframe, a new round of organizational assessments became relevant. Questions were being asked about the individual components of the fraternity, broken down by our territorial districts and queries about the history and involvement of our individual chapters. I have previously noted my role as chairman of the History and Archives Committee for the Third District, which encompasses Washington, D.C. and the state of Virginia. Above, I referred to the lack of adequate planning and resources, which hampered the best efforts of the respective 12 districts to showcase their fraternal history during the Centennial Celebration Grand Conclave. But before I leave the subject of my involvement with the Third District's history book project, I must underscore that all too often the lending of one's time and talent to an otherwise important project is sometimes not sufficiently appreciated. My efforts on behalf of this project was one such instance.

## 50+ OMEGA INSPIRED YEARS

As previously noted, my mission as the Chairman of History and Archives Committee was threefold. First, we were to write and publish the initial history book on the district. Second, the committee was charged with assessing the official Omega website on the Internet, to see what updates, if any, should be made to the Founders biographical statements. Third, the Committee was requested to write the Statement for the Centennial Souvenir Journal, which would be an overview of the last 25 years (1986-2011), but also look into the near future.

Our H&A committee worked diligently towards meeting all three charges, but time and resources proved to be in short supply. We decided that, given the constricted parameters, there was no need to adjust the existing biographical information on our Founders, and that we should concentrate on the first and third charges, as each of them would have an immediate and lasting effect upon the history of Omega. Thus we were not prepared for a fourth charge – to create a comprehensive Third District history display - which came at very short notice and likewise without ANY additional resources being made available. And it was from this point that Brother District Representative Anthony Knight and I began to part company, although I did not yet realize it. My concept of how Omega's history should be portrayed at its Centennial Celebration and his were clearly not the same. I saw something that should be "Grand," while he apparently saw something that was far less. How much less, I still am not certain.

## Alpha Omega Observes 90 Years As A Graduate Chapter

It was realized, certainly as far back as 1917, when the first of the two War Chapters of Omega operated, that the Omega fraternal experience should be much more than just an undergraduate experience. The men who were in military training at Fort Des Moines, Iowa, were drafted into service and drawn from many colleges and universities. As well, many were recent graduates, no longer a part of their former undergraduate institutions. Once they were introduced to Omega, they soon likewise appreciated that they had little in common with a typical 18 year old college freshman who was also aspiring to join the fraternity.

## OMEGA, IN ITS SECOND CENTURY, 2012 AND BEYOND

These older men wanted the friendship and fraternity, just as their undergraduate counterparts so desired, but it had to be on a different level. Although no formal graduate chapters yet existed for the fledgling Omega, most assuredly there was talk of how we can continue this grand idea, this scheme of things, to accord older men the benefits of Omega membership. The sentiment for continued affiliation was again evident the following year (1918) at Camp Howard, located on Howard University's campus. Although I have no documents to support what is obvious to me, the older men must have pulled themselves aside and determined to periodically convene in the name of Omega, without the need to be a part of Alpha Chapter, the sole Omega chapter in the area.

These D.C.-based brothers, many of whom had come to the nation's capital city for the limited work opportunities that Negroes were accorded at the time, had come from such diverse educational institutions as Harvard, Yale, Morehouse, Bowdoin, Dartmouth, Tuskegee, West Virginia College, and Hampton Institute, to name but a few. They had friends and Omega brothers who lived in other places, and most assuredly their conversations revealed that a new concept, the graduate chapter, was taking hold. The first was Lambda (now Lambda Omega) established in Norfolk, Virginia in 1920. Eventually the Washington, D.C. brothers, under the leadership of Bro. Charles Herbert Marshall, Sr. (Alpha Chapter 1920), Founding Basileus, petitioned the Grand Chapter for a charter to start a graduate chapter, and did so on or about October 1, 1922. Thus Alpha Omega Chapter, to which I owe my allegiance and affiliation, was born.

From that date until the present, Alpha Omega has continued to be a leader among men, and certainly one of Omega's most dynamic chapters. It was only natural, considering that Washington, D.C. is not only the nation's capital, but also the world's capital city. Power resides there, whether it be the White House, Congress, the Supreme Court, or the many non-governmental organizations that are located in this area. It iss only natural, then, that much of that power and influence has come to rest within the membership ranks of Alpha Omega.

## 50+ OMEGA INSPIRED YEARS

I elect not to enumerate here who many of these well known, and sometimes even famous, brothers were. Many now reside in Omega chapter, but their good work and diversified legacies will live on as a result of how they each made a difference, whether it be in civil rights, education, the sciences, or social justice. I am so very pleased, and likewise humbled, to be able to count myself to have known many of these great men, being an Omega Legacy, whose father made it his business to make himself known to many of these "Greats," with me often tagging along as well.

In 1997 Alpha Omega Chapter observed its Diamond Jubilee (1922-1997), the details of which event have, unfortunately, faded within a fairly short time. In 2012, when the decision was made to observe Alpha Omega's 90th anniversary, the planning committee, of which I was an integral part, determined that such should not reoccur. We appreciated that the chapter still had many older brothers who had been quite active in their younger years, and felt that we should not wait another 10 years, for a centennial milestone. Rather, we were of the opinion that we should honor those most senior brothers by having a 90th anniversary celebration, and let the Centennial events be taken care of at a later time.

With all due respect, nothing is promised, and for brothers who are in their late 80s, or even their 90s, now is the time to give due recognition. And of course, we must also acknowledge that Omega's most senior brother, Dr. David H. Reid, Jr., age 104 years, (Upsilon, 1927) is also the first Omega son to earn an 85-year membership recognition from the fraternity. Thus the planning committee, headed by Bro. Gregory Boykin, executed the plans for the celebration, which was hosted by The Alpha Omega Social Action and Scholarship Foundation, a 501 (c)(3) entity that the chapter established in 1991 to serve as the chapter's "giving arm." Thus, it was decided that the 90th Anniversary Celebration should be significantly more than just a party, but rather a fundraiser to benefit our "giving arm." As well, the below-enumerated activities of the foundation underscore the chapter's ongoing pursuit of meeting the mandated programs directive that the Grand Chapter has determined should be ongoing throughout the fraternity.

## OMEGA, IN ITS SECOND CENTURY, 2012 AND BEYOND

We convened the celebration on November 2, 2012, at the Samuel Riggs IV Alumni Center, at the University of Maryland. It was an excellent venue to hold such a celebration. Under the able chairmanship of Bro. Welton Belsches, the foundation continues to meet its goals which are to provide: 1) College scholarships based on academic achievement; 2) College scholarships based on talent achievements; 3) Food for families at Thanksgiving and Christmas; 4) Mentoring programs for high school students; and 5) health education programs and social awareness events for the local community.

I played one of many key roles in making the event of that evening a success, working closely with Bro. Boykin, event chair, and the other committee members, to set the protocol of how the events should unfold. I undertook some historical research and writing assignments, drew upon my personal knowledge and Omega legacy background. When Alpha Omega is identified with its activities, I believe that they must be done correctly. And certainly a $90^{th}$ anniversary event is one such activity. Several brothers joined with me in creating the program and then determining the Order of Program. Bro. Walter Hill, Chapter Keeper of Finance, served as master of ceremonies, while Rev. Bro. Courtenay Miller, chapter chaplain, did the invocation. I crafted three documents, "The Occasion," which was delivered by Bro. Norman Senior; "Alpha Omega Chapter: An Historical Retrospect," which I delivered; and the biographical statement of Bro. Dr. Charles Herbert Marshall, Sr. (Alpha Chapter, 1920), Alpha Omega's 1922 Founding Basileus.

Doing the bio statement was both a labor of love and a pleasure. Although I had grown up with Charles Marshall, III, now deceased, who was Bro. Marshall, Sr.'s grandson, we were not close personal friends. Still, I knew that both his grandfather and his own dad, C. Herbert Marshall, Jr. (Alpha Chapter, 1917) were each pillars of Omega. So I reached out to Charlie's son, Raleigh Marshall. I did not know the 28 year old young man, but Bro. Donnie Lucas (Alpha Omega, 2011) came to my rescue. As we were researching information on Dr. Marshall, Sr., Donnie mentioned that he lived in their home one summer while in college at the University of Virginia, and knew Raleigh well. Bingo!

### 50+ OMEGA INSPIRED YEARS

*For over 100 years Omega has functioned as a guiding and constructive force for men of all ages. This truth was, is, and always will be the manifest genius of Founders Love, Cooper, Coleman, and Just. To the initiated, Omega teases out and ensures the courage of our convictions by illuminating the possibilities of life, while also providing the enabling resource of the example of the like-minded who came before us. Each Omega soul and his life's story are but another unbreakable link in the Omega chain of promise. Many of us recognize this most powerful phenomenon as "the bridge". Where this bridge is properly girded by Omega's principles and precepts, great things are not only possible; great things happen. It is this bridge that all Sons of Omega should seek to cross again and again as we embark on the next millennium of internal and external relevance. Bro. Quander, thank you for bearing your Omega soul. Thank you for your story. Thank you for extending the bridge.* -Brother Donald G. Lucas, 11-FA2011-Alpha Omega

He called Raleigh, and made an appointment for me to visit. During the visit, I secured an appropriate photograph and obtained an autobiographical statement that his great grandfather had written about himself, tracing his birth to 1862 in Amissaville, Virginia, one of nine children. Born free just before the 1863 Emancipation Proclamation, his parents were also free at the time of his birth. Raleigh also directed me to a file kept by the Georgetown Public Library, located on R Street, N.W., just off Wisconsin Avenue, which maintained an historical file on the family. There I found newspaper clippings and many favorable comments that had been made by the community about both Doctors Marshall, father and son.

Along the way of my research, I learned a few other matters of significance as well. Dr. Marshall, Sr., began his medical practice in 1890, the same year that he graduated from the Howard University School of Medicine. He was most active in the local community, and when he served his patients in their homes, he could be seen driving his horse and buggy through the streets in all kinds of weather and at odd hours, if necessary.

## OMEGA, IN ITS SECOND CENTURY, 2012 AND BEYOND

His son, Dr. Marshall, Jr., followed in his footsteps, likewise graduating from Howard's School of Medicine, and was so active in the community that he was dubbed "Mayor of Georgetown." Of course it was an unofficial title, as no black man was ever elected to such a distinguished post at that early stage in our local history. Still, it was a nice honor and recognition among those citizens who appreciated the service that both his father and he provided to the community, both in medicine and community service.

As I was conducting my research for the 90th Anniversary program, I recalled a fond memory that will stick with me for the rest of my life. In February 1965, when I was still an Alpha Chapter neophyte, the dean of pledgees invited Dr. Marshall, Jr., to be the guest speaker for the Alpha Chapter annual recruitment smoker. He was delighted to accept the invitation and kept us laughing and joking for the better part of 45 minutes, while he spoke on a variety of life subjects, including his experiences as an Alpha Chapter brother in 1917. Looking back, I was so young and so naïve. I did not then realize nor appreciate that valuable and unique historical information was being freely given.

I had no appreciation at that time that I was in the presence of greatness. Not just "Omega greatness," but greatness at large. Dr. Marshall, Jr., beyond medicine, was a civil and humanitarian rights man. He was a well-respected churchman and deacon at the 19th Street Baptist Church. He gave freely of his time, talent, and treasure, and in the process, he made a great difference in the plight of the African American population in this town. And in the process, he extended his own father's stellar legacy, as the senior Bro. Marshall set the tone and discharged himself in the manner that set the precedent for his son to follow.

One additional note. I discovered that during the time that Bro. Charles Herbert Marshall, Sr., served as Alpha Omega's Founding Basileus (1922-1928), his son, Bro. Marshall, Jr., served Omega in the capacity as Grand Marshal for the December 1924, 13th Annual Grand Conclave, that was held in Washington, D.C. Truly, father and son were examples of how Omega was bringing the best men home. As well, an anomaly occurred in their fraternal lives. Personally, I know of no other instance in which the son was inducted into Omega, and subsequently sponsored his dad into the same chapter of the fraternity at a later date.

Bro. Marshall, Jr., was inducted into Omega by way of Alpha Chapter in 1917. Three years later, in 1920, Bro. Marshall, Sr., was likewise inducted. Although the induction records for Bro. Marshall, Sr., appear to be lost, since Omega kept very poor records in its early history, secondary sources, including an obituary article in the fall 1929 *Oracle,* refer to his 1920 induction into Omega. Interestingly, though, the article states that he was inducted via "Alpha Omega" chapter, an entity which did not exist in 1920, and did not come into existence until October 1922, fully two years later. Logic dictates, and I am reasonably certain that it happened in this manner, Bro. Marshall, Sr., at age 58 years, surrendered his person to the much younger college age men of Alpha Chapter, and was thus inducted into the fraternity by them, but under the personal sponsorship and watchful eye of his son. Had this ever happened before? Has it ever occurred since? Indeed, he was spurred on by the desire to make Omega more than just a college-era experience. It certainly must have been an interesting time. I am certain Dr. Marshall, Sr., came to the situation with his eyes open, aware of what he was doing, and likewise wanting to be a part of the Omega brotherhood.

Over time, he would call to his side mature men of like ideas and the desire to create and sustain Omega as a life-long journey. Older than most, and perhaps the oldest Omega man at the time, he was likewise wiser. He assuredly saw a brotherhood of men who were friends, and felt that he wanted to be a part of it, despite the age difference. And when time came for the formal chartering of Alpha Omega, as the first graduate chapter in the entire Washington, D.C. area, it was at his behest and best efforts, resulting in the brotherhood recognizing his leadership qualities and selecting him as their Founding Basileus. He served in that capacity from 1922, until health considerations dictated that he give up the helm. He died in Washington, D.C. in 1929, but not before making an indelible mark upon all of that which is Omega to follow.

I salute the Brothers Marshall, father and son, and recognize their valuable contributions to both Omega and the community at large. They were truly great examples of how Omega brought the best men home. And I would hope that we would continue to do so. And where we are failing to follow their examples, then we should refocus and call to mind the words of Bro. Walter H. Mazyck, former Grand Keeper of Records and Seal.

**Members vs. Men**[91]

> *The Greek Letter Societies among our group appear to have entered upon a period of mad competition for obtaining members. Pledgees are increasing in numbers. Scarcely a student on the college campus but wears a pledge pin or a Frat pin. Are the Fraternities forgetting their original high standards? Can it be said that every man who enters college is of Fraternity material? If in any place, Omega has entered this mad race for members, pause and consider.*
>
> *The value of our Fraternity is not in numbers, but in men, in real brotherhood. Eight men thoroughly immersed in the true Omega spirit are far greater assets than eighty with lukewarm enthusiasm. If any chapter has reached the maximum in numbers for efficient work and brotherly cooperation, let it initiate each year only a number of men equal to those leaving the chapter by way of graduation or otherwise.*
>
> *Men, real men of Omega caliber, strive for that which is most difficult of attainment. Keep Omega the most difficult Greek letter Society in which to obtain membership and be assured that Omega material will never be found lacking.*

Undoubtedly, the highlight of the 90th Anniversary Celebration was the conferring of awards upon worthy brothers for their sustained service on behalf of Omega. Choosing carefully from among many qualified candidates, the planning committee decided to give five category awards, and one special recognition award. Naturally, the Four Cardinal Principles befittingly lent themselves to the occasion. We conferred the Manhood Award upon Bro. William H. Deane (Omega Chapter), who served as Alpha Omega basileus for

---

[91] *The Oracle Spring 1925, Pp. 4 & 5. This issue was edited by Brother Walter H. Mazyck, then the Grand KRS.*

about six years in the 1980s. We chose Bro. Ralph J. Briscoe, Jr., for the Scholarship Award; Bro. Dewayne Wynn for the Perseverance Award; and Bro. Edward L. Baldwin, Jr., former Alpha Omega Basileus, for the Uplift Award.

In recognition of Bro. Dr. Marshall, Sr., we also created the Charles Herbert Marshall, Sr., Leadership Award, which we conferred upon Bro. Judge Herbert B. Dixon, Jr., former Alpha Omega basileus, and senior judge at the Superior Court of the District of Columbia. Finally, we issued a special 85-year membership recognition award to Bro. Dr. David H. Reid, Jr., (Upsilon, 1927), our beloved 104 year old brother. Although he was unable to be present, his son, Dr. David H. Reid, III, was present and accepted the award on his dad's behalf. As David later related to me, when he returned home about midnight in Fairfax, Virginia, his dad was waiting up, and wanted to know about everything that had occurred earlier that evening.

Presenting the award and recognition to his dad, the senior Bro. Reid had tears in his eyes, and expressed both excitement and appreciation for this recognition. He added too, that he had no idea that he would live so long and likewise still be an active member of Omega, although age has slowed his steps and prevented his being able to attend fraternity functions. As they talked into the night, David reminded his dad that in two weeks, on November 17, the brothers would convene at Cramton Auditorium for Founders Day, and if his dad felt up to it, he would gladly take him to Howard University for the convocation. The senior Bro. Reid agreed, and then went to sleep for the night.

Then, as planned and promised, David brought his dad to Howard for the 101st anniversary convocation to commemorate Omega's founding. At an earlier time, David mentioned to me that he intentionally did not bring his dad to the Centennial Convocation in 2011, because the crush of the crowd would have been simply too much. Although his dad is in reasonably good health, still it is always advisable to exercise caution and discretion when taking him out. In the excitement of the moment, David felt that to add his dad to the scene in the Centennial year observance might have caused a stampede or at least too much crowding around him, if there was a

## OMEGA, IN ITS SECOND CENTURY, 2012 AND BEYOND

joint recognition of Omega's Founding Day, plus the presence of Omega's oldest member of then 84 years.

By the following year, November 17, 2012, things had cooled down some. The crowd was smaller and the scene much more manageable. The Doctors Reid arrived at Cramton, using a side entrance. A cadre of brothers had been alerted, and immediately swung into action, to lift Dr. Reid from the car into his wheelchair, although he was quite capable of doing so himself. But more importantly, the intent was to prevent a crowd from forming around him. With the rumor widely circulated that he would be present, the objective was to get him into Cramton auditorium and lifted up on the stage as quickly as possible, to separate him from the crowd of brothers. As well, because of his elevated position, everyone could easily see him.

> *As a proud Omega Man, I truly value our cardinal principles, Manhood, Scholarship, Perseverance, and Uplift. I try my best to uphold these principles in everything that I do. As "The People's Frat," I love the way we pride ourselves on being of the community, never proceeding, patronizing or transcending it. I also truly appreciate the love and zeal we hold for our brothers, in real brotherhood. I am most proud of the rich history that our Founders and other distinguished members left before us. As a youth, I was a proud member of the Beautillion, a program that introduces young men into society. This program was run by members of Omega Psi Phi Fraternity Inc.*
>
> *While serving in the U.S. Air Force, I encountered and was mentored by Omega Men throughout my career. I presently serve as the Chapter Reporter for Alpha Omega Chapter, as well as a member of several fraternity committees. Lastly, I believe that we need to always continue to pay recognition and homage to the Brothers who came before us and laid the blueprint for us to follow. In Friendship!* - Bro Norm Senior, 4-2011, Alpha Omega Chapter

The order of program was one, including greetings from brothers, the introduction of District Representative Robert Warren, and all Grand and District Officers. A few remarks were made about the occasion, with a focus upon the need for Omega men to step up and make certain that our second century is ever more grand than our first century was. But unquestionably, the highlight of the evening was the introduction of Bro. Dr. David H. Reid, Jr.

A brief highlight of his life was given, noting when he was inducted into the Lampados Club (1926), when and where he was inducted into the fraternity (November 17, 1927, in the sub-basement of the home of Bro. Col. Charles Young, a former station on the Underground Railroad), and how long he has been a member of Omega Psi Phi (85 years). As the brothers stood and cheered Bro. Reid, the 85 year recognition award was re-presented to him. The award had initially been presented at the Alpha Omega 90th Anniversary Celebration, but it was deemed appropriate to borrow the award from Bro. Reid, and present it again before a much larger audience.

Bro. Reid signaled that he wished to speak to the brotherhood. The room got so quiet that you could have head a pin drop. Well more than 1,000 Omega men were in the house, but not a word, other than those of Dr. Reid, was heard. Taking the microphone, he thanked the fraternity for bestowing this award and recognition upon him, adding that he never imagined that such would ever happen, reflecting back to the date of his induction into the fraternity.

Next, he shared some of his experiences of the 1926-1927 pledge period, noting that it was 14 months long, during which time he was able to bond with his two line brothers and all of the other members of the Lampados club, as well as the big brothers in Upsilon Chapter. Then, when the brothers deemed that he was ready, he was taken from the residence hall one evening, blindfolded, and carried to the home of Bro. Charles Young, then deceased. After he entered the house, not yet knowing where he was, he was taken down to the basement, and then to a dirt-floored sub-basement, where the blindfold was removed.

He was then told that he was standing on hallowed ground, the ground where many of our enslaved ancestors had hidden as they were trying to escape the oppression, brutality, and physical pain of slavery, seeking to find freedom and opportunities in the north. That the subbasement existed was a secret known only to a few, and that as an Omega man, he would be sworn to uphold the secret that a subbasement existed. Why? Although slavery had ended, protecting the legacy and historical significance of the Young home, was still a priority, and considered to be a secret that would be known only to a few, including the men of Upsilon Chapter. And then, with "Mother Young," as she was lovingly and most respectfully called, also in the house, but on an upper floor, he was put through the steps of the induction process into the sacred brotherhood that is Omega.

On his knees, he held his right hand high and took his oath of fealty to Omega with his left hand placed on a Bible. Arising from the dirt floor, he stood as a new member of the Omega Psi Phi Fraternity. Presented his pin on site, he never looked back. Returning home for Thanksgiving, he proudly wore his pin, displaying it to the brothers in the Raleigh area, primarily students or recent graduates from Shaw and St. Augustine Universities, many of whom he had previously known from his high school days.

He concluded his remarks with a word of advice to the younger Omega brothers, with the audience laughing and noting that everyone in the room was "younger" by Dr. Reid's standard. He said, "Remember the Cardinal Principles and the meaning of each of the Pearls. Walk tall, excel in education, yet be humble in the face of God."

The program concluded, most of the brothers adjourned to the Memorial to the Founders, located in front of Ernest E. Just Hall, where they sang *Omega Dear*, the official hymn, and later spent time on site discussing Dr. Reid's sage words of advice, and how they could put his words to use to make them better and more effective in pursuit of their fraternal oath and the principles that are recited therein.

# 50+ OMEGA INSPIRED YEARS

# XXIX – Homecoming Stretch

With 2012 behind me, I now enter the homestretch of writing these Omega-based memoirs. At one time I thought that the homestretch would be a wind down, and that I would slowly close out my endeavor with a sweet "Thank you and good night!" But anyone who really knows me also knows that I never operate that way. Not that I was looking for a "Big Bang" upon which to curtail my story, but events keep coming and with them a demand for some additional personal involvements. And 2013 was no exception. Therefore, I elect to address five particular activities, four of which are fraternal, and the other, a health issue. Fortunately, they all turned out well, and I am much the better for it.

Alpha Phi Alpha, Alpha Kappa Alpha, Kappa Alpha Psi, Omega Psi Phi, Delta Sigma Theta, and Phi Beta Sigma have each had their Centennial Celebrations, and due recognition appertaining thereto. Each organization has earned its proper due, for all of them share a common purpose as related to brotherhood/sisterhood and service to all mankind.

During the December 2012 Alpha Omega Chapter monthly meeting, Bro. Philip Thomas, Basileus, reminded the chapter that Delta Sigma Theta, our sister sorority, was observing its Centennial during the calendar year 2013. Of couse we already were well aware of their plans, but not necessarily the details. He requested volunteers from the brotherhood to serve as transportation hosts for the Delta Dears, senior sorors who are 62 years old and older. Our assignment was to drive these sorors around Howard University's campus on January 11, 2013, in battery powered carts. More than 10,000 Delta women were expected to converge on the campus as a component of their January 10-13, 2013, multi-day observance of the founding of Delta on January 13, 1913. My hand went up and I became one of the dozen or so chapter brothers who agreed to serve in this capacity.

With the new year underway, I was hanging out with the frat on Wednesday, January 9th at the Omega house, throwing back some Omega "oil," when Bro. Frank Boris reminded me that Bro. Steve Johnson, Howard's Assistant Vice President for Protocol and Events, needed to confirm which brothers would drive the Delta Dears to various locations on campus during the weekend of their Centennial Convocation. Howard was renting several golf cart type vehicles for the dozen brothers of Alpha Omega Chapter to host and drive the sorors throughout the campus. We were directed to be in place by 7:00 a.m. on Friday, January 11th. I awoke at 5:30 a.m., and was out of the house by 6:40 a.m., arriving at the Twin Towers, a residency building on Howard's campus at 7:05 a.m.

By 7:30 a.m., we were in place to meet a continuing fleet of arriving buses at the front of Cramton Auditorium. We picked up the Delta Dears and transported them to Burr Gymnasium, just a block away. Still it was a challenge to several of the older sorors, some of whom had canes, walkers, and even wheelchairs. Joining with me were Alpha Omega chapter brothers: Adamio Boddie, Steven G. Johnson, Wilson T. Bland, Curtis Malik Boykin, Frank S. Boris, Gregory "Uncle Phil" Boykin, Courtenay L. Miller, Anthony D. Carrell, and Damon Green. As well, there were also some other Omega men present and in service to Delta, but I do not have their names. It was about 12 of us in total.

While it was a task, it was also a great joy to me, personally. It was good for the Men of Omega to serve our Delta sisters in their hour of both celebration and need. Although the brother-sister relationship is not official, the close relationship goes back to the earliest days of both organizations, and was cemented by a marriage between Omega Founder Frank Coleman, and his beautiful bride, Edna Brown Coleman, a AKA, who was later a Delta Founder. As well, Founder Love was courting Marguerite Young (Alexander), another AKA-Delta Founder, although they did not marry.

The sorors were very pleased that the men of Omega, appropriately sporting their own colors, were visibly present and available to be of service to them. I heard over and over again, "My husband in an Omega." "My father was an Omega." "My son is an Omega." And to all of these comments and compliments, I added, "And Omega men are gentlemen. We are not dogs." Smiles abounded everywhere throughout the day. I got into one little testy match with a middle-aged Delta soror, when I pointed out the AKA Founders Memorial, located on Howard's campus in front of the Middle School

## HOMECOMING STRETCH

building, the site of the former Clarke Hall, where AKA was founded in 1908. She replied, "Who cares!" and was dismissive about whatever I was trying to say. When I mentioned that this is the site also where Nellie Quander apparently met with the young sorors who were contemplating a breakaway from AKA, she looked at me and said, "You wouldn't know anything about that, and besides whatever you think is probably not true anyway." I was appalled at her rudeness, and so were the other four sorors who were in the golf cart.

One of them, from Alexandria, Virginia, knew that I was a Quander, and that Nellie Quander was my relative. She spoke up and said, "This Omega man is a Quander, and a relative of Nellie Quander. We all know who she is, and he probably does know a lot more about that issue than we do." I smiled, and stated that I had written the book on Nellie Quander's life, and that during my research cycle, I visited the Delta archives at Howard, and reviewed the statements made by several of the Delta Founders, including the late Jimmy Bugg Middleton, my next door neighbor, who died in the late 1960s before we purchased our house. I then added that several of the Delta Founders had quite a bit to say about the breakup and formation of Delta. As well, I had read, *In Search of Sisterhood*, the definitive history of Delta, written by Soror Paula Giddings, my fellow Howard classmate, and that I assuredly knew what I was talking about.

After hearing my retort, and the dress down from her fellow sorors, the testy soror did say, "Well, I guess you probably do know what you are talking about." She departed the cart, asking me if I was a member of Kappa Alpha Psi? I was floored. Where has she been all day? Not one Kappa was driving a golf cart, and all Omegas, including me, had some paraphernalia on, indicative of our fraternal affiliation. My purple hat, which I obtained while attending the 76th Grand Conclave in Raleigh, North Carolina in July 2010, was perched prominently upon my head for all to see. Well, it takes all kinds.

Although I drove from 7:30 a.m., until 4:15 p.m., shuttling sorors back and forth to the university bookstore, the Freedmen's Building for a health seminar, the medical school library for a press conference, the Delta Founder's Memorial, "Fortitude," and other campus sites, the highlight of my day came when my cart and I were commandeered, and directed to Rankin Chapel to pick up Grace Elizabeth White-Ware, the 92 year old daughter of Delta Founder Madree Penn-White. I had heard of Soror Penn-White, and knew that she was respected for her great intelligence and personal drive and accomplishment. Later, I looked up her bio on the Internet, and learned several additional interesting things about her life, as noted in the following paragraphs.

She is widely accredited as "the driving force and inspiration behind Delta." Originally from Atchison, Kansas, the family moved to Omaha, Nebraska, where she graduated as the highest ranking student in her high school class. As a newly minted member of Delta, she drafted the sorority's first constitution and set of by-laws. She also selected the Greek letter symbols and created the initiation ritual. Her focus and determination was to make Delta a truly national organization, and in that capacity she set in motion the mechanism for creating other chapters. Penn White conducted the first individual Initiation Ceremony for Ruby Martin, an undergraduate from Wilberforce College, Ohio, who returned to her campus and established Beta Chapter in February 1914.

According to Grace White Ware, her daughter, Madree was also the second president of the sorority at the time that it was a fledgling single chapter organization. As well, she was also the first female to be on the staff of the *Howard University Journal,* also serving as editor. In her professional life, she was Founder and President of the Triangle Press Company in St. Louis, Missouri. She became an accomplished linguist, speaking German, French, Greek and Latin. Naturally, her high intelligence and linguistic skills were put to service in the founding of Delta Sigma Theta, an idea primarily conceived by her while a dissatisfied member of Alpha Kappa Alpha.

White Ware recounted how her mother served as the second president of Delta, beginning in 1913. Serving in that capacity, of course she knew Nellie Quander well. Having severed her membership with AKA, she concurrently served as both Alpha Chapter and Delta's national president, while Nellie Quander did the

## HOMECOMING STRETCH

same for AKA (1911 until 1919).[92] Soror Penn White also served as the first woman editor of the campus paper, *The Howard University Journal.* Her participation in the March 1913 Woman's Suffrage March led to her being the first Delta ever to have an audience with a President of the United States.

When Penn White's daughter, Soror Grace, emerged from Rankin Chapel, she was accompanied by an entourage of several sorors, all jockeying for a more favorable camera angle, pushing and shoving each other in a sisterly context, everyone trying to get a closer look at her and to get photographs with her, if possible. If not, then at least a glance. Accompanied and assisted by two volunteers, Howard University students who were not members of Delta, she slowly climbed into the middle row of the three row seated golf cart, where an impromptu press immediately ensured.

Several questions were asked, and in such rapid fire that she could hardly answer them. How old are you? Where and when were you born? Are you also a Delta? How does it feel to be a Founder's daughter? What are some of the recollections that you have of what your mother told you about the founding and earliest days of Delta? The questions were fast and furious, and virtually nonstop. After a few moments of this mad dash for firsthand information, one of the volunteer escorts said to me, "Mr. Quander, I think it's time for us to depart for the medical school library. Mrs. Ware has an appointment there for Delta's ongoing medical forum."

And with that, we departed, but not before I had my picture taken sitting at the wheel of my cart, with Soror White Ware, sitting behind me at an angle, clearly visible over my right shoulder. Turning to her, I said, "Mrs. Ware, I want this picture for my Omega legacy, and it will appear in my forthcoming book on my life as a 50+ year member of Omega Psi Phi." She retorted, "My father, James Eathel White, was

---

[92] *This above information came from two primary sources: a) my interview of Grace White Ware, daughter of Madree Penn White, during her January 2013 visit to Washington, D.C. for the start of Delta's Centennial Celebration, and follow up telephone conversations with Mrs. Ware and her son, Oloye Adeyemon, director of the Legacy Program ; b) the Internet, on the life of Madre Penn White.*

## 50+ OMEGA INSPIRED YEARS

an Omega man, and a good man too. In fact, he was one of the very first men who joined the fraternity, here at Howard University." When I asked her what year that was, she indicated that she was not certain, but that it was very early in the existence of the fraternity, adding that he knew all of the Omega Founders well.[93]

After letting Mrs. Ware off at the medical school library, I continued to transport the Delta Dears to and fro. About an hour later, as I was letting a group of sorors out at the corner of Sixth and Bryant Streets, near the Howard bookstore, I saw a man waving at me, as though trying to flag down a taxicab. I did not know who he was, but waited until he crossed the street to speak to me. He said, "I saw you about an hour ago transporting my mother to the medical school library. They have completed their interview and business, and I was wondering if you could transport her back up to the buses, so we can go back to the hotel." I said, "Why, of course!" He climbed into the passenger seat next to me, introducing himself as Oloye Adeyemon. He volunteered that he was Madree Penn White's grandson, and the son of Grace Elizabeth White Ware, whom I had transported to the medical library during the prior hour.

I asked about his name, to which he replied, "Yes, some of my paternal ancestors were from Nigeria, including those who came to study at universities in the U.S., and elected to stay in the United

---

[93] *Unable to find Bro. James Eathel White's (1887-1971) name on the induction list of Alpha Chapter, I called to International Headquarters in Decatur, Georgia, for them to check their records. They informed me that the records reflect that Dr. White was inducted into Omega by way of Delta Chapter (Meherry/Fisk) in 1919, and not Alpha Chapter, as his daughter believed. In a follow up conversation on another day, Mrs. Ware stated that her father was a member of a study group of men, many of whom joined the fraternity while Omega Founders were still enrolled at Howard. As she stated to me, "My dad said that he was an Omega before my mother was a Delta." Therefore, she thought that he was inducted by way of the Mother Pearl before the 1913 founding of Delta Sigma Theta. Why he did not join Omega via Alpha Chapter in not known. Further research uncovered that Dr. White was also a Charter Member and first basileus of Upsilon Chapter (now Upsilon Omega), founded in St. Louis in 1921.*

## HOMECOMING STRETCH

States. Yes, my names are Nigerian, both of them." I asked if he was an Omega man, to which he replied, "No, I'm not, but my grandfather, Dr. James White, my grandmother Madree Penn's husband, surely was, an early man in Omega."

As we wound our way to the medical library, located at Fourth and Bryant Streets, I introduced myself. Immediately picking up on the name, "Quander," he added that that surname is very famous, well known, and historical. I had not even mentioned that fact to him. Asking him how he knew that, since he was from Cincinnati, he replied that he worked for the Legacy Program, an historical organization that researches and publishes information on historical subject matter.

It is of further interest to note that Penn White and Nellie Quander became friends, although they assuredly had a rocky start to that relationship. Penn White's daughter, Grace Elizabeth, had fond memories of Nellie Quander staying in their St. Louis home when visiting the area. Although she recalled no particular details, she did remember them discussing "the old days," when the young chapter members of AKA decided to reform the sorority, and frustrated at the opposition from the more senior sorors, decided in October 1912 to break away and form a new organization.

Several months after we had served our Delta sisters in January 2013, my chapter was privileged to provide the same transport service for the Deltas during their centennial convention, convened here in D.C. in July 2013. Because I was due to leave the city for our Martha's Vineyard vacation, my time was greatly restricted. But I did serve Delta on Thursday, July 11, 2013, the first day of their Centennial Celebration. Arriving at Howard's campus about 8:45 a.m., I drove steadily until 6:30 p.m. It was a long haul, but still a delight to serve these sorors who had come from every state in the union and a number of foreign countries as well.

Only this time, there was a very noticeable difference. Sitting with the brothers at about 8:30 a.m., waiting for the crowd to swell, we observed several well-dressed younger Deltas tip toeing about in their finest, some even wearing six-inch high heel shoes. They were dressed quite differently from that cold day last January. One brother said, "She sure thinks that she is cute," to which another brother retorted, "She is cute now, but by 5:00 p.m., those 'dogs' are going to be singing and she probably won't be able to take another step because her feet will be killing her."

Sure enough, almost on the dot of 5:00 p.m., this same cute soror, about 30 years of age and about whom the comment had been made earlier, flagged me down in front of Rankin Chapel, and begged me to drive her up to the Drew Hall parking lot where she had left her vehicle earlier. She added, "I can't take another step. My feet are just killing me." Smiling, and beckoning her to get in, I told her what the brothers had said about her earlier this morning. She retorted, "Yeah, and they sure were right. I don't know why I didn't stick a pair of flats in my bag. It's more than big enough and would have been so much better at this hour. They were so right!"

So happy to get a ride, despite not yet being a Delta Dear, she tried to tip me for my service. Naturally I refused, as I had likewise done all day. I added that brothers and sisters must always stay vigilant and help one another at times such as this, and that service by Omega to Delta today, will come back 100-fold in some way, yet unknown. As she alighted towards her vehicle, she thanked me profusely, adding, "I don't dare take my shoes off here and walk barefoot. Between here and my car, my feet might swell up very badly, and I won't be able to get them into the old shoes that I keep in the car." We both smiled, as we bid each other adieu.

# XXX – Omega Men Gather At The White House

On February 19, 2013, I was one of 14 brothers of the Omega Psi Phi Fraternity, Inc., among approximately 75 invited guests, who gathered at the White House for a Black History Month 2013 event. The occasion was initiated by the Association for the Study of African American Life and History (ASALH), the organization founded by Omega Bro. Dr. Carter G. Woodson in Chicago, Illinois on September 9, 1915, with the mission to "promote, research, preserve, interpret and disseminate information about Black life, history and culture to the global community."

The program was officially sponsored by the White House Office of Public Engagement and Inter-Governmental Affairs, and featured greetings from President and Mrs. Obama delivered by Michael Strautmanis, Deputy Assistant to the President. Dr. Woodson's message, to educate all Americans about the sustained contributions of African Americans since 1619, when the first Africans were imported to this country, continues to ring true.

In 1920, the Omega Psi Phi Fraternity, Inc., acted favorably upon the request of Omega brother, Dr. Woodson, for assistance in creating a venue and places for learning about and sharing the contributions of African Americans throughout this country's history. Omega then created the fraternity's Negro History and Literature Week (retitled Achievement Week), and observed in November of each year. In 1926, Dr. Woodson created a separate Negro History Week effort, which is now titled Black History Month. ASALH selects the official theme, which it encourages all celebrants to embrace for the theme in February of each year.

Befittingly, the Official Theme for 2013 was: "At the Crossroads of Freedom and Equality: The Emancipation Proclamation and the March on Washington." This theme recognized the 150th anniversary of President Abraham Lincoln's issuance of the proclamation that freed the enslaved, and likewise an acknowledgement that 100 years later, 1963, the United States as a nation and our government had done very little to address and correct the many inequities. We, as

African Americans, were still denied at that time our basic constitutional rights. Such is still the case in many instances today.

President Barack H. Obama, our first recognized African American president, issued a Proclamation on January 31, 2013, officially recognizing the significance of Black History Month, and the selected theme for 2013. In the first few sentences of the Proclamation, President Obama stated:

> *In America, we share a dream that lies at the heart of our founding: that no matter who you are, no matter what you look like, no matter how modest your beginnings or the circumstances of your birth, you can make it if you try. Yet, for many and for much of our nation's history, that dream has gone unfilled.*
>
> *For African Americans, it was a dream denied until 150 years ago, when a great emancipator called for the end of slavery. It was a dream deferred less than 50 years ago, when a preacher spoke of justice from Lincoln's memorial. This dream of equality and fairness has never come easily – but it has always been sustained by the belief that in America, change is possible.*

In addition to the welcome and greetings by Mr. Strautmanis on behalf of President and Mrs. Obama, the Statement of the Occasion was delivered by Daryl L. Scott, ASALH National President, with additional comments from Sylvia Cyrus, the ASALH National Director. That was followed by a moving musical rendition of Lift Every Voice and Sing, brilliantly sung by Omega brother James A. Green, Musical Choir Director of Providence Baptist Church, Baltimore, Maryland.

Five nationally accredited African American historians and communicators, all with a Ph.D. degrees and stellar credentials, served as panel participants. They were: Dr. Claudrena Harold, a Professor of History and African American Studies at the University of Virginia, who served as the moderator, and Dr. William Jelani Cobb, Associate Professor of History and Director of the Institute of African American Studies, University of Connecticut; Dr. Edna Greene Medford, Professor of History and Chairperson of the

## OMEGA MEN GATHER AT THE WHITE HOUSE

Department of History, Howard University; Dr. James Braxton Peterson, II, Director of Africana Studies and Associate Professor of English, Lehigh University; and Dr. Karsonya Wise Whitehead, Assistant Professor of Communications and an Affiliate Assistant Professor in African American History, Loyola University, Maryland.

The panelists spoke as a group, interchanging their thoughts and perspectives about the many challenges that lie ahead for African Americans, but universally agreeing that getting a quality education is the key to working ourselves out of the depths of despair into the light of acknowledgement. Education opens doors, makes more of us both prepared and equal, and provides the means of taking care of our families, being able to realize our goals and objectives, and the means to sustain ourselves for generations to come. As well, the decision-makers, whether local, state level, or federal, still have not come to terms with the adverse effects that denial of access has created among those who do not have, especially African Americans.

Among the guests were two younger persons, Kofi Whitehead, age 12, and Amir Whitehead, age 10, the sons of Johnnie and Dr. Kaye Wise Whitehead, a panelist, she a proud member of the Delta Sigma Theta Sorority, Inc. With some of the other guests commenting that the brothers were not in school today, Kofi replied, "No! While I am not in my regular classroom, this is a very special occasion, and my brother and I will both be giving our classmates a full report of what we saw today. This place is today's school for us."

The general consensus was that we need to lobby officials to address the issues of lack of education and poverty, both of which affect our ability to get decent jobs and enjoy decent housing. But, and even more importantly, we must learn to better help ourselves and each other. African Americans cannot sit back and bemoan out plight. We must pick ourselves and each other up and go forward. Mentoring and the rendering of service at all levels were universally agreed as central to any successes that we hope to enjoy. It was noted that there are several service-oriented organizations within the African American communities whose missions are to render service. We must support these organizations and work to help them meet their goals.

## 50+ OMEGA INSPIRED YEARS

It was noted as well that far too many of the upper class African Americans have abandoned their less fortunate brothers and sisters, as much out of fear as anything. This too must be addressed and changed. Effective mentoring and a better appreciation for hard work, values, and a sense of accomplishment are lacking among the lower class blacks, which only leads to more frustration and a sense of hopelessness, much of which plays out in the form of violence and fear of one another.

The program concluded with comments and questions from the audience. The White House-sponsored program did not end with this one program. It will be edited and shown throughout the nation's schools and in other educational and public venues, in a continuing effort to create a greater appreciation for ASALH's historical mission, and likewise for all Americans to develop a greater appreciation for the adverse effects that poverty and the lack of a quality education each impose upon those who do not have the benefits that others enjoy.

On February 23, 2013, ASALH held its 87th Annual Luncheon, at the Marriott Wardman Park Hotel, Washington, D.C. The event was based upon the 2013 Black History Month theme, and also honored the memory and contributions of Dr. Woodson. More than 1,000 people assembled for the luncheon, at which Dr. Mary Frances Berry, former Chair of the U.S. Civil Rights Commission, gave a rousing keynote address which focused upon African American successes, but with a recognition that we still have a long way to go.

Dr. Andrew A. Ray, 39th Grand Basileus, attended the luncheon, and made a surprise donation of $10,000 to ASALH, to help the organization further its mission of educating everyone about the history and contributions of African Americans to the legacy that is our great nation. At the conclusion of the event, 13 brothers of Omega sat for a photograph, which was taken by their 14th Omega brother, an official photographer for the program.

# XXXI – Salute To Colonel Charles Young

On June 5, 2013, my wife and I had the distinct pleasure and privilege to attend a Wreath Laying Ceremony in recognition of the 90th Anniversary of the Interment of Bro. Charles Young, a legendary soldier and diplomat. The event and evening banquet were sponsored by the National Coalition of Black Veteran Organizations (NCBVO), with major contributions and assistance from the brothers of the Omega Psi Phi Fraternity. Among Omega's sons, Bro. Col. Matt Coleman, 13th District Representative, Bro. Col. James Mullen, International History and Archives Military Achievement Sub-Committee Chairman, and Bro. Col. Conrado Morgan worked diligently to make the event's ceremony the quality that it was. Brothers Mullen and Morgan each did an outstanding job arranging and coordinating the presence and participation of Omega Generals at Arlington, while Bro. Robert Warren, Third District Representative, managed Grand Basileus Andrew A. Ray, his delegation, and other members of the Supreme Council who were present.

L-R, Bro. Antonio Knox, First Vice Grand Basileus, Dr. Andrew A. Ray, 39th Grand Basileus, and Bro. Quander, and others, at gravesite of Bro. Colonel Charles Young, June 1913

Omega's star shone particularly bright with the presence of many Omega's active and retired Generals, Colonels, other officers, enlisted members of the armed services, our Grand Basileus, 1st Vice Grand Basileus, current and former Supreme Council members and civilian brothers of Omega Psi Fraternity Inc. Each of them was present to give tribute and recognition to one of Omega's brightest stars, a man who through his sustained personal sacrifices paved the way for so many to follow, and have their paths lighted as they proceeded to make their own personal presences felt.

## 50+ OMEGA INSPIRED YEARS

On March 8, 1912, Bro. Young became the second honorary member of the Omega Psi Phi Fraternity, Inc., an honor and status which he took most seriously. An additional purpose for this historic gathering, which has now become a "Cause," is to persuade the U.S. Congress to posthumously award Bro. Young a promotion to the rank of Brigadier General in the U.S. Army. He earned the right to this elevation through a life of service to his country during his many years of distinguished military service. Yet he was denied the honor, majorly because of his skin color, which circumstance also contributed to there being a dearth of supportive information to justify the posthumous promotion.

This is a clear example of a situation where the deliberate non creation of data has, many years later, helped to create a vacuum in Col. Young's distinguished military record, which adversarial persons seek to use as justification for no promotion action being taken. Therefore, we, who are left to mourn, have a duty to remember and likewise correct a major historical act of racial discrimination. Further, his belated promotion would underscore that people of color, and African Americans in particular, have always shown great loyalty to a nation and rendered service in a time of national danger.

### *In Memory of Charles Young,* a poem by Countee Cullen[94]

*Along the shore the tall thin grass,*
*That fringes that dark river,*
*While sinuously soft feet pass*
*Beings to bleed and quiver.*

*The great dark voice breaks with a sob*
*Across the womb of night;*
*Above your grave, the tom-toms throb*
*And the hills are weird with light.*

---

[94] *Countee Cullen was a famed Harlem Renaissance poet. A contemporary to Bro. Langston Hughes and Zora Neale Hurston, he wrote the above tribute poem In Memory of Charles Young in about 1925.*

## SALUTE TO COLONEL CHARLES YOUNG

*The great dark beast is like a well*
*Drained bitter by the sky,*
*And all the honeyed lies they tell*
*Come there to thirst and die.*

*No lie is strong enough to kill*
*The roots that work below,*
*From your rich dust and slaughtered will*
*A tree with tongues shall grow.*

Bro. Young was an intellectual, and read voraciously, and wrote many poems to bide his time in foreign lands, and to challenge his intellectual abilities. After his death, Countee Cullen, a famed Harlem Renaissance poet, penned the above poetic tribute, to commemorate and observe the pain that many mothers felt as they mourned the loss of their sons on Flanders Field and elsewhere during the Great War (1914-1918). Although a man of peace, Bro. Young realized as well, that all too often, the pursuit of peace can only come after a sustained conflict, in which many a son will be slain or maimed on the battlefield.

The program of the afternoon was held near the gravesite of Bro. Young, and was initiated with the Pledge of Allegiance and the National Anthem, plus the posting of the colors by the Tennessee 13th United States Colored Troops, an Infantry reenactment unit that came to Washington for the occasion. As well, this unit had several ladies appropriately adorned in late 19th Century clothing, which lent an additional ambience to the occasion. This group also attended the banquet in the evening. Towards the conclusion of the gravesite program, this honorary military unit sang two traditional songs that the Negro troops from the Civil War favored, *Lord, I Know I've Been Changed,* and *Oh Freedom.*

## 50+ OMEGA INSPIRED YEARS
### *Negro Mothers' Cradle Song,*
### by Bro. Col. Charles E. Young[95]

*Sleep, little son! Rest ebon head*
*Sad your mother mourns your soldier father dead*
*Who on the soil of France bravely fought and bled;*
*Sleep! Sleep!*

*When grim and gruesome war took its terrific toll,*
*And gray grief filled the heart with sorrowing of soul*
*He answered then the call of the world for freedom's right*
*Sleep little son! Good Night.*

*Shade of my dead, O warrior one!*
*Watch from your realm upon our little son,*
*Teach him that you died that all might rise and run;*
*Watch! Watch?*

*Make for him a place in the world's new March of Man*
*And be, O spirit fine, his leader in the van.*
*Ah grant, dear husband mine, your sad wife's fond request*
*Rest warrior on. Then rest.*

It is an historical fact of American history that our race was not previously given the recognition and respect for how we served this nation with distinction through many decades, even centuries, when our national security was threatened. The life's work of Bro. Young and the many Buffalo Soldiers who served with him and elsewhere, is only now being recognized on a sustained basis. With the National Coalition of Black Veteran Organizations (NCBVO) and the men of the Omega Psi Phi Fraternity banned together, our mission is clearer than ever – to have the U.S. Congress award Col. Charles Young his general's star, thus elevating him to his rightful place in American history.

Further, to have the story of the Buffalo Soldiers, known for their fierce fighting spirit, their brown and black skin, and their dark curly hair which resembled the coat of a buffalo, be firmly woven into

---

[95] *This poem was first widely read and enjoyed in the June 1928 issue of the Oracle, published several years after Col Young's death in 1922.*

## SALUTE TO COLONEL CHARLES YOUNG

American history, where future generation, yet unborn, will have cause to stop and give them the proper respect and recognition that they rightly have earned and deserve.

This most distinguished event was coordinated and sponsored by NCBVO, with the full participation of the membership of the Omega Psi Phi Fraternity. Founded in Oakland, California in 2008, to raise public awareness about the importance of minority Americans' history and contemporary contributions in the defense of our country, NCBVO consists of approximately 20 veterans groups and organizations. During both the Wreath Laying Ceremony, and later at the evening dinner held in the Rayburn House Office Building of the U.S. Congress, Charles Blatcher, III, NCBVO Founder and CEO, paid great tribute to the Men of Omega.

Blatcher told the assembled audience that Col. Young may well have been forgotten after his death, were it not for the Men of Omega, who for the next 65 years worked virtually alone to perpetuate his memory, his loyalty to country, his service, and devotion to Omega Psi Phi. Finally, the rest of the world seemed to be catching up, and in the late 1980s, there was a renewed interest in Charles Young, and along with it, a call to correct a great historical, but deliberate, oversight.

> *NCBVO's aim is to get Col. Charles Young the star that he earned and deserves, but which was denied to him because he was the wrong color at that time. Col. Young paved the way for many, and every minority flag officer has stood on his shoulders as they climbed the ladder to earn their own stars.*[96]

Bro. Dr. Andrew A. Ray, 39th Grand Basileus, was also present at both the Wreathing Laying Ceremony and the banquet in the evening. On both occasions he brought greetings from Omega to the assembly.

> *Each of you is here this afternoon to help keep Charles Young's memory alive. It's up to us to do that, to stand firm, and we would be remiss of our personal duties and responsibilities if we*

---

[96] *Extracted from Remarks delivered by Charles Blatcher, III, Founder, CEO, and Chairman, NCBVO, at the graveside Wreathing Laying Ceremony, Arlington National Cemetery, June 5, 2013.*

*fail to give our military personnel their proper due. Bro Young's contributions are immeasurable. And he was followed by many quality men and women who gave their lives, when called for, to this nation, even when the nation did not appreciate it or acknowledge them. As well, it was another Omega Man, Grant Reynolds, a former Grand Basileus [21st 1951-53], who was at the heart of convincing President Harry S. Truman in 1948 to sign Executive Order #8891, to end segregation in the U.S. armed forces. Surely, it was in significant part based upon the courage, education, and bravery previously demonstrated by Col. Charles Young and other military personnel which convinced the president that it was time to act.[97]*

Present at the graveside program were several Young family descendants, including Dennis Russell, Charles Young's great grandson, who brought greetings from the Young family and words of appreciation for the efforts being extended on behalf of his ancestor. He also brought the same message to the banquet guests, later that evening. As well, the afternoon event featured several guest speakers, including Rev. Dr. Fred Douglas Smith, Jr., a faculty member of the Washington Theological Seminary, Washington, D.C. His remarks, covering both Charles Young and the role of the Buffalo Soldiers, were greatly inspired, and likewise inspiring.

Preaching on the theme, *May Our Souls Find Rest,* Rev. Dr. Smith noted that Charles Young was a man who demonstrated dogged strength, asking what does it take to be serving in a military which does not respect your manhood and humanity? How can one tolerate having to fight for the rights of others, when you do not have those rights yourself to enjoy? Yet, Col. Young lived that life every day. A proud American, proud to serve his country, yet he was forced to carry in his heart that racism, that prejudice and discrimination throughout all of his personal and professional life.

Surely Charles Young was well aware of the sins of America and his limited place in its society. He was smart enough to appreciate

---

[97] *Extracted from Remarks delivered by Dr. Andrew A. Ray, 39th Grand Basileus, Omega Psi Phi Fraternity, at the graveside Wreathing Laying Ceremony, Arlington National Cemetery, June 5, 2013.*

## SALUTE TO COLONEL CHARLES YOUNG

that the America promised on paper was not yet realized as to him and others similarly situated. Yet he had a duty, and was loyal to a cause greater than himself, and in the end gave his life to it and for it. His strength of character allowed him to tolerate insults and being constantly put down by others, because his calling was higher and his duty was to lean towards a moral universe where justice would be realized. And it is into this inheritance that we are rooted today. For indeed, Col. Charles Young's life was not one lived in vain.

> *It does us no good if we let lies told on Charles Young stand. It's about all of us, and the truth, humanity, and each human reaching his potential* – W.E.B. DuBois, in putting Col. Charles Young in proper perspective.

As a member of Omega Psi Phi, in reviewing the words of Dr. Smith, I am further moved indeed by the life of my brother, Charles Young. Although Rev. Dr. Smith noted that he is not a member of our fraternity, still he preached a sermon about Charles Young that was in every respect consistent with our Four Cardinal Principles - MANHOOD, SCHOLARHSIP, PERSEVERANCE, AND UPLIFT. Rev. Dr. Smith, wittingly or otherwise, cited several examples, some of which are not reflected in this document, where Bro. Young, despite the continuing adversities that he faced in his profession as the Negro race's highest ranking military officer, proved himself to be both a Man and a Scholar. Further, Smith cited instances where Perseverance was the word and order of the day, as Young uplifted his race, and also others who were adverse to his race.

Truly, Brother Colonel Charles Young, was a man for all seasons.

At the conclusion of the program at Arlington, Bro. Col. Conrado Morgan, who was chosen to present a ceremonial star wreath, led the audience about 150 feet to Col. Young's final resting place. Bro. Morgan then placed the six point star-shaped red, white, and blue floral wreath at the large stone marker that Omega Psi Phi placed on Bro. Young's grave in 1926. On December 29, 1924, during the Thirteenth Annual Grand Conclave, convened in Washington, D.C., the brothers of Omega met with President Calvin Coolidge at the White House. Immediately thereafter, they reassembled at Bro. Young's gravesite later in the afternoon. Observing that no fitting head stone was in place, but only a wooden marker, they resolved to quickly rectify the situation with an appropriate stone marker.

> *The phase of the Young memorial that challenged Omega was the erection of the monument. Mrs. Young, the widow, had been importuned by various organizations to permit them to solicit funds for the erection of an appropriate memorial. She refused each request. Then came the request of Colonel Young's fraternity, which had been dear to his heart. Mrs. Young readily consented. That consent was the great responsibility of Omega. One feature of the Thirteenth Conclave, which met in Washington, D.C, in December 1924, was a pilgrimage of the brothers to the grave of Colonel Young, the happy warrior, the inspirer of youth. After laying thereon a wreath in the name of the Omega Psi Phi Fraternity the brothers, while uncovered, bowed their heads in reverence and in shame; for the grave of their dear friend was marked only with a wooden slab. So greatly were they chagrined that they resolved that Omega should erect for him at Arlington a fitting monument, since they regarded his life as an epitome of the ideals of our Fraternity.*[98]

The shape of the wreath was symbolic of the hoped for posthumous Brigadier General's star that we are aiming to have approved by Congress. The site is situated on a hill overlooking the head stones of many other men and women who served their nation with pride. In placing the marker, the fraternity exercised its determination to not let the memory of one of its most stellar sons die in vain. Inscribed on the primary side of the marker is a single word, "Young." On the reverse side, the stone states, "Colonel Charles Young, 1864-1922." Before we left the site, Carmen and other photographers took several photographs of different groups of people at the stone marker, to include the Young family, alone; Blatcher and the Youngs; representatives of the Omega Supreme Council; and Grand Basileus Ray, along with several members of the fraternity, including me. While the 13th Tennessee Infantry, U.S. Colored Troops

---

[98] *The History of Omega Psi Phi Fraternity, Herman Dreer, 1940, P. 138.*

re-enactors posted the colors at the outset of the program, several representative re-enactors from the 10th Infantry, U.S. Colored Troops, were on hand at the gravesite, each man dressed in an authentic uniform beginning with the U.S. Civil War and up to World War I.

Closing out the evening banquet held in the Rayburn House Office Building, U.S. Congress, Dr. Sandra Jowers Barber, who attended Howard University with me some years ago, underscored to the guests that our generation, consisting of mostly older citizens, had both a duty and responsibility to educate our younger citizens, not just those of African American ancestry, but ALL young Americans about our history, and to give them a complete and balanced story about what all Americans have accomplished.

Noting that today's policy determination are tomorrow's history, she underscored that we must act correctly now, when those policy determinations are being made, so that we will not have to come back in the future and try to correct the many errors of the past, and particularly those that have inaccurately portrayed people of color in American society. Just think of all the energy that is being spent currently in efforts to undue lies, to find and shore up the truth. Think about the conflicts and denials of our own ancestors' many, but still unknown, accomplishments. Those accomplishments will stay hidden unless we take it upon ourselves to bring them to light. It is our duty, like it is now being jointly undertaken by NCBOV and the Omega Psi Phi Fraternity, to bring Col. Charles Young to his rightful place in history.

Dr. Bowers concluded her remarks by noting that we cannot stop now. Congress seems on the verge of doing something to correct this major historical anomaly. But doing just that will not, in itself, be enough. There are many other stories that are begging to be told, and they will not be unless we are vigilant in assuring that they become known.

> *George L. Vaughn of Upsilon Omega chapter, St. Louis, was elected as Omega's Eleventh Grand Basileus in December 1924. Under his leadership the fraternity erected and dedicated at Arlington National Cemetery, a monument in memory of Col. Charles Young. Vaughn was a well-known lawyer and civil*

*rights activist in St. Louis. Under his leadership, the fraternity's observance was re-designated as National Negro, Achievement Week in 1925, now observed as Black History Month. Vaughn was able to use his national prominence as a lawyer to advocate the establishment of the celebration in every black community. It was determined that the purpose of the celebration should be to present the important achievements of black people which might otherwise escape notice and thus not be properly recorded. The Fraternity hoped, in the face of public ignorance, imposed segregation through legislation, and state sanctioned private discrimination, to engender sensitivity to the potential and capabilities of black people in this regard. In short, the national observance of Achievement Week was to inspire race pride and the pubic appreciation of our potential as a people.[99]*

---

[99] *Information extracted from the Internet and the History of Upsilon Omega chapter, St. Louis, Missouri.*

## XXXII – Omega Verses Alpha, Who Is Number One?

*The challenges facing the rejuvenation of Omega at the outset of our Second Century are multifaceted. Yet, inspired by the clear messages imbued in the meaning of our Four Cardinal Principles, Omega men must take the helm and step up to assume their rightful places in the forefront of leadership. It is not an African American "Thing!" It is an American thing. Our brothers have fought long and hard, seeking to attain our rightful places in the American society. Now that we have achieved same, although the struggle is still faced with many challenges, we have a duty to serve, to carry the torch, and to pass it on in due season.*[100]

With so much new information gleaned as a result of our reaching out to many brothers, chapters, and beyond, two things were quite obvious. First, it was not realistic to complete the Third District history book project with the publication of a high quality hard cover history book before the Centennial Conclave. Second, Omega Men stand alone. The latter statement requires some expansion. For years, and now at least a full century, the discussion, and some would say "argument" has been, "Which fraternity is truly Number One? Which black Greek Letter Organization has proven itself to be the most prestigious over time?"

When I asked this question of my Omega brothers, naturally they put on their suit of bias, and proclaimed that "Omega is No. 1." This was their hands down conclusion, although I would venture to say that this is more of an emotional statement, than anything else. Perhaps one brother put it best, when he said, "Alpha was the prototype, but Omega is the finished product." I will not take issue with him, but I feel that we need to look at that question and

---

[100] *"Omega - In the Last Quarter Century, 1986-2011, Centennial Souvenir Journal Statement, P. 33, authored by Rohulamin Quander, Chairman, Third District History and Archives Committee, June 2011.*

approach it in the most intellectually balanced manner. And perhaps, after a fuller analyzation of the issue, we may conclude that there is no answer of any real significance, as both organizations are committed to their members, to service to others, and to friendship and brotherhood.

Alpha Omega Chapter brothers on steps of Thirkield Hall, Howard University, 2013

Because of my own affiliation, many might say that my answer would be biased, unobjective. They would proffer that I have a predisposition towards Omega that clouds my thinking in formulating an objective, balanced answer to such a sensitive question. And perhaps they are right. Still, I must at least attempt to address and answer the central question, and do it in a manner that does not offend – too much. I say "too much," because no matter my answer, someone will be offended, even angered. But my intent is not to do that, as I recognize that each of the five fraternities that are counted among the Divine Nine, has a mission and purpose, with their own goals and cardinal principles, and are like-minded in their commitment to service.

## OMEGA VERSES ALPHA, WHO IS NUMBER ONE

Truly, the existence of the five Black Greek letter fraternities, plus the four sororities, have made all of us better. The competition, the striving, the public display, has lifted us all onto a higher plain. And may we continue to be cooperative to the extent that we are all elevated and inspired to do something for ourselves, and most importantly, for others. Nowhere is the expression, "A rising tide lifts all boats," more applicable than in the story of our brotherly and sisterly existence. Sibling rivalry is a part of growing up, maturing, and living. So why should it be different here?

Nellie Quander, when addressing that date in October 1912, when 22 young members of Alpha Kappa Alpha broke away and founded Delta Sigma Theta the following January, stated that the breakaway was a very good thing, looking back on the event. Further, she added that the crisis made all of us stronger, helped us to focus, and to better appreciate that everyone is not of like or single mind. On many occasions, when called upon to comment, and after making light of the separation and telling a short story or two about the painful experience, she was effusive in paying compliments to the women who founded Delta, and their current membership as well.

Without conceding to the question of which sorority was the "most prestigious," she preferred to point out that there were great women in all of the sororities, and that "most prestigious" was something that was of less importance, than the commitment of the membership, both individually and collectively, to meeting the organizations' goals and objectives. As well, it matters not what your colors are, as all four of the sororities were committed to service, and in the vein of forbears like Mary McLeod Bethune (Delta), Mary Church Terrell (Delta), and Anna Julia Cooper (AKA), each was committed to the uplift of their people.

Now to the question, "Is Alpha, the Beginning, or Omega, the Final Word, the more prestigious fraternal organization?" I assure that there are as many answers to that question as brothers who are asked. Yes Alpha rightfully claims Dr. Martin Luther King, Jr., Thurgood Marshall, and Frederick Douglass (Honorary) as brothers. And indeed, many would argue that these three men represent perhaps the greatest triumvirate of achievement among our race. On the other hand, taking a look at that same claim, and stepping back to reflect how much achievement was attained over the sustained period of time, one naturally must see other achievers whose long-term effects are of a likewise similar and lasting nature.

No one can fully examine Dr. King's achievements without noting that he was molded and shaped in many of his philosophies by Bro. Dr. Benjamin E. Mays, then president of Morehouse College. Surely, the scholarship and academic prowess of Founder Ernest E. Just, Bro. Percy Julian, Bro. Charles R, Drew, and Bro. Carter G. Woodson inspired Thurgood Marshall in his legal work in the courts to underscore that we were not mentally deficient or otherwise incapable, and that all we really needed was a fair and equal opportunity.

Alpha's recited aims are "manly deeds, scholarship, and love for all mankind." Its motto is *First of All, Servants of All, We Shall Transcend All.* Through the years, beginning initially during the 1930s, Alpha Phi Alpha evolved into a primarily service organization and provided leadership and service during the Great Depression, World Wars, and Civil Rights Movements. It addresses social issues such as apartheid, AIDS, urban housing, and other economic, cultural, and political issues of interest to people of color. The Martin Luther King, Jr. National Memorial and World Policy Council are programs of Alpha Phi Alpha. It also conducts philanthropic programming initiatives with March of Dimes, Head Start, Boy Scouts of America, and Big Brothers and Big Sisters of America.

Omega's stated purpose is to attract and build a strong and effective force of men dedicated to its Cardinal Principles of Manhood, Scholarship, Perseverance, and Uplift. As well, we live by the motto, *Friendship is Essential to the Soul.* Likewise, during the 1930s, as America's black population cried out in agony and pain during the hard years of the Great Depression, the fraternity modified its program to expand its focus to include service. With time and continuing to today, several mandated programs were established to include: Achievement Week; The Charles R. Drew Scholarship Program; diverse Social Action Programs to uplift society, which include each chapter maintaining a life membership in the NAACP, voter registration, health initiatives, literacy programs, mentoring programs, such as the National Fatherhood Initiative and Stop the

## OMEGA VERSES ALPHA, WHO IS NUMBER ONE

Violence Campaigns; Talent Hunt Program to encourage young people to expose themselves to the Performing Arts; fundraisers, and support for charitable organizations such as the American Diabetes Association, United Way, and the Sickle Cell Anemia Foundation.

Both organizations have proven their worth, not only to themselves, but to the world at large. Both organizations have attracted men of great promise and molded them into men of greater promise, stellar achievements, and movers and shakers who have literally changed the world. As well, the listing of the awardees of the venerable and much sought after Spingarn Medal is replete with the names of men who were Alpha and Omega men, four of whom – Ernest E. Just (Omega), Charles Hamilton Houston (Alpha), Carter G. Woodson (Omega) and Thurgood Marshall (Alpha) come to mind immediately as shining lights, men who made a difference in the lives of not just men of Alpha and men of Omega, but humankind as a whole. So in answer to the initial question of "Which fraternity is #1, the most prestigious?" the answer must be another question, i.e., What difference does it make? Joined by the brothers of Kappa, Sigma, and Iota, we are all on the same mission – to help one another and to help others lift as we ourselves climb.

In a recent article that appeared in the *Emory Wheel*, Emory University, regarding the role and objectives of the membership organizations that subscribe to the National Pan-Hellenic Council, it was noted that although our mission statements and goals may differ from organization to organization, we all seek to achieve several common objectives. We provide such a force in the community that enriches the college experience at Emory for not only black students, but all students.[101] In the words of a distinguished Alpha man, Thurgood Marshall, "None of us got where we are solely by pulling ourselves up by our bootstraps. We got here because somebody — a parent, a teacher, an Ivy League crony or a few nuns — bent down

---

[101] *Statement extracted from "Letter to the Emory Community," The National Pan-Hellenic Council Encourages Acting for Change, The Emory Wheel, Emory University, April 2, 2013.*

and helped us pick up our boots."[102] We, the NPHC, are here to pick up the boots of our fellow council members and Emory Community, to hold each other accountable, to make a difference — together.

---

[102] *Statement of Thurgood Marshall that appeared in the article, "Letter to the Emory Community," The Emory Wheel, Emory University, April 2, 2013.*

# XXXIII – Fifty Years In Omega

**November 17, 2013 – A Crisis Day in Omega's History**

On April 4, 2014, I crossed over - crossed over a major milestone in my fraternal journey. For that was the day that I became a "senior brother." The AKAs have their "Golden Sorors." The Deltas have their "Delta Dears." And Omega has its "Senior Brothers." We are all a "special lot," for we have each demonstrated over time that we are indeed all just that – special. To become a "Senior Brother" in Omega, one must have been a member of the sacred brotherhood for at least 50 years. You cannot enter Omega at age 65, and be bestowed with the privilege and title of "Senior Brother" at age 70. Therefore, relatively few men of Omega attain that hollowed status. Although they may still be living, they have fallen by the wayside, and ceased to be financial and active.

This is one of the thorns in Omega's side, not being able to retain or reclaim more of our fallen away brothers. We are all busy in one endeavor or another, and in the course, too many of us neglect to keep Omega on our short list of important obligations. But for those of us who do remain active, and continue to align ourselves with the sacred brotherhood, the rewards are most treasured. I am blessed to count myself among the ranks of the latter group.

Tracing my Omega Legacy from 1931, I witnessed both my uncle (Bro. Joseph P. Quander, Theta Psi 1931) and my dad (Bro. James W. Quander, Alpha Omega 1958) in their Omega-related activities, not initially dreaming or appreciating that I was witnessing Omega history in the making. Both of them, and particularly my dad, took active roles in Alpha Omega's social action projects. They were likewise involved in social events, the Talent Hunt, judged the essay contests, and represented Alpha Omega before the Pan-Hellenic Council. They both set a tone and a stage for me to follow.

And now, at age 70, I realize just how full, rich, and diverse my grounding in Omega was. In December 1959, at age 16, I attended the 45th Grand Conclave in New York City. There, I met at least four or five current or former grand basilei, as well as a cross-section of national officers. These were men of great achievement, and they paved the way for the society that we inherited. I distinctly remember meeting Bro. Lawrence Oxley, 14th Grand Basileus (1932-35), and a family acquaintance. He said to me, "Young man, one day you will be a fine Omega man." Little did he know just how much his words meant to me. During that same Grand Conclave, my dad motioned to me to step over to meet the man and woman that he was talking to. At that time, I made the acquaintance of Bro. I. Gregory Newton, then the 24th Grand Basileus (1958-61), and his wife, Dr. Eunice Shaed Newton. She was friendly with my dad back in D.C., so it was only natural for them to stop and chat in the hallway of the Hotel New Yorker.

Dr. Newton asked me where I was in school (Archbishop John Carroll, Washington, D.C.) and did I plan to follow in my dad's Omega footsteps (Yes!). Simple! But encouraging! It was during that time that I determined that I *would* be an Omega, Not that I wanted to be, but that I "would" be. Arriving back home to D.C., it was not three weeks before I assembled classmates who joined me in founding *Les Jeunes Hommes,* which became an Alpha Omega Chapter sponsored interest group. Over time, the club led several men to Omega, two of whom are Bro. David Reid, III, my 1964 line 21 Titans" line brother, and Bryant VanBrakle, who followed us on the 1965 Alpha Chapter line, "The Seldom Seen 17." All three of us were John Carroll graduates.

My particular point is that I became interested in Omega's history at a very early age, which interest allowed me to meet and make the acquaintance of many men of stellar achievement, including Founders Love, Cooper, and Coleman. In all three instances, I made their acquaintance more than once. And armed and inspired by those contacts, I dedicated myself to knowing, understanding, and appreciating Omega's history. Further, I have known, Kathy Just, granddaughter of Founder Ernest E. Just, since high school. She too inspires, as she related stories about her grandfather and his many achievements. More than in the case of the other three Founders, the details of her stories underscore Founder Just as a real human being, someone who faced many challenges in life, yet continued to persevere.

## FIFTY YEARS IN OMEGA

She has shown me how his life was by no means a crystal stairway, and that he frequently became frustrated by the limitations that were placed upon his creativity and intellectual potential, all because of his sable persuasion. Kathy characterized her grandfather with some degree of sadness, adding that the many adversities that he faced also caste some negative pall over the Just family, even to the present generation. But this is true life, one that shows the strong character and nature of the men who founded Omega and the brothers who came this way at an earlier time. In them, not only was there an ideal, but also many realities. That said, I move on.

Having underscored my historical journey to this point, I feel an obligation to comment in significant part upon the disaster that occurred on November 17, 2013, the day that the latest "official" Omega history book was released. Billed, prior to availability, as the latest and most comprehensive history of Omega, the forthcoming book was touted as one that all Omega men could be proud of, a document that was worthy of being placed in the carrels of the Library of Congress as well as with the inventory of items that Omega was scheduled to donate to the new Museum of African American History and Culture, slated to open in late 2015.

Personally, I was excited about the new Omega history book, but likewise approached the publication with some trepidation. Having been appointed as an at large member of the fraternity's History and Archives Committee, in late June 2013, I travelled to IHQ for a three-day meeting on Omega's history. The Committee was aware that a new history book was in the planning stage, but very few of us had been apprised of the fact that such a book was this close to publication. Representing the 13 districts of the fraternity, plus about four members-at-large, the committee members were gravely concerned about what was rapidly taking shape, i.e., the issuance of a new official history book, a book which not one of the committee members had seen.

In preparation for my trip, I contacted Robert Warren, my District Representative, and expressed my concerns, advising him that I planned to raise that issue at the meeting. He advised me to follow my conscience, and to update him upon my return to D.C. Once in session, the topic was raised and discussed. Everyone pretty much felt the same way, but I expressed the greatest concern, noting that I was getting wind of the fact that many major Omega events, several of which occurred in the Third District, were not mentioned at all, or perhaps were far too summarily mentioned, thus reducing the historical significance of certain key events or Omega's participation in making American history.

## *THIS HISTORY DOCUMENTSHOULD NOT BE ALLOWED TO GO FORWARD!*[103]

*Dear Bro. Barnes:*

*I was requested by Dr. Andrew A. Ray, 39th Grand Basileus, the Omega Psi Phi Fraternity, Inc., through Bro. Robert Warren, the Third District Representative of the Fraternity, to address with some degree of specificity my previously expressed concerns about several aspects of the recently published Omega history book. I, as well as a significant number of Omega brothers, have alleged that numerous errors are apparent, which errors should be promptly reviewed and corrected. It is not my intent to personally or unjustly criticize, as it took sustained effort to obtain this current result. Still, something major must be done before this publication can bear the name of Omega*

*The authors of our first two official Omega history books had vision. They wanted future generations of Omega men to understand that their predecessors took pains to record events, so that those who came after would learn and be inspired. That mission remains the same today. The tone having been set, any subsequent history book on Omega must be a document worth collecting, remembering, and a treasure, one from which future generations of Omega men and readers at large can gain a perspective of who we are and what we stand for as Omega men.*

---

[103] *Extract from my third letter of grave concern, written at the request of Grand Basileus Ray, a comprehensive report dated January 1, 2014, directed to Bro. Kenneth Barnes, National Executive Director, Omega Psi Phi, with copies to Grand Basileus Ray and Third District Representative Warren.*

## FIFTY YEARS IN OMEGA

*In my considered opinion, The History of the Omega Psi Phi Fraternity, Inc., 2013 Edition, as presently constituted, does not meet that standard. I doubt whether this document can be fixed. Rather, I am of the opinion that the amount of reworking, coupled with the fiscal investment that will be required, mandates that this book be scrapped and the project started de novo, including the replacement of the entire team of brothers who served as the volunteer book-writing committee.*

Upon my return to D.C., I authored a stern letter to my Bro. Warren, raising several pertinent points and asking him to forward the letter on to Omega's leaders. Although he did just that, there was no action taken to fully address either the committee's or my concerns. I received some comments from other committee members reminding me that I was only speaking for myself, and had no authority or capacity to speak out on behalf of the committee. Nothing happened!

Until November 17, 2013! On that day the brotherhood was assembled in Cramton Auditorium, Howard University, for our 102nd anniversary convocation. Cramton, which seats about 1,500 people, was about 75% full. Prior to the convocation, the brothers lined up in the lobby to obtain an autographed copy of the new book, *The History of the Omega Psi Phi Fraternity, Inc.,* by Rev. Dr. Charles D. Fletcher, Jr. Bro. Fletcher was inducted into Omega via Pi Chapter, Morgan State University in 1970. Following the usual course, I solicited Bro. Fletcher's personal autograph. He wrote, "Rohulamin Quander, Friendship is Essential to the Soul. Rev. Dr. Fletcher, 5 Pi 70."

At home that evening, I initially undertook to read the new history book. My first effort was to quickly scan it, to look at the pictures and gather a sense of the content and how it was presented. I was immediately struck by several factors that I quickly noted were not consistent with what I felt was a high quality product. While I will not enumerate the details here, as this is not the focus of this memoir, I immediately undertook a comprehensive evaluation of the book, writing margin notes in red pen, and likewise made notes on a notepad, as my comments often could not fit in the margin.

## 50+ OMEGA INSPIRED YEARS

Run on sentences; sentence fragments; poor format, lay out, and stylization; failure to properly emphasize events of great historical significance in Omega; and the non-inclusion of a relevant photograph of the Third District, Omega's birthplace, cradle, and early nurture, were but some of the adverse characteristics. Heartbroken, I immediately crafted a multi-page letter to my district Representative, titled, in red pen, "THIS HISTORY DOCUMENT SHOULD NOT BE ALLOWED TO GO FORWARD." My subtext was "STOP THE PUBLICATION OF THE OMEGA HISTORY BOOK NOW." At last I got attention of the leadership. Some of our leaders were seemingly shocked at my boldness, but were forced to pay closer attention to my clanging noise, as telephone calls and other written communications began to come to their attention, noting the same objections to the book as presented.

During the quick response and initial reaction, it was revealed that apparently no one on the Supreme Council, including the Grand Basileus, had expended required time to review the manuscript, and that even the Supreme Council meeting of late June 2013, on which the review of the history book was allegedly on the agenda, very little time was devoted to the history book, and no one supposedly read the manuscript extracts that Bro. Fletcher presented at the meeting. As well, even if they had looked at the manuscript, the meeting agenda was skewed, and no one would have had the time to critically evaluate and comment upon the document in any intellectual way.

Without equivocation, I am very happy to say – *I am the Omega man who stopped Omega from making a bigger fool of itself.* Oh yes, we did make fools of ourselves, by letting something so important slip past us. And we are all to blame for being too lackadaisical about protecting our fraternal organization. This statement transcends to more than just our history. It affects our whole Omega being. This is not an indictment or criticism of Dr. Andrew A. Ray, 39th Grand Basileus. He inherited a mess in 2010, and has spent the last four years trying to straighten it out. But he cannot do it alone. We all have to bear our share of responsibility for this serious mess, and likewise can take our share of the credit when the matter is finally straightened out.

## 50 Years at Last

January 1, 2014, is the day on which Omega's roles officially reflect my status as a "Senior Brother." The posture is to carry the brother in that status from the first day of the year in which he is inducted into the fraternity. Therefore, I was not required to wait until April 4th, to be accorded my newly acquired status. I relish this new status, and will do nothing to tarnish my ascension.

Still, it is nostalgic as I look back over these last 50 years of my membership, and likewise reflect upon my Omega-related history even before April 4, 1964. But I will focus upon the present. For much of the prior year, I have been in a countdown mode. The readers' reference to the many congratulatory letters that appeared at the beginning of this book mostly reflect that the letters are dated April 2013, a full year ago. That is when I began my countdown to the present. I asked the writers to reflect my countdown, as I

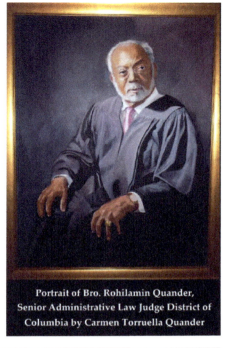

Portrait of Bro. Rohilamin Quander, Senior Administrative Law Judge District of Columbia by Carmen Torruella Quander

Rohulamin Quander and Carmen Toruella Quander at George Washington's Mount Vernon Plantation for event, c2007

anticipated a full year of contemplating before I reached my actual **induction date.**

And the interim between then and now did not disappoint. On June 5, 2013, I was privileged to be in attendance at the Bro. Col. Charles Young commemorative memorial service at Arlington

## 50+ OMEGA INSPIRED YEARS

National Cemetery and the banquet later that evening. On November 17, 2013, noted above, I was likewise in attendance at the 103rd anniversary convocation at Howard University. Other Omega-related events of my 50th year included the December 19, 2013, 138th commemorative birthday celebration of Bro. Dr. Carter G. Woodson, and then on February 22, 2014, at the 88th Annual Association for the Study of Afro American Life and History Luncheon, at which event Omega donated $20,000.00 to the Woodson home restoration fund.

Beyond that, I was also present at two other very significant events. The first was the February 4, 2014, funeral celebration of life of Bro. Dr. David H. Reid, Jr., who was Omega's oldest and longest serving brother. Born in Raleigh, North Carolina on May 17, 1909, he was inducted into Omega on Founders Day, November 17, 1927, and was a faithful man of Omega for more than 86 years. It was my deep honor to serve Bro. Reid as an honorary pall bearer at his funeral service. As you note from above, his son, David, III, and I are childhood friends, high school and college classmates, and line brothers.

Later in the same week, I revisited Lincoln University, Pennsylvania, to attend some of Beta Chapter's Centennial Celebration events. There I stood by the grave of Sister Charlotte "Lottie B." Wilson, as the brothers of Beta paid a memorial tribute to the woman who made the founding of Beta Chapter possible in February 1914, thus creating a venue whereby Omega could expand to become a national organization.

Although I had not visited Lincoln's campus in many years, "going home" was still of great spiritual significance, for at Beta chapter, I gained new and wider insights into just what Omega meant to those who were beyond just the Howard University campus. To be in the presence of Dr. Ray, as he addressed the brothers and guests about what Beta represents in the expanded history of Omega, was most inspiring. It imbued in me a great sense of the significance of my being a 50-year brother.

Thus, as the weeks grew short, and the 50th anniversary day drew closer, I was singularly focused on being there. Being there on the campus of Howard University, and strolling down the "Long Walk," the symbol of many great Howard University events. The location is not only an historic tribute to Benjamin Banneker, but the dial also bisects the Upper Quadrangle between Founders Library and the College of Fine arts. For me, the inscription on the brass plate, "Grow Old Along With Me, For The Best Is Yet To Be," has taken on an even more significant meaning. While I do not consider myself as "old," the reality is that I am not 20 years old anymore, the age of my induction.

I am wiser now, have greater vision, but likewise have most of my life behind me. Yet, truly the best is yet to be. As I get closer to the day when I will be enshrined in Omega Chapter, it is my vision and hope that my efforts on behalf of Omega, including the penning of this memoir, will help to perpetuate the memory of me by those who follow. This is not a vanity statement, but rather a desire that the brothers will more fully appreciate what I have tried to accomplish, and render on behalf of our beloved fraternity.

The challenges, and they are many, that we face can undue us, if we let it happen. But we must not let it happen – ever. We must celebrate and commemorate the many good things that Omega has done and continues to do. We must not let ourselves be overcome by fear, anxiety, blame, and self-pity. But it is all a matter of education, to inculcate into our membership that the future of Omega's survival rests primarily in their hands. So do not destroy it, and do not let others take it away from us.

## Fifty Years To The Day – My Revisit To The Long Walk

On April 4, 2014, 50 years to the day of my induction into the sacred brotherhood, I returned to the Long Walk and the iconic Omega Psi Phi Fraternity sun dial. Nostalgia! As fate would have it, that was the same day on which the 2014 pledge line would engage in their open pro demonstration. Things have changed a lot since my induction, and in this instance, the 14 men were already members of the fraternity, having been inducted in mid-March, after a shortened induction period of just three weeks. However, their intent and enthusiasm was no less than mine was 50 years ago.

They looked just a mean, tough, and focused as the 21 Titans did when we marched double file down the long walk. The big brothers cleared a path, moving back the screaming young ladies. The guys, many of them aspiring freshman, who I put in the category of "men seeking" Omega, looked on with anticipation in their eyes and hearts, imaging themselves doing exactly the same thing, this time next year. I know that is how I approached it before I was inducted.

Bro. Quander in his original sweater April, 2014

Line Brothers, L-R, David H. Reid, Gilbert Brown, Quander, Howard University, April 4, 2014

Appreciating the significance of this day, I contacted several of my line brothers, although they are scattered across the country. I was not able to locate many of them, although several are still in the local area. At least three are in Omega Chapter (Derrick C. Brown, Ralph M. Durham, and George Garrison) . Still, I reached David Reid, Larry Davis, H. Patrick Swygert (President, Howard University 1995-2008), Gilbert Brown, LaSalle Petty, and Will Singleton, asking them to join me in observing our 50 years in Omega. All of them said "Yes!" All were local, except Singleton, who came down from Massachusetts, his home state. We were joined by Taft "Chuck" Broome, our dean of pledgees. And between the dial on Friday and lunch on Saturday, all seven of us came together, joined by "Big Brother" Broome.

## FIFTY YEARS IN OMEGA

It was a great event, and brought back so many memories of a bygone era. Bro. David Reid and I, being life-long friends from childhood, agreed that we would wear our original fraternity sweaters from 50 years ago. Only, the question for me was how well would it fit, if at all. I have both gained and lost weight, and am blessed now to say that my sweater still fits. I elected to call it a "cozy" fit, but I did not look stuffed into it like a sausage, once I pulled it over my head and adjusted it. Meeting David at the dial in our somewhat faded purple sweaters adorned with gold, including large "'64" numbers on each, we looked at each other with "days of joy," as we hugged and reminisced where we had come from, and how our journeys have each brought us to this point in our lives.

Once again, I placed my hands on the top of the dial, and ran my fingers along the inscribed poetic words of poet Robert Browning, *Grow old along with me, the best is yet to be.* Although we know the history of how the dial got to be, and that it was a conceived tribute to Benjamin Banneker, I have seen nothing that indicates why those truly prophetic, but highly appropriate, words were selected to adorn the brass plate. Without further comment, my life in Omega has been governed by many components, and Browning's words are among them.

We expected to be the subject of some adulation, and we were. Fifty years, and in our original sweaters, too. As the many brothers present congratulated us wholeheartedly, which greetings likewise continued later via e mails, many of the young students likewise extended their congratulations and best wishes. As we passed groups of students who were lining the Long Walk waiting for the probate demonstration, David and I "pranced" like the noble men that we are, adorned in Royal Purple and Old Gold. But before we could get too full of ourselves, we each heard comments to the effect, "1964! They are old! My parents weren't even born then." It brought us back to earth and kept it real.

# 50+ OMEGA INSPIRED YEARS

## XXXIV – My Parting Words

Brothers, as I conclude this Omega Memoir, 50 years in the making, and tracing my Omega Legacy back to 1931, there are a number of observations that I must make before I feel comfortable in drawing this document to a close. What I am about to say about the future of Omega is not easy to digest. There has been much Rah! Rah! Rah! over the years. There have been many days of joy, but also some years of pain. But as I look both backwards and forwards, I see much joy, but perhaps even more pain ahead.

Omega is a way of life, a journey that begins on the day that we arise from our knees, having pledged our fealty and devotion for life. In Alpha Chapter, and likewise in many other chapters, we best captured the words and our sentiment in a song that was very popular, colloquially called, *Omega Psi Phi.* That is not a particularly original title, and actually may not be the correct original title, but it served our purpose, and we sang it weekly around the dial on Friday afternoons on Howard's campus. It goes like this (partial words):

**Omega Psi Phi Fraternity** (verse one)
*Omega Psi Phi Fraternity,*
*We'll always leave and honor thee.*
*Omega Psi Phi Fraternity,*
*We pledge our loyalty to thee.*
*In after years when 'ere we sing,*
*We'll always let Omega ring.*
*For we are bound by ties of love,*
*Fraternally, Eternally.*

These were not just words, but rather a continuing pledge to love, be friends, and to do so eternally. I look back over the years, and see that, for the most part, we Men of Omega were committed to that pledge, committed to "Ties of Love, Fraternally, Eternally." But in more recent times, I have to really question our focus, and ask, Where is Omega going? What are we doing to ourselves? Will we last another century? The answers and perspectives are not particularly encouraging. Yes, we have leadership that is committed to making us a better fraternal organization. But our leadership has not been consistently good. Yes, we have high-minded programs, that if fully pursued and executed, would make us a much better fraternal organization, one clearly focused upon its "Five Cardinal Principles."

Yes, I know that there are only Four Cardinal principles, but I say "Five" here, in living tribute to Founder Oscar J. Cooper, who was asked in December 1941, if there was anything that he would change about Omega at that time. Thinking carefully, he said, "Yes, we should have added a fifth Cardinal Principle, 'Service,' because that is what Omega must be about." Going further, he then stated that the lack of Service as a recited Cardinal Principle was not all that bad, as Service was clearly implied in the other Four Cardinal Principles, as Manhood, Scholarship, Perseverance, and Uplift each implied that some measure of Service was due from all Omega men.

I entreat all of you, my Omega brothers, to take Founder Cooper's words to heart and be of and about Service. Yes, we have great service-related programs, and the brothers are to be congratulated for their spirit, enthusiasm, and dedication to all of Omega's uplifting programs that benefit others. And we must never loose site of that obligation. Whether it be the Fatherhood Initiative; Stop the Violence Campaign; Omega Men Feed Homeless Men; Self Awareness, Self Esteem; Talent Hunt; or scholarship, fundraising and economic development programs, Omega is leading the way. We are there. We are recognized on a national level, and have been saluted by no less than President Barack Obama, whose administration has given a shout out to the men of Omega for our record of service.

But we certainly cannot afford to rest upon any laurels that we have accumulated. I was privileged to serve as co-author and principal editor of the Diamond Jubilee Souvenir Journal Historical Overview Statement for the 64th Grand Conclave, held in Washington, D.C. between July 25 - August 1, 1986. The three-page Statement was largely self-congratulatory, and highlighted Omega's stellar achievements from November 17, 1911, to 1986. While it was very inspiring to read about all the great things that Omega Psi Phi had accomplished in the intervening 75 years, the contrast between where we were in 1986, looking back 75 years, and where we have now devolved is stark.

## MY PARTING WORDS

Yes, Omega still brings the "Best Men Home." That is our trademark, and we continue in that vein, and likewise are men of significant achievement. But we are also a fast moving train, whose rail alignment may well be about to come undone. A train wreck, if you will! Having penned the Statement for the Diamond Jubilee in 1986, I was deeply honored to be asked by Bro. Bernal Coulon, 31st Grand Basileus and chairman of the Centennial Souvenir Journal Committee, to write an updated Statement for the Centennial Souvenir Journal. The directive was to craft an overview statement that addressed the status of Omega from 1986 to 2011.

In taking on the assignment, I crafted, "Omega – In the Last Quarter Century, 1986-2011." However, as I researched and assembled information to support my various suppositions and comments, I realized that I had an obligation to do more than just review the past 25 years. Rather, I concluded that I had a more important obligation, i.e., to look forward, to issue a Clarion Call – Omega is in Deep Trouble.

**A Clarion Call – Omega is in Deep Trouble**
*Omega – In the Last Quarter Century, 1986-2011,*
*By Brother Rohulamin Quander*[104]

*As the Diamond Jubilee Celebration drew to a close in August 1986, the euphoria that settled over the membership was not long to last. While many of the brothers viewed this time as an occasion for self-congratulation and elected to rest on their laurels, several pressing issues clouded the clarity of the moment. Not the least of them was the continued plague imposed by hazing and brutality. Despite the fraternity's officially adopted policies and efforts to address the issue, and discipline imposed against those brothers who continued to violate Omega's adopted policies, recalcitrant brothers have made it difficult for the rest of us. Operating under the guise of "making a new brother in the right way," the issue, while less serious than in past eras, has caused the fraternity to face liability suits and other challenges*

---

[104] *Omega Centennial Commemorative Journal, 1911-2011, P. 30.*

*which undermines us as a brotherhood as well as an organization of professional men.*

*As we look back over these last 100 years, the Omega Psi Phi Fraternity, Inc., has much to be proud of. But there is still room for improvement. As we reflect over the many things, both good and bad, which have had an impact on the current state of the brotherhood, we can link much of the behavior and traditions that we exhibit back to several common foundations.*

*The pledging process and subsequent fraternal affiliation has been frequently likened to the military, where a group of individuals from diverse backgrounds and exposures are, within a short time period, joined together into a cohesive unit with a common cause. This military influence makes it easy to trace how men were traditionally brought into Omega's fold, and how those experiences still hold sway to this day.*

*Now, as we reflect over the past century of the fraternity's history and the harsh physical hardships that were sometimes imposed as a means of bringing men together, the question arising is whether this level of training and treatment is necessary or, even more so, counterproductive for achieving the desired goals of the Fraternity?*

*The days and times have changed from what was tolerated and accepted from Omega's inception, earlier days, and for many decades in our existence. From at least 1938, the calls for the end to physical hazing have been sounding, and with it the threat that the fraternity might sustain the severest of penalties, if we did not heed and bring this brutal practice to an end. The struggle has been significant, as the psyche of what it means to be an Omega man, is often impaired when brothers challenge the validity and quality of another's membership, based upon how many strokes he took, or whether he joined Omega through an undergraduate or graduate chapter.*

It is indeed this pervasive attitude which threatens to bring us down. For as much as we love Omega and proclaim her from the highest hill, as did our Founders and the many stellar men of

## MY PARTING WORDS

achievement who preceded us, it will only take one or two "bad apples" (recalcitrant brothers) to destroy the barrel (Omega). For as much good as the men of Omega, acting individually or collectively, have done, it only takes one negative incident to ruin our image, which is already a fragile one. My brothers, we simply cannot afford to let that happen.

**Omega – Facing the Challenges of its Second Century**

Where do we go from here? At the outset of Omega's Second Century, many brothers are of the opinion that there are two different Omegas. While co-existing on the surface, we appear to be drifting in different directions. Accolades for our most prominent and highest achieving brothers are loudly touted. We continue to keep a count of who, among the brotherhood, has been selected to head a Fortune 500 firm, become president of a prominent university, appointed to the Presidential Cabinet, or named as an ambassador.

Yet, we have also comfortably settled into mediocrity, a potential death knell, inconsistent with what Omega is supposed to be about. We are rapidly approaching a crossroad, and I am sounding a clarion call for all to hear that if the "Olde Ship of Omega" does not right itself and come back together – and quickly – the already badly listing ship will tilt to the point of no return. If that happens, all that the Founders and early membership steadfastly pursued could be lost. Plainly put, Omega continues to have strong pockets where standards of high achievement, coupled with brotherhood and friendship, embrace the true meaning as initially intended by our Founders. However, in parallel, we have also warily endured the last 25 to 30 years, challenged by the negative effects of mediocrity and subjected to voices within the brotherhood that seek to compromise our initial standards. For those within our ranks who advocate such, most often in an effort to increase our numbers, they should find no welcome, comfort, or solace in Omega.

When previously confronted with the issue of increasing the size of the membership, particularly in light of the other fraternities' efforts to become significantly larger than Omega, Bro. Walter H. Mazyck (Alpha Chapter 1913), former Grand Keeper of Records and Seal, and one of Omega's most stall worth early members, addressed the issue of "Members vs. Men." While editing the first issue of the 1925 ORACLE, he wrote that "The value of our Fraternity is not in numbers, but in men, in real brotherhood. Eight men thoroughly immersed in the true Omega spirit are far greater assets than eighty with lukewarm enthusiasm." His comments were clearly a rejection of mediocrity, the byproduct of a mad race to increase our numbers, and a call for Omega to retain its higher standards and to bring only the best men home. Mazyck's words were relevant then and remain ever more so today.

The survival of Omega as a unit of high achieving men and a solid brotherhood demands that we carefully and comprehensively reassess ourselves, and then focus on restoring and preserving our legacy of greatness. The reclamation of the brothers who have fallen asleep, as well as the retention of continuing interest from among the active membership, are integral parts of whatever plans and efforts are put forth. We cannot wait any longer, drifting from one uncertainty to another, before we decide what we must do, and how to do it. In addition to seeking men who already demonstrate their leadership and determination to achieve, to address and stem the inflow of mediocrity, the fraternity should create an internal program designed to teach its own members how to become tomorrow's leaders, men who will take up the Founders' and early members' mantles, and carry them forth.

Our Mandated Programs, such as the Charles Drew Memorial Scholarship Fund, the Talent Hunt, and get out the vote drives, are an essential component of Omega's true mission, and have continued to be among our most visible social service efforts. Yet the support for each is paltry. Still, in recent years, we have quickened the pace with the Fatherhood Initiative and the Stop the Violence Campaign, both initiated in the Third District, now fully embraced and spreading rapidly across the entire fraternity. Feeding the hungry and homeless, clothing drives, fighting illiteracy, and health fairs continue to be our mainstay, but likewise have become stale, with the brothers support being uneven from district to district or year to year.

Criticism about Omega being too social and not sufficiently social action oriented is not new. But we must be ever mindful that our Founders chose four words Cardinal Principles - Manhood,

## MY PARTING WORDS

Scholarship, Perseverance, and Uplift - and that social service to the less fortunate is how we, as Omega men, demonstrate our belief in these principles and live by them in our daily lives. It is upon this base that Omega was built, and upon this base we will continue to grow and serve. Otherwise, we might as well declare ourselves as dead, and cease to function.

Dr. Andrew A. Ray, 39th Grand Basileus, in his message to the brotherhood, in the pre-Centennial Celebration Winter 2011 edition of the ORACLE, stated, "The existence and success of Omega has been and continues to be a result of dedication, tradition, pride, and enthusiasm. I am constantly reminded of the many sacrifices our Founders made as they created this great organization. They built a solid foundation and remained active to assure that like-minded men would represent Omega well, while uplifting their communities. As I reflect on the time I met Founders Cooper and Love, they said, ' ... young brothers, we gave birth to Omega, but it is up to you to keep Omega alive.' I will never forget those words and the spirit and passion in which they were shared. To that end, it is our obligation to take the necessary steps to make sure Omega thrives for future generations."

If we fail to act, or further delay in moving Omega forward, we will inflict irreparable damage upon ourselves. Many of those who are counted among the most famous of the brotherhood will seek memberships and accolades elsewhere, electing other venues in which to have their achievements noted. As well, those who are our audience, the men and women who follow our endeavors and sing our praises, will find other fields to plow.

The challenges facing the rejuvenation of Omega at the outset of our Second Century are multifaceted. Yet, inspired by the clear messages imbued in the meaning of our Four Cardinal Principles, Omega men must take the helm and step up to assume their rightful places in the forefront of leadership. It is not an African American "Thing!" It is an American thing. Our brothers have fought long and hard, seeking to attain our rightful places in the American society. Now that we have achieved same, although the struggle is still faced with many challenges, we have a duty to serve, to carry the torch, and to pass it on in due season.

But it has become a tug of war, with forces pulling in opposite directions. My above-noted words have taken the high road, the place where we really need to be, if we are to continue to be at all. Too much traction is being given to negative forces, the forces of our potential undoing. Dr. Walter M. Kimbrough, a member of Alpha Phi Alpha and the president of Dillard University in New Orleans, published an article in the *Atlantic* magazine on March 17, 2014, titled *"Black Greek 101: The Culture, Customs, and Challenges of Black Fraternities and Sororities."*

He observed many continuous and disturbing trends within the ranks of Black Greek-letter fraternal organizations, and attributed much of it to an underground culture of making the new members "right," which trend and attitude was in direct conflict with the loudly and publicly stated positions and directives of each organizations' leadership. Among his findings he noted:

> *[D]ark power or force exists in black groups, one that also creates tragic problems. It invades undergraduates who have been members of a group for a year or two, and miraculously overnight are the authorities on their group and how one should become a member. Their national leaders, scholars, lawyers, and experts, all who say don't haze, have no credibility with these young geniuses. And so they employ an "old school" approach to hazing, and I mean old, as in 1800s when all college students had few resources, so the upperclassmen physically punished freshmen during that first year. In 2014 alone, black fraternity members were arrested at the University of Central Arkansas for paddling and being pelted with raw eggs. Six members of another black fraternity (my fraternity) were arrested for paddling that sent one student to the hospital for a month. And at the University of Georgia, 11 black fraternity members were arrested after allegedly lining up potential new members along a wall and striking them.*
>
> *They all must know hazing is illegal. They must know it is against their respective fraternity and campus policies. They must know that if caught there could be harsh sanctions, including legal ones. And year after year, they beat people.*

## MY PARTING WORDS

*Undergraduates all start off with these noble intentions in their groups, but they become exposed to the dark side. For black groups, ... they are ... men and women actively convincing new members that hazing is the only way. They are an insidious group, operating inconspicuously on campuses but causing great harm.*

Dr. Kimbrough's assessment on the plight of Black Greek-Letter Organizations is as tame, as the article, "The End of Black Greek-Letter Organizations," by Gregory Parks, is alarming. An Assistant Professor of Law at Wake Forest University School of Law, who, like Dr. Kimbrough, is also a member of Alpha Phi Alpha, Professor Parks' stories and experiences about Greek life in African American organizations are equally applicable, and perhaps more than that, to the climate and culture within Omega. In his April 2, 2014, article, he wrote (selected extracts):

*For many years now, at least as long as I have been a brother of Alpha Phi Alpha—17 years—I have heard that "we are one lawsuit away from being out of business." I am sure other Black Greek Letter Organizations (BGLO) members have heard the same thing. I always took it as hyperbole; and over the years, maybe it was such or at least a scare tactic. Having been a researcher on BGLOs for the past 14 years and a law professor who has studied BGLOs for the past 3 years, I would bank on the fact that within 25 years the Divine Nine will be the Great Eight, Stellar Seven or Six...maybe the Fabulous Five or Four. Honestly, at the rate that BGLOs are going, I can only foresee two having any longevity. Given their sizes, financial resources, and frequency of hazing litigation, my prediction is that the organizations will fall by the wayside in the following order: Omega Psi Phi, Kappa Alpha Psi/Phi Beta Sigma, Zeta Phi Beta, Sigma Gamma Rho, Iota Phi Theta, Alpha Phi Alpha, Alpha Kappa Alpha/Delta Sigma Theta.*

After setting forth the general and main premise that BGLOs are on their way out, Mr. Parks enumerates in some detail several reasons that underlie his position. The details are beyond the scope of this chapter, so I will not elucidate further, other than to say that, should Omega cease to exist, possibly within the next 25 years, we will have no one to blame but ourselves. Our inattention to the culture of hazing, brutality, and focus on ever expanding our membership, which is translated into generating dollars for grander and grander events, has placed us at a level comparable to prostitution, which is itself inherently illegal. With pitiable resources with which to buy our way out of trouble, and insurance companies increasingly less willing to insure both fraternities and sororities, it become just a matter of time when we can be, and most likely will be, sued out of existence. With a lack of resources with which to satisfy legal challenges, we cannot hope to survive in the face of a serious legal challenge.

Parks notes that the ironic thing about BGLOs is that, for the most part, they have tremendous intellectual capital, given the nature of alumni membership within these groups, but the vast majority of this intellectual capital goes untapped. So, BGLOs remain in an information vacuum due to their own actions or inactions.

Parks concluded his article, based upon his extensive study of BGLO, by noting:

*I am hopeful about the longevity of BGLOs but not optimistic. Their demise will be blamed on 19-23 year-olds, but how responsible can you expect "kids" to be, even those who espouse high ideals? The end of BGLOs will ultimately have resulted from the failure of the adults, especially those in leadership, from doing, not simply something(s) about hazing, but all that needed to be done. Within BGLOs, there is not the will to be transformative. These are inherently conservative organizations where new modes of thinking are strenuously resisted, organizational politics prevails, and provincialism rules the day. Only time will tell; but time is not on their side.*

Brothers, when are we going to wake up and do something about this crisis that is daily facing us, and ever more pressing? Leadership within BGLOs seem to believe that their current efforts are the best possible. Most assuredly, that is not the case. There is no easy, simple, lasting, or singular solution. Parks suggests that at least one approach might be to educate our membership differently, by

## MY PARTING WORDS

teaching BGLO members how hazing will destroy our fraternal organizations. He notes, and I fully agree, that laying out the case systematically and regularly, is far different from just telling the member, "Don't do it!" But that all turns on having sufficient information—e.g., aggregating the major hazing incidents across BGLOs, resultant injuries, lawsuits, settlement/judgment figures, criminal convictions, and sharing more openly information between the organizations, to learn the best and most effective practices—to make such a case.

Will that approach work? We do not know. But it is worth at least a full court press effort. The alternative, i.e., a failure to act more aggressively, will hasten our demise. We cannot not do nothing. This sentence is a triple negative for a reason, to get the brothers' attention, and light a fire under them to get them to act quickly. Omega's future and continued existence is at stake, and we must step up in an immediate and forthright manner to assure that we prevail.

# XXXV – Our Founders A Retrospect

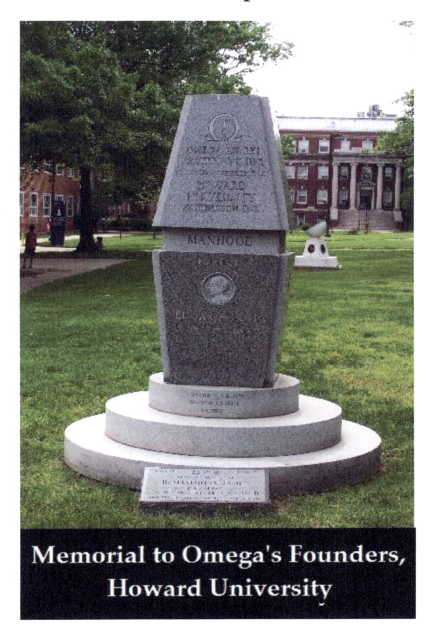

Memorial to Omega's Founders, Howard University

## 50+ OMEGA INSPIRED YEARS
**Founder Oscar J. Cooper - letter to George Isabelle, 10th GKRS, December 17, 1941 –**
*Let it be said of Omega of the future that, we live to serve our fellow man.*

Bishop Edgar A. Love – on Omega's Purpose –
Quoting from the preamble to the original constitution, *Believing that men of like attainment and of the same ideals of fellowship, scholarship and highest manhood should bind themselves together in order to approach these ideals, we have banded ourselves together under the name, Omega Psi Phi upon the ideals of the Fraternity.*

**Founder Frank Coleman – on Service -**
*Any institution which fails to render its meed of service to society must lead a tortuous and uncertain existence if indeed it continues to exist at all.* "The Negro Greek-Letter Men's Opportunity for Service," *Oracle*, 1930.

**Founder Ernest E. Just – The Challenge, to Omega men -**
*These times demand clean men, of clear vision, or straight thinking, of unselfish doing. And every Omega man must accept this challenge.* - Initial Issue of the ORACLE, 1919.

*Mother to Son*[105]
**By Langston Hughes (1902-1967**
*Well, son, I'll tell you:*
*Life for me ain't been no crystal stair.*
*It's had tacks in it,*
*And splinters,*
*And boards torn up,*
*And places with no carpet on the floor — Bare.*
*But all the time*
*I'se been a-climbin' on,*
*And reachin' landin's,*
*And turnin' corners,*

---

[105] Langston Hughes, "Mother to Son" from *The Collected Poems of Langston Hughes*, Vantage Books, 1994.

## OUR FOUNDERS A RETROSPECT

*And sometimes goin' in the dark*
*Where there ain't been no light.*
*So boy, don't you turn back.*
*Don't you set down on the steps*
*'Cause you finds it's kinder hard.*
*Don't you fall now—*
*For I'se still goin', honey,*
*I'se still climbin',*
*And life for me ain't been no crystal stair.*

In a sense, this is where I leave you. Omega, my brothers, over the last 50 years of my faithful membership, ain't been no crystal stair. There have been ups and downs, periods of uncertainty, and sometimes even bordering on despair, as I see my beloved fraternity making twists and turns that I know can sometimes lead to destruction or at least a diminution. Yet, we have still survived, persevered, and even prospered in the mode of the intent of our Four Founders – Oscar J. Cooper, Frank Coleman, Edgar A. Love and Ernest E. Just.

There is a strong message to all Omega Men embedded in Bro. Hughes' poem. He too knew what it was to have tacks, splinters, and torn boards. And so must we too understand that the key is to keep climbing, to keep reaching, to keep turning, despite the occasional lack of light, and the lost sense of direction.

Omega is in her second century, and as Bro. Hughes noted, "Don't you turn back. Don't you set on the steps. ... Don't you fall now." And this is my parting message to each of you – my beloved Omega brothers. The future is bright, but we must keep lifting, always climb higher, take the turns as they come, and be not afraid of the dark. For as surely as day follows night, we too will come into the bright light as we continue to advance, imbued by the value and determination of high aspiration.

Omega was founded on these values and must continue to pursue, obtain, and maintain them.

**Peace!**

CPSIA information can be obtained at www.ICGtesting.com
Printed in the USA
BVOW11s0018290814

364744BV00004B/6/P